Lecture Notes in Artificial Intelligence 5934

Edited by R. Goebel, J. Siekmann, and W. Wahlster

Subseries of Lecture Notes in Computer Science

Stefan Kopp
Ipke Wachsmuth (Eds.)

Gesture in Embodied Communication and Human – Computer Interaction

8th International Gesture Workshop, GW 2009
Bielefeld, Germany, February 25-27, 2009
Revised Selected Papers

 Springer

Series Editors

Randy Goebel, University of Alberta, Edmonton, Canada
Jörg Siekmann, University of Saarland, Saarbrücken, Germany
Wolfgang Wahlster, DFKI and University of Saarland, Saarbrücken, Germany

Volume Editors

Stefan Kopp
Bielefeld University, CITEC
P.O. Box 100131, 33501 Bielefeld, Germany
E-mail: skopp@techfak.uni-bielefeld.de

Ipke Wachsmuth
Bielefeld University, Faculty of Technology
P.O. Box 100131, 33501, Bielefeld, Germany
E-mail: ipke@techfak.uni-bielefeld.de

Library of Congress Control Number: 2010924334

CR Subject Classification (1998): I.2, I.3.7, H.5.2, H.1.2, I.5.4, I.5, I.4

LNCS Sublibrary: SL 7 – Artificial Intelligence

ISSN   0302-9743
ISBN-10   3-642-12552-2 Springer Berlin Heidelberg New York
ISBN-13   978-3-642-12552-2 Springer Berlin Heidelberg New York

springer.com

© Springer-Verlag Berlin Heidelberg 2010
Printed in Germany

Typesetting: Camera-ready by author, data conversion by Scientific Publishing Services, Chennai, India
Printed on acid-free paper   06/3180

Preface

The International Gesture Workshops (GW) are interdisciplinary events for those researching gesture-based communication across the disciplines. The focus of these events is a shared interest in understanding gestures and sign language in their many facets, and using them for advancing human–machine interaction. Since 1996, International Gesture Workshops have been held roughly every second year, with fully reviewed proceedings published by Springer.

The International Gesture Workshop GW 2009 was hosted by Bielefeld University's Center for Interdisciplinary Research (ZiF – Zentrum für interdisziplinäre Forschung) during February 25–27, 2009. Like its predecessors, GW 2009 aimed to provide a platform for participants to share, discuss, and criticize recent and novel research with a multidisciplinary audience. More than 70 computer scientists, linguistics, psychologists, neuroscientists as well as dance and music scientists from 16 countries met to present and exchange their newest results under the umbrella theme "Gesture in Embodied Communication and Human–Computer Interaction."

Consistent with the steady growth of research activity in this area, a large number of high-quality submissions were received, which made GW 2009 an exciting and important event for anyone interested in gesture-related technological research relevant to human–computer interaction. In line with the practice of previous gesture workshops, presenters were invited to submit theirs papers for publication in a subsequent peer-reviewed publication of high quality. The present book is the outcome of this effort. Representing the research work from eight countries, it contains a selection of 28 thoroughly reviewed articles.

An invited contribution by keynote speaker Asli Özyürek (Radboud University Nijmegen and Max Planck Institute for Psycholinguistics) addressed behavioral and brain research on the mechanisms that underlie processing of high-level multimodal semantic information conveyed through speech and hand gestures during production and comprehension of utterances. The invited contribution by keynote speaker Antonio Camurri and colleagues (InfoMus Lab, DIST – University of Genova) presented a survey of their research on analysis of expressive gesture and how it is evolving toward the analysis of expressive social interaction in groups of users. Further included is the extended abstract of keynote speaker Alex Waibel's contribution on multimodal interfaces in support of human–human interaction.

The papers in this book are ordered in eight sections pertaining to the following themes:

- Brain and Behavioral Analysis of Gesture
- Concepts of Gesture
- Gesture Recognition
- Gesture Processing
- Gesture Simulation
- Gesture-Based Interfaces
- Sign Language

The work presented in these papers encompasses a multitude of research areas from among: cognitive and psychological mechanisms of gesture; gestures in context and multi-modality; theoretical conceptions of gesture; automatic recognition, interpretation, and synthesis of gestures and sign language; specification and computational representation of gestures; real-time and continuous gesture and human-movement tracking; automatic processing and analysis of gestural behaviors; gesture and musical performances; user issues and interface paradigms; application in interactive systems.

We are grateful to the authors of the articles in this volume as well as to the international reviewers who provided very helpful input. We hope that the results of their hard work will be perceived as a timely and inspiring reference for an interdisciplinary audience of researchers and practitioners interested in gesture in embodied communication and human–computer interaction. Thanks also to the local committee, Kirsten Bergmann, Hendrik Buschmeier and Petra Udelhoven, as well as Marina Hoffmann and the whole ZiF team for hosting the event and contributing to a well-attended and lively meeting. Last but not least, financial support by the ZiF, as well as by the Center of Excellence "Cognitive Interaction Technology (CITEC)" and the Collaborative Research Center "Alignment in Communication," is gratefully acknowledged.

January 2010
Stefan Kopp
Ipke Wachsmuth

Notes

Webpages for GW 2009 can be accessed under http://www.gw2009.de/.

ZiF
Zentrum für interdisziplinäre Forschung
Center for Interdisciplinary Research
Universität Bielefeld

Alignment in Communication
SFB 673

CITEC
Cognitive Interaction Technology
Centre of Excellence
Bielefeld University

Reviewers

Table of Contents

Gesture Processing

Gesture Simulation

Gesture and Multimodal Interfaces

Sign Language

The Role of Iconic Gestures in Production and Comprehension of Language: Evidence from Brain and Behavior

Asli Özyürek

Radboud University Nijmegen, Center for Language Studies &
Max Planck Institute for Psycholinguistics

Abstract. Speakers in all cultures and ages use gestures as they speak (i.e., cospeech gestures). There have been different views in the literature with regard to whether and how a specific type of gestures speakers use, i.e., iconic gestures, interacts with language processing. Here I review evidence showing that iconic gestures are not produced merely from the spatial and/or motoric imagery but from an in interface representation of imagistic and linguistic representation during online speaking Similarly, for comprehension, neuroimaging and behavioral studies indicate that speech and gesture influences semantic processing of each other during online comprehension. These findings show overall that processing of information in both modalities interacts during both comprehension and production of language arguing against models that propose independent processing of each modality. They also have implications for AI models that aim to simulate cospeech gesture use in conversational agents.

Keywords: iconic, cospeech gesture, interface, production, comprehension, brain, behavior.

1 Introduction

Face-to-face communication involves continuous coordination and processing of information across modalities such as from speech, lips, facial expressions, eye gaze, hand gestures etc. Previous studies investigating multi modal processing during communication have focused mostly on the relationship between lip movements and speech (e.g., McGurk effect, [1]). However, during everyday face-to-face communication, we almost always use and view meaningful hand movements, i.e., gestures, along with speech. Although both gestures and lip movements are examples of the natural co-occurrence of auditory and visual information during communication, they are fundamentally different with respect to their relationship to the speech they accompany. Whereas there is a clear one-to-one overlap of speech sounds and lip movements in terms of their form, the mapping between the forms of gesture and speech is different [2]. Consider for example an upward hand movement in a climbing manner when a speaker says: "He climbed up the ladder". Here, the gesture might depict the event as a whole, describing the figure (crawled hands

S. Kopp and I. Wachsmuth (Eds.): GW 2009, LNAI 5934, pp. 1–10, 2010.

representing as that of the agent, 'he'), manner ('climb') and direction ('up') simultaneously. In speech, however, the message unfolds over time, broken up into smaller meaningful segments (i.e. words). Because of such differences, the mapping of speech and gesture information has to happen at a higher, semantic level. In this paper I will address the question of what are the mechanisms that underlie processing of such high level multi-modal semantic information, specifically conveyed through speech and hand gestures both during production and comprehension of utterances.

Speakers use gestures at all ages (starting from around 9 months) and cultures. The use of gesture is so robust in human communication that it is visible in people blind from birth, when people talk on the phone –albeit less than during face-to face communication [3]- and can be found in sign languages where the same modality is used for both sign and gesture (see for a review [4]).

Research on gestures that people produce while speaking has identified different types of gestures [2],[5]. Some of the hand gestures that speakers use, such as emblems, are highly conventionalized and meaningful even in the absence of speech (e.g., a thumbs up gesture for O.K.). Some others, such as pointing gestures are meaningful in the context of both the speech and the extra linguistic context of the utterance that the point is directed to (e.g., pointing to a lamp and say " turn on that lamp"). However, others are less conventionalized, represent meaning by their resemblance to different aspects of the events they depict (e.g., wiggling fingers crossing space to represent someone walking) and rely more on speech for their meaning. The latter have been called iconic or representational gestures in the literature and how they are processed in relation to speech both during production and comprehension of utterances is the topic of this paper.

It is important to note here that previous research has shown evidence both of speaker-oriented (cognition centered) as well as addressee-oriented (context centered) factors in shaping gestures and their relation to speech. Here I will review speaker-oriented evidence to explain the interactions between speech and gesture-without denying that social context or communicative intention to convey a message designed for the addressee are also additional factors that shape iconic gesture production (e.g., [3], [5], [14]) and are needed for a full account of speech and gesture production and comprehension.

2 Previous Studies on Relations between Gesture and Speech

Previous work by McNeill ([6],[2]) has shown that iconic gestures reveal speakers' imagistic representations during speaking. For example, a circular hand gesture representing the shape of a table, which accompanies the speech referring to the table, provides information about the speaker's mental image of the table at the moment of speaking. Due to differences in modality, iconic gestures reveal information in a different schema than verbal expressions. Gestures represent meaning as a whole, not as a construction made out of separate meaningful components as in speech.

However, although gestures reveal the information in a different representational format than speech, the two modalities are systematically related to each other and convey the speaker's meaning together as a "composite signal" [7]. This unified meaning representation is achieved by semantic relatedness and temporal congruity between speech and gesture [2]. First of all, there is semantic overlap between the representation in gesture and the meaning expressed in the concurrent speech, although gesture usually also encodes additional information that is not expressed in speech. Consider the example of a narrator telling an animated cartoon story. In the relevant scene, a cat that has swallowed a bowling ball rolls down the street into a bowling alley from left to the right on the TV screen. The narrator describes this scene with the sentence "the cat rolls down the street" accompanied by a hand gesture consisting of the hand moving from left to right while the fingers wiggle repetitively. In this example, a single gesture exhibits simultaneously the manner, the change of location, and the direction of the movement to the right. Speech expresses the manner and the path of the movement, but not the direction. Thus there is informational overlap between speech and gesture, but also additional information in the gesture [8].

The second systematic relationship between speech and gestures is temporal. A gesture phrase has three phases: preparation, stroke (semantically the most meaningful part of the gesture), and retraction or hold [2]. All three phases together constitute a gesture phrase. McNeill [2] has also shown that in 90% of speech-gesture pairs, the stroke coincides with the relevant speech segment, which might be a single lexical item or a phrase. For example the stroke phase of the climb up gesture exemplified above is very likely to occur during the bracketed part of the following utterance "he [climbed up] the ladder".

Thus research has shown that, at least at the surface level, there is semantic and temporal coordination in the production of semantic information in the two channels during communication. The question I address here it whether two streams of communication interact and are integrated during the language production and comprehension process or alternatively can be conceived as two independent but parallel streams of communication. Most studies and models of gesture processing have been designed for production but less is known about the interaction processes between the two for comprehension. The purpose of this paper is then to review recent evidence showing that speech and gesture interact during both production (section 4.1) and comprehension (section 4.2) of language. Before that I briefly outline some competing views proposed about the relations between speech and gesture during processing in section 3.

3 Models of Speech and Gesture Processing: Competing Views

Even though the speech and gesture seem tightly coordinated according to behavioral measures, there is controversy in their literature with regard to their underlying interaction during the production and comprehension processes.

According to some views ([9],[10],[11]) speech and gesture are processed independently and in a parallel fashion (i.e., that explains their overt coordination at the behavior level). According to these view gestures are generated and processed directly and solely from the spatial and motoric representations, whereas speech is generated from propositional representations and without interactions between the two during the production process. For example according to Krauss [10], gestures are generated from spatial representations, "prelinguistically", and independent from how certain information is linguistically formulated. One of the functions of gestures is to keep memories of such representations active and facilitate lexical retrieval through cross-modal priming (from gesture to speech). However how information is semantically or grammatically encoded for example would not change the representational format of such gestures. Also according to a new framework, Gesture as Simulated Action (GSA) [9], gestures arise simply out of simulations of actions and do not interact with the language production process.

However, according to other views ([12],[13],[2],[8],[14]) there is interaction between the production of two systems either at the conceptual, or grammatical encoding level of speech production process–even though there is further controversy with regard to which level the interaction occurs and to what extent among the latter set of researchers.

Even though most models have been proposed for production but not comprehension, the existing production models also have different views for how listeners/viewers might comprehend information from both modalities. The independence models claim that gesture is used–if ever–as "add-on" information during comprehension and only after speech has been processed [15]). However, interaction models [16] claim that there are mutual, simultaneous and even obligatory interactions between processing of speech and gesture during comprehension.

Below I review studies from my own collaborative work that provide evidence for the fact that speech and gesture processing interact during *both* in production and comprehension of utterances, arguing against the independent and sequential models of processing.

4   Evidence for Interactions between Speech and Gesture

4.1 Production

As a first step to test whether speech and gesture processing interacts during production we investigated whether gestures of the same motion event would differ according the language- specific semantic and grammatical encoding of spatial information in different languages The independence models would predict that the way certain elements of an event are encoded linguistically will not change the form of gestures, since gestures are generated from and shaped solely by spatial representations (i.e., which would be similar across speakers of different languages). However according to interaction models (i.e., specifically the Interface Model [8], the linguistic encoding of the event would change the shape of gestures, due to an interaction between linguistically formulating the message (i.e., specific for requirements of each language) and the formation of the gesture during online production.

The cross-linguistic variation in gestural representation was demonstrated by comparing how Japanese, Turkish, and English speakers verbally and gesturally express motion events, which were presented as a part of an animated cartoon ([8], [17]). Japanese and Turkish differed from English typologically which allowed us to look whether and how gestures of the same event differed due to linguistic encoding possibilities among the speakers of these languages. Two analyses were carried out. The first analysis concerned an event in which a protagonist swung on a rope like

Tarzan from one building to another. It was found that English speakers all used the verb swing, which encodes the arc shape of the trajectory, and Japanese and Turkish speakers used verbs such as go, which does not encode the arc trajectory. In their conceptual planning phase of the utterance describing this event, Japanese and Turkish speakers presumably got feedback from speech formulation processes and created a mental representation of the event that does not include the trajectory shape. If gestures reflect this planning process, the gestural contents should differ cross-linguistically in a way analogous to the difference in speech. It was indeed found that Japanese and Turkish speakers were more likely to produce a straight gesture, which does not encode the trajectory shape, and most English speakers produced just gestures with an arc trajectory ([18], [8]).

The second analysis concerned how speech and gesture express the Manner and Path of an event in which the protagonist rolled down a hill. It was found that verbal descriptions differed cross-linguistically in terms of how manner and path information is lexicalized [19]. English speakers used a Manner verb and a Path particle or preposition (e.g., he *rolled down* the hill) to express the two pieces information within one clause. In contrast, Japanese and Turkish speakers separated Manner and Path expressions over two clauses, path as in the main clause and manner as in the subordinated clause (e.g., he descended as he rolled). Given the assumption that a clause approximates a unit of processing in speech production ([20], [21]), presumably English speakers were likely to process both Manner and Path within a single processing unit, whereas Japanese and Turkish speakers were likely to need two processing units. Consequently, Japanese and Turkish speakers should be more likely to separate the images of Manner and Path in preparation for speaking so that two pieces of information could be dealt with in turn, as compared to English speakers. The gesture data confirmed this prediction ([17], [8]). In depicting how an animated figure rolled down a hill having swallowed a bowling ball in the cartoon, Japanese and Turkish speakers were more likely to use separate gestures, one for manner and one for path and English speakers were more likely to use just one gesture to express both manner and path.

These findings were further replicated in a recent study where Turkish and English speakers were asked to talk about 10 different motion events that involved different types of manner (jump, roll, spin, rotate) and path (descend, ascend, go around). Furthermore in cases where only manner or only path was expressed in an utterance, speakers of both languages were more likely to express congruent information in gesture to what is expressed with speech (e.g., he went down the slope: Gesture: index finger moving down expressing just the path information) [22].

In addition to the cross-linguistic variation in gestural representation, it was found that gestures encoded certain spatial details of motion events that were never verbalized due to modality. For example, in the description of the above two motion events, none of the participants in any of the languages verbally encoded whether the motion was to the right or to the left, but this information was reflected in the direction of the gestures very accurately [8].

These findings are. line with the view (i.e., Interface Hypothesis, [8]) that the representations underlying a gesture is shaped simultaneously by 1) how information is organized according to easily accessible linguistic expression in a given language and at the moment of speaking and 2) the spatio-motoric properties of the referent which may or may not be verbally expressed. These findings are counter evidence for the models that argue that the only source that shapes gestural information is spatial representations independent of linguistic conceptualization for speaking.

However one concern regarding the above studies was that different gestures produced by speakers of different languages could have still originated from spatial representations that are shaped differently due to difference cultural ways of thinking or habitually using language in a certain way-i.e., in line with Whorfian Hypothesis [23]. If this were the case the difference in gestures across speakers of different languages would not be evidence for the online interaction between gesture and language production processes but rather gestures could still be considered to be originated and shaped solely by the spatial representations (i.e., shaped in language-specific ways a priori to the encoding of each message). To clear out which of these processes could be responsible for our initial findings about gestural differences across languages, we asked English speakers to describe motion events using different syntactic frames –one in which manner and path expressed in one verbal clause (i.e., roll down) and one where manner and path are in separate clauses (i.e., went down the hill rolling) (less preferred but not ungrammatical for English speakers). We found that English speakers gestures changed with the syntactic frames they chose reflecting differences in the same way we found between English and Turkish speakers' gestures [24]. These findings rule out the possibility that spatial gestures are generated from language- or culture-specific spatial representations prior to the online linguistic formulation of the event. If the former were the case, we would have expected English speakers to use also conflated gestures when they used the less preferred syntactic frame –but instead they used segmented gestures as Turkish speakers. This finding provided further evidence that iconic gestures are shaped by speaker's online syntactic choices rather than a priori by habitual language-specific representations.

4.2 Comprehension

Neural Evidence: If speech and gestures are two interacting systems of communication in comprehension as well as in production then we expect speech and gesture processing to use similar neural resources during comprehension. Even though previous research has shown that listeners/ viewers pay attention to gestures and pick up information from gestures [25], only recently researches have begun to investigate the interactions between speech and gesture during language comprehension. In two studies we investigated the neural correlates of speech and gesture comprehension.

One of these studies used an ERP (event related potentials) technique, which measured electrophysiological responses to events by electrodes attached to the scalp as listeners/viewers listened sentences and saw accompanying gestures. In the sentence-gesture pairs we manipulated the semantic fit of a verb or of a temporally overlapping iconic gesture to the preceding sentence context (see Table 1). In the control condition both a critical verb and accompanying gesture fitted semantically to the previous sentence context. In the experimental conditions either speech or gesture or both did not fit semantically to the previous context. Recordings were measured, time-locked to the beginning of the critical verb and stroke of gesture, which were presented simultaneously. The results showed similar N400 effects (showing

Table 1. Examples from speech gesture pairs used in [26]

Control condition (speech and gesture match to previous context)

   (1) He slips on the roof and [rolls down]

G: ROLL DOWN

Experimental conditions (speech and/or gesture (in bold) mismatch to previous context)

   (2) He slips on the roof and [**writes**] a note (speech mismatch only)

G: ROLL DOWN

   (3) He slips on the roof and [rolls down] (gesture mismatch only)

G: WRITE

   (4) He slips on the roof and [**writes**] a note (speech and gesture mismatch)

G: WRITE

---

detection of semantic unfit) for sentences where either language or gesture did not fit semantically to the previous context. These results show that the information form both speech and gesture are integrated to previous context of the utterance at the same time providing evidence against independent and sequential models of speech and gesture comprehension processes [26]. Note that if gesture was processed after the verb or vice versa we would have expected either speech or gesture anomaly to be detected later than 400 ms but we did not.

In the second study we used fMRI technique to identify brain regions activated during understanding iconic gestures versus verbs in a sentence context using the same stimuli (Table 1) in the ERP study above. Integration load was expected to vary with this manipulation due to the increased load of semantic integration, thereby showing regions specific for speech and gesture processing as well as areas common to the integration of both information types into the prior sentence context.

Analysis of both gesture and speech mismatch versus correct conditions showed overlapping areas for both comparisons in the left inferior frontal gyrus, (LIPC) corresponding to Brodmann area (BA) 45. That is, gesture mismatches as well as speech mismatches recruited LIPC showing common areas of processing of semantic information from both modalities. Intraparietal and superior temporal regions also showed gesture and language specific responses respectively for mismatches than matches [27].

Gesture-mismatch activating similar areas as those of language mismatch are in line within a neurobiological theory of language, 'Broca's complex' (including BA 47, 45, 44 and the ventral part of BA 6) in the left frontal cortex, serves as a unification space for language comprehension, in which lexical information retrieved from memory (i. e. from the mental lexicon) is integrated into a unified representation of a multi-word utterance, such as a sentence ([28], [29]). The current findings further suggest that integration of semantic information from linguistic elements as well as from both language and gesture share similar processes during comprehension.

Behavioral Evidence: Thus both the ERP and the fMRI measurements show that the brain comprehends speech and gesture in relation to a previous sentence context in similar ways; both are processed as semantically, using similar time course and neural correlates. However these studies do not directly show whether the semantic processing of each modality interacts with the other. Thus in a third study we investigated this possibility in a behavioral experiment [16]. We asked whether listeners/viewers do process the meaning of speech and gesture separately or whether the meaning of one interacts with processing the meaning of the other during comprehension. We presented participants with action primes (someone chopping vegetables) and bi-modal speech and gesture targets. Participants were faster and more accurate to relate primes to targets that contained congruent (Speech: "CHOP"; gesture: CHOP) versus incongruent information (Speech: "CHOP"; gesture: TWIST). Moreover, the strength of the incongruence affected processing, with fewer errors for weak (Speech: "CHOP"; gesture: CUT) versus strong incongruities (Speech: "CHOP"; gesture: TWIST). Furthermore, this influence was bi-directional. A follow up study demonstrated that gesture's influence on speech was obligatory. That is even though subjects were asked only to decide whether the verb followed an action prime matched to the prime, whether gesture was congruent or incongruent to the accompanying verb influenced subjects responses. These results show that listeners/viewers process the meaning of one modality in relation to the meaning of the other rather than processing each in an independent manner.

5 Conclusion

Both the results of the production and the comprehension studies reported above suggest that multi modal semantic information, specifically from speech and gesture, is processed in an interactive way -at both semantic and syntactic levels for production and semantic for comprehension- and recruiting similar neural correlates brain rather than being processed in a distinct modular fashion. It is important to note here that the model proposed by Interface Hypothesis [8] for production is also successfully implemented in AI models that try to simulate iconic gesture production in conversational agents [30]. In the future it would be useful to see whether AI models can be also extended to comprehension which simulates the interaction between the two modalities as proposed in Integrated Systems Hypothesis [16].

Further research is necessary to delineate the exact level where these cross modal semantic interaction processes take place during processing as well as the role of communicative intentions of the speakers in gesture processing and to situate gesture production and comprehension in a larger interactional-situational context than we have done so far.

Acknowledgements. The research reviewed here was supported by Netherlands Organization for Scientific Research (NWO), 051.02.040; US National Science Foundation (NSF) and the Max Planck Institute for Psycholinguistics, Netherlands.

References

1. Calvert, A.: Crossmodal processing in the human brain: Insights from functional neuroimaging studies. Cerebral Cortex 11, 1110–1123 (2001)
2. McNeill, D.: Hand and mind. University of Chicago Press, Chicago (1992)
3. Bavelas, J.B., Gerwing, J., Sutton, C., Prevost, D.: Gesturing on the telephone: Independent effects of dialogue and visibility. Journal of Memory and Language 58, 495–520 (2008)
4. Özyürek, A.: Gesture in sign and spoken language. In: Pfau, R., Steinbach, M., Woll, B. (eds.) Sign language: An international handbook. Mouton, Berlin (in press)
5. Kendon, A.: Gesture. Cambridge University Press, Cambridge (2004)
6. McNeill, D.: So you think gestures are nonverbal? Psychological Review 92, 350–371 (1985)
7. Clark, H.: Using language. Cambridge University Press, Cambridge (1996)
8. Kita, S., Özyürek, A.: What does cross-linguistic variation in semantic coordination of speech and gesture reveal?: Evidence for an interface representation of spatial thinking and speaking. Journal of Memory and Language 48, 16–32 (2003)
9. Hostetter, A.B., Alibali, M.W.: Visible embodiment: Gestures as simulated action. Psychonomic Bulletin and Review (2008)
10. Krauss, R.M., Chen, Y., Gottesman, R.: Lexical gestures and lexical access: A process model. In: McNeill, D. (ed.) Language and Gesture, pp. 261–284. Cambridge University Press, Cambridge (2000)
11. Feyreisen, P., Lanoy, J.D.: Gestures and speech: Psychological investigations. Cambridge University Press, Cambridge (1991)
12. De Ruiter, J.P.: The production of gesture and speech. In: McNeill, D. (ed.) Language and Gesture, pp. 284–312. Cambridge University Press, Cambridge (2000)
13. Mayberry, R., Jaques, J.: Gesture productino during stuttered speech: insights into the nature of speech-gesture integration. In: McNeill, D. (ed.) Language and Gesture, pp. 199–215. Cambridge University Press, Cambridge (2000)
14. Özyürek, A.: Do speakers design their co-speech gestures for their addressees? The effects of addressee location on representational gestures. Journal of Memory and Language 46, 688–704 (2002)
15. Krauss, R.M., Morrel-Samuels, P., Colasante, C.: Do conversational hand gestures communicate? Journal of Personality and Social Psychology 61, 743–754 (1991)
16. Kelly, S., Özyürek, A., Maris, E.: Two sides of the same coin: Speech and gesture interact to enhance comprehension. Psychological Science (in press)
17. Özyürek, A., Kita, S.: Expressing manner and path in English and Turkish: Differences in speech, gesture, and conceptualization. In: Hahn, M., Stoness, S.C. (eds.) Proceedings of the twenty first annual conference of the Cognitive Science Society, pp. 507–512. Lawrence Erlbaum, Mahwah (1999)
18. Kita, S.: How representational gestures help speaking. In: McNeill, D. (ed.) Language and Gesture, pp. 261–284. Cambridge University Press, Cambridge (2000)
19. Talmy, L.: Semantics and syntax of motion. In: Shopen, T. (ed.) Language typology and syntactic description. Grammatical categories and the lexicon, vol. 3, pp. 57–149. Cambridge University Press, Cambridge (1985)
20. Bock, K.: Towards a cognitive psychology of syntax: Information processing contributions to sentence formulation. Psychological Review 89, 1–47 (1982)
21. Levelt, P.: Speaking. MIT Press, Cambridge (1989)

22. Özyürek, A., Kita, S., Allen, S., Furman, R., Brown, A.: How does linguistic framing influence co-speech gestures? Insights from cross-linguistic differences and similarities. Gesture 5, 216–241 (2005)
23. Pederson, E., Danziger, E., Wilkins, D., Levinson, S.C., Kita, S., Senft, G.: Semantic typology and spatial conceptualization. Language 74, 557–589 (1998)
24. Kita, S., Özyürek, A., Allen, S., Brown, A., Furman, R., Ishizuka, T.: Relations between syntactic encoding and co-speech gestures: Implications for a model of speech and gesture production. Language and Cognitive Processes 22(8), 1212–1236 (2007)
25. Beattie, G., Shovelton, H.: Do iconic hand gestures really contribute anything to the semantic information conveyed by speech? An experimental investigation. Semiotica 123, 1 (1999)
26. Özyürek, A., Willems, R., Kita, S., Hagoort, P.: On-line integration of information from speech and gesture: Insight from event-related potentials. Journal of Cognitive Neuroscience 19(4), 605–616 (2007)
27. Willems, R., Özyürek, A., Hagoort, P.: When language meets action. The neural integration of speech and gesture. Cerebral Cortex 17, 2322–2333 (2007)
28. Hagoort, P.: How the brain solves the binding problem for language: a neurocomputational model of syntactic processing. Neuroimage 20, S18–S29 (2003)
29. Hagoort, P., Hald, L., Bastiaansen, M., Petersson, K.M.: Integration of word meaning and world knowledge in language comprehension. Science 304, 438–441 (2004)
30. Kopp, S., Bergmann, K., Wachsmuth, I.: Multimodal communication from multimodal thinking – Towards an integrated model of speech and gesture production. Semantic Computing 2(1), 115–136 (2008)

Speakers' Use of Interactive Gestures as Markers of Common Ground

Judith Holler

School of Psychological Sciences,
Coupland Building 1,
University of Manchester,
Manchester M13 9PL, UK
judith.holler@manchester.ac.uk

Abstract. This study experimentally manipulates common ground (the knowledge, beliefs and assumptions interlocutors mutually share [6]) and measures the effect on speakers' use of interactive gestures to mark common ground. The data consist of narratives based on a video of which selected scenes were known to both speaker and addressee (common ground condition) or to only the speaker (no common ground condition). The analysis focuses on those interactive gestures that have been described in the literature as 'shared information gestures' [4]. The findings provide experimental evidence that certain interactive gestures are indeed linked to common ground. Further, they show that speakers seem to employ at least two different forms of shared knowledge gestures. This difference in form appears to be linked to speakers' use of gesture in the grounding process, as addressees provided feedback more frequently in response to one of the gesture types.

Keywords: common ground, interactive gestures, gestural markers, pointing, palm up open hand gesture.

1 Introduction

Much research in the field of gesture has focused on those speech-accompanying movements representing semantic information related to the content of speech. McNeill [1], [2] has termed these iconic and metaphoric gestures. Co-speech gestures that have received far less attention are those termed 'interactive gestures' [3], [4], [5]. In contrast to iconic and metaphoric gestures, interactive gestures do not represent any propositional information. Instead, they are closely tied to the social context in which they occur; speakers direct interactive gestures at their addressees, thus involving them in the interaction. The specific functions they fulfil at any given moment depend on the context in which they are embedded.

Bavelas et al. [4], [5] have shown through systematic, fine-grained analyses that it is possible to interpret the functions of individual interactive gestures when considering the gestures in social context. These studies have led to a categorisation scheme including four broader categories (delivery gestures, citing gestures, seeking gestures and turn gestures), and twelve specialised sub-categories. The present paper

S. Kopp and I. Wachsmuth (Eds.): GW 2009, LNAI 5934, pp. 11–22, 2010.

focuses on one of the sub-categories of delivery gestures, called 'shared information gestures', which comprises gestures that refer to information the addressee is assumed to already know. Their meaning can be paraphrased as 'as you know'. Bavelas et al. [4] provide the example of a speaker referring to the subject he studies, and referring back to this information about a minute later (while still talking to the same addressee). Together with this second reference, 'his hand quickly came up from his lap and rotated toward the addressee; his fingers uncurled to point at the addressee; then his hand returned to his lap' ([4] p.395). The meaning and function of this type of interactive gesture is, in their analyses, based on the analyst's interpretation (in the form of a verbal explication), supported by strong inter-observer agreement between several independent judges. In addition, Bavelas et al. [4] have provided empirical evidence that the functions of interactive gestures they attributed to the different gesture categories do indeed elicit the predicted addressee responses.

The knowledge, beliefs and assumptions that are mutually shared by interlocutors in a conversation tends to be referred to as their *common ground* (e.g., [6]). We already know from a host of experimental and field studies that this kind of common ground influences our use of verbal language. For example, the use of definite references, such as in the utterance 'Have you ever seen the movie showing at the Roxy tonight?' [7] presupposes mutual knowledge, here about the fact that a film is playing that evening, which film is being shown, and what the Roxy is. Experimental studies have shown, for example, that speakers tend to use fewer words [8], [9], [10] and less informative utterances [11] when more common ground exists.

The vast majority of studies investigating the influence of common ground on language have focused on the verbal side of utterances. However, some studies have started to explore the connection between speech, co-speech gesture and common ground (e.g., [12], [13], [14], [15], [16]). These studies have yielded mixed results. Some suggest that gestures become less precise, carry less information and are produced at a lower rate when common ground exists compared to when it does not, whereas others have shown that gesture rate increases and that the gestures often remain informative and full-blown. More research is clearly needed in this area.

Another aspect which we know very little about is the use of interactive gestures in connection with common ground. The studies mentioned above have focused exclusively on iconic, metaphoric and abstract deictic gestures. In terms of interactive gestures, all we know (such as from the example by Bavelas et al. [4], cited above) is that certain gestures seem to refer specifically to mutually shared knowledge (i.e., 'shared information gestures', in their terms). The present paper is a step to advance this area of research. It aims to do so by experimentally testing the claim that certain interactive gestures are specifically used to mark mutually shared information. So far, we have evidence that independent analysts can reliably identify and agree on the paraphrasing of these shared information gestures [4]. While this is compelling evidence that the respective gestures evoke the same interpretation in different observers of an interaction, critics could argue that this does not necessarily mean that individuals directly participating in it actually use these gestures with the intent to mark common ground.

Experimental studies manipulating common ground and measuring speakers' use of such gestures could provide further insights here. In the present study, dyads either had pre-existing mutual knowledge about parts of a video one speaker was telling the other about, or they did not. Thus, the experiment involved a manipulation of the kind of common ground which is based on 'prior physical co-presence' [7]. The focus of the analysis is on the narrative of those parts of the video that formed part of the interlocutors' common ground in one condition but not in the other. If there are indeed interactive gestures whose function is to mark common ground, then speakers in the Common Ground condition (CG) should use more of these gestures than those in the No Common Ground condition (NCG). (Of course, in the NCG condition some common ground-related gestures may still occur due to the fact that mutually shared knowledge also accumulates over the course of an interaction [based on 'linguistic co-presence' [7]]; however, this should be the same in both conditions and therefore should not interfere with the experimental manipulation.)

The second way in which the study explores the link between interactive gestures and common ground is by examining differences in the form of these shared information gestures. When eye-balling the data it was noticeable that speakers appear to use two forms of gestures here. One is a deictic gesture, pointing directly at the addressee, with a clearly protruding index finger (in a couple of cases the middle finger was also extended) and with the palm facing either to the side, down or upwards. The second type of gesture involves a flat hand (although the fingers may be slightly curled in), no individual finger protruding distinctly, and with the palm facing upwards (Palm Up Open Hand, or PUOH [17], see also [18]; the example provided by Bavelas et al. [4], cited above, also seems to belong into this category, as all of the fingers are pointing towards the addressee). In both cases the gestures motion towards the addressee, although the pointing gestures tended to often flick out more rapidly and with more emphasis. Of course, this difference in hand shape might seem small and may not matter at all. In fact, Bavelas et al. [4] state that, while all interactive gestures share the general feature of palm or finger orientation towards the addressee, the function of interactive gestures does not depend on the exact form, which is idiosyncratically determined and improvised. In other words, unlike with emblems [19], for example, there is no simple form-function mapping. A PUOH gesture can, for instance, have the function of someone handing over the speaking turn to another (thus belonging to the class of 'turn gestures'), but it can also be used to indicate someone else's earlier conversational contribution (thus falling into the category of 'citing gestures') or to provide new information (thus being a 'delivery gesture'). However, we also know that, in certain contexts at least, the form of gestures (in particular pointing gestures) is not idiosyncratic, with the morphological parameters and exact hand configuration being 'a patterned component of the utterance ensemble' ([18], p.223). The second part of the present analysis focuses on differences in the form of gestures which have the same general function (i.e., both are 'delivery gestures' used to mark shared information). In other words, this analysis focuses on differences *within* one of the sub-categories established by Bavelas and colleagues. From their 1995 analysis, it is clear that there is some variation in addressee responses to interactive gestures from the same sub-category. For example, for shared knowledge gestures (as for some other categories, too), they predicted a 'confirming response *or* no new response (Bavelas et al. [4], p.402, emphasis added). The second part of the present analysis therefore aims to uncover whether there is any particular pattern underlying this variation which is based on morphological differences in gesture form.

The rationale behind this idea is that hand gestures are believed to have evolved from manipulations of the physical world (e.g., [20], [21]). As such, using a PUOH gesture is like offering, presenting or giving something imaginary placed on the surface of the hand, such as the current discourse focus, or to receive something, such as feedback or a comment ([18]; see also [17]). A pointing gesture, on the other hand, does not direct attention to something that is placed on top of the palm. Rather, it has a trajectory which singles out a referent in the surrounding environment (or in fictive space). Here, the gesture's trajectory singles out the addressee. It thus reaches, through its vector, into the addressee's gesture space. If we assume that gestures evolved from object manipulation and acting in a physical world, then one possibility is that pointing gestures evolved from touching or reaching with the index finger. This would mean that through the trajectory the interactive pointing gesture is somewhat like touching the addressee. As such, this pointing gesture may be perceived as somewhat more imperative, a more demanding request for a response than one which *offers* something that may be *considered* for responding to, or not.

Speakers' use of these two different kinds of gesture forms to mark common ground may relate to Clark's [6] notion of 'projected evidence'. In order for the joint activity of conversation to be successful, interactants need to ground their discourse contributions [22]. Grounding is the process by which interactants establish the mutual belief that they have understood the meaning of a discourse contribution 'to a criterion sufficient for current purposes' ([22], p. 129). For this to happen, contributors require from their partners some form of positive evidence of understanding (or, in case of negative evidence, the contributor can rephrase or in some other form repair their previous contribution). One way in which addressees often provide such positive evidence is through acknowledgements, such as 'yeah', 'ok' or 'uhu'. A might say to B 'I'm gonna go to a gig at the Academy tonight' to which B responds 'uhu'. In this case, A's contribution has been grounded. Another basic form of positive evidence is continued attention. In face-to-face interaction, speakers can express their undisturbed attention through eye gaze (e.g., [22]). In order to ground contributions in discourse, and thus to accumulate common ground in a conversation, contributors signal when they need positive evidence of understanding from their addressee. Further, by presenting an utterance in a particular way, speakers project which kind of evidence they require [6]. According to Clark [6], gestures are one way by which speakers can elicit this evidence, including interactive gestures. The idea tested here is that speakers may use different forms of shared-knowledge gestures depending on what kind of positive evidence they require and how urgent this response is. The focus is on how speakers use interactive gestures in grounding references to common ground that they acquired through prior physical co-presence with their addressee.

In sum, the first part of the analysis aims to provide experimental evidence for speakers' use of interactive gestures in association with experimentally induced common ground. The second part of the analysis tests whether two forms of gestures occurring with references to common ground function the same or differently in terms of involving the addressee in the communication process. To test this, the focus is on two aspects, namely whether a new response occurs or not, and how quickly this response is elicited.

Of course, it would be interesting to also consider a range of other aspects. Because of this, and because the present study uses a dataset that is more monologue-like in nature with one person in each dyad having the speaking part, the present analysis needs to be considered work in progress. However, it offers a first insight into how speakers may use interactive gestures in the context of common ground.

2 Method

2.1 Participants and Design

80 students (40 female and 40 male) from the University of Manchester took part in the experiment (for either payment or experimental credits). All individuals were right handed native English speakers, unacquainted with each other prior to the experiment. Each participant was allocated to a same-sex pairing, which was then randomly assigned to one of two experimental conditions: 1) a 'common ground' (CG) condition, in which mutually shared knowledge about the stimulus material was experimentally induced, and a 'no common ground' condition (NCG), in which participants did not share any experimentally induced common ground.

2.2 Apparatus and Materials

A video recording, about 8 minutes in length, from a children's television program (showing various characters involved in a range of everyday activities, such as grocery shopping, playing in a barn) was used as the stimulus material ('Neues aus Uhlenbusch', ZDF, Germany; the video was played without the sound, but was still easily understandable). Six individual scenes, each just a few seconds long, were selected from this video and recorded onto a second tape to induce common ground. Participants were filmed split screen with two wall-mounted video cameras, each providing a view of one of the participants.

2.3 Procedure

In both the CG and the NCG condition the participants were randomly allocated to a speaker and to an addressee role. The speaker was asked to watch the stimulus video while the addressee was absent. However, in the CG condition, both participants first watched the six selected scenes together before the speaker saw the entire video. (In the NCG condition, the speaker also watched the six scenes, alone, to keep salience and memory constant across conditions). The addressee was then asked back into the room and the speaker was instructed to tell them what happened in the story as a whole. In the CG condition, the speaker-participant was reminded that the addressee already shared some knowledge about the video with them. In the NCG condition they were reminded that their addressee had no pre-existing knowledge about the story. In both conditions, addressees were told to not interrupt the speaker with questions but that they could signal their understanding or lack thereof in any other way they deemed appropriate (such as backchannel responses, *uhum, yeah, ok*, or nonverbally). The reason for this restriction was that the dataset was also used for an analysis of gesture rate [14], and differences in the number of questions asked by addressees would affect gesture frequency [23] and thus could result in a confound with differences due to the experimental manipulation of common ground.

2.4 Analysis

Gesture Categorisation. In the first instance, all gestures identified were categorised according to Bavelas (e.g., [3]) into 'topic' and 'interactive' gestures. The inter-observer reliability between two independent coders using these two categories to code the data from six randomly selected participants (three from each condition) was 95%.

Then, the gestures were divided into more detailed categories, distinguishing iconic, metaphoric and abstract deictic gestures [1], as well as interactive pointing gestures towards the addressee with the hypothesised function of marking common ground, and palm up open hand gestures [17] related to common ground. In addition, a category including all other forms of interactive gestures was used, as well as a category for pragmatic gestures [18]. The agreement of two independent judges categorising all gestures using these seven categories was 86%.

The data from this experiment were subjected to a range of different analyses. However, the present study focuses exclusively on common ground related pointing gestures made towards the addressee (hereafter termed CG-ADD-pointing gestures) and common ground related palm up open hand gestures (hereafter termed CG-PUOH gestures), as described in the Introduction. Only gestures accompanying parts of speech that referred to content from the six selected scenes were considered (see [14], for more detail on the segmentation of the narratives)).

Addressee Responses. The second and third analyses take into account i) whether addressees responded, and ii) how promptly this response was issued. In terms of addressee responses, both verbal and nonverbal responses were included. Usually, the responses consisted of either a head nod or a backchannel response (such as *uhu, yeah, ok*), or a combination of the two. These were 'new' responses in a way, as addressees usually respond through continued attention, signalled, for example, through eye gaze directed at the speaker. The responses coded here were therefore new responses which occurred in addition to continued eye gaze. With regard to response timing, the delay from the peak of the gesture to the onset of the addressee's immediate response was evaluated, with a maximum delay of two seconds being considered immediate. Although this criterion is somewhat arbitrary, the decision was based on Bavelas et al.'s statement that most of the addressee responses to interactive gestures occurred within a 2 second window in their analysis ([4], p. 402-403). Two delay categories were used, *0s delay*, capturing responses whose onset coincided with the peak of the gesture (or even preceded it due to the response starting towards the end of the preparation phase of the gesture), and up to *2s delay*, which captured any other new responses occurring after the peak of the gesture. A third category called 'no response' captured those cases where either no new response occurred at all, or the delay was longer than two seconds and therefore the response did not seem directly related to the gesture.

3 Results

This section reports three analyses. The first one tests the link between shared information gestures and common ground. The second and third one consider the two forms of shared information gestures found in the present dataset individually to compare the frequency with which they elicit addressee responses, and how prompt these responses are.

3.1 Do Interactive Gestures Mark Common Ground?

This analysis tests the claim that there are indeed certain kinds of interactive gestures associated with the delivery of shared information. If this is the case, speakers in the CG condition should use more CG-PUOH and more CG-ADD-pointing gestures when referring to the six selected scenes than speakers in the NCG condition. While the latter group of speakers may, on occasion, use these gestures to refer to information they have already provided (i.e., when referring to shared knowledge that has accumulated during the conversation), speakers in the CG condition should use them also when referring to the information from the six experimental scenes as common ground. And this is what we found (see Table 1). A Mann-Whitney U test showed that speakers in the CG condition used significantly more CG-PUOH gestures and CG-ADD-pointing gestures towards the addressee (combined data) when referring to the six selected scenes ($Mdn = 1.5$, $Range = 6.00$) than speakers from the NCG condition ($Mdn = 0.00$, $Range = 2.00$), $U = 59.50$, $n_1 = 20$, $n_2 = 20$, $p = .0001$.

Table 1. Frequency of CG-ADD-pointing and CG-PUOH gestures in the common ground (CG) and no-common ground (NCG) conditions

	Interactive gesture type	
	ADD	PUOH
CG	31	11
NCG	1	3

3.2 Do CG-PUOH and CG-ADD-Pointing Gestures Differ in the Amount of Addressee Responses They Elicit?

This analysis focuses only on speakers in the CG condition. It compares the frequency with which addressees provide a feedback response immediately following the two kinds of interactive gestures marking shared information. Goodman and Kruskal's Tau (dependent variable = response) showed a significant association between interactive gesture type and response frequency ($\tau_B = .098$, $p = .045$), with CG-ADD-pointing gestures eliciting proportionally more responses than CG-PUOH gestures.

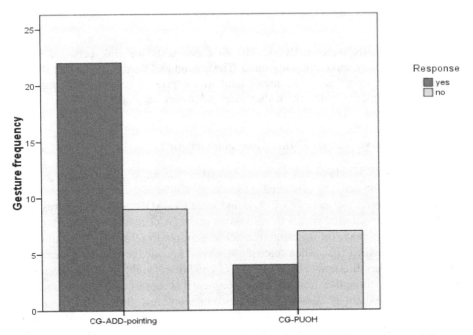

Fig. 1. Frequency of CG-ADD-pointing gestures and CG-PUOH gestures receiving an addressee response

3.3 Do Addressees Respond More Promptly to Either CG-PUOH or CG-ADD-Pointing Gestures?

This analysis is based on those gestures examined in section 3.2 that did receive a response within the 2s time window (see Table 2). It tested the hypothesis that the two different forms of the common ground related interactive gestures identified in the present corpus affect the speed with which addressees respond. When speakers refer to the information that constitutes common ground and mark this with the respective interactive gestures which aim to involve the addressee, then addressees should provide some feedback as to whether they have understood and recall the respective aspects of the video. One idea is that they may do so with more urgency in response to CG-ADD-pointing gestures, as they could be viewed as more imperative and a more direct demand for feedback (compared to the possibly more 'subtle' CG-PUOH invitation to provide feedback). However, although we see a pattern that could be interpreted as suggestive of such an association (in that in almost a third of the cases participants' responses coincided with the peak of the CG-ADD-pointing gesture, whereas for CG-PUOH gestures, none of the responses coincided with the peak of the gesture), no significant association was found, $\tau_B = .055$, $p = .243$.

(Only two CG-ADD-pointing gestures occurred within the 2nd second following the peak of a gesture; although the pattern becomes slightly stronger when excluding these two cases when reducing the time window to 1 second as an alternative analysis (with almost half of the responses to CG-ADD-pointing gestures then coinciding with the gesture peak), the association remains statistically non-significant, $\tau_B = .067$, $p = .216$.)

Table 2. Frequency of gestures eliciting addressee responses coinciding with (0s) or following (2s) the gesture

	Response delay	
	0s	up to 2s
CG-ADD-point	6	16
CG-PUOH	0	4

4 Discussion

The present analysis set out to show two things. First, it tried to experimentally validate the claim that one particular category of interactive gestures fulfils the function of marking shared knowledge. Previous studies have provided some evidence for this in that independent analysts agree in their identification of such gestures and on the interpretation of the function they fulfil. The present analysis has provided supporting experimental evidence for this claim. From examining the data, it appeared that there are at least two different forms of interactive gestures that speakers use for marking common ground (i.e., two different gesture forms that would both fall into Bavelas et al.'s [4] category of 'shared information gestures'). One is a flat hand shape, the palm facing up, fingers (either slightly curled or extended) facing towards the addressee, without any individual fingers protruding distinctly more than the others in an indexical manner. This type of hand gesture has been termed 'palm up open hand' (PUOH) by Müller [17] and is considered to be part of the 'open hand supine' (OHS) family of gestures [18]. The other form is a common pointing gesture, with the index finger (and in a few cases also the middle finger) clearly protruding more than any other finger, and with the point being directed at the addressee. Here, we termed these gestures CG-PUOH and CG-ADD-pointing, respectively.

The findings from the first analysis showed that, indeed, speakers who talk to addressees with whom they share experimentally induced common ground (based on a prior shared visual experience and experimental instructions) use significantly more of both of these types of interactive gestures than speakers who talk about the same semantic events but without these being part of the common ground. This is clear evidence that common ground between interlocutors encourages the use of interactive gestures which fulfil the specific function of marking this mutually shared knowledge for the addressee. Important to note is that co-speech gestures were *not* more frequent in the common ground condition in general. An earlier analysis based on data from the same experiment [14] focused on iconic and deictic gestures (here pointing gestures used in a non-interactive manner) and found no significant difference between the CG and NCG conditions; in fact, the tendency was in the opposite direction, with numerically more gestures being used in the NCG than in the CG condition. In addition, this earlier analysis also found that speakers in the CG condition used significantly fewer words than when no experimentally induced common ground existed. This means that, in the present analysis, the higher number of common ground related interactive gestures in the CG condition can*not* be accounted for simply by the fact that speakers talked more and therefore had more opportunity to produce more of these gestures. As another side point, the present findings relate mainly to common ground based on prior co-presence, but in some cases shared knowledge gestures were also used for the kind of common ground that builds up during conversation (based on linguistic co-presence) [7].

Whereas the first analysis combined the two different gesture forms to tap the general category of shared information gestures, the second and third analyses considered them individually. They showed that the difference in form seems to be functional at a micro-level (i.e., *within* the category of shared knowledge gestures established by Bavelas et al. [4]). There was a clear association between CG-ADD-pointing gestures and new addressee responses, whereas this was not the case for CG-PUOH gestures. (Although the third analysis also revealed a tendency for CG-ADD-pointing gestures being responded to more promptly than CG-PUOH gestures, this association was not significant.) It therefore seems that, in the context of communicating mutually shared knowledge, pointing gestures directed at the addressee are perceived as somewhat more urgent requests for addressee feedback than palm up open hand gestures are.

Although the relationship between form and function of interactive gestures is idiosyncratic with no fixed one-to-one mapping (e.g., a PUOH gesture may occur in any of the main categories of interactive gestures [4]), it seems that within one sub-category, small differences in the morphological form of gestures may impact on the interactive process between speaker and addressee (at least in the case of shared knowledge gestures). Thus, within the group of gestures sharing the general function of marking common ground, CG-ADD-pointing gestures may be considered the more imperative form of common ground related interactive gestures. With reference to Clark [6], we may conclude that different gestural signals are used by speakers to project different kinds of evidence of understanding. Whereas in some cases the speaker may perceive continued attention (e.g., expressed by the addressee's eye gaze) a sufficient indicator that their contribution has been understood 'well enough for current purposes', they may require more explicit evidence in others (such as a new response in the form of a verbal or nonverbal acknowledgement). This suggests that interactive gestures may play an important role in the process of grounding – at least in the context of grounding speakers' reference to common ground based on prior physical co-presence.

However, because the present analysis constitutes work in progress, we have to be tentative with interpretations. After all, there are a host of additional, unexplored factors that may play a role here. One of the most important next steps is to examine the interplay of these interactive gestures with the verbal components of the utterances they form part of. Also, the kinds of responses addressees provided have here been grouped together. A more fine-grained analysis differentiating verbal, nonverbal and multi-modal responses (including gaze, facial expressions and intonation) is needed. Moreover, the current findings are restricted in generalisability as they are based on more monologue-type contexts where one person speaks and the other provides backchannel responses, similar to telling an anecdote, a close-call story, a joke, and so forth. More dialogic interactions may potentially differ in terms of how speakers mark common ground and how addressees respond to these markers. Yet another avenue for advancing this work is to apply a more micro-analytic procedure taking into account morphological differences also at other parameter levels, such as differences in palm orientation (for pointing gestures). This may yield further sub-classifications. It is obvious that much work remains to be done on this issue, but the present study has thrown light on some potentially very important associations between interactive gestures, common ground and grounding.

Acknowledgements. I would like to thank two anonymous reviewers for their very helpful input into this article, Katie Wilkin for her help with collecting the data, and the Economic and Social Research Council for funding this research (RES-061-23-0135).

References

1. McNeill, D.: So you think gestures are nonverbal? Psychological Review 92, 350–371 (1985)
2. McNeill, D.: Hand and mind: What gestures reveal about thought. University of Chicago Press, Chicago (1992)
3. Bavelas, J.B.: Gestures as part of speech: methodological implications. Research on Language and Social Interaction 27, 201–221 (1994)
4. Bavelas, J.B., Chovil, N., Coates, L., Roe, L.: Gestures specialized for dialogue. Personality and Social Psychology Bulletin 21, 394–405 (1995)
5. Bavelas, J.B., Chovil, N., Lawrie, D., Wade, A.: Interactive gestures. Discourse Processes 15, 469–489 (1992)
6. Clark, H.H.: Using language. Cambridge University Press, Cambridge (1996)
7. Clark, H.H., Marshall, C.R.: Definite reference and mutual knowledge. In: Joshi, A.K., Webber, B., Sag, I. (eds.) Elements of discourse understanding, pp. 10–63. Cambridge University Press, Cambridge (1981)
8. Clark, H.H., Wilkes-Gibbs, D.: Referring as a collaborative process. Cognition 22, 1–39 (1986)
9. Fussell, S.R., Krauss, R.M.: The effects of intended audience on message production and comprehension: Reference in a common ground framework. Journal of Experimental Social Psychology 25, 203–219 (1989)
10. Isaacs, E.A., Clark, H.H.: References in conversations between experts and novices. Journal of Experimental Psychology: General 116, 26–37 (1987)
11. Fussell, S.R., Krauss, R.M.: Coordination of knowledge in communication: Effects of speakers' assumptions about what others know. Journal of Personality and Social Psychology 62, 378–391 (1992)
12. Gerwing, J., Bavelas, J.B.: Linguistic influences on gesture's form. Gesture 4, 157–195 (2004)
13. Holler, J., Stevens, R.: An experimental investigation into the effect of common ground on how speakers use gesture and speech to represent size information in referential communication. Journal of Language and Social Psychology 26, 4–27 (2007)
14. Holler, J., Wilkin, K.: Communicating common ground: how mutually shared knowledge influences the representation of semantic information in speech and gesture in a narrative task. Language and Cognitive Processes 24, 267–289 (2009)
15. Jacobs, N., Garnham, A.: The role of conversational hand gestures in a narrative task. Journal of Memory and Language 56, 291–303 (2007)
16. Parrill, F.: The hands are part of the package: gesture, common ground and information packaging. In: Newman, J., Rice, S. (eds.) Empirical and experimental methods in cognitive/functional research. CSLI, Stanford (in press)

17. Müller, C.: Forms of the uses of the Palm Up Open Hand. A case of a gesture family? In: Posner, R., Müller, C. (eds.) The semantics and pragmatics of everyday gestures, pp. 234–256. Weidler Buchverlag, Berlin (2004)
18. Kendon, A.: Gesture: Visible action as utterance. Cambridge University Press, Cambridge (2004)
19. Ekman, P., Friesen, W.V.: The repertoire of nonverbal behavior: Categories, origins, usage, and coding. Semiotica 1, 49–98 (1996)
20. LeBaron, C., Streeck, J.: Gestures, knowledge, and the world. In: McNeill, D. (ed.) Language and gesture: Window into thought and action, pp. 118–138. Cambridge University Press, Cambridge (2000)
21. Roth, W.-M.: From action to discourse: The bridging function of gestures. Journal of Cognitive Systems Research 3, 535–554 (2002)
22. Clark, H.H., Brennan, S.A.: Grounding in communication. In: Resnick, L.B., Levine, J.M., Teasley, S.D. (eds.) Perspectives on socially shared cognition. APA Books, Washington (1991)
23. Beattie, G., Aboudan, R.: Gestures, pauses and speech: an experimental investigation of the effects of changing social context on their precise temporal relationships. Semiotica 99, 239–272 (1994)

Gesture Space and Gesture Choreography in European Portuguese and African Portuguese Interactions: A Pilot Study of Two Cases

Isabel Galhano Rodrigues

Faculdade de Letras da Universidade do Porto,
Via Panorâmica, s/n,
P-4150-564 Porto, Portugal
irodrig@letras.up.pt

Abstract. This pilot study focuses on aspects of cultural variation in cospeech gestures in two interactions with Angolan and European Portuguese participants. The elements compared are gesture features - extension, drawn path, articulation points - and generated gesture spaces. Posture, interpersonal distance and other speech-correlated movements were taken into account as essential parameters for the definition of different kinds of physical spaces. Some differences were obvious: gestures performed by Angolan speakers were articulated at the levels of the shoulders, elbows and wrists, thus tracing considerable larger angles than those traced by gestures performed by Portuguese speakers. As the Angolan participants sit close to one another, their extended arms constantly invade the other participants' personal spaces.

Keywords: gesture, cultural variations in cospeech gestures, gesture space.

1 Introduction

As is well known, gesture choreography and gesture space vary considerably from culture to culture. The paths followed by gestures, the hand configuration, as well as the amplitude of shoulder, elbow, and wrist angles have distinct features and reveal not only individually but also culturally determined tendencies (Chienki, Müller, 2008, Efron, 1972, Hall, 1974, Müller, 1998). The same can be said concerning distances and positions of interactants' bodies in relation to each other (Argyle, 1994, Özyürek, 20002, Sweetser, Sizemore, 2006). The analysis of face-to-face interaction offers the possibility of considering, among numerous other aspects, both gesture amplitude and the paths pursued by fingers, hands and arms, as well as issues regarding proxemics and haptics. Comparing interactions in Portuguese spoken in Portugal with Portuguese spoken in Luanda (Angola) can show cultural tendencies gesture choreography and gesture space. The next section of this paper explores the different kinds of *space(s)* in the context of face-to-face interaction as well as the

S. Kopp and I. Wachsmuth (Eds.): GW 2009, LNAI 5934, pp. 23–33, 2010.
© Springer-Verlag Berlin Heidelberg 2010

topics of *body contact* and *touch*. This is followed by a description of some examples of how gesture space[1] and gesture features are generated.

2 Physical Spaces

Within the context of this paper, space(s) in interaction are understood to mean the areas defined by the orientation and the movements of the participants' bodies in a face-to-face interaction. The dimensions of these spaces depend on different factors:

a) engagement in interaction, state of mind (Yngve, 1970) or socio-cognitive state (Rodrigues, 2007b: 245);

b) common ground (Holler, 2007);

c) size of the bodies (when standing, taller people have the tendency to keep their hands at a lower level (lap), while short people prefer to perform gestures at a higher level (chest, shoulder height), arm length;

d) individual variables like age, gender, status and other socio-cultural elements;

e) physical setting (size of space participants are in, posture, postural habits: sitting on a chair, on the floor, standing, lying on a sofa, on the floor).

f) the orientation of the participants' bodies (location of the space shared by participants) (Özyürek, 2002);

g) affect display rules (Ekman, Friesen, 1969). (This item is inspired by the works of several authors (Efron, 1972, Hall, 1974, Müller, 1998, Chienki, Müller, 2000, Kendon, 2004) who focus on cultural tendencies related to gesture amplitude and gesture articulation points.)

As pointed out by Kita (2009: 5), the physical space around us has some influence in the organization of space in our brain. I believe in the reflexivity (as commented by Tuan (1977, 8-18) already some decades ago) between, on the one hand, bodily experience in the world and conceptualization of space, and, on the other hand, space definition/mapping according to this bodily experience in a certain environment. Also Hall emphasizes the experienced aspects of the relation between body and environment (which involves parameters like population density, topography, living habits) when he writes, "people from different cultures inhabit different sensory worlds [...] they do not structure space differently, but experience it differently" (Hall, 1974, 207).

Several researchers have defined different kinds of spaces which are to be considered in face-to-face interaction:

---

[1] In the literature *gesture space* is generally defined as follows: "the space speakers use to gesticulate." I would be careful with the word *use,* as it seems to assign static properties to the concept of gesture space; I prefer expressions like "the space defined by...", as space is a dynamic dimension. Space in general only exists as the result of the imposition of limits, marks or borders, and gesture space is the space defined/mapped by gesticulation, thus being subjected to changes of its dimensions and location in the course of face-to-face interaction. So gesture space should be seen as a continuously changing area, with more or less considerable variations according to different movement units.

Personal space – the area an individual feels as his/her territory, the body buffer zone (Wallbott, 1995) whose dimensions can vary according to individual, cultural and context (topographic and relational) features. These features determine the proximity-distance maintained by interactants, which can be individually or culturally determined. There are in fact cultural tendencies, so that we could say that, while in some societies people position themselves close to each other and often touch each other when they interact, in other societies touch and proximity are avoided.

Gesture space - the area determined by the performance of gestures, created through the movements of hands/arms. Generally the definition of gesture space does not include the position/movements of trunk and head, but in my opinion these modalities have an important influence on the physical area where a gesture is performed and, consequently, on the mapping of the gesture space itself. Özyürek (2002, 690) defines it as "the intersection of the individual gesture space of the participants". She also explores the fact that gesture space varies according to the position of the participants in relation to each other (side-by-side, face-to-face). Furthermore, as Sweetser and Sizemore argue, "there is no fixed size for a person's gesture space" as it depends on cultural and linguistic community and it is polyfunctional: "it can be used for interactional regulation, as well as to gesture about content (…) when gestures reach outside their personal space it is a sign that (1) they are engaged in regulating the speech interaction and (2) that the regulation is highlighted rather than backgrounded" (Sweetser, Sizemore, 2006, 33).

Interactional space – (*inter-speaker space* (Sweetser, Sizemore, 2006, 31) is the area defined by the orientation of the interaction partners' bodies. I should say this space corresponds to the *shared space* ("the intersection of the individual gesture spaces of the participants") (Özyürek, 2002, 690) together with a possible *in-between space* (Sweetser, Sizemore, 2006, 32) if the interactants are not seated too close to each other. The location and the size of the interactional space clearly depend on the position of participants and on the location of their gesture spaces. In addition, in the case of the recordings made for this pilot study (where the interactants are seated in a semi-circle in front of the camera) it can also be argued that the interactional space includes the area between the camera and the interactants. In fact, it should, at least when the interactants look at the camera while speaking. The definition of spaces in interaction should also account for the level of abstraction, as suggested by Haviland (2000), who distinguishes between a local and a narrated space besides the interactional space.

Conceiving different types of spaces is important not only for the description and definition of the areas (spaces) crossed by hands, arms and other body parts in the performance of co-speech gestures, but also for the explanation of the relation between performed concepts and interactional signals, and spoken concepts and interactional signals.

3 Gesture Choreography

I use the expression *gesture choreography* to refer to: a) the paths traced by the upper limbs along several axes, creating a three-dimensional space in front of the speaker's

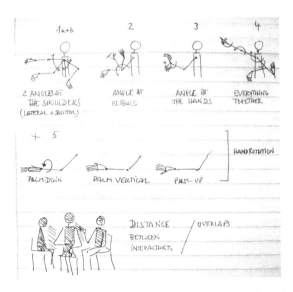

Fig. 1. Representation of the vertices, angles and hand rotation

body, b) the movement features (energy or tension put in the performance of a gesture), as well as the movement speed (how fast gestures are performed) and movement frequency (how many gestures are performed per unit of time), c) the way fingers, hands and arms articulate, and d) hand shape – the anatomy of hand and fingers allows a remarkable accuracy in the micro-representation of concepts, as well as more or less culturally determined movements related to habitual activities and (emotional) experiences. For this reason, the variables 'hand shape' and 'hand rotation' (palm orientation, degree of openness, fingers and thumb flexibility) are of great importance for the description of a gesture.

The vertices shoulder (1), elbow (2) and wrist (3) were used to describe gesture extension. Fig. 1 illustrates the angles that can be formed at these vertices, as well as hand rotation (hand shape). Obviously, it is the degree of the angles formed at the shoulders and elbows that determines the range of gesture space. Furthermore, other modalities (such as head and trunk movements) can also be taken into account when they are present in the gesticulation process, as can be frequently witnessed, for instance, in South European and African cultures.

4   Analysis of Two Case Studies

The analysed corpus consists of two interactions: one between three Portuguese male students and another between three Angolan male students. They were instructed to position their chairs in a semicircle in front of the camera (so that the video camera could capture the full image of their bodies) and they were asked to discuss about several themes, like the adoption of children by homosexual couples, or women's roles in different societies around the world. Their communication is spontaneous, although this laboratorial context may condition the quality of their movements. Due to the limit of pages imposed in this paper, preference was given to the description of the interaction between Angolans, as the movement features of the African students are considerably different from the movements of Portuguese, which were already described in detail in previous publications (Rodrigues, 2006, 2007a, 2007b).

4.1 Interpersonal Distance and Defined Spaces

Interpersonal distance - as we can see from the frames below (Fig.2), the three participants are engaged in a face-to-face interaction. They are sitting in semicircle so they can easily look at each other. They maintain a certain distance from each other and they do not touch each other. The first image represents the gesture with the biggest amplitude in the whole sequence (these four images were selected from the whole sequence). In this interaction, gesture space does not go beyond the personal space of any of the speakers.

Fig. 2. Interaction between Portuguese students

Fig. 3. Location and orientation of the interactants' bodies

As represented in Fig.3, the circles around speakers' heads roughly correspond to the space defined by the movements of their arms and hands, i.e., the gesture space. The small grey circle in front of the three speakers is the video camera.

As for the interaction between the three Angolan students, the situation is quite different: they placed their chairs side-by-side and close to each other so that they could all directly face the camera. Their lower limbs come into physical contact. The frames below show that they move their hands beyond the limits of the area generally defined as personal space and 'invade' the other participants' personal space (cf. Fig 4, pictures 5, 7, 8, 9, 10, 11, 14).

Pictures 5-8 illustrate a sequence where the participant in the middle has his turn. He opens his arms wide to both sides, entering the other participants' territory.

Fig. 5 illustrates the gesture space of the Angolan interactants. It is formed by the total extension of the speakers' arms of towards the interactional space.

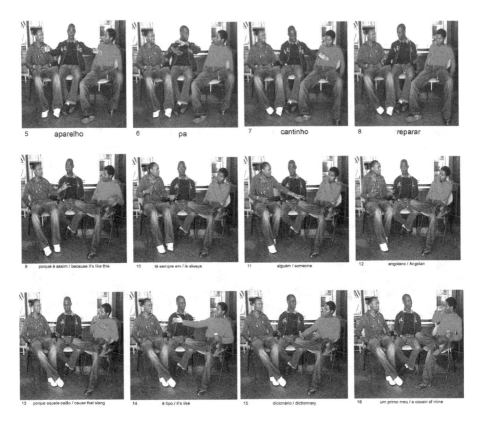

Fig. 4. Interaction between Angolan students

Fig. 5. Location and orientation of the interactants' bodies

Pictures 9 and 14 show how gestures enter the personal space of both the first and the third participant. In both cases the speaker focuses on an important part of his speech. In the first case, the gesture, together with the linguistic elements "porque é assim", functions as an announcement (Rodrigues, 2007) of what is going to be said and done next; in the second case, it introduces an aside to the utterance which is being produced. Both speakers orient their gestures to the centre of the interactional space, to the others [2].

---

[2] As this paper concerns the theme gesture choreography and gesture space, detailed description about gesture functions and forms were omitted. Further descriptions on this sequence can be read in Rodrigues (2007a, 2008).

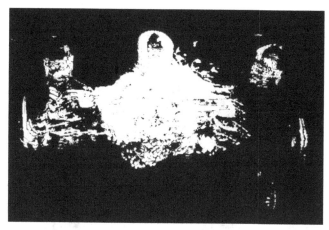

Fig. 6. a video of three seated figures is transformed into a sequence of moving silhouettes, and the sequence is then viewed as a single 2D image. The large white region in the center reveals the wide and varied range of the central speaker's hands over time.

Pictures 10-12 illustrate a moment when Speaker 1 moves his trunk forwards and raises his shoulders, modifying the dimension and location of his gesture space. This new posture is relevant at the interactional level since it reveals the speaker's intention to keep his turn. Leaning forwards and towards the other participants, the speaker also creates an atmosphere of more intimacy: it is a way of catching their attention and eliciting their cooperation as hearers[3].

Defined spaces - The images below are visualizations of a small sequence of the second interaction, kindly created by Jeremy Douglas, with the support of Lev Manovich[4]. Using McNeill's scheme (McNeill, 1992) of several areas in gesture space, we can say that the speaker's hands frequently move in the peripheral space.

Fig. 7 shows a longer sequence of frames from another perspective. In this sequence, Speaker 2 and Speaker 3 have the floor at different times. For each of the speakers, gesture space is the area defined by the positions of their hands in different points in space. As the extension of the movements reaches a location beyond the place occupied by their bodies, the gesture spaces of each of the interactants overlap. In other words, the shared space is created by the three speakers' overlapping gesture spaces, i.e., gesture space of speaker 1 overlaps with gesture space of speaker 2; gesture space of speaker 2 overlaps with the gesture spaces of both other participants; gesture space of speaker 3 overlaps with gesture space of speaker 2. As none of the participants seem to be bothered by the closeness of their body parts, we can suppose that these overlaps are common, and that this is a culturally determined feature of co-

---

[3] These aspects are similar to the results obtained by Özyürek (2002), although the position of the speakers here is different from the position of those described in her experiments.

[4] Jeremy Douglass (http: jeremydouglass.com) and Lev Manovich (http:www.manovich.net), University of California in San Diego. Lev Manovich is the director of the Software Studies Initiative at the California Institute for Telecommunications and Information Technology (Calit2). Jeremy Douglass and Lev Manovich are engaged in the development of cultural analytics projects.

verbal gestures in Angolan speakers. However, it is evident that further analyses of Angolan speakers (considering also age, gender and status), as well as of speakers from other cultures, are needed.

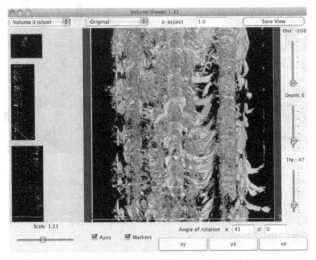

Fig. 7. Here a video of three seated figures is transformed into a sequence of moving silhouettes, and the sequence is then viewed as a 3D volume view to reveal the shared gestural space. The three fairly stationairy heads form three ridges, with the rhythms of arm motions between the figures appearing as a texture in the furrows.

Gesture type in gesture space - regarding the distribution of the different types of gestures (iconic, metaphoric, deictic) in gesture space, it can be noted that gestures referring to oneself were generally performed in the upper central region (according to McNeill's scheme of gesture space); presenting gestures (metaphoric) were more often found in the peripheral lower areas in the form of palm-ups; while gestures illustrating movements and objects were more frequently performed in peripheral upper areas. It is important to emphasize the qualitative – and not quantitative – nature of this study, which takes into account only three speakers. The pictures below illustrate three of these situations for speaker 2:

Fig. 8. McNeill's grid defining different areas of gesture space

4.2 Gesture Choreography

As mentioned before, describing gesture space implies the reference to the movement features of the body parts which are responsible for the dimensions of the generated space. The following drawings show the different kinds of movements performed by speaker 2 in a few seconds of this interaction:

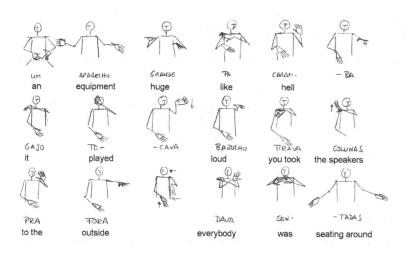

UM	APARELHO	GRANDE	PA	CAMAM-	— BA
an	equipment	huge	like	hell	

GAJO	TO -	— CAVA	BARULHO	TIRAVA	COLUNAS
it	played		loud	you took	the speakers

PRA	FORA		DAVA	SEN -	— TADAS
to the	outside		everybody	was	seating around

Fig. 9. Drawings at some crucial points of speaker's movements

This representation shows the following approximate measures for the different angles:

shoulders:	45° – 90°
elbows:	15° - 180°
wrists:	90° to the outside / 90° to the inside
	(degree 0° corresponds to the axis of the arm)

The hand-shape and hand configuration were characterized by a frequent rotation at the wrists as well as the articulation of the fingers / thumbs. As for the energy/tension of the movements performed, it is to be noted that the movements were relaxed and the focus of tension was located at shoulder level: as if the motion force was located at that level, elevating the limbs from there. Because the bodies are relaxed, the force that causes the articulation of hands and arms seems to result from the swinging of the whole arm.

In the case of the Portuguese speakers, the approximate measures of the angles are:

shoulders:	45°(to the side) and 60° (to the front),
elbows:	45° - 115°
wrists:	around 10° to the outside / 45° to the inside.

In these movements, the focus of tension is in the hands. As the strokes are shorter, these movements also seem to be performed with a higher degree of tenseness.

5 Final Remarks

The objective of this pilot study was to look for interesting cues regarding cultural variations in the performance of gesture when using the same language system. As Portuguese is spoken in several parts of the world, it offers an interesting research field for studies which seek to compare gesture features, the relation of gestures to the linguistic content of the utterances they accompany, the rhythm of speech and body movements, as well as the functions of spatial parameters in face-to-face interaction. By focusing on such aspects as gesture space and gesture choreography, it was possible to observe a number of differences between Angolan and Portuguese speakers, differences which are mostly related to the extension of the movements as well as the articulation of several parts of the upper limbs. In particular, the proximity between the Angolan interactants and the overlap of their spaces (personal – gesture – interactional) led to a closer examination of gesture space and interactional space. Thus, it became evident that there is a need for a more flexible definition of concepts such as personal space, gesture space and interactional space and the further research is needed to validate the results obtained.

References

1. Argyle, M.: The psychology of interpersonal behavior. Penguin, Harmondsworth
2. Chienki, A., Müller, C. (eds.): Metaphor and Gesture. John Benjamins, Amsterdam (2008)
3. Efron, D.: Gesture, race and culture. Mouton, The Hague [1941] (1972)
4. Ekman, P., Friesen, W.: The repertoire of nonverbal behavior: categories, origins, usage and coding. Semiotica 1(I), 49–98 (1969)
5. Hall, E.: Proxemics. In: Weitz, S. (ed.) Nonverbal communication, pp. 205–229. Oxford University Press, New York (1974)
6. Haviland, J.: Pointing, gesture spaces and mental maps. In: McNeill, D. (ed.) Language and Gesture, pp. 11–46. Cambridge University Press, Cambridge (2000)
7. Holler, J.: The effect of common ground on how speakers use gesture and speech to represent size information. Journal of Language and Social Psychology 26(1), 4–27 (2007)
8. Kendon, A.: Conducting Interaction. Patterns of behavior in focused encounters. Cambridge University Press, Cambridge (1990)
9. Kendon, A.: Gesture. Visible action as an utterance. Cambridge University Press, Cambridge (2004)
10. Kita, S.: Cross-cultural variation of speech-accomapanying gesture: A review. Language and Cognitive Processes 24(5), 145–167 (2009)
11. McNeill, D.: Hand and Mind. Cambridge University Press, Cambridge (1992)
12. Müller, C.: Redebegleitende Gesten. Kulturgeschichte-Theorie-Sprachvergleich. Verlag Arno Spitz, Berlin (1998)
13. Özyürek, A.: Do speakers design their cospeech gestures to their addressees? The effects of addressee location on representational gestures. Journal of Memory and Language 46(6), 688–704 (2002)
14. Rodrigues, I.: Konversationelle Funktionen der verbalen und nonverbalen Signale in der portugiesischen Interaktion: eine Reparartur. In: Endruschat, A., Kemmler, R., Schäfer-Prieß (eds.) Grammatische Strukturen des europäischen Portugiesisch, pp. 215–245. Calepinus Verlag, Tübingen (2006)

15. Rodrigues, I.: Interaktioneller Raum im Vergleich: Angolaner und Portugiesen. In: Grenzgänge (ed.) Beiträge zu einer modernen Romanistik, vol. 28, pp. 58–83 (2007a)
16. Rodrigues, I.: O corpo e a fala. FCG/FCT, Lisboa (2007b)
17. Rodrigues, I.: Espaço e gesto: interacções no português de diferentes culturas. Africana Studia 11, 81–127 (2008)
18. Sweetser, E., Sizemore, M.: Personal and interpersonal gesture spaces: Functional contrasts in language and gesture. In: Tyler, A., Kim, Y., Takada, M. (eds.) Language in the Context of Use: Cognitive and Discourse Approaches to Language and Language Learning, pp. 31–58. Mouton de Gruyter, Berlin (2006)
19. Tuan, Y.-F.: Space and Place. The perspective of experience. University of Minneapolis Press, London (1977)
20. Wallbott, H.: Analysis of nonverbal communication. In: Quasthoff, U. (ed.) Aspects of oral communication, pp. 480–490. Walter de Gruyter, Berlin (1995)
21. Yngve, V.: On getting a word in edgewise. Papers from the 6th regional meeting, Chicago Linguistic Society, April 16-18, pp. 567–578 (1970)

The Embodied Morphemes of Gaze

Isabella Poggi, Francesca D'Errico, and Alessia Spagnolo

Dipartimento di Scienze dell'Educazione – Università Roma Tre
Via del Castro Pretorio 20, 00185 Roma, Italy
poggi@uniroma3.it, francesca.derrico@uniroma1.it,
alessia.spagnolo@istruzione.it

Abstract. The paper presents some empirical studies aimed at singling out the meanings of specific items of gaze and of some of their parameters. It argues that the values on some parameters of gaze items are not comparable to phonemes in a verbal language, but rather to morphemes, since by themselves they convey some specific meanings. The different positions of the upper and lower eyelids are combined and the meanings conveyed by their possible values are investigated. It is found that wide open upper eyelids and raised lower eyelids convey activation and effort, while half open and half closed upper eyelids convey de-activation and relaxation. These embodied morphemes, stemming from particular physical states, become part of the meanings of gaze items conveyed by the combination of these eyelid positions.

Keywords: multimodality, gaze, lexicon, morphemes, embodied.

1 Gaze Communication

After the pioneering studies of Kendon (1967) and Argyle & Cook (1976), communication through gaze has captured attention in the last ten years. In Psychology and Linguistics, gaze has been investigated as to the evolutionary differences between humans' and apes' (Tomasello, 2007), as to its role in imagery and text comprehension (Underwood, 2005), in face-to-face interaction (Goodwin, 2000; Bavelas, 2000; Rossano, 2005; Allwood et al., 2005; Poggi and Roberto, 2007) and persuasion (Poggi & Vincze, 2008). In the field of Embodied Agents, gaze has been studied as a sign of interest (Peters et al., 2005), for its semantic subleties (Poggi, Pelachaud & de Rosis, 2000; Heylen, 2005), and for simulation in Virtual Agents (Cassell, 2000; Bevacqua et al., 2007; Maatman et al., 2005; Poel et al., 2009).

Most of these studies, though, generally deal with a single dimension: gaze direction. Which has, in fact, many important functions: looking at the interlocutor asks him to follow or to provide feedback; averting gaze tells you are thinking, trying to retrieve words; and if you are the interlocutor, gazing at the speaker assures about your interest and attention. Yet, beside eye direction many other aspects of eye behavior are relevant, and their function is not only to establish the setting for interaction, but to tell things: gaze conveys specific meanings, it is a rich and consistent communicative system that deserves being described in a systematic way.

S. Kopp and I. Wachsmuth (Eds.): GW 2009, LNAI 5934, pp. 34–46, 2010.
© Springer-Verlag Berlin Heidelberg 2010

Some research in these domains has been done; Eibl-Eibesfeldt (1972) and Ekman (1979) analyzed some of the conversational, emotional and syntactic functions of the eyebrows; Sign Language scholars (Baker-Schenk, 1985; Volterra, 1987; Thompson et al., 2006) have studied the syntactic and semantic role of gaze in ASL (American Sign Language) and LIS (Italian Sign Language). In Hearing people, the repertoire of gaze meanings has been investigated by Kreidlin's "Oculesics" (2002), and Poggi (2007) proposed to write a lexicon of gaze, arguing it is a communicative system as complex and sophisticated as facial expression or gesture can be.

2   The Communicative System of Gaze

According to Poggi (2007), beside being used to see, to look, to feel, and to favour thought processes, gaze can be seen as a communication system, i.e. a system of rules to put signals and meanings in correspondence, just like a verbal system, or a system of symbolic gestures, where a particular combination of sounds, or a particular shape and movement of the hands, corresponds to a specific meaning. In gaze, the signals – the perceivable stimuli an interlocutor can see and interpret by attributing them some meaning – are morphological features and muscular actions exhibited in the eye region, that includes eyebrows, eyelids, eyelashes, eyes and eye-sockets. The meanings are imagistic or conceptual representations that, in the minds of both S and A, are linked to those signals.

Given this definition of gaze, its communicative system can be analysed on both the signal and the meaning side. On the signal side you can find the elements that compose all the possible signals of gaze, and their combination rules, thus writing the "optology" ("phonology" of gaze), while on the meaning side, the correspondences between signals and meanings ("lexical items" of gaze) can be found.

As to the former issue, to describe the signal of gaze Poggi (2007) proposed, like did Stokoe (1978) for the Signs of Sign Languages, a set of parameters to analyze the morphological features and muscular movements that form items of gaze. As shown by Stokoe (1978) and Klima & Bellugi (1979), any Sign can be analyzed in terms of a small number of parameters – handshape, orientation, location and movement –, where for each parameter the Sign can assume a number of possible values, and the combination of values in all parameters allows to describe the Sign thoroughly.

Also to establish the "optology" of gaze you can single out its parameters and their possible values, and describe each single item of gaze as a combination of specific values in all parameters. The parameters considered pertinent for gaze (in that changing a value on a parameter implies switching the gaze item analyzed to no meaning or to a different meaning) are the following (Poggi, 2007):

- movements of the eyebrows (for example, eyebrow frowning means worry or concentration, eyebrow raising, perplexity or surprise)
- position, tension and movement of the eyelids (in hate one lowers upper eyelids and raises lower eyelids with tension; in boredom upper eyelids are lowered but relaxed)

- various aspects of the eyes: humidity (see the bright eyes of joy or enthusiasm), reddening (bloodshot eyes in rage), pupil dilation (a cue to sexual arousal); focusing (stare out into space when thoughtful), direction of the iris with respect to direction of the Speaker's head and to the Interlocutor (which allows a deictic use of eyes)
- size of the eye sockets (to express tiredness)
- duration of movements (a defying gaze focuses longer over the other's eyes).

Through careful analysis of videos, items of gaze in conversation have been described in terms of these parameters (Poggi, 2007; Poggi & Vincze, 2008).

To find the meanings of gaze items, a deductive method was first adopted: a list was produced of the types of information that people may need to convey; then, analysing videorecorded data, the types of meanings hypothesized and their corresponding gaze items were found. Fragments of a lexicon of gaze were described, showing that gaze conveys very specific meanings by exploiting the richness of its optology.

It bears information about entities (its deictic use: gazing at something or someone to refer to it) or about properties (squeezing eyes to mention something very little, opening eyes wide for something big: an iconic use of gaze). Eyelid shape reveals Western vs. Eastern ethnicity; bright eyes reveal aspects of personality. Gaze can also tell how certain we are of what we are saying (a slight frown means "I am serious, not kidding"; raised eyebrows with half open eyes means "I am perplexed, not sure"), and what is the source of what we are saying (eyes left-downward mean "I am retrieving from memory"). Further, gaze communicates the goal of our sentence (staring at the Interlocutor conveys a performative of requesting attention; a frown communicates a question; a fixed stare, defiance); topic-comment distinction (by averting vs. directing gaze to Interlocutor); turn-taking moves (gazing at the Speaker to take the floor) and feedback (frowning to express incomprehension or disagreement, see Heylen, 2005; Poggi, 2007; Bevacqua, 2009).

3   Subtle Differences in the Meanings of Gaze

To investigate some specific items of gaze two empirical studies were conducted (Poggi & Roberto, 2007).

The first study aimed to assess whether people attribute specific meanings to specific items of gaze in a systematic way, and whether the meaning attributed to each item is shared. 10 static items of gaze were constructed by using "Greta face-library" (Bevacqua et al., 2007), a tool that allows to set Greta's face on whatever facial expression, by changing facial parameters of head, mouth and eye region. The following parameters were varied in the eye region:

1. Eyelids aperture: half closed (upper eyelids lowered and lower eyelids raised), half open (upper eyelids lowered), wide open up (upper eyelids raised showing the sclera over the iris), wide open up and down (upper eyelids raised showing the sclera over the iris, and lower eyelids lowered showing the sclera under the iris)
2. Eyes direction: forward, upward, downward, rightward, left-downward
3. Eyebrows position: default, all raised, internal parts raised, internal parts lowered and external parts raised.

By combining these parameters 10 items of gaze were constructed, and for each a hypothesis was made about its meaning. The 10 items were submitted to 100 students of a high school near Rome, between 18 and 20, 86 females and 14 males, through a questionnaire of multiple choice questions. For each item, the meaning hypothesized was mentioned among three distractors, in random order, with a further open alternative offered ("other…").

Six of the meanings hypothesized were confirmed by more than 75% subjects (*bothered* 88%, *tired* 86%, *amazed* 85%, *hate* 81%, *repent* 79%, *exasperated* 76%), three by more than 43% (*absorbed* 58%; *scanning* 54%; *terrorised* 43%)(*absorbed* 58%; *scanning* 54%; *terrorised* 43%) and one (*cautious*) only by 28%. However, from the analysis of the subjects' answers to the "other" alternative it resulted that also the meanings freely proposed by subjects generally shared some semantic components with those hypothesized. For example, the gaze items whose target meaning was *terrorized* was also interpreted as *astonished, deranged, impressed, dismayed, stupefied, amazed*, while *amazed* also as *alarmed, terrorized, surprised, astonished*.

The second study aimed to assess if specific values in some parameters have an "optological" value, thus distinguishing minimal pairs. It focused on eyelids aperture; the hypothesis was for example that, keeping eye position in the default value (center of the sclera), eye direction forward, and eyebrow raised, simply changing eyelids aperture from wide open, to default, to half closed could switch the meaning, respectively, from *surprise*, to *perplexity*, to *contemptuous* (Figures 1, 2, 3).

Fig. 1. Surprise   **Fig. 2.** Perplexed   **Fig. 3.** Contemptuous

A questionnaire of 15 items was submitted to 100 high school students near Rome, between 16 and 20, 82 females and 12 males. The meanings hypothesized were generally confirmed. Again, some common semantic element is generally shared between the target meaning and the chosen distractors or the meanings freely proposed. For example, in all the items with internal parts of eyebrows raised, whatever the position of the iris in the sclera, upward, downward or forward, a meaning of an unpleasant emotion with low activation is always present: the attributed meanings range from trouble, to grief, sorry, disappointed, resigned, sad.

The results of the second study show that even single values in the parameter of eyelids aperture have a distinctive function; wide open, default, and half-closed eyelids contrast items of gaze with each other; they distinguish minimal pairs, thus having a "phonemic" value. Thus gaze seems to entail an "optology": a system for the construction of signals, whose units of analysis, equivalent to phonemes, we might call "optemes".

4   Gaze Morphemes?

However, as we have seen, in these cases a specific value on a parameter is not simply distinctive of a meaning against another, like for words, where phonemes are not meaningful per se; these values seem to bear some meaning themselves, thus having not barely a phonemic, but a morphemic nature.

More than words, gaze resembles the signs of a Sign Language, or the gestures of the Hearing, where sometimes a single value of a parameter may bear a specific meaning by itself. In various signs in LIS (Italian Sign Language) the index finger protrusion bears a meaning of uniqueness (Boyes-Braem, 1981; Volterra, 1987); a progressive movement from left to right gives the idea of numbering (Calbris, 2003); gestures touching or pointing at the head refer to mental functions (Kendon, 1992). Works by Boyes-Braem (1981) and Volterra (1987) in the domain of Sign Languages, and by Calbris (1990; 2003) and Kendon (2004) for Hearings's gestures seem to converge on a "morpho-semantics" hypothesis (Boyes-Braem, 1981), according to which shared kinesic features correspond to shared semantic themes. So, like some gestures are "stylized and conventionalized versions of various manipulatory actions" (Kendon, 2004, p.224), also gaze communicative actions might derive from the ritualization (Posner, 2003) of actions that people do when pursuing some goal, feeling some emotion, showing some attitude to other people. For example, opening eyes wide to widen the visual field, or squeezing eyes to see better, stem from – and then reveal, *mean* – a need for knowledge. Each particular feature of a gaze item endows it with its particular meaning, that combines with the other meanings provided by other features. In other words, we might think that some "embodied morphemes of gaze" exist, having their roots in the physiological reactions that are driven by, or linked to, specific affective or cognitive states. This could account for the different interpretations of gaze items provided by subjects in the second study above. For item 3 *I judge you*, the subjects proposing meanings like *defiance*, *determination, I dare you, I am looking at you* might have relied on the feature of eye direction forward, as a defying gaze to the Interlocutor, while those proposing *surprise, astonished, impressed* might have focused on the raised eyebrows typical of unexpected information and search for knowledge.

In this work we present a study to further investigate this topic.

5   Eyelid Morphemes

To test our hypothesis about the morphemic value of some optemes, we designed an empirical study on the position of the eyelids.

5.1   Hypotheses

Our general hypothesis is that, in a single item of gaze, even the different values in one parameter may have a "morphemic" value, in that, both singularly and in combination with values in other parameters, they convey a specific meaning. This specific meaning is not necessarily the global meaning attributed to a whole item of gaze, but rather a – sometimes very general and abstract – semantic theme conveyed by all the items that contain that particular value in that particular parameter: in short, a morpheme.

Our specific hypothesis is that, in a single item of gaze, the different values in the parameters "position of upper and lower eyelids" convey different levels of activation of the subject displaying that gaze. This activation may be of a physiological, emotional or mental kind.

5.2 Experimental Design

To test the hypothesis about the meaning conveyed by different eyelids aperture, we designed an empirical study. The factorial design is 3 x 3 between subject with two independent variables being the different positions of upper eyelids (*wide-open, half-open, half-closed*) and lower eyelids (*lowered, default, raised*), and dependent variables being the meaning of the resulting gaze.

5.3 Procedure

We constructed a multiple choice questionnaire of 9 items of gaze. The items were built by using the "face-library" of Greta. This tool is very useful to build pictures because, different from actors' posed photographs, it allows you to set the FAPs (Facial Animation Parameters) very precisely. In some cases you even see a threshold in changing from one to another meaning, as if discreteness in gaze held just as for words or acoustic parameters of voice: at a certain point, a very slight change in the value of the parameter suddenly changes the resulting meaning. For example, combining half closed upper eyelids with progressively lowering lower eyelids, if you change the FAP values of the lower eyelids from 540.00 to 400.00, the resulting meaning is still "I am trying to remember", but suddenly if you pass to 340.00 the meaning changes into "I am sad".

With Greta's Face Library, we combined the three positions of the upper eyelids (*wide-open, half-open, half-closed*) with the three positions of the lower eyelids (*lowered, default, raised*), resulting in 9 items of gaze.

Then, for each gaze we made a hypothesis about its meaning, by using the method of Chomskian Speaker's judgments. As previously argued (Poggi & Roberto, 2007), not only for words or sentences, but also for non-verbal "lexical" items (Poggi, 2007), one of the methods for research on gaze is to make hypotheses about their meanings based on the intuitive judgments of speakers. Finally, for each item, after making a hypothesis about its meaning, we constructed a multiple choice question including the verbal phrasings of the hypothesized meaning and of three distractors. Distractors were progressively more distant from the target meaning, with the extreme one opposite to it.

Combining the value "*wide-open*" of parameter "upper eyelid" with the values "*lowered*" vs. "*default*" and "*raised*" of parameter "lower eyelid", we proposed the following choices for the resulting items. For gaze number 1, Upper/wide-open + lower/lowered, (a) *I want to see clearly*, (b) *I fear*, (c) *astonished*, (d) *I can't see*, with *astonished* as hypothesized meaning; for n.7, Upper/wide-open + lower/default, we proposed the meanings (a) *I don't mind*, (b) *look at me*, (c) *I am surprised*, (d) *I fear*, with *I fear* as target meaning; for n.4, Upper/wide-open + lower/raised, (a) *dismay*, (b) *I couldn't care less*, (c) *don't you dare*, (d) *I implore you*, with *dismay* as target.

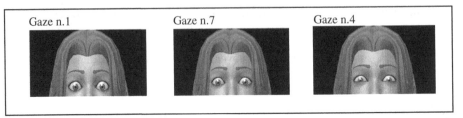

Fig. 4. Upper/Wide open

The possible choices for Upper/half open were the following: n. 8, Upper/half-open + lower/lowered, (a) *I am surprised*, (b) *I am sorry*, (c) *sad*, (d) *look at me*, (*sad* as target); n. 2, Upper/half-open + lower/default, (a) you *bother me*, (b) *how boring*, (c) *I am trying to understand*, (d) *I feel superior*, with *how boring* as target; n.5, Upper/half-open + lower/raised, (a) *I am ready to act*, (b) *exhausted*, (c) *sleepy*, (d) *I am sorry*, target *sleepy*.

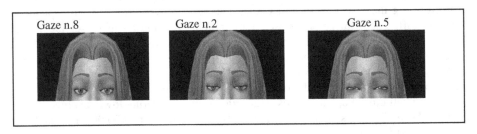

Fig. 5. Upper/Half Open

For combinations with Upper/half closed, we proposed: for n.3, Upper/half closed + Lower/lowered, (a) *how boring*, (b) *I am feeling sick*, (c) *you bother me*, (d) *sleepy*, with *how boring* as target; for n.6, Upper/half closed + Lower/default, (a) *you annoy me*, (b) *I couldn't care less*, (c) *teeny tiny*, (d)*I feel superior*, with *I feel superior* as target; for n.9 Upper/half closed + Lower/raised, that we hypothesized to mean *teeny tiny*, the choices were (a) *I am about to cry*, (b) *I hate you*, (c) *teeny tiny*, (d) *I am trying to remember*. We were thus testing the hypothesis that a narrow opening of eyes can also be iconically used to refer to very little things.

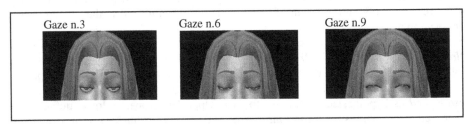

Fig. 6. Upper/Half Closed

The questionnaire was submitted to 360 subjects (208 females and 152 males, range 7 - 86 years old, mean age 36.8).

5.4 Results

We present the percentages of the meanings attributed to the upper eyelids by grouping them according to their combination with the three positions of the lower eyelids, *lowered, default, raised*. A *chi-square* analysis was performed for each position of the upper eyelids while changing that of the lower eyelids and the total sum of percentages amounts to the sum of the four alternatives presented for each item.

Upper/Wide-Open
The meanings attributed by subjects to the gaze items with wide-open upper eyelids (Figure 7), whether the lower eyelids with which it was combined was lowered, default or raised, in general concern emotions, but all sharing a component of **high activation** and sense of alert. For instance, picture 1 was attributed the meaning *sbalordita* = astonished by 53.10% of subjects; n.7 was interpreted as *ho paura* = I fear, by 43.30 % subjects, and *sono sorpresa* = I'm surprised by, 43,60%. In both meanings it shared a component of **cognitive novelty**. Moreover, in 7 and 4 (*sgomento* = dismay, 36.40%), a component of **thwarted goal** is added to the alert, which is also present in the performative meaning, also attributed to 4, *ti supplico* = I implore you (33.6'%) [Fig.7].

That an idea of activation is present in all these items is confirmed also by the very low percentage (2.8%) of subjects that, for gaze n. 4, chose the opposite distractor *Non mi fai nè caldo nè freddo* = I couldn't care less [$\chi^2(359)$; $p<0.000$].

In all other cases, that the Agent is still active is plausible because, even if the situation is worrying, a possibility still exists that s/he can do something to recover. As I *implore*, something bad has happened or is going to happen, but I still believe that someone can help. Even in *dismay* there is still a difference from, say, *despair*. Thus in all of these cases a common idea holds of the Agent being oriented to the present time or even to the future, different, as we shall see, from the cases below.

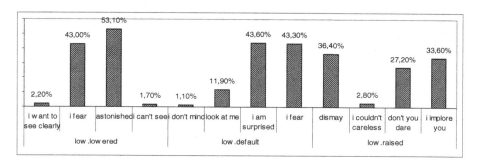

Fig. 7. Meanings for Upper/Wide Open

Upper/Half Open

Coherent with the Darwinian principle of antithesis (Darwin, 1872), the *half-open* upper eyelid carries meanings of de-activation, that can be caused by a physical state (like in 2, *assonnata* = sleepy, 37.50%, *esausta* = exhausted, 31.10%), a cognitive (5, *che noia* = how boring, 44,40%) or emotional state (8, *triste* = sad, 58,50% and *mi dispiace* = I am sorry, 30,50%). As to the timeline, these meanings are oriented to past or present: past both for the physical state of tiredness in 2, that might be caused by a previous effort or waste of energy, and the emotional state of sadness (8); and present for boredom (5) [$\chi^2(359)$; p<0.000]. The Agent showing upper eyelids half open may either afford relaxing because nothing serious is attracting his attention (like for *boredom*) or because something irreversible already happened that it is waste time to struggle for (*sad* and *sorry*).

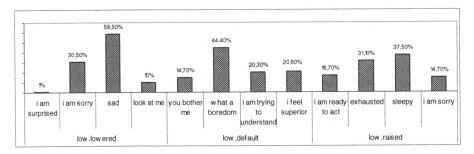

Fig. 8. Meanings for Upper/Half open

Upper/Half Closed

Also the *half closed upper eyelids* bears **deactivation** (3. *che noia* = how boring, 43,90%; 6. *non mi fai nè caldo nè freddo* = I couldn't care less, 39,60%), except for when combined with raised lower eyelids (see below), which add a component of **effort** (9.*sto cercando di ricordare* = I am trying to remember 42,20%, or *mi viene da piangere* = I am about to cry, 37,50%)[$\chi^2(359)$; p<0.000].

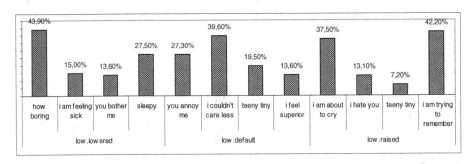

Fig. 9. Meanings for Upper/Half closed

Lower Eyelids

Results for *lower eyelids* are less clear. In general the *default* and *lowered* positions convey the same meaning of the upper eyelid position with which they are combined, that is, **activation** when combined with *wide-open* and **deactivation** when with *half-open* and *half closed* upper eyelids; but the *raised lower eyelids* definitely bear a component of **effort**, hence of **activation**, when combined with *half closed* upper eyelids. See the cognitive activation of 9, that is interpreted mainly as *sto cercando di ricordare* = I am trying to remember (42,20%), or as *mi viene da piangere* = I am about to cry (37,50%), which seems to evoke the **effort** of one who is trying to refrain from crying.

In fact, raising the lower eyelids implies some muscular tension; but why should this tension only appear with half-closed and not with half-open eyelids? A possible account, focused on the Receiver's perception, is that the meaning of effort intervenes when the measure of the eyelids' aperture is under a given threshold. There might be a default unmarked value of aperture that is seen as "natural"; so when, during a social encounter (in which, of course, people are not supposed to fall asleep), a person's eyes are more closed than that, she might be supposed to deliberately – then actively – strive for half-closing them, hence making the meaning of effort salient.

An alternative account might be that a value of a parameter does not always have the same morphemic role, but it becomes morphologically salient only in some cases. An analogous example in verbal language might be the "false diminutives" of Derivative Morphology: like for the ending *-let*, which is a derivative morpheme in the word *booklet*, but not in the word *outlet*.

6 Conclusion

We have investigated the semantic role of the position of the eyelids in the communicative system of gaze, and found that the wide open upper eyelids typically carry meanings of activation and alert, generally caused by external stimuli, while the half open eyelids convey a component of de-activation. Another meaningful eyelid position is lower eyelids raised, that convey a meaning of effort.

To set analogies between the structures of verbal languages and ones of communicative systems in other modalities is far from trivial. In a verbal language we have five levels of units: distinctive feature, phoneme, morpheme, word and sentence. A complete item of gaze, with its combination of values in all parameters, generally corresponds to a sentence, since in its meaning it includes its performative (Poggi, 2007). Distinctive features are analogous to our parameters with different values: our eyelid aperture, with its values "wide open", "half open", "half closed" and "closed" correspond to a distinctive feature like voicing, with its values "voiced" and "non-voiced"; the only difference being that the latter is a binary alternative. A distinctive feature distinguishes two phonemes, for instance, /f/ and /v/, which in their turn distinguish two words, like *veal* and *feel*. Yet, here ends the analogy: a distinctive feature or a phoneme distinguish two words, but they do not have meaning in themselves. Here instead a single value in a parameter, e.g. "half closed upper eyelid", bears meaning by itself: it does not have simply a phonemic, but a morphemic import. Is it a bound or free morpheme? Once again, the analogy is not straightforward, because in a verbal language a bound morpheme combines in sequence with another: after a root, an affix comes. But in gaze the values on various parameters – eyelid position, eye direction, eyebrow position – combine with each other at the same time: while I may say *"boy"* instead of *"boys"*, I may not keep my eyelids half closed without directing my iris in some direction. So *wide open* and *half open upper eyelids*, or *raised lower eyelids*, may be viewed like roots or themes, more than like words, both because they combine and because the meanings they bear are very general – activation, deactivation, effort.

Future work will investigate more lexical items and morphemes of gaze. New procedures might use (like Bevacqua, 2009) not only static images but videoclips, to keep into account the dynamic flow of gaze items and its influence on semantic interpretation. Moreover, future study about morphemes of gaze might adopt the so called *representative design* based on Brunswik's "lens model" (1955), to support the attribution of meanings trough differentiation of gaze contexts, by varying, for instance, eyebrows' position and eyes' direction.

The study might also be replicated in different cultures, to assess whether the morphemes found are culture specific or not. But if they are, as we maintain, "embodied morphemes of gaze", stemming from physiological reactions driven by, or linked to, universal affective or cognitive states, what may be subject to cultural variation is not their meaning but their norms of use, that is, the rules stating when and to whom gaze items embedding morphemes with a particular meaning can be used (Poggi, 2007).

New research will widen our knowledge on gaze and elucidate the structure of this charming communication system.

Acknowledgment

This research is partially supported by the Seventh Framework Program, European Network of Excellence SSPNet (Social Signal Processing Network), Grant Agreement Number 231287.

References

Allwood, J., Ahlsén, E., Lund, J., Sundqvist: Multimodality in Own communication management. In: Allwood, J., Dorriots, B., Nicholson, S. (eds.) Multimodal communication. Proceedings from the Second Nordic Conference on Multimodal communication, Gothenburg Papers in Theoretical Linguistics, Department of Linguistics, Goteborg University, pp. 43–62 (2005)

Argyle, M., Cook, M.: Gaze and mutual gaze. Cambridge University Press, Cambridge (1976)

Bavelas, J., Coates, L., Johnson, T.: Listeners as Co-narrators. J. Pers. & Soc. Psyc. 79(6), 941–952 (2000)

Baker-Schenk, C.: Nonmanual behaviors in sign languages: methodological concerns and recent findings. In: Stokoe, W., Volterra, V. (eds.) SRL 1983, Sign Language Research. Linstock Press, Silver Spring (1985)

Bevacqua, E.: Computational model of listener behavior for Embodied Conversational Agents. PhD Thesis, Université Paris 8 – Università di Roma "La Sapienza" (2009)

Bevacqua, E., Mancini, M., Niewiadomski, R., Pelachaud, C.: An expressive ECA showing complex emotions. In: Language, Speech and Gesture for Expressive Characters, AISB 2007, Newcastle, UK (2007)

Boyes-Braem, P.: Significant Features of the handshape in American Sign Language. Unpublished PhD. Thesis, University of California, Berkeley (1981)

Brunswik, E.: Representative design and probabilistic theory in a functional psychology. Psychological Review 62, 193–217 (1955)

Calbris, G.: The semiotics of French Gestures. Indiana University Press, Bloomington (1990)

Calbris, G.: L'expression gestuelle de la pensée d'un homme politique. Ed. du CNRS, Paris (2003)

Cassell, J.: Nudge nudge wink wink: Elements of Face-to-face-Conversation for Embodied Conversational Agents. In: Cassell, J., Sullivan, J., Prevost, S., Churchill, E. (eds.) Embodied Conversational Agents. The MIT Press, Cambridge (2000)

Darwin, C.: The Expression of the Emotions in Man and Animals. Appleton and Company, New York (1872)

Eibl-Eibesfeldt, I.: Similarities and differences between cultures in expressive movements. In: Hinde, R. (ed.) Non-verbal communication, pp. 297–314. Cambridge University Press, London (1972)

Ekman, P.: About brows: Emotional and conversational signals. In: von Cranach, M., Foppa, K., Lepenies, W., Ploog, D. (eds.) Human ethology: Claims and limits of a new discipline: contributions to the Colloquium, pp. 169–248. Cambridge University Press, Cambridge (1979)

Goodwin, C.: Il senso del vedere. In: Fabbri, P., Marrone, G. (eds.) Pratiche sociali della significazione. Meltemi, Roma (2003)

Heylen, D.: A closer look at gaze. In: Pelachaud, C., André, E., Kopp, S., Ruttkay Z.M. (eds.) Creating Bonds with Embodied Conversational Agents. AAMAS Workshop, pp. 3–9 (2005)

Kendon, A.: Some functions of gaze direction in social interaction. Acta Psych. 26, 1–47 (1967)

Kendon, A.: Abstraction in Gesture. Semiotica 90(3-4), 225–250 (1992)

Kendon, A.: Gesture. Visible action as utterance. Cambridge University Press, Cambridge (2004)

Klima, E.S., Bellugi, U.: The signs of language. Harvard University Press, Cambridge (1979)

Kreidlin, G.E.: Neverbal´naia semiotika: Iazyk tela i estestvennyi iazyk. Novoe literaturnoe obozrenie, Moskva (2002)

Maatman, R., Gratch, I., Marsella, S.: Natural behaviour of a listening agent. In: Panayiotopoulos, T., Gratch, J., Aylett, R.S., Ballin, D., Olivier, P., Rist, T. (eds.) IVA 2005. LNCS (LNAI), vol. 3661, pp. 25–36. Springer, Heidelberg (2005)

Peters, C., Pelachaud, C., Bevacqua, E., Mancini, M., Poggi, I.: A model of attention and interest using gaze behavior. In: Panayiotopoulos, T., Gratch, J., Aylett, R.S., Ballin, D., Olivier, P., Rist, T. (eds.) IVA 2005. LNCS (LNAI), vol. 3661, pp. 229–240. Springer, Heidelberg (2005)

Poel, M., Heylen, D.K.J., Nijholt, A., Meulemans, M., van Bremen, A.: Gaze Behavior, Believability, Likability and the iCat. AI and Society. Nijholt, A., Stock, O., Nishida, T. (eds.) The Journal of Human-Centred Systems 24(1), 61–73 (2009)

Poggi, I.: Mind, hands, face and body. A goal and belief view of multimodal communication. Weidler, Berlin (2007)

Poggi, I., Pelachaud, C., de Rosis, F.: Eye communication in a conversational 3D synthetic agent. AI Communications (13), 169–181 (2000)

Poggi, I., Roberto, E.: Meaningful eyes. In: Ahlsén, E., Henrichsen, P.J., Hirsch, R., Nivre, J., Abelin, A., Stroemqvist, S., Nicholson, S., Dorriots, B. (eds.) Communication – Action – Meaning. A festschrift to Jens Allwood, Department of Linguistics, Goteborg University, Goteborg, pp. 325–341 (2007)

Poggi, I., Vincze, L.: The persuasive import of gesture and gaze. In: Proceeding on the Workshop on Multimodal Corpora, LREC, Marrakech, pp. 46–51 (2008)

Posner, R.: Everyday gestures as a result of ritualization. In: Rector, M., Poggi, I., Trigo, N. (eds.) Gestures. Meaning and Use. Edicoes Universidade Fernando Pessoa, Porto (2003)

Stokoe, W.C.: Sign Language Structure: An Outline of the Communicative Systems of the American Deaf. Linstock Press, Silver Spring (1978)

Rossano, F.: When it's over is it really over? On the effects of sustained gaze vs. gaze withdrawal at sequence possible completion. In: 9th International Pragmatics Conference, Riva del Garda, July 10-15 (2005)

Thompson, R., Emmorey, K., Kluender, R.: The relationship between eye gaze and verb agreement in American Sign Language: an eye-tracking study. Natural Language & Linguistic Theory 24, 571–604 (2006)

Tomasello, M., Hare, B., Lehmann, H., Call, J.: Reliance on head versus eyes in the gaze following of great apes and human infants: the cooperative eye hypothesis. Journal of Human Evolution 52(3), 314–320 (2007)

Underwood, G. (ed.): Cognitive Processes in Eye Guidance. Oxford University Press, Oxford (2005)

Volterra, V.: La Lingua Italiana dei Segni. Il Mulino, Bologna (1987)

On Factoring Out a Gesture Typology from the *Bielefeld* Speech-and-Gesture-Alignment Corpus (SAGA)

Hannes Rieser

Bielefeld University
hannes.rieser@uni-bielefeld.de

Abstract. The paper is based on the Bielefeld Speech-And-Gesture-Alignment corpus (SAGA). From this corpus one video film is taken to establish a typological grid for iconic and referring gesture types, i.e. a multiple inheritance hierarchy of types proceeding from single gestural features like hand shape to sequences of entities filling up the whole gesture space. Types are mapped onto a partial ontology specifying their respective meaning. Multi-modal meaning is generated via linking verbal meaning and gestural meaning. How verbal and gestural meaning interface is shown with an example using a quantified NP. It is argued that gestural meaning extends the restriction of the original quantified NP. On the other hand it is shown that gestural meaning is not strong enough to resolve the underspecification of the lexical information.

Keywords: SAGA corpus, iconic gesture, gesture typology, partial ontology, speech-gesture interface.

1   Intro: Typology and Typology Work in Gesture Research

Typology is the study of types. Types are configurations of structural features. Typologies have been developed in many research fields, for example in anthropology, archaeology, biology, linguistics or psychology. There are linguistic typologies which classify languages according to word order or verbal entities according to parts of speech. Both typologies are in turn used in theory of grammar explanations: Here you have an example showing that typologies can serve a theoretical purpose. A useful distinction can be made into qualitative typology where you compare structures descriptively and quantitative typology where statistics for a well-defined field, e.g. a corpus of data is used. This paper is about a typological grid set up for statistical investigations which will be based on it. Essentially, a typological grid is a complex structure exhaustively covering one subset of given data set up to investigate whether it can be generalised to the rest. The grid we'll develop here is a set of types organised in a multiple inheritance hierarchy. In gesture research there is a veritable typology tradition, all of it qualitative research, for example there is the seminal paper of Ekman and Friesen (1969), a chapter on types of gestures in McNeill's (1992) book, Poggi (2002) is an example for the use of gesture typology in generation tasks, Kendon (2004) contains two typology chapters, Kita's collection (2003) concentrates on pointings. This paper is based on one route-description dialogue out of the *Bielefeld Speech-And-Gesture-Alignment* Corpus, SAGA, to which I now turn.

S. Kopp and I. Wachsmuth (Eds.): GW 2009, LNAI 5934, pp. 47–60, 2010.
© Springer-Verlag Berlin Heidelberg 2010

2   The Bielefeld Speech-and-Gesture-Alignment Corpus, SAGA

The SAGA corpus contains 25 route-description dialogues taken from three camera perspectives using body tracking technologies. The setting comes with a driver "riding on a car" embedded in a VR-setting, called "router", passing five landmarks, sculpture, town-hall, two churches, chapel, fountain. The landmarks are connected by streets. After his ride the router narrates his experience in detail to a follower who is supposed to organise his own trip following the router's instructions. We collected video and audio data for both participants, for the router body movement tracking data due to markers on head, wrist, elbow and eye-tracking data. The tracking data generated traces in Euclidean space and provided exact measurements for positions of head, elbow, wrist *etc.* The dialogues have all been annotated, the functional predicates like *indexing, modelling, shaping etc.* used were rated. Roughly, participants can point to objects of the VR representation, model objects by gesture or shape them. To describe these actions one needs a set of annotation predicates (details are given in Bergmann et al. 2007 and 2008). These annotation predicates are called "functional" here. "Functional" stands in opposition to single features which capture hand-shape, wrist position, angle of back of hand *etc.* but which on their own do not have the power to depict and hence designate. An example of a gesture annotation is given in Fig. 4, describing the router's gesture in Fig. 3. The corpus contains ca. 5000 gestures. Roughly 400 gestures have been investigated for establishing the typological grid detailed below.

3   Preliminary Observations, Expected Gain, Coverage of Gesture Research, Focus of Paper

SAGA clearly demonstrates (Rieser et al. 2007) that there are recurrent patterns in one individual's gesture behaviour in a chosen video film and these patterns generalize to the gesture behaviour of other agents in other films. However, there is variation across speakers as shown in the paper by Bergmann and Kopp (this volume): the variation observed ranges from the frequency of using gestures observed with agents or preferences for practices in gesture use to the extent of gestures, the latter meaning how much of the McNeillan gesture space a gesturer habitually uses in gesturing; here the opposition would be large vs small gestures, lap-oriented *vs.* torso-oriented ones, scale used *etc.*

  The information of interest here is captured in the multi-modal annotation of the data; examples are provided in sections five and six. The information of interest can be factored out and assembled in types; the types can be represented as typed feature structures and coded in AVMs (examples of AVMs are given in Fig. 5.). This way we can make use of AVM-technology (Carpenter 1992) to structure a really diverse domain. We will see in a short while which kind of structures types are. There is no *a priori* decision about the kind of structures that qualify as types. One has to find them out investigating which information packages enter larger informational structures and can be used in different gesture contexts. Feature bundles using a combination of hand-shape, palm, back of hand or wrist are good candidates for a type as are feature bundles associated with depicting gesture "Gestalts" such as lines, regions or three-dimensional entities. Comparing pointing gestures, line gestures and "box" gestures we see that types can be ordered along dimensions and complexity (points have zero dimension, lines are one-dimensional, signs for flat surfaces two-dimensional, gestures for containers three-dimensional *etc.*). To clarify further: "line gestures" are lines drawn in gesture space using the extended index finger; frequently these depict routes, directions or edges of three-dimensional objects; "box gestures" are formed with both hands indicating a container shaped like a box. Since there exists an ordering along a scale of complexity and since there is a finite source for all gesturing, we may assume that an inheritance hierarchy can be established for all the gestures going into a typological grid and finally into a full-fledged typology. Some types, the more basic ones, will pass their information "further down" to other types. The more complex types will get their information from different less complex ones higher up in the hierarchy. As a consequence, we will have multiple branchings from the top and multiple branchings from the bottom, this gives us a multiple inheritance hierarchy.

What will be the expected gain of heading towards a systematic gesture typology? The types factored out will first of all substantiate the very notion of a gesture morphology, which, for an appropriate use of the word 'morphology', presupposes stable, context-independent forms. This is a methodological gain. If we find out that gestures are built out of regular, stable parts, then we will learn something fundamental about the compositionality property of gestures. Here the gain is both on the empirical and the theoretical side. Finally, we can use the types isolated for gesture generation and gesture understanding, since on the one hand, we can establish a finite set of gesture building blocks as some sort of generating set triggering motor behaviour, on the other hand we can associate conventionalised descriptions of partial ontology with these blocks, whose INTERFACE with verbal meaning is conventionalised. Again, the gain is on the side of application and theory here.

Looking at the range of gestures investigated, we see that some are fairly well known, for example beats, emblems, pointing gestures and iconic gestures (McNeill, 1992, p. 76 for these types); however, there is a large under-researched area (double quotes in the following indicate that the terminology, coming originally from formal semantics, pragmatics and the theory of discourse, is used in a liberal sense)[1]: We certainly have "quantificational" gestures which might perhaps qualify as iconic gestures. Some gestures seem to operate on the propositional content in the role of "modifiers". Furthermore, gestures can have pragmatic functions as is shown by gestural "denials", others may even express full "illocutionary acts". A fairly difficult question is whether there are gestures related to turn allocation and dialogue structure, however, self-selection of next speaker or next speaker selection by current speaker can both be done by demonstration. Finally, we have complex gestures produced by more than one agent in successive turns. In sum, we see that there is evidence that gesture is not a mere construction-related or even propositional phenomenon but can permeate all of the talk. The topic of this paper is restricted to pointing and iconic gestures co-occurring with Noun-phrases (NPs). Iconic gestures co-occurring with verb-phrases (VPs) and adverbial phrases (AdvPhs) were excluded, because these follow a different ontology, namely one for states or events. So, we are concentrating on a more easy part here (cf. the remark above about well-understood gestures).

---

[1] Most of these are dealt with from a phenomenological perspective in Kendon (2004).

4   Form and Meaning of Iconic Gestures

Since we are dealing with iconic gestures (IGs for short) here, especially with their meaning and their interface potential, we set out with some simple hypotheses concerning these. First, we start with a *caveat*: IGs are in no way similar to the entities they somehow deal with. The similarity assumption belongs to the everlasting myths of research in IGs since Peirce's times (Houser and Kloesel 1992). Instead of resorting to similarity, we assume that IGs carry information and moreover that the information is tied up with depiction. Binding these two things together we say that IGs are structures encoding meaning. This assumption does not in itself commit us to a particular stance towards the type of meaning we have to use as will be made clear below. However, it is further assumed that IGs can form "meaning coalitions", they have the special property of being able to interface with verbal meaning. This is due to various properties of IGs the most important one being that they transport meaning in a way verbal expressions do as well. The interface point between IG meaning and verbal meaning is the gesture stroke and perhaps the main accent of the NP tone group, *i.e.* the intonation contour superimposed on syntactical material classified as NP[2] (remember that we are dealing only with NPs here). So, gestures are full triadic Peircian signs (Hartshorne and Weiss 1965) exhibiting compositionality and interface potential, *i.e.* they can combine with other gestural constructions yielding larger gestural units (cf. section 5) and fuse with verbal meanings (cf. section 6.4). Especially the latter property implies that gestures designate on the whole in a conventional way, i.e. on the meaning level they do essentially not behave differently from words. Consequently, gestures come with form-and-meaning properties. As we will see, semantics and pragmatics, especially the perspective of the gesturer play a central role. The form is given by dynamically generated postures of hands, wrists *etc.* (see below). The existence of form-and-meaning properties implies that IGs have a controlled variation of shape and controlled relation to types of objects or situations. In this paper the focus will be on objects indicated. Let us look at the form-meaning relation of IGs in more detail: form emerges from hand postures and movements of hands/wrists. Single agents use one hand/wrist or two; two agents cooperate in the production of gesture ensembles, so we get two-agent composites.

Meaning is associated with rated structures by stipulation. It takes the form of (the description of) a partial ontology. Let me explain. Gestures come in depictional fragments. They do not exhaustively delineate objects such as bent lines, locations, regions, circles, cylinders *etc.*, besides that they are irregular and vague. So, gestures do not set up clear geometrical forms as in geometry school books, they generate weird topological structures: cones with hollows, instead of cylinders' surfaces surfaces with dents where none should be and so on. Clearly, this is due to the aspect that gestures are tokens, *i.e.* signs produced, but that's not all. To see that, think for a moment about how gestures differ from word tokens: in whichever bad state a word-token is in, if one still can decode it one has something like a lexeme and hence a lexical definition for it. This is not the case for gesture tokens. If they are in too bad a state of corruption, they cannot produce a meaning interfacing with the verbal meaning. Stipulated gesture meaning

---

[2] I owe this assumption (not tested as yet) to Andy Lücking.

interacts with verbal meaning and context. If the work is all done and the interface describing the interaction of the verbal and the gestural meaning is set, there is always a *post festum* way of evaluating the meaning attributed. It might not fit, it might not have been inserted into the right position *etc.*, roughly, it must behave like an argument to a function in the mathematical sense.

So far, I did not say much about the notion of meaning I propose. Well, there are various options for meaning reconstruction shown below and commented upon thereafter. In order to keep things simple, I will not deal with the question which theory of meaning one should apply, extensional, intensional or structured, static or dynamic meaning, DPL-, DRT- or SDRT-like and so on. These are questions to discuss if the very principles and foundations are laid, which I set out to do here.

Perhaps the most straight-forward way to start with a theory of speech-gesture interaction is to forget about gesture irregularities and to work with idealised gesture shapes. This leads, for example, to considering a cone-gesture with erratic hollows as a standard cylinder-shape. Proceeding in this way one has a clear idea about what the cylinder shape depicts and hence the meaning to be attributed to the shape is also quite clear. As a precondition for the interface of speech-meaning and gesture-meaning one may assume that speech and gesture express the same type of meaning and that only the way they render it on two channels is different. So one gets the same regular meaning for both types of signs, say an extensional one[3]. Still keeping to the idealisation assumption one might really doubt that gesture meaning and speech meaning operate on the same level, since, for example, speech meaning might override gesture meaning. Indeed, some data related to contradictory information (Goldin-Meadow 1997) for speech and gesture in the SAGA Video Film 5 indicate that this might be the case. In this case we may do the following: take the chosen regular meaning for speech and a reconstruction relying on implicature for gesture. The latter amounts to using some default inference reconstruction for gesture meaning. It might be achieved as follows: The default inference (Reiter 1980), might be tied to a set of gesture features. It has to be observed, however, that the resulting implicature is not Gricean (Grice 1967) any more, since we deal with non-verbal information. Setting up a paradigm in this way has also the consequence that we do not get a unified notion of inference (Karttunen and Peters 1979). So much for the side of the idealisations in Fig. 1. The other main branch of the tree in Fig. 1 takes into account that gesture shapes usually show irregularities in various ways, they are "garbled", accepting that one can't idealise *tout court*. Since the irregularity at stake amounts to fragmentary gestural forms one has to reside to partiality and underspecification. Finally, if one still wants to do more, i.e. apply inferences and provide an "indirect" semantics for the gesture information, one can for example treat partiality *via* metonymy resolution (mostly *pars pro toto*) and underspecification *via* resolution using relevant Gestalt principles. The approach to bind the information together would presumably have to be abduction (Paul 1993) confronting us, however, with massive non-monotonicity, since inferred information need not be stable.

The approach most faithful to the data is, of course, "garbled" and "indirect". So much is certain, the option chosen determines the interface constructions for speech and

---

[3] This is not very realistic given the extreme context-dependence of gestures, but let us accept that for the moment on didactic grounds.

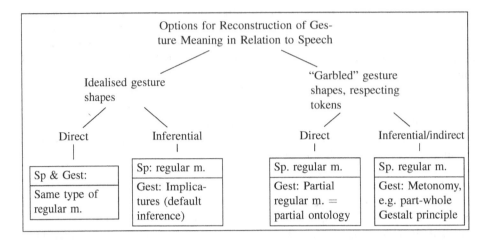

Fig. 1. Possible strategies for establishing an interface between verbal meaning and gestural meaning

gesture: roughly, the farther to the right in the tree one moves, the more complicated it gets. The point of view in the paper is the "garbled"-direct-partial-regular-meaning path. The resulting meaning concept is called "partial ontology", since we are mainly dealing with partially specified objects due to the NPs.

5   A Typological Grid for "NP"-Gestures and How It Has Been Extracted from the SAGA Video Film 5

As stated before, the typological grid established covers NPs and gestures co-occurring with them, for example an utterance of *the bridge* overlapped by a cuboid gestured with left hand and right hand extending from the middle stressing the horizontal axis of the bridge. The main question is now 'What can we take as parameters in order to get at types'? Obviously, we need a means, instrument or source slot to start with, a plausible option is to install agency as a root feature dominating the role features router and follower. Next we need the router's and the follower's left and right hands and both their hands, all subsumed under handedness. Handedness materialises in the single features of the hands. As single features we use all the annotation features from the chosen annotation set laid down in the two manuals developed for SAGA (Bergmann, K. et al 2007 and 2008). These are *HandShape, PalmDirection, BackofHandDirection, WristMovement, PathofWristMovement, PositionInGestureSpace etc.* Bundles of features form recurrent feature clusters. Up to now we dealt with the fine grain of ontology, now we move on to more every-day objects. Feature clusters yield large classes of objects like curved, vertical, horizontal *etc.* entities. These are used to build up *shapes* of different dimensions[4]: we have abstract objects of 0 dimension to which belong McNeill's

---

[4] Here *geometric* names are used mnemonically. (No Platonic shapes exist, cf. the comments on "garbled" above). Partiality and underspecification will become clear ultimately from the specification of the partial ontology for the types.

Agency
|
Handedness
|
Two-Handedness
|
Features
|
FeatureClusters
|
0-DimensionalEntities
|
1-DimensionalEntities: Lines
|
Composite 1-DimensionalEntities
|
2-DimensionalEntities: 2-DimensionalShapes
|
2-DimensionalEntities: Segments
|
2-DimensionalComposites
|
3-DimensionalEntities
|
3-DimensionalEntities: Segments
|
3-DimensionalComposites
|
MixedComposites
|
SequencesofComposites

Mother Category	Instantiating Categories
Agency	Router, Follower
Handedness	LeftHand, RightHand, Two-Handedness
LeftHand	Features
RightHand	Features
TwoHandedness	TWH-Movement, TWH-Configuration
Features	$Feature_1$ ... $Feature_n$
$Feature_1$ ... $Feature_n$	Feature-Clusters
Feature-Clusters	$Feature\text{-}Cluster_1$ ... $Feature\text{-}Cluster_n$
Feature-Clusters, TWH-M, TWH-C	0-Dimensional Entities
Feature-Clusters, TWH-M, TWH-C	Lines: Straight Lines, Bent Lines
Straight Lines, Bent Lines, TWH-M, TWH-C	Composite Lines
Feature-Clusters, TWH-M, TWH-C	2-Dimensional Shapes
2-Dimensional Shapes, TWH-M, TWH-C	Segments&Wholes: Circles, Rectangles, Regions, Locations
2-Dimensional Composites, TWH-M, TWH-C	Circle $\oplus$ Region, ...
Feature-Clusters, TWH-M, TWH-C	3-Dimensional Entities
3-Dimensional Entities, TWH-M, TWH-C	Segments&Wholes: Cylindroids, Frustra, Prisms, Spheroids
3-Dimensional Composites, TWH-M, TWH-C	2 Prisms ...
0-Dimensional Entities, Lines, 2-Dimensional Shapes, 2-Dimensional Composites, 3-Dimensional Entities, 3-Dimensional Composites, TWH-M, TWH-C	Mixed $Composites_{router}$, Mixed $Composites_{follower}$, Mixed $Composites_{router\&follower}$
Sequences of Composites, TWH-M, TWH-C	$X+Y+Z+...$

Fig. 2. Left-hand side: Simplified hierarchy of features and shapes. Right-hand side: the multiple inheritance hierarchy in tabular form.

abstract deixis and the demonstration of discourse referents. Next we have one dimensional things: *lines straight* or *bent*. Among the twodimensional things we encounter *locations, regions, rectangles, circles etc.* Then the three dimensional sorts come up: *cuboids, cylinders, frustra, prisms, spheres* and so on. Among the most interesting objects are composites of shapes of various sorts. Abstract deixis can go with a two-dimensional thing, a two-dimensional area may be singled out in a larger region, a line may touch a shpere. A prism may be set up on a flat ground. An example involving two parallel prisms will be given below. Finally, we have sequences of shapes. These can come in all sorts of variations. A line may extend up to a prism, a curved line may go around a circle, one three-dimensional object may be set on the top of another one and so on. In Fig. 2 you see the hierarchy (left) and the inheritance relations of the typological grid in tabular form (right), both simplified.

Anticipating the *two towers* example below, which involves two gestured partial prisms, we comment on feature inheritance for the **2 Prisms** type (right column, third segment from the bottom). The *2 Prisms* type inherits information from the type of

The verbal expression overlapping with the gesture is
... *und hat zwei Türme/and has two towers*. One can see
that the two tower bases are indicated by the loose C
shapes produced by the right and the left hand, respectively. The wrist movements are upwards, stressing the
vertical dimensions of the two objects signed. The gesture and the verbal expression are reasonably matched.

Fig. 3. The router gesturing two prism fragments to the follower

3-Dimensional Composites and two-handed features. Since two prisms taken collectively are made up of two *single prisms* they depend on *3-Dimensional single Entities*,
again the features of both hands may play a role here. *3-Dimensional Entities* are made
up of *Feature-Clusters*, again, both hands can be involved. *Feature-Clusters* are bundles of *single Features*. Features belong to the *RightHand*, the *LeftHand* or *both hands*.
Hands are either the hands of the *Router* or the *Follower*, both of whom are *agents*.

6   The Two-Towers Example

6.1   Datum and Gesture-Annotation

I now want to explain the role of the typological grid in setting up a speech-gesture
interface. First I present the router's turn and a still (Fig. 3) with the situation of the
router gesturing two partial prisms to the follower.

> Router: ... und [subject-ellipsis] hat zwei Türme.
> ... and [subject-ellipsis] has two towers.

Observe that we have an ellipsis here. The term going into the ellipsis slot is *the church*.
Hence the proposition expressed by the locution is *The church has two towers*.

Now let us have a look at the annotation of the left and the right hand carried
out in ELAN depending on the two manuals (Bergmann *et al.* 2007 and 2008). Here
comes a detailed comment on the left column in Fig. 4 line for line: The annotation
prefix is *R.G.Left* for *R.outer, G.esture, Left*, respectively. We have an *iconic Phrase*.
What semantically matters is the *stroke Phase* (the gesture's most articulated form)
being the carrier of the semantic and pragmatic information. The *hand-shape* is *loose
C*. The *direction of palm* is *away from body* and *towards right*. The *direction of the
back of the hand* is *up*. The *path described by the wrist* is a *line*. The *movement of
the wrist* is *up, down, up*. The *extent* is *medium*. The functional predicate characterizing the gestures is shaping, intuitively, shaping the two towers of the church. The
perspective is the router's which can be exploited in the pragmatic interpretation (cf.
the discussion in section 6.5). The right hand is characterised by corresponding annotation predicates, starting with *R.G.Right* for *R.outer, G.esture, R.ight*, respectively. What
matters are the complementary properties of the palms and the two-handed configurations. The two hands together express the "mirror"-predicate *Mirror-sagittal*. In
addition, the annotation contains the wording and the time span used up in gesturing.

Next we show how gesture types are extracted from the annotation.

R.G.Left.Phrase	iconic	R.G.Left.Practice	shaping
R.G.Left.Phase	stroke	R.G.Left.HandShapeShape	loose C
R.G.Left.PalmDirection	PAB/PTR	R.G.Left.BackOfHandDirection	BUP
R.G.Left.PathOfWristLocation	LINE	R.G.Left.WristLocMoveDirect	MU>MD>MU
R.G.Left.Extent	MEDIUM		
R.G.Left.Perspective	speaker		
R.Two-handed.configuration	BHA	R.Move.relative.to.other.Hand	Mirror-sagittal
Transcription	*und hat zwei Türme*		
TC	0:04:47.00 - 00:04:40.220		

Fig. 4. Annotation for the example in Fig. 3 comprising the router's left hand positions

6.2   Gesture Typology, AVMs

The potential types (remember that we are establishing a hypothesis) are obtained collecting the non-0 valued annotation predicates and their values from the annotation grid. We get three gesture types here, *two One-Handed-Prism-Segment*s and one *Two-Handed-2-Prism-Segment* generated by unification of the two single types plus the information coming from both hands. The hypothesis is motivated by the idea that the hand-postures form a kind of Gestalt to be interpreted and that in the end the Gestalt will be recurring in the datum chosen, in the SAGA corpus and beyond. Indeed, the intuition connected with these shapes is that they form prisms or cylinders, something in between a lengthier box and a tube.

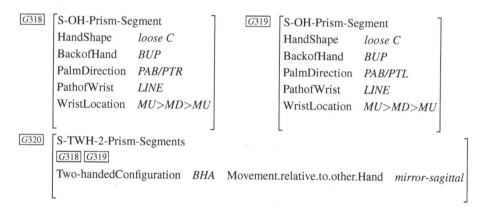

Fig. 5. Two single types and one composite type

6.3   Description of Partial Ontology and Position of Type Used in Typological Grid

In section 4 I argued that IGs have meaning and that they interface with verbal meaning. How do we get at the meaning of words? Easy, we look up the Oxford English Dictionary (OED). But, how do we get at the meaning of IGs? The OED will not tell us. In principle we could rate and annotate as for the gesture shapes. However, this is far more complicated and would mean a tremendous lot of annotation work. Therefore, at the moment one has to resort to stipulation. What do we stipulate? We associate with HandShape-*looseC* the information of the base of the prism-segment *base(b$_l$, p$_l$)*, read b$_l$ is the base of the

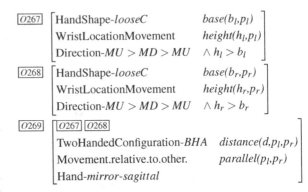

Fig. 6. Description of partial ontology

left prism-segment p$_l$. We map the WristLocationMovementDirection-*MU>MD>MU* onto the *height h$_l$* of the prism-segment and fix at the same time that the *height* extends the *base*, which is a short-cut for a more complex logical formula. So we have the information that the gesture depicts or means something which has a base and is high. The same is done for the gesture type coming from the right hand. What do we get in the complex type? First of all, two based objects that are high, in addition, the information that there is a distance *d* (TwoHandedConfiguration-*BHA*) between the two prism-segments and that they are parallel (Movement.relative.to.otherHand-*mirror-sagittal*). Where does the underspecification come from? It is for example tied up with the base, since no form is given for it; it might be triangular, circular and so on. In principle any two-dimensional shape would do. It is not expressed either which object the two prisms are related to or are part of. This underspecification is, however, resolved by the proposition expressed which says that *The church has two towers*.

As far as I can see, the roofs of the towers are in no way indicated by gestures. Whether the description of the partial ontology should be richer is a matter of dispute, some possible extensions are discussed in sect. 6.5.

6.4 Interface of Verbal and Gestural Meaning

Why did we develop annotation, gesture types and descriptions of partial ontology in the first place? The answer is, in order to build an interface where verbal meaning and gestural meaning meet. How this is accomplished is the topic of the present section. The interface is presented in Fig. 7.

We already discussed the gesture part of Fig. 7. It proceeds from annotation up to the description of the partial ontology. The left side is still to be explained. The grammatical framework used is LTAG (lexicalised tree adjoining grammar, Abeillé *et al.* Eds., 2000). For the verbal part under discussion, *two towers*, we need two LTAG-projections, one for the quantifier *two* and the other for the noun *tower* as well as a substitution rule for embedding the noun in the quantifier projection. This is simple.

How do we know about the meaning of terminals like *tower*? Let us assume that we can look up the OED in order to get the information about *tower* we are interested in. The OED says:

(2) *tower: = A tall narrow building or structure, usu. of square, circular, or rectangular section, either standing alone or forming part of a castle, church etc.*

Remember that the proposition expressed by the verbal contribution of the router is *The church has two towers*. In other words, we have something like 'There are two towers which are part of the church'. This means that we can eliminate non-relevant information from our lexical entry by disjunctive syllogism. I do not show how that is done in detail, it is fairly trivial anyway. Let us accept that *building* is also out such that the relevant remaining part of the OED entry is

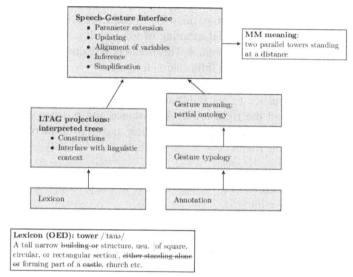

Fig. 7. The speech-gesture interface

(3) *tower: = A tall narrow structure, usu. of square, circular, or rectangular section, forming part of a church.*

Taking (3) as a sort of explicit definition, we can substitute the *definiens* for *tower*. We also do not carry out that here. We are now in the second box from the top. The semantics which we can assume at this stage is

(4) $\exists x \exists z.tower(x) \wedge tower(z)$

Next we come to the interface box1 which demands that we unify verbal and gestural meaning. In order to do so, we have to open up the closed formula and extend the parameters in it. Then we update the opened formula with the partial ontology information. Alignment of variables is done for us by λ-conversion

(5) $\lambda R(\exists x \exists z.tower(x) \quad \wedge \quad tower(z) \quad \wedge \quad R(x)(z)))(\lambda pl \lambda pr.parallel(pl, pr) \quad \wedge$ $distance(d, pl, pr))$.

In the end we arrive at the formula for the multi-modal meaning which is $(\exists x \exists z.tower(x) \wedge tower(z) \wedge parallel(x, z) \wedge distance(d, x, z))$. We do not show the role of inference and simplification here.

6.5   Discussion of the Two-Towers Example

The remarkable features shown by the example are: In the multi-modal meaning the restriction of the quantifier *two* has been changed if we compare it to the uni-modal verbal expression: from *two towers* we come to *two parallel towers standing at a distance*. Hence, multi-modality gives us richer information than verbal meaning: Any model which satisfies the multi-modal quantifier phrase will also satisfy the verbal one but not *vice versa*. In other respects, however, we do not get more: gestural information is not able to resolve the underspecification of the lexical information of *tower* taken from the OED; the multi-modal meaning of tower still contains the disjunction of *square, circular or rectangular section*. This is essentially due to the *loose C* shape which only provides partial ontology information for bases.

The information contained in the example's description of the partial ontology might not fully do justice to our intuitions. I will briefly comment on four pertinent issues, (a) the left and the right tower, (b) distance and position of towers, (c) the models determined by the multi-modal description, and on (d) Is there a quantificational gesture indicated by the router?

(a) The left and the right tower. The *left-right*-information is present in the gesture but not represented in (5). Essentially, it would presuppose integration of the router's perspective into (5).
(b) Distance and position of towers. This information is also present in the gesture. Distance is indicated by hands and wrists. The hands also indicate that the towers are situated on a horizontal line running orthogonally to the router's position, information which is missing in (5) as well. (a) and (b) show that the partial ontology is essentially speaker-dependent.
(c) The models determined by the multi-modal description: This is one of the most intriguing questions for multi-modal meanings like (5). People experienced in the use of model theory will readily have observed that (5) is satisfied by models which intuitively won't fit the stimulus or our world knowledge. For example, according to (5), the distance between the two towers might be minimal or too large. This shows that the models need to pass the "filter" of world-knowledge giving us a preference order wrt models containing churches with two towers.
(d) Is there a quantifier gesture indicated by the router? This is a controversial point among the raters, related to the interpretation of the down-up-down movement of the router's arms. If we assume that there is, we would have compositionality between a quantifier-gesture and an N-Bar-gesture. This would have to be reconstructed in two steps: first the quantifier gesture would have to be combined with the quantifier *two* and the towers-gesture would have to be aligned with *towers*. Finally, as the second step, the whole multi-modal quantifier gesture would have to be formed by compositionality. We would need quite a lot of apparatus to get there but the solution is straightforward.

7   What Remains to Be Done

I briefly describe here some ongoing work. Given that the typological grid shown in Fig. 4 has been extracted from one SAGA video-film, we have to test it with respect to other MM dialogues in the corpus. Then statistical investigation will be employed to yield a full-fledged typology for SAGA, essentially providing us with information about which clusters of gestural features are recurrent in the corpus. The typological grid described above has been designed for NPs. Hence, additional typological grids must be developed for dynamic iconic gestures co-occurring with VPs, iconic space and movement in space going together with AdvPhs. This having been accomplished, one has to unify the typologies and the result can be used for establishing MM propositions (*i.e.* propositions arising from verbal and gestural content) by compositionality.

Acknowledgements

Work on this Paper was supported by the German Research Foundation, CRC 673, 'Alignment in Communication', Bielefeld University. Thanks go to my fellow SAGA corpus annotators, Kirsten Bergmann, Oliver Damm, Andy Lücking, Florian Hahn, and to Stefan Kopp and Ipke Wachsmuth for general support. Special thanks go to my 'co-typologist' Florian Hahn and to two anonymous reviewers who came up with many suggestions for how to improve the original paper.

References

Abeillé, A., Rambow, O.: Tree Adjoining Grammars. CSLI Publications, Stanford (2000)
Bergmann, K., Kopp, S.: Systematicity and idiosyncrasy in iconic gestures – A probabilistic model of gesture use. In: Kopp, S., Wachsmuth, I. (eds.) GW 2009. LNCS (LNAI), vol. 5934, pp. 179–191. Springer, Heidelberg (2010)
Bergmann, K., Fröhlich, C., Hahn, F., Kopp, S., Lücking, A., Rieser, H.: Wegbeschreibungsexperiment: Grobannotationsschema. MS., Univ. Bielefeld (June 2007)
Bergmann, K., Damm, O., Fröhlich, C., Hahn, F., Kopp, S., L'ucking, A., Rieser, H., Thomas, N.: Annotationsmanual zur Gestenmorphologie. MS., Univ. Bielefeld (June 2008)
Carpenter, B.: The Logic of Typed Feature Structures. CUP, Cambridge (1992)
Ekman, P., Friesen, W.: The repertoire of nonverbal behavior: categories, origins, usage and coding. Semiotica 1, 49–98 (1969)
Essler, K.: Wissenschaftstheorie I. Definition und Reduktion. Freiburg, Alber (1970)
Goldin-Meadow, S.: When gesture and words speak differently. Current Directions in Psychological Science 6, 138–143 (1997)
Grice, H.P.: Logic and Conversation. The William James Lectures. Harvard University, Cambridge (1989) Published as Part 1 of Grice; Grice, H. P.: Studies in the Way of Words. Harvard University Press, Cambridge (1967)
Karttunen, L., Peters, S.: Conventional Implicature. In: Syntax and Semantics 11: Presuppositions, pp. 1–56. Academic Press, London (1979)
Kendon, A.: Gesture: Visible Action as Utterance. CUP, Cambridge (2004)
Kita, S. (ed.): Pointing: Where Language, Culture and Cognition Meet. Lawr. Erlb., Mahwah (2003)
McNeill, D.: Hand and Mind. What Gestures Reveal About Thought. Univ. Chic. Press, Chicago (1992)
Paul, G.: Approaches to abductive reasoning: an overview. Artificial Intelligence Review 7, 109–152 (1993)
Peirce, C.S.: Syllabus. In: Hartshorne, C., Weiss, P. (eds.) Collected papers of Charles Sanders Peirce, vol. 2, p. 274. Belknap Press of Harvard Univ. Press (1965)

Peirce, C.S.: On the Algebra of Logic. In: Houser, N., Kloesel, C. (eds.) The Essential Peirce, vol. 1, p. 226. Indiana Univ. Pr., Bloomington (1992)

Poggi, I.: From a Typology of Gestures to a Procedure for Gesture Production. In: Wachsmuth, I., Sowa, T. (eds.) GW 2001. LNCS (LNAI), vol. 2298, pp. 158–168. Springer, Heidelberg (2002)

Reiter, R.: A logic for default reasoning. Artificial Intelligence 13, 81–132 (1980)

Rieser, H., Kopp, S., Wachsmuth, I.: Speech-Gesture Alignment. In: ISGS Abstracts, Integrating Gestures, Northwestern University, Evanston, Chicago, pp. 25–27 (2007)

Function and Form of Gestures
in a Collaborative Design Meeting

Willemien Visser

LTCI, UMR 5141, CNRS – INRIA,
46 rue Barrault, 75013 Paris, France
willemien.visser@TELECOM-ParisTech.fr

Abstract. This paper examines the relationship between gestures' function and form in design collaboration. It adopts a cognitive design research viewpoint. The analysis is restricted to gesticulations and emblems. The data analysed come from an empirical study conducted on an architectural design meeting. Based on a previous analysis of the data, guided by our model of design as the construction of representations, we distinguish representational and organisational functions. The results of the present analysis are that, even if form-function association tendencies exist, gestures with a particular function may take various forms, and particular gestural movements as regards form can fulfil different functions. Reconsidering these results and other research on gesture, we formulate the assumption that, if formal characteristics do not allow differentiating functional gestures in collaboration, context-dependent, semantic characteristics may be more appropriate. We also envision the possibility that closer inspection of the data reveal tendencies of another nature.

Keywords: Gestural interaction, Cognitive design research, Collaborative design, Collaboration, Architectural design, Gesticulations, Emblems.

1 Introduction

Dependent on researchers' aims, gestures have been analysed from several perspectives: for example, semiotic analysis [1], language development [2], human-computer interaction [3], gesture recognition and generation in interactive dialogue systems [4], and collaborative task-completion tools [5].

Working in the domain of cognitive design research [6], we are interested by the role of gesture in design collaboration. The aim of our research is double. Its main objective is an epistemic socio-cognitive psychology one—to understand the use of the different interaction modalities in professional collaboration. A long-term cognitive-ergonomics purpose is to contribute to the specification of remote collaborative-design environments, especially to facilitate the use of various semiotic modalities (multi-modal interaction) by designers working on remote locations.

In the study presented here, we examine if, in a collaborative design setting, gestures with a particular function have a particular form and/or if gestures with a particular form have a particular function. This question is relevant for several

S. Kopp and I. Wachsmuth (Eds.): GW 2009, LNAI 5934, pp. 61–72, 2010.
© Springer-Verlag Berlin Heidelberg 2010

reasons. Data on the function-form relationship may present arguments for the debate concerning the idiosyncratic nature of gestures (cf. our Discussion and Conclusion). Further, such data may contribute to the specification of collaborative-design systems—or other multimodal interactive systems—in providing elements for the "translation" of functional, communicative, or semantic specifications into gestural movements [cf., for example, 7, but cf. also our Discussion and Conclusion].

Before introducing our analysis of the relationship between gestures' function and form, we shortly present our viewpoint on design and review previous research on gestural interaction in design collaboration. In the main section, we introduce the empirical study that provided the data that we use for our present analysis [8]. In the final section, we discuss further perspectives of this work.

2   Gestures in Design Collaboration

In this section, we introduce the viewpoint from which we analyse design and we review previous research on gestural interaction in design collaboration.

2.1 A Cognitive Perspective on Design

Design is an important, all-pervading domain of human activity. Not only are new sport cars and mobile phones the object of design, but so too are artefacts as diverse as traffic signals [9], route plans [10, 11], software [12], and, of course, buildings of all kinds [13].

This paper presents a study on architectural design, focusing on the types of socio-cognitive processes and structures implemented by designers collaborating on architectural projects.

In accordance with our theoretical framework, we consider designing as the construction of representations [6]. "Globally characterised, designing consists in specifying an artefact, *given requirements* that indicate—generally neither explicitly, nor completely—one or more functions to be fulfilled, and needs and objectives to be satisfied by the artefact, under certain conditions expressed by constraints. At a cognitive level, this specification activity consists in developing (generating, transforming, and evaluating) representations of the artefact *until they are so concrete, detailed, and precise* that the resulting representation—the *specifications* of the artefact—specify explicitly and completely the implementation of the artefact." [14, p. 117] Designing does not consist in *implementing* the specifications: it is not the fabrication of the artefact product, that is, in case of architectural design, the construction of the building. The representations that come out of architectural design are drawings and models of this artefact product. These representations are also artefacts, that is, entities created by people, "man-made as opposed to natural" [15].

"Cognitive design research" is the qualification for studies that examine design focusing on its cognitive aspects [6, 14]. Researchers from the engineering domain often use the term "design thinking" [16].

Design always involves several people—at least two, a client and a designer, or a designer and a user. Yet, given that design projects generally require the integration of information and knowledge from a variety of domains, they usually involve multiple competencies, and thus collaboration between people from different areas of expertise, working together in meetings. We consider as "designers" all those who, in such meetings, contribute to the specification of the artefact—even if their payslip may qualify them as, for example, "draftsman" or "programmer."

2.2 Gestural Interaction in Design Collaboration: Previous Studies

Compared with verbal and graphical interaction, gestural expression has barely been studied in collaborative design. In an analysis of the rare empirical studies on this use of gesture [17-19], we highlighted two functions [8]. (1) Gesture offers specific possibilities to render spatial (especially 3D) and motion-related qualities of entities, and to embody action sequences through their mimicked simulation. (2) Gesture plays an important organisational role.

In our previous research on gestures, we have developed a description language for graphico-gestural design activities [20]. Using this language to analyse the interaction in an architectural meeting, we have interpreted co-designers' graphico-gestural actions according to their functional roles in the project and in the meeting [21]. We also examined different forms of multimodal articulation between graphico-gestural and verbal modalities in parallel interactions between the designers, revealing alignment and disalignment between the designers regarding the focus of their activities [22, 23].

3 Analysing Function and Form of Gesture in a Design Meeting

This section presents the data we analysed to examine the function-form question, the functions of gestures we identified in a previous study, and our analysis of the relationship between function and form of gestures used in design collaboration.

3.1 Data: An Architectural Design Meeting

The data analysed come from the dataset for DTRS7 [The 7th Design Thinking Research Symposium, 24; DTRS7 dataset, P. Lloyd, J. McDonnell, F. Reid and R. Luck, 2007. These data are not publicly available for general distribution]. These data were provided to 24 researchers/research groups from different disciplines in order to confront, through different analyses of a same dataset, a representative variety of today's perspectives on design thinking. The dataset was made up of videos regarding naturally occurring design activity in the authentic setting of design practice. These were face-to-face, synchronous professional design meetings taking place in two different design firms (architecture and product design). We analysed the first architectural meeting, A1.

The A1 meeting took place in the pre-planning application stage of a project to design a new municipal crematorium with chapel, to be set in a landscaped site where existed already another crematorium. Data supplied were a video; a transcript of the audible part; plans at different scales, elevations, sketches, and orthographic projections referred to during the meeting; a 30-min video of an informal interview with the principal architect describing the background to the project. The video

Fig. 1. Three-view video of the A1 architectural meeting (from the DTRS7 dataset, 2007, P. Lloyd, J. McDonnell, F. Reid, and R. Luck)

provided three views: top-view, medium-view, long-view (see Figure 1). The meeting took 2h 17min. The transcript had 2,342 transcript lines, corresponding to 987 speaker turns.

The meeting involved three participants: Adam, the architect in charge of the project, and two clients, Anna, registrar of the cemetery, and Charles, an officer from local government representing the municipality's interests. A DTRS7 organiser (sitting at the end of the table) observed A1. Even if different roles can be distinguished among the three participants, we qualify them all as "designers," given our view of design as a cognitive activity, not necessarily the activity of somebody whose profession is "designer."

In our DTRS7 study [8], we analysed the entire meeting. However, we did not describe (as in the examples in Tables 1 and 2) all the gestures: our aim in this first study was to identify as much functions as possible. We therefore viewed the A1 video numerous times: during the first series of viewings, we noted and described an episode when we came across a gesture with a function not yet identified in our current analysis; afterwards, we went again through the video many times, searching for other instances of these functions.

We restricted our analysis to (1) gesticulations, that is, spontaneous, speech-accompanying gestures, and (2) emblems, quasi-linguistic, lexicalised gestures, with conventional forms and meanings, and which are not necessarily speech-accompanying [25, 26]. The qualification "gesture" is used for both in this paper.

In the DTRS7 study, we identified some 130 functional episodes (where an episode contains one or more gestures, see the two examples provided below in Tables 1 and 2, each one qualified "one episode"). We distinguished five main families of gestures, two of which each with two sub-families, two of which each again with their own two or three sub-families: representation (designation: identification, qualification, and comparison; specification), organisation (discourse and interaction management: management of one's own discourse, management of co-participants' interaction; functional design-action management), focalisation, modulation, and disambiguation. We did not retain all these distinctions for the analysis presented in this paper (see below).

Both in the DTRS7 and in the present analysis, we were the only judge for the identification of gestures, their function, and their form. In the identification of functions, we were guided by our model of design [6] (see below).

3.2 Functions of Gestures Used in Design Collaboration

We suppose that the activities that are performed or supported by gestures in design meetings fulfil one or more of the functions that cognitive design research has shown design activities to have [6]: (1) to contribute to the design *per se,* or (2) to have an organisational function.

The first family of activities—"representational gestures"—contributes to the construction of the representations that are to result in the specifications of the artefact. We indeed identified gestures that play a role in the generation, modification, or evaluation of such representations. Besides these representational specification gestures, we identified a second type of representational gestures, that is, representational designation gestures. Indeed, in addition to their classical function, that is, to point out an entity to one's co-participants, we observed that designational gestures can also have a distinctive design function: a designer can *design* an entity *through its designation* [8]. As regards data analysis, we wish to stress that it is difficult for an external observer (and for a designer's co-participants in a meeting) to distinguish between entities that "existed" already before their being designated and entities that are being designed through their designation. Designing is a continuous process: design working meetings generally are not events where a definitely finished project is being reported (and once the meeting over, design generally continues) [27] [cf. also 28's distinction between gestures that depict—iconic gestures—and gestures that conceive an entity].

Gestures also served organisational functions: the gestures of this second family— "organisational gestures"—contributed to the management of interaction [Bavelas' "interactive" gestures, 29] and to the organisation of functional design actions.

Relative to the DTRS7 study, we brought back to two main families (each with two subfamilies) the five families distinguished in our first analysis [8]. Identification, qualification, and comparison are no longer differentiated as separate functions. Management of one's own discourse and management of co-participants' interaction are both considered management of interaction now. Focalising, modulating, and disambiguating gestures are considered all three organisational now.

One may notice that the representational gestures in this study refer to a particular kind of representations. "Representational gestures" as identified by other authors [30, 31] receive this name because they "[represent] attributes, actions, or relationships of objects or characters" [30, p. 377], they "[represent] an aspect of the content of an utterance" [31, p. 160]. Here, the criterion for qualifying a gesture as "representational" is its contribution to the construction of a cognitive artefact, that is, a representation that is to result in the entity to be designed.

We chose the label "designational gestures" because it allows covering in an elegant way both the classical "deictics" or "pointing gestures" and the gestures that *design* through their designation.

3.3 The Relationship between Function and Form of Gesture in Design Collaboration

Do gestures with a particular function have a particular form, and do gestures with a particular form fulfil a particular function?

Data Analysed. To examine this question, we reanalysed the episodes of A1 that the DTRS7 study allowed identifying the functions of gesture in design collaboration, associating this time the form of the gestures to their function.

Specifying Form. Form can be specified and analysed at various levels (as function can be). We have to establish the relevant level(s). Most formal characterisations use rather low-level physical kinetic features, such as hand shape, palm orientation, movement, and location in gesture space. Our cognitive-ergonomics aim to contribute to the specification of collaborative-design environments is not yet formulated in terms of well-circumscribed specifications. We therefore adopt a medium or even high-level characterisation, using McNeill's [30] form-related subcategories for gesticulation: pointing, iconics/metaphorics [32], and beats. Rather than covering gestures with one particular form, these categories refer to families of forms: pointing gestures all share a movement towards the *designatum* [31]; iconics/metaphorics (re)present an object through the physical display of one or more of its characteristics; beats take the form of the hand beating time. If such broad categories allow for an association between gestures' function and form, a next step could be to examine the function-form relationship in terms of more low-level formal features (but cf. our Discussion and Conclusion section).

Results. We did not find a one-to-one function-form relationship.

Gestures with a Particular Function do not Systematically have a Particular Form. Representation was of course often performed using iconic/metaphoric gestures and emblems. However, it could also be through a pointing gesture. The episode presented in Table 1 gives an example of a pointing gesture, rather than an iconic/metaphoric gesture, that represents an entity. Through their designation, three possible itineraries are brought into life—that is, designed. Consecutively pointing with a finger three different routes on the plan, Adam indeed designs three possible itineraries for entering the cremator area. We will come back upon this analysis in the Discussion and Conclusion section.

Table 1. Designing three itineraries using pointing gestures

The first description line indicates, between square brackets, the identity of the gesturer and the duration of the gesture by reference to that of the corresponding portion of the verbal protocol

The second line presents a brief description of the gestural movement

34	Adam	obviously there are numerous ways of getting into this accommodation
35		that's route number one the second route is round the end of the pond [g_Ad.. *tracing with a finger consecutively three lines over the plan*
36		and the third route is through the chapel so there's numerous ways of ....]

Table 2. Modulating discourse components using various forms of gesture
lchoag = long continuous hands opening, advancing gestures
This table corresponds to Extract 6 from [8]

34	Anna	yes she's been to have a look at our existing we're mentioned in the [g_Anna................ *points to the book*
35		book quite a bit with the existing chapel she was quite impressed ....]
36		because we've also got quite a lot of photographs and other things and [g_Anna.............................] *long continuous hands opening, advancing gestures*
37		plans like the forward plan of extending the chapel originally the original [g_Anna.......................................] *long continuous hands opening, advancing gestures*
38		idea so that was quite forward thinking in nineteen eighty or seventy
39		whenever seventy eight when they decided on that + so I've sent off for
40		that but you try and get them to raise a SAP order for it and you get how [g_Anna.....................................] [g_Anna....... *lchoag* *sequence of*
41		often will we need the SPIRE BOOKS COMPANY I said well we'll never use ....] [g_Anna............] *detached short beats* *lchoag*
42		them again probably why do you need to do that oh for god's sake [g_Anna..........] *lchoag*
43		so I just went out and bought it and the one above as well a history [g_Anna....................] *lchoag*
44		of cremations that's what we have at home on the bookshelf
45		cheerful reading like you when you go on holiday with your part- your [g_An *lchoag*
46		husband and wife + you see a sign for crematorium straight away na.................] [g_Anna......] *enacting how one*
47		ignoring them whether you're abroad or in this country the [g_Anna.......................................] *holds a car steering wheel* *enacting how one suddenly changes direction*
48		first thing you do straight away oh not another cemetery they go oh dear

There were nevertheless tendencies. Specification (the main representational design function) mostly occurred using iconic/metaphoric gestures. Designation in its classical signalling function (indicating something that already exists) was chiefly performed through pointing. By definition, designation in its design function was performed through pointing.

Gestures with a Particular Form do not Systematically Fulfil a Particular Function. We mentioned some tendencies above. Nevertheless, pointing had other uses than its signalling designation function; iconic/metaphoric gestures did not always specify design entities (cf. the example in Table 2). Pointing was also used to design (as illustrated in Table 1), to manage the interaction or design actions [cf. examples in 8], or to modulate components in one's discourse, another organisational function (cf. the example in Table 2).

Table 2 presents an episode in which Anna uses a variety of gestural movements to modulate elements of her discourse. It shows how Anna presents a book in which the author ("she" in line 34) mentions the already existing crematorium. When Anna wanted to order the book, she encountered many administrative problems, so she bought it herself. Telling this, she both highlights content elements and expresses their emotional loading, using different types of gestures.

- Pointing to the book, Anna uses this deictic gesture to highlight that "[they]'re mentioned in the book."
- Through long continuous hands opening, advancing gestures, she metaphorically emphasises discourse components.
- She also uses a sequence of detached short beats with this emphasis function (the "classic" use of beats).
- Enacting how a person holds a car steering wheel and then suddenly changes direction, Anna uses these iconic/metaphoric gestures to highlight her idea that people, normally, do not wish to visit cemeteries during their holidays.

The Multifaceted Nature of Gesture. The results presented in the two previous sub-sections showed the multifaceted nature of gesture. Another example of this quality of gesture was that—as we already saw in these sub-sections—neither functional nor form categories were exclusive: a particular gesture could have various functions or combine various form-related characteristics. In A1, certain gestures used to specify could also serve focalisation, modulation, or disambiguation, that is, have an organisational function. The same observation was made for certain organisational gestures, which fulfilled other functions as well in a number of situations. As also mentioned already, gestures used to designate could have in addition an organisational function.

4 Discussion and Conclusion

We wish to highlight several outcomes with respect to the question examined in this paper and envision extensions of our study.

Our analysis did not allow attributing particular forms to particular functions—and v.v. A gesture with a particular function could take various forms, and a particular gestural movement as regards form could fulfil different functions. There were tendencies—designation being mostly performed through pointing gestures, and specification mainly through iconic/metaphoric gestures—but, as we mentioned, the distinctions between McNeill's [30] form-related categories are very global: a characterisation of the gestures in more low-level formal characteristics might not have shown such tendencies (but we are not going to examine this possibility, cf. below).

Another example of the multifaceted nature of gestures observed in the study was that functional and form categories were not exclusive. On the one hand, a particular gesture could fulfil different functions; on the other hand, one gesture could combine different form-related characteristics. Kendon [31] has also observed this in a detailed analysis of pointing (which he analyses as a function): pointing can be combined with other functions, for example, with a representational one (pp. 202-205). Nevertheless, Kendon notes as well that there are gestures that are "specialised" for pointing. Other authors have analysed as iconics, gestures that superficially may seem pointers (cf. our example in Table 1), observed that iconic gestures may be used as pointers [33], or shown that iconicity is not restricted to "iconic" gestures [34]. Doing so, they privilege other than formal features: they favour semantic or semiotic relations between the referent and its gestural expression.

If the formal characteristics we adopted do not allow differentiating functional gestures in collaboration, our next concern could be to find other features—formal or not—that allow such differentiation. Given our results—and, even more, on the basis of observations by other authors in the domain of gesture studies [35, 36]—we think that, rather than more low-level formal features, these will be context-dependent, semantic characteristics.

More tendencies than those identified here might exist—but especially tendencies of another than a formal nature seem to us more relevant at present. Many studies have shown indeed that formal features of gestural movements are not enough—and even not the most relevant attributes—to characterise gestures [7, 35, 36].

"Inter-speaker systematics" [35] has been searched for—and found—in several directions. "Representation techniques" [31] and "modes of representation" [34] are two related ones. Analysing iconicity (cf. above), Müller [34] identifies four different modes of representation that are used to "construct gestural meaning" (p. 321). In his detailed analysis of pointing gestures, Kendon [31] concludes that the specific form of these gestures "might vary systematically in relation to semantic distinctions of various sorts.... The form of the pointing gesture is not a matter of idiosyncratic choice or variation unrelated to the other things the speaker is doing." (p. 223) The author identifies seven different hand shape and hand shape/forearm orientation configurations.

Referring to Kendon [31], Bergmann and Kopp [35] analysed the use of iconic gestures in spatial descriptions. The authors examined the differential use of five representation techniques as a candidate for such "inter-speaker systematics." Analysing if there was a relationship between these representation techniques, Bergmann and Kopp observed inter-subjective correlations, but they also noticed individual differences (idiosyncratic aspects of gestures) [also underlined in 36].

To conclude, the study presented in this paper has illustrated again the complex relationship between gestures' function and form. It has pointed out some tendencies concerning form-function relationships, but we decided to not investigate further this specific issue. Instead, closer inspection of the data might reveal tendencies—or even regularities—of another nature (especially semantic and/or context-related).

Acknowledgments. The author wishes to thank an anonymous reviewer, whose questions, remarks, and suggestions in relation to an earlier version of this text have helped to advance her reflections on gesture and its relevant dimensions.

References

1. Calbris, G.: The Semiotics of French Gestures. Indiana University Press, Bloomington (1990)
2. Goldin-Meadow, S.: The Resilience of Language: What Gesture Creation in Deaf Children Can Tell Us About How All Children Learn Language. Taylor & Francis, New York (2003)
3. Mitra, S., Acharya, T.: Gesture Recognition: A Survey. IEEE Transactions on Systems, Man, and Cybernetics, Part C: Applications and Reviews 37, 311–324 (2007)
4. Cassell, J.: A Framework for Gesture Generation and Interpretation. In: Cipolla, R., Pentland, A. (eds.) Computer Vision in Human-Machine Interaction, pp. 191–215. Cambridge University Press, New York (1998)
5. Kraut, R.E., Fussell, S.R., Siegel, J.: Visual Information as a Conversational Resource in Collaborative Physical Tasks. Human-Computer Interaction 18, 13–49 (2003)
6. Visser, W.: The Cognitive Artifacts of Designing. Lawrence Erlbaum Associates, Mahwah (2006)
7. Cassell, J., Stone, M.: Living Hand to Mouth: Psychological Theories About Speech and Gesture in Interactive Dialogue Systems. In: AAAI 1999 Fall Symposium on Psychological Models of Communication in Collaborative Systems, North Falmouth, MA, pp. 34–42 (1999)
8. Visser, W.: The Function of Gesture in an Architectural Design Meeting. In: McDonnell, J., Lloyd, P., Luck, R., Reid, F. (eds.) About: Designing. Analysing Design Meetings, ch. 15, pp. 269–284. Taylor & Francis, London (2009)
9. Bisseret, A., Figeac-Letang, C., Falzon, P.: Modeling Opportunistic Reasonings: The Cognitive Activity of Traffic Signal Setting Technicians. Institut National de Recherche en Informatique et en Automatique, Rocquencourt, France (1988), http://www.inria.fr/rrrt/rr-0898.html
10. Hayes-Roth, B., Hayes-Roth, F.: A Cognitive Model of Planning. Cognitive Science 3, 275–310 (1979)
11. Chalmé, S., Visser, W., Denis, M.: Cognitive Effects of Environmental Knowledge on Urban Route Planning Strategies. In: Rothengatter, T., Huguenin, R.D. (eds.) Traffic and Transport Psychology. Theory and Application, pp. 61–71. Elsevier, Amsterdam (2004)
12. Détienne, F.: Software Design. Cognitive Aspects. Springer, London (2002)
13. Lawson, B.R.: Design in Mind. Butterworth, London (1994)
14. Visser, W.: Designing as Construction of Representations: A Dynamic Viewpoint in Cognitive Design Research. Human-Computer Interaction, Special Issue Foundations of Design in HCI 21, 103–152 (2006), http://hal.inria.fr/inria-00117249/en/
15. Simon, H.A.: The Sciences of the Artificial (3rd, Rev. Ed. 1996; Orig. Ed. 1969; 2nd Rev. Ed. 1981) (3rd ed.). MIT Press, Cambridge (1999/1969)
16. Cross, N.: Designerly Ways of Knowing. Springer, London (2006)
17. Tang, J.C.: Findings from Observational Studies of Collaborative Work. International Journal of Man-Machine Studies 34, 143–160 (1991)
18. Bekker, M.M., Olson, J.S., Olson, G.M.: Analysis of Gestures in Face-to-Face Design Teams Provides Guidance for How to Use Groupware in Design. In: DIS 1995, Conference on Designing interactive systems: Processes, practices, methods, & techniques, pp. 157–166. ACM Press, New York (1995)
19. Murphy, K.M.: Collaborative Imagining: The Interactive Use of Gestures, Talk, and Graphic Representation in Architectural Practice. Semiotica 156, 113–145 (2005)

20. Détienne, F., Visser, W., Tabary, R.: Articulation des Dimensions Graphico-Gestuelle et Verbale dans l'Analyse de la Conception Collaborative [Articulation of Graphico-Gestural and Verbal Dimensions in the Analysis of Collaborative Design]. Psychologie de l'Interaction. Numéro spécial Langage et cognition: Contraintes pragmatiques, pp. 283–307 (2006)

21. Détienne, F., Visser, W.: Multimodality and Parallelism in Design Interaction: Co-Designers' Alignment and Coalitions. In: Hassanaly, P., Herrmann, T., Kunau, G., Zacklad, M. (eds.) Cooperative Systems Design. Seamless Integration of Artifacts and Conversations-Enhanced Concepts of Infrastructure for Communication, pp. 118–131. IOS, Amsterdam (2006), http://hal.inria.fr/inria-00118255/en/

22. Visser, W., Détienne, F.: Articulation entre Composantes Verbale et Graphico-Gestuelle de l'Interaction dans des Réunions de Conception Architecturale [Articulating the Verbal and Graphico-Gestural Components of the Interaction in Architectural Design Meetings]. In: Actes de Scan 2005, Séminaire de Conception Architecturale Numérique [Digital Architectural Design Seminar]: Le Rôle de l'Esquisse Architecturale dans le Monde Numérique [The Role of the Architectural Sketch in the Digital World], Charenton-le-Pont, France (2005), http://hal.inria.fr/inria-00117076/en/

23. Visser, W.: Co-Élaboration de Solutions en Conception Architecturale et Rôle du Graphico-Gestuel: Point de Vue de la Psychologie Ergonomique [Co-Elaborating Architectural Design Solutions and the Role of the Graphico-Gestural: The Ergonomic-Psychology Viewpoint]. In: Détienne, F., Traverso, V. (eds.) Méthodologies d'Analyse de Situations Coopératives de Conception: Corpus Mosaic [Methodologies for Analysing Cooperative Design Situations: The Mosaic Corpus], ch. 5.3, pp. 129–167. Presses Universitaires de Nancy, Nancy (2009)

24. McDonnell, J., Lloyd, P., Luck, R., Reid, F.: About: Designing: Analysing Design Meetings. Taylor & Francis, London (2009)

25. Kendon, A.: Gesture. Annual Review of Anthropology 26, 109–128 (1997)

26. McNeill, D.: Gesture and Thought. University of Chicago Press, Chicago (2005)

27. Gasser, L., Scacchi, W., Ripoche, G., Penne, B.: Understanding Continuous Design in F/Oss Projects. In: ICSSEA 2003, the 16th International Conference on Software Engineering and its Applications, Paris (2003)

28. Streeck, J.: Gesture and Illusion: Methods of Depicting the World by Moving the Hands. International Conference "Il gesto nel Mediterraneo: Studi recenti sulla gestualità nel sud d'Europa [Gesture in the Mediterranean: Recent research in Southern Europe], Procida, Italy (2005)

29. Bavelas, J.B., Chovil, N., Lawrie, D.A., Wade, A.: Interactive Gestures. Discourse Processes 15, 469–489 (1992)

30. McNeill, D.: Hand and Mind. What Gestures Reveal About Thought. University of Chicago Press, Chicago (1992)

31. Kendon, A.: Gesture: Visible Action as Utterance. Cambridge University Press, Cambridge (2004)

32. Krauss, R.M., Chen, Y., Gottesman, R.F.: Lexical Gestures and Lexical Access: A Process Model. In: McNeill, D. (ed.) Language and Gesture, pp. 261–283. Cambridge University Press, New York (2000)

33. Pozzer-Ardenghi, L., Roth, W.-M.: Photographs in Lectures: Gestures as Meaning-Making Resources. Linguistics and Education 15, 275–293 (2004)

34. Müller, C.: Iconicity and Gesture. In: Santi, S., Guaïtella, I., Cavé, C., Konopczynski, G. (eds.) Oralité et Gestualité, Communication Multimodale, Interaction: Actes du Colloque Orage 1998. L'Harmattan, Paris (1998)

35. Bergmann, K., Kopp, S.: Increasing the Expressiveness of Virtual Agents. Autonomous Generation of Speech and Gesture for Spatial Description Tasks. In: Decker, K.S., Sichman, J.S., Sierra, C., Castelfranchi, C. (eds.) AAMAS 2009, the 8th Int. Conf. on Autonomous Agents and Multiagent Systems, Budapest, Hungary (2009)
36. Sowa, T., Kopp, S., Duncan, S., McNeill, D., Wachsmuth, I.: Implementing a Non-Modular Theory of Language Production in an Embodied Conversational Agent. In: Wachsmuth, I., Lenzen, M., Knoblich, G. (eds.) Embodied Communication in Humans and Machines, pp. 425–449. Oxford University Press, Oxford (2008)

Continuous Realtime Gesture Following and Recognition

Frédéric Bevilacqua, Bruno Zamborlin, Anthony Sypniewski, Norbert Schnell, Fabrice Guédy, and Nicolas Rasamimanana

Real Time Musical Interactions Team,
IRCAM, CNRS - STMS,
1, Place Igor Stravinsky, 75004 Paris, France
`Frederic.Bevilacqua@ircam.fr`

Abstract. We present a HMM based system for real-time gesture analysis. The system outputs continuously parameters relative to the gesture *time progression* and its *likelihood*. These parameters are computed by comparing the performed gesture with stored reference gestures. The method relies on a detailed modeling of multidimensional temporal curves. Compared to standard HMM systems, the learning procedure is simplified using prior knowledge allowing the system to use a single example for each class. Several applications have been developed using this system in the context of music education, music and dance performances and interactive installation. Typically, the estimation of the *time progression* allows for the synchronization of physical gestures to sound files by time stretching/compressing audio buffers or videos.

Keywords: gesture recognition, gesture following, Hidden Markov Model, music, interactive systems.

1 Introduction

Gesture recognition systems have been successively developed based on methods such as Hidden Markov Models (HMM), finite state machines, template matching or neural networks [1]. In most cases, gestures are considered as "unbreakable units" that must be recognized once completed. Typically, on-line systems output the recognition result at the end of each gesture. Motivated by the development of interactive systems in performing arts, we present here a different approach for online gesture analysis : the system updates "continuously" (i.e. on a fine temporal grain) parameters characterizing the performance of a gesture. Precisely, these parameters are made available during the temporal unfolding of the performed gesture.

We are first particularly interested in computing the *time progression* of the performance, or in other words answering the question "where are we within the gesture ?". We refer this as *following* the gesture. Second, we are interested in computing *likelihood* values between a performed gesture and pre-recorded gestures stored in a database. This can be used to perform a *recognition* task, but

S. Kopp and I. Wachsmuth (Eds.): GW 2009, LNAI 5934, pp. 73–84, 2010.

also to characterize gestures. As this will be illustrated by application examples, these parameters are particularly useful to build systems enabling expressive gestural control of sonic and/or visual media. Moreover, the estimation of both the *time progression* and *likelihood* values enable another important feature of such a system: the possibility to predict the evolution of the current gesture.

We assume here that *gestures* can be represented as multidimensional temporal curves. Importantly, our approach focuses on a detailed modeling of temporal profiles. High resolution temporal modeling is indeed essential for the estimation of the *time progression* of a gesture. This approach is thus especially suited for cases where the gesture temporal evolution are intrinsically relevant, and performed in a consistent manner. This is typically found in performing arts: measurements of dancers or musicians gestures reveal very consistent temporal profiles[2,3].

Our system is essentially based on Hidden Markov Models, with a particular implementation guaranteeing precise temporal modeling of gesture profiles and allowing for a simplified learning procedure. This latter point is essential for making such a system workable in the context of performing arts. As a matter of fact, building general gesture databases can reveal to be unpractical, as also discussed in Ref.[4], since gesture data are typically highly dependent on the artistic contexts and idiosyncrasies of performers. For these reasons, we developed a particular learning scheme based on a single recorded example only, using a priori knowledge. In this case, the learning phase is simple to operate and can be easily achieved during the normal flow of rehearsals. This approach has been iteratively designed through several specific cases[5,6,7] and implemented in a software called the *Gesture Follower*.

This paper is structured as follows. After a short summary of related works, we describe the algorithm, along with numerical simulations using synthetic data assessing quantitatively the algorithm. Second, we present typical applications of this system related to music and dance practices.

2   Related Works

The use of machine learning techniques for gesture recognition has been widely covered. Hidden Markov Models represents one of the mostly used methods [1,8,9]. Taking notice that training Hidden Markov Models might represent a cumbersome task, several authors proposed various approaches to facilitate the training process. Bobick and Wilson have proposed a state-based approach using a single prototype [10]. Using HMM they also later proposed an online adaptive algorithm for learning gesture models [11]. Rajko et al. also proposed a HMM based system, with the aim of reducing training requirements and allowing precise temporal gesture modeling [4,12,13]. Artieres et al. [14] proposed a recognition scheme based on segmental HMM that can be trained with very few examples.

Concerning realtime recognition Bloit and Rodet [15] developed a modified Viterbi decoding, called short term Viterbi, that allows for low latency recognition.

Mori et al. [16] proposed a system for early recognition and anticipation, based on continuous dynamic programming.

These works are generally principally oriented towards recognition tasks. The case of *following* a gesture in realtime, i.e. determining the time progression of a gesture during a performance, is generally not explicitly covered with the exception of score following systems for musical applications. Several authors have proposed systems based on HMM (or Semi-Markov Models) [17,18]. Nevertheless, in such cases, the Markov structure is essentially built from a symbolic representation given by the musical score, and not from continuous gesture data.

3   Gesture Modeling and Analysis Algorithm

As generally found in machine learning techniques, the system operation is separated into two procedures, learning and decoding. Our approach is based on Hidden Markov Models but with a modified learning schema. The algorithm fundamentally works with any type of regularly sampled multidimensional data flow.

3.1   Learning

Our system has been developed with the constraint that only few examples will be available. This constraint is incompatible with the use of statistical training (for example using the Baum-Welch algorithm), as found in standard implementations of Hidden Markov Models (HMM) [8].

The learning procedure is illustrated in Figure 1. The recorded temporal profile is used to create a left-to-right Hidden Markov Model. We build a model that fits the recorded reference by directly associating each sampled points to a state in a left-to-right Markov chain.

Each state i emits an observable O with a probability b_i, following a normal distribution (the vectorial case can be generalized in a straightforward way):

$$b_i(O) = \frac{1}{\sigma_i\sqrt{2\pi}}exp[-(\frac{O-\mu_i}{2\sigma_i})^2] \qquad (1)$$

μ_i is the *ith* sampled value of the recorded reference. The σ_i parameter can be interpreted as the standard deviation of differences in x occurring between performances. Obviously, σ_i cannot be estimated from a single example. Therefore, it is either estimated for a given context based on prior experiments and/or knowledge. The influence of this parameter will be further discussed in section 3.4.

This HMM structure statistically models the recorded data sequence, considering additional assumptions on the transition probabilities. We define a limited number of permitted transitions by setting the transition probabilities a_0, a_1, a_2 (self, next, skip transitions, see Figure1). These probabilities a_0, a_1, a_2 must satisfy the Equation 2.

$$a_0 + a_1 + a_2 = 1 \qquad (2)$$

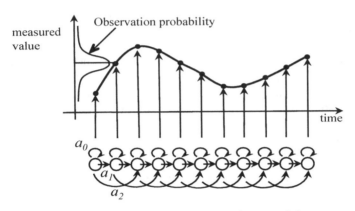

left to right Hidden Markov Model

Fig. 1. Learning procedure: a left-to-right HMM is used to model the recorded reference

As for σ_i, these parameters cannot be precisely estimated from a single example. Nevertheless, their values can be set based on prior knowledge or measurements in specific applications. The following discussion clarifies the role of these parameters.

1. $a_0 = a_1 = a_2 = 1/3$: this case corresponds to have equal probabilities slower or faster performance of the gesture.
2. $a_0 < a_1$ and $a_2 < a_1$ this case corresponds to have lower probability for speeding up or slowing down.
3. $a_0 < a_2$ this case corresponds to have lower probability for slowing down than speeding up
4. $a_0 > a_2$ this case corresponds to have higher probability for slowing down than speeding up.

Note that the relative maximum speed (between the performed and reference gesture) is 2 in the example shown in Figure1. This value can higher by setting additional transitions (for example $a_3 > 0$).

Based on experiments (see section 4), we found that empirical values such as $a_0 = a_1 = a_2 = 1/3$ or $a_0 = a_2 = 0.25$ and $a_1 = 0.5$ work for a large set of applications. A similar discussion can be found in [4].

We also implemented a further simplified HMM structure. As described in [6], a HMM structure with only two possible transitions, self and next transitions can be used considering $a_0 = 1/n$ and $a_1 = 1 - 1/n$, and downsampling the recorded reference by a factor n. This configuration has been used for the assessments described in section 3.4.

3.2   Decoding

As explained in the introduction, we are interested in two types of quantities: *time progression index* and *likelihood* values, computed from the online comparison between the gesture being performed and recorded references. Similarly to score following algorithms [17], we base our decoding scheme on the standard forward procedure in HMM [8].

Consider the partial observation sequence $O_1, O_2, ...O_t$. The forward procedure requires the computation of the $\alpha_i(t)$ variable which corresponds to the probability distribution of the partial observation sequence until time t, and state i . It is computed inductively as follows:

Initialisation

$$\alpha_1(i) = \pi_i b_i(O_1) \qquad 1 \leq i \leq N \tag{3}$$

where π is the initial state distribution, and b is the observation probability distribution.

Induction

$$\alpha_{t+1}(i) = [\sum_{i=1}^{N} \alpha_t(i)a_{ij}]b_i(O_t) \qquad 1 \leq t \leq T-1, 1 \leq j \leq N \tag{4}$$

where a_{ij} is the state transition probability distribution.

From the $\alpha_i(t)$ variable we can compute two important quantities:

1. Time progression of the sequence, related to the recorded example

$$time\ progression\ index(t) = argmax[\alpha_t(i)] \tag{5}$$

   Note that this *index* can be alternatively estimated by the mean (expected value) of the distribution $\alpha_i(t)$.
2. Likelihood of the sequence.

$$likelihood(t) = \sum_{i=1}^{N} \alpha_t(i) \tag{6}$$

This quantity can been used directly as a *similarity measure* between the gesture being performed and the recorded reference. Other similarity measures could also be derived by combining the *likelihood* and the smoothness of the *time progression* index.

3.3   Windowing Technique

A major limitation of the algorithm described above is the large number of states of the HMM when dealing with long phrases, which can be an issue for real-time computation. For example, with a data sampling rate of 100 Hz, the number of states is typically 600 for an one minute phrase. Typically, a number of states larger than 1000 might be too CPU intensive for our applications. To avoid this problem, we developed a sliding window technique that uses a fixed number of

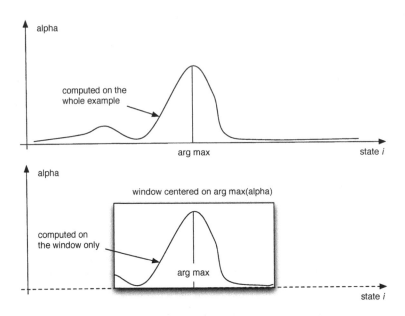

Fig. 2. Windowing technique used in the decoding scheme to reduce the CPU load

states, thus limiting the computation load, similarly to beam search techniques. The method is illustrated in Figure 2.

As explained earlier, the decoding procedure requires the computation of the probability $\alpha_i(t)$. In the basic algorithm, this probability distribution is computed on the entire state structure. In the windowed version, this computation is limited to a section of the state structure. Precisely, it is evaluated on a window centered around the arg max of the $\alpha_i(t)$ distribution, i.e. around the *time progression index*. At each new step of the evaluation, the window location is moved. α_i values that were not considered in the previous window are initialized to zero in the new window.

This technique allows for the computation with a fixed number of states, that is adjustable by the user. Thus the CPU load remains a constant value independent of the length of the gesture data. Tests showed that this method was effective.

Importantly, this technique can also be seen as adding constraints to the estimation of the *time progression index*, since the range of possible values is reduced at a given time. This procedure can make the estimation of the *time progression index* more robust to outlier data that could otherwise provoke unrealistic jumps.

3.4 Assessments on Synthetic Data

Simulations were performed with Matlab using synthetic signals to evaluate quantitatively the accuracy of the *time progression index*. As shown in Figure 3,

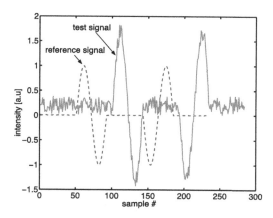

Fig. 3. Synthetic signals used for the algorithm assessment

reference and test signals were created by concatenating truncated sine functions and constant signals.

Precisely, the reference signal was obtained by concatenating the following parts: constant zero signal (50 samples), one period of a sine signal (40 samples), constant zero signal (50 samples), one period of a sine signal (40 samples), constant zero signal (50 samples) (total length = 230 samples). The tests signals were obtained from the reference signal by applying various transformations in the amplitude, offset and noise level.

The algorithm was applied to these altered test signals, and average errors obtained in the *time progression* index were computed. These error values can be associated to a time jitter. For example, with a sampling rate of 200 Hz, an error of one sample would correspond to a jitter of 5 ms.

The assessments reported here were performed in the case of the simplified HMM state structure, where we retain only two types of possible transitions, *self* and *next* transitions ($a_0 = a_1 = 0.5$). As noted in section 3.1, a downsampling of a factor 2 was thus applied to the reference signals. In this simplified case, the standard deviation σ_i is the only parameter to be adjusted. We performed a complete set of assessments varying the σ_i values.

Interestingly, we found that, as long as σ_i values lies in an given interval, the results for the *time progression* index are weakly affected by the σ_i absolute value. For example, considering reference signals normalized between -1 and 1, we found that σ_i should lie approximately in the interval [0.1 0.5]. This result confirmed us that our algorithm can operate in cases where the σ_i values are known only approximately.

Figure 4 (a), (b) and (c) show the results for three different signal alterations: scaling the amplitude, adding a constant offset and adding gaussian noise, respectively. The value σ_i is = 0.2 in all cases. These results show that, as expected, the accuracy in the estimation of the *time progression index* decreases while increasing the alteration level. Nevertheless, it is important to note that the errors

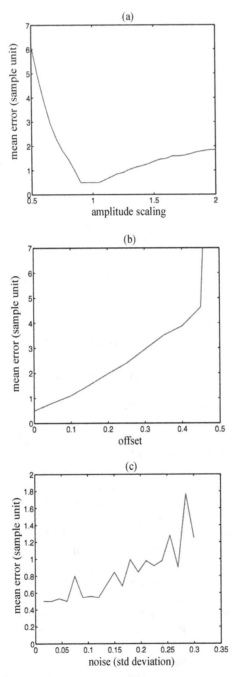

Fig. 4. (a) Error in the time progression index for various amplitude scaling of the test signals. (b) Error in the time progression index for various offset of the test signals. (c) Error in the time progression index for various noise levels of the test signals. In all cases, value $\sigma_i = 0.2$, and the reference signal were normalized between -1 and 1. In the cases of (a) and (b), a fixed gaussian noise of 1% was also added.

remain at an acceptable level considering relatively large alterations. For example, a test signal of amplitude twice the reference signal induces an average error less than 2 samples, for a total signal length of 250 samples (see Figure 3). Interestingly, the algorithm is more sensitive to a decrease than to an increase of the test signal amplitude. These results indicate that theses limits can be large enough to work with real data, which has been confirmed later during our applications as described in section 4.

4   Implementation and Applications

The system described in this paper is implemented as a collection of modules in the Max environnement[1] called the *Gesture Follower*, taking advantage of the data structures of the FTM library[2] such as matrices and dictionaries[19,20]. Recently, the core algorithm was developed as an independent C++ library and can therefore be implemented in other environnements.

We applied the *Gesture Follower* to build interactive systems in music and dance performances. The system was also applied to design experiments aimed at studying gesture and movement sonification [21].

Most of the applications make use of the *time progression index* given by the *Gesture Follower*. Particularly, this parameter allows for the design of applications based on a time synchronization paradigm: digital media and effects can be synchronized to any particular moments of a given reference gesture. This reference gesture is set by the user by a simple recording. Thanks to the windowing technique (section 3.3), there is no limitation other than the computer memory for the gesture length. This opens interesting perspectives, such as following an entire music performance. A particular interesting case is illustrated in Figure 5, were the *time progression index* is used to synchronize the speed of the playback of an audio recording. For example, audio time stretching/compressing can be performed using phase vocoder techniques.

Specific cases of this paradigm were experimented in the context of music pedagogy [22]. In particular, "virtual" conducting was achieved using a wireless sensor module transmitting hand gesture accelerations to the *Gesture Follower* (Figure 6). With this system, students were able to control precisely the playing speed of an orchestra recording.

A particular interesting feature of our system resides in the possibility to continuously compare the live performance with different interpretations previously recorded. For example, the *likelihood* value can be therefore used to control the sound intensity (see Figure 5) and further sound transformation.

Other applications were achieved in the fields of dance performance and interactive installations. Experiments showed that the system was able to distinguish easily between fifteen short dance phrases, based on 3D accelerometers wore on a dancer wrists. Since the *likelihood* parameters were continuously updated, it was

---

[1] http://www.cycling74.com
[2] http://ftm.ircam.fr

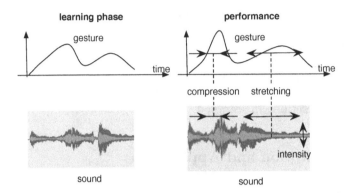

Fig. 5. Gesture synchronization to audio time stretching/compression

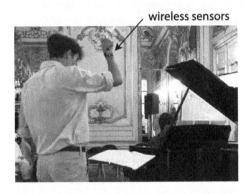

Fig. 6. "Virtual" conducting using wireless motion sensors (accelerometers and gyroscopes and the *gesture follower*. The system synchronizes the gesture with the playback of an orchestra recording.

possible to recognize a gesture early, without waiting for its completion to operate a choice in the interaction process. Parallel to this recognition procedure, it was possible to effectively synchronize video materials to the dancer movements using the *time progression index*.

5   Conclusion and Future Work

We presented a HMM based system for real-time gesture analysis. The system relies on a detailed temporal modeling and outputs continuously two main parameters: the *time progression index* and *likelihood* values which can be used to estimate *similarities* between a gesture being performed and recorded references. One advantage of this system resides in the simplified learning process.

Various applications, mainly based on a *following* paradigm, were built with this system, and proved the validity of our approach. Refinements of this system are currently implemented and further applications are foreseen, especially taking advantage of the prediction capabilities of this system.

Acknowledgements

We acknowledge partial support of the following projects: The EU-ICT i-Maestro project, the EU-ICT Project SAME and the ANR project EarToy (French National Research Agency). We would like to thank Remy Muller for his important contribution in the early development of this work, Richard Siegal, Jean-Philippe Lambert, Florence Baschet, Serge Lemouton and the students of "Atelier des Feuillantines" for contributing to experiments.

References

1. Mitra, S., Acharya, T., Member, S., Member, S.: Gesture recognition: A survey. IEEE Transactions on Systems, Man and Cybernetics - Part C 37, 311–324 (2007)
2. Rasamimanana, N.H., Bevilacqua, F.: Effort-based analysis of bowing movements: evidence of anticipation effects. The Journal of New Music Research 37(4), 339–351 (2009)
3. Rasamimanana, N.H., Kaiser, F., Bevilacqua, F.: Perspectives on gesture-sound relationships informed from acoustic instrument studies. Organised Sound 14(2), 208–216 (2009)
4. Rajko, S., Qian, G., Ingalls, T., James, J.: Real-time gesture recognition with minimal training requirements and on-line learning. In: CVPR 2007: IEEE Conference on Computer Vision and Pattern Recognition, pp. 1–8 (2007)
5. Muller, R.: Human Motion Following using Hidden Markov Models. Master thesis, INSA Lyon, Laboratoire CREATIS (2004)
6. Bevilacqua, F., Guédy, F., Schnell, N., Fléty, E., Leroy, N.: Wireless sensor interface and gesture-follower for music pedagogy. In: NIME 2007: Proceedings of the 7th international conference on New interfaces for musical expression, pp. 124–129 (2007)
7. Bevilacqua, F.: Momentary notes on capturing gestures. In: (capturing intentions). Emio Greco/PC and the Amsterdam School for the Arts (2007)
8. Rabiner, L.R.: A tutorial on hidden markov models and selected applications in speech recognition. Proceedings of the IEEE 77(2), 257–286 (1989)
9. Fine, S., Singer, Y.: The hierarchical hidden markov model: Analysis and applications. In: Machine Learning, pp. 41–62 (1998)
10. Bobick, A.F., Wilson, A.D.: A state-based approach to the representation and recognition of gesture. IEEE Transactions on Pattern Analysis and Machine Intelligence 19(12), 1325–1337 (1997)
11. Wilson, A.D., Bobick, A.F.: Realtime online adaptive gesture recognition. In: Proceedings of the International Conference on Pattern Recognition (1999)
12. Rajko, S., Qian, G.: A hybrid hmm/dpa adaptive gesture recognition method. In: International Symposium on Visual Computing (ISVC), pp. 227–234 (2005)

13. Rajko, S., Qian, G.: Hmm parameter reduction for practical gesture recognition. In: 8th IEEE International Conference on Automatic Face and Gesture Recognition (FG 2008), pp. 1–6 (2008)
14. Artieres, T., Marukatat, S., Gallinari, P.: Online handwritten shape recognition using segmental hidden markov models. IEEE Transactions on Pattern Analysis and Machine Intelligence 29(2), 205–217 (2007)
15. Bloit, J., Rodet, X.: Short-time viterbi for online HMM decoding: evaluation on a real-time phone recognition task. In: International Conference on Acoustics, Speech, and Signal Processing, ICASSP (2008)
16. Mori, A., Uchida, S., Kurazume, R., Ichiro Taniguchi, R., Hasegawa, T., Sakoe, H.: Early recognition and prediction of gestures. In: Proceedings of the International Conference on Pattern Recognition, vol. 3, pp. 560–563 (2006)
17. Schwarz, D., Orio, N., Schnell, N.: Robust polyphonic midi score following with hidden markov models. In: Proceedings of the International Computer Music Conference, ICMC (2004)
18. Cont, A.: Antescofo: Anticipatory synchronization and control of interactive parameters in computer music. In: Proceedings of the International Computer Music Conference, ICMC (2008)
19. Schnell, N., Borghesi, R., Schwarz, D., Bevilacqua, F., Müller, R.: Ftm - complex data structures for max. In: International Computer Music Conference, ICMC (2005)
20. Bevilacqua, F., Muller, R., Schnell, N.: Mnm: a max/msp mapping toolbox. In: NIME 2005: Proceedings of the 5th international conference on New interfaces for musical expression, pp. 85–88 (2005)
21. Viaud-Delmon, I., Bresson, J., Pachet, F., Bevilacqua, F., Roy, P., Warusfel, O.: Eartoy: interactions ludiques par l'audition. In: Journées d'Informatique Musicale - JIM 2007, Lyon, France (2007)
22. Rasamimanana, N., Guedy, F., Schnell, N., Lambert, J.P., Bevilacqua, F.: Three pedagogical scenarios using the sound and gesture lab. In: Proceedings of the 4th i-Maestro Workshop on Technology Enhanced Music Education (2008)

Multiscale Detection of Gesture Patterns in Continuous Motion Trajectories

Radu-Daniel Vatavu[1], Laurent Grisoni[2], and Stefan-Gheorghe Pentiuc[1]

[1] University Stefan cel Mare of Suceava, Romania
[2] Laboratoire d'Informatique Fondamentale de Lille, France
vatavu@eed.usv.ro, laurent.grisoni@lifl.fr, pentiuc@eed.usv.ro
http://www.eed.usv.ro/~vatavu

Abstract. We describe a numerical method for scale invariant detection of gesture patterns in continuous 2D motions. The algorithm is fast due to our rejection-based reasoning achieved using a new set of curvature-based functions which we call Integral Absolute Curvatures. Detection rates above 96% are reported on a large data set consisting of 72,000 samples with demonstrated low execution time. The technique can be used to automatically detect gesture patterns in unconstrained motions in order to enable click-free interactions.

Keywords: gesture recognition, pattern detection, multiscale, curvature, integral of curvature, motion trajectory.

1 Introduction

Gestures have become more and more present in today's human-computer interfaces with the recent advances in robust recognition techniques as well as in acquisition devices that became more and more available and affordable [7,9,13,16,17,20]. However, current gesture-based interfaces still isolate gestures by making use of user-driven discrete events such as mouse clicks, stylus up/down movements, pushing buttons on tracking devices or by requiring users to hold a specified hand posture in vision-based processing. Recognition techniques are further applied on such user-segmented gestures by using shape similarity methods well established in the pattern recognition community [7,9]. By adopting this self-segmentation approach, it is the users that let the system know when and where the gesture commands start and end with a direct impact on the fluidity of the interaction process. The alternative would be to automatically detect gestures in constraint-free continuous motions for which we propose a novel fast technique. The challenge is a difficult one cause of the multiscale problem: given two motion curves $G(s)$ and $\Gamma(s)$, find the occurrences of gesture $G(s)$ in the user-input trajectory $\Gamma(s)$ irregardless of scale.

2 Related Work

Gesture motions may be acquired using the mouse, stylus [7,16], WiiMote [15], specialized trackers, gloves and vision-based computing with dedicated

S. Kopp and I. Wachsmuth (Eds.): GW 2009, LNAI 5934, pp. 85–97, 2010.

algorithms for detecting and tracking various regions of interest such as hands, arms or the full body. Moeslund et. al [9] and Poppe [11] provide excellent surveys on the trends in video-based human capture and visual analysis of human movement while Pavlovic et al. [10] focus on hand gestures. Also, good courses on sketching recognition are available [7]. With respect to gesture recognizers, several robust approaches have been proposed such as the Rubine's classifier [13], the $1 recognizer [20] or elastic matching techniques [17].

Common approaches for segmenting gestures make use of predefined hand postures that simulate click events: Vatavu et al. [17] signal the beginning and end of a gesture by pointing and retracting the index finger; Wilson [19] uses the pinch gesture in the TAFFI interface; Vatavu and Pentiuc [18] combine hand open and hand close. Not only posture but location has been used as well: Cerlinca et al. [4] use predefined regions of interest around the human body in order to facilitate segmentation and recognition of free hand gestures; Marcel [8] defines a body-face space with various motion and color sensitive zones.

Several attempts have been made with regards to the automatic detection of gestures in unconstrained motion. Reng et al. [12] pose the problem of identifying primitives in body motions and consider an error measurement based on density. Dong et al. [5] propose a greedy approach for segmenting body motions from long video sequences into a predefined set of motion templates. The authors do not report execution times nor complexity orders and the technique was evaluated for off-line segmentation. Arvo and Novins introduce fluid sketching [1,2] as a technique for on-the-fly recognition and morphing of users sketches to predefined classes of simple geometric shapes such as circles, boxes, lines or Bezier shapes by least-squares approximation. The motion doodles of Thorne et al. [16] represent a technique for parsing sketches into predefined tokens using a corner detection algorithm and classifying segments into straight or curved. The approach is simple and limited to 4 orientations of the straight lines and 2 directions of the curved segments.

Non-template-based approaches that split continuous motions into meaningful gestures without previous learnt templates are worth pursuing in the context of natural gesturing. Segmentation is handled in this case using various cues such as pauses in motion, hand tension or movement effort [14].

2.1   Contribution

Detecting gesture patterns in unconstrained motions is a difficult problem and current approaches address it partially by limiting the patterns to simple shapes. The problem is hard due to the multiscale issue: a (naive) algorithm that would try to match all the possible candidates would fail within the constrains of real-time interfaces. The main contribution of this paper is represented by a fast technique that rejects the majority of weak and unfit candidates. We introduce for this purpose the notion of integral of absolute curvature by taking an approach from differential geometry. By making use of a curvature-based representation, our gesture detection is rotation invariant as well. Reported results show detection rates above 96% for a large dataset of 72,000 samples.

3   Motion Representation

For all our further discussions, we will consider a gesture motion as a point moving in time, $c(t) : [0, T] \rightarrow \Re^2$ in the continuous domain as well as a sequence of sampled points, $C = \{p_i = (x_i, y_i), i = \overline{0, n-1}\}$ in the discrete case. We limit our method to 2D gesture motions only. Also, we are not particularly interested in the acquisition device as long as we dispose of the discrete representation of the captured motion. For example, development of the technique was carried mostly on motions acquired using the mouse while the actual testing described in section 5 and the performance results are discussed on gestures captured using a stylus as it best matches the real-world experience (i.e. the pen).

We briefly describe below the main notions employed throughout the paper. When considering the continuous case of a motion curve, $c(t) : [0, T] \rightarrow \Re^2, c(t) = (x(t), y(t))$, we make use of arc-length $s(t) = \int_0^t \|c'(u)\| \, dt$ where $\|c'(u)\|$ represents the norm of the vector $c'(u)$, $\|c'(u)\| = \sqrt{x'^2(t) + y'^2(t)}$. The curve c may be re-parametrized by taking the arc-length s as the new parameter which leads to $c(s) : [0, L] \rightarrow \Re^2$ where L is the length of the curve, $L = \int_0^T \|c'(u)\| \, dt$. We equally employ the notion of curvature defined as the signed magnitude of the second derivative of the motion curve, $\kappa(s) = c''(s)$. Equivalently, curvature may be expressed as the rate of change of the tangential angle with respect to arc-length, $\kappa(s) = \frac{d\phi}{ds}$. All the above notions pertain to the differential geometry of curves [3].

Although the reasoning will be performed using differential geometry, the associated algorithms need to work with the discrete representation of a curve, $C = \{p_i = (x_i, y_i), i = \overline{0, n-1}\}$, for which we have the corresponding definitions of arc-length and curvature:

$$s_i = \sum_{j=0}^{i-1} \|p_j - p_{j+1}\|, \quad \kappa_i = \frac{\langle p_{i-r} p_r, p_i p_{i+r} \rangle}{\|p_{i-r} - p_r\| + \|p_i - p_{i+r}\|} \tag{1}$$

where $\langle \cdot, \cdot \rangle$ represents the angle between two line segments and r is a fixed value representing the sliding window size for discrete curvature computation.

3.1   Acquisition and Preprocessing of Motion Trajectories

Acquired motions, irrespective of the capture device, are usually composed of points sampled at a given time interval τ depending on the working frequency of the device: $\{p_i = p(\tau \cdot i) = (x_i, y_i) \in \Re^2, i = \overline{0, n-1}\}$. The initial trajectory is usually raw and noisy so it needs preprocessing with a polyline reduction technique. We use the fast version of the Douglas-Peucker algorithm [6] which provides a set of significant points $\{p_{i_k}, k = \overline{0, m-1}\}$ and then re-sample each interval $[p_{i_k}, p_{i_{k+1}}]$ at equal length with a given resolution r ($r = 3$ points in our approach) in order to get a smoother version of the initial data. Figure 1 shows the result on a continuous motion trajectory including a star pattern. Preprocessing also acts as a data reduction strategy where the initial 210 points of the star motion are reduced to 52 with 18 most significant points.

Fig. 1. Preprocessing of user-input motion: acquisition data (left); simplified motion with significant points over imposed (middle); final re-sampled motion (green points, right)

4   Multiscale Detection of Gesture Patterns

Let $G(s)$ and $\Gamma(s)$ be two curves sampled by arc-length s normalized in $[0, 1]$. Also, let $G = \left\{ s_i / i = \overline{0, m-1} \right\}$ and $\Gamma = \left\{ s_j / j = \overline{0, n-1} \right\}$ be two discrete samplings of the curves into m and n points. We pose the problem of finding the occurrences of gesture G in the longer motion Γ irregardless of scale.

4.1   A Naive Search Algorithm

A naive algorithm would choose every pair $p < q$, $p, q \in [0, n-1]$ from the Γ curve and employ a gesture recognizer R in order to get the matching result between G and the extracted part of Γ, $\Gamma_{[p,q]}$. The reported start location p' and scale $(q' - p' + 1)/n$ would be those for which the recognizer outputs the minimum distance (or maximum similarity):

$$(p', q') = \min_{0 \leq p < q \leq n-1} R\left(G, \Gamma_{[p,q]}\right) \tag{2}$$

The algorithm below illustrates this idea. Although the approach taken here is brute (search for all pairs $p < q$), there is no other option when aiming at scale invariance. Similar approaches in the literature perform this kind of multi-scale searches in order to achieve the invariance goal.

Algorithm 1. Naive-Detection(G, m, Γ, n)

1: **for** $p = 0$ to $n - 1$ **do**
2:     **for** $q = p + step$ to $n - 1$ **do**
3:         // compute distance between gesture G and part $[p, q]$ of Γ
4:         $distance \Leftarrow Recognizer(G, \Gamma_{[p,q]})$
5:         **if** $min > distance$ **then**
6:             $min \Leftarrow distance,\ p' \Leftarrow p,\ q' \Leftarrow q$
7:         **end if**
8:     **end for**
9: **end for**
10: **return** p', q'

The naive algorithm fails in practice due to over computations which cause big response times. The discussion from the Results section 5 gives an overview of the bad performances of this algorithm which do not meet the constraints of real-time interaction. For example, searching for a pattern inside a longer motion Γ sampled into $n \approx 100$ points returned a response in ≈ 167 ms, not acceptable when searching for multiple gestures.

4.2   The Gesture Recognizer

We use the elastic matching recognizer of Vatavu et al. [17] that computes the minimum alignment cost between the curvature functions of a gesture and a given template. The curvature signature function $\kappa(s)$ of a planar curve $C(s)$ parameterized by arc-length s fully prescribes the original curve up to a rigid motion transformation [3] which makes curvature suitable for gesture recognition. Figure 2 illustrates the alignment process between the curvature functions of two gestures. The complexity of the recognizer is $O(m \times n)$ where m and n are the sampling resolutions of the curves to be matched.

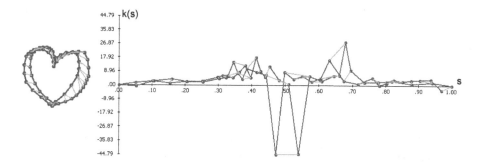

Fig. 2. Gesture recognition by measuring the cost of alignment between the signature function of a gesture (green) and that of a stored template (red)

4.3   Integral of Absolute Curvature

The Naive-Detection algorithm presented previously provides a good starting point for the scale-invariant detection problem if we set as goal filtering as many unnecessary intervals $p < q$ as possible. We build on top of the curvature representation of Vatavu et al. [17] and introduce the principle of summed area tables for the 1D case of the curvature signature function associated to a gesture motion. We thus define the *Integral Absolute Curvature*, $K(s)$, of a curve $C(s)$ parametrized by arc-length s:

$$K(s) = \int_0^s |\kappa(s)|\, ds \qquad (3)$$

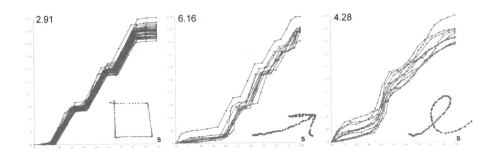

Fig. 3. Integral of absolute curvature for several gestures (multiple instances displayed overimposed): rectangle (right), arrow (middle) and pigtail (right)

Similarly, we can define the integral absolute curvature for a portion of a curve between arc-lengths s_1 and s_2 as follows:

$$K(s_1, s_2) = \int_{s_1}^{s_2} |\kappa(s)|\, ds = K(s_2) - K(s_1) \tag{4}$$

Figure 3 illustrates the integral curvature functions for a few gesture types.

The integral absolute curvature presents a few interesting properties as given by the following theorems:

Theorem 1. $K(s)$ *is positively increasing.*

Proof. Demonstration follows easily from the definition: $K(s + h) = \int_0^{s+h} |\kappa(s)|\, ds = \int_0^s |\kappa(s)|\, ds + \int_s^{s+h} |\kappa(s)|\, ds \geq K(s)$ *for* $\forall s \in [0, L]$ *and* $h \geq 0$. *This means we can uniquely associate a given value* $K(s)$ *to an interval of arc-length* Δs.

Theorem 2. $K(s)$ *is scale invariant (Figure 4 illustrates the concept).*

Proof. Let $c(t) : [0, T] \to \Re^2, c(t) = (x(t), y(t))$ *be a curve defined over time and let* $\gamma(t) : [0, T] \to \Re^2, \gamma(t) = \lambda \cdot c(t)$ *be the scaled version of* $c(t)$ *with a given scale* λ. *If we re-parametrize each curve by its arc-length we obtain* $c(s_c) : [0, L_c] \to \Re^2$ *with* $s_c(t) = \int_0^t \|c'(u)\|\, du$ *and* $\gamma(s_\gamma) : [0, L_\gamma] \to \Re^2$ *with* $s_\gamma(t) = \int_0^t \|\gamma'(u)\|\, du$. *It follows immediately that* $s_\gamma(t) = \lambda \cdot s_c(t)$ *and* $L_\gamma = \lambda \cdot L_c$ *and in consequence we have* $\gamma(s_\gamma) = \lambda \cdot c(s_c)$ *where* $s_\gamma \in [0, L_\gamma]$ *and* $s_c \in [0, L_c]$.

If we compute the curvature of $\gamma(s_\gamma)$ *we get consecutively:*

$\gamma'(s_\gamma) = \frac{d\gamma(s_\gamma)}{ds_\gamma} = \frac{d\gamma(s_\gamma)}{ds_c} \cdot \frac{ds_c}{ds_\gamma} = \frac{d(\lambda \cdot c(s_c))}{ds_c} \cdot \frac{1}{\lambda} = \frac{dc(s_c)}{ds_c} = c'(s_c)$

$\kappa_\gamma(s_\gamma) = \gamma''(s_\gamma) = \frac{d\gamma'(s_\gamma)}{ds_\gamma} = \frac{d\gamma'(s_\gamma)}{ds_c} \cdot \frac{ds_c}{ds_\gamma} = \frac{dc'(s_c)}{ds_c} \cdot \frac{1}{\lambda} = \frac{1}{\lambda} \cdot c''(s_c)$ *hence*

$\kappa_\gamma(s_\gamma) = \frac{1}{\lambda} \cdot \kappa_c(s_c)$ *where* $s_\gamma \in [0, L_\gamma]$ *and* $s_c \in [0, L_c]$.

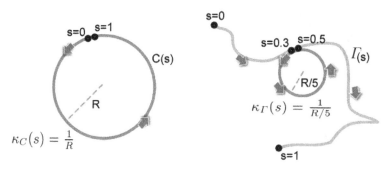

Fig. 4. The left circle $C(s)$ has been scaled down with a factor of 1:5 and inserted in the longer motion $\Gamma(s)$ from the right at location $s = 0.3$. The arrows show the direction of motion. Both curves are normalized with respect to arc-length hence the length of the downsized circle becomes 0.2. While curvature is not scale invariant: $\kappa_C(s) = \frac{1}{R}$ and $\kappa_\Gamma(s) = \frac{1}{R/5}$, the integral absolute curvature is: $\int_0^1 \frac{1}{R} \cdot ds = \int_{0.3}^{0.5} \frac{1}{R/5} \cdot ds = \frac{1}{R}$.

As for the integral of absolute curvature for $\gamma(s_\gamma)$: $K_\gamma(L_\gamma) = \int_0^{L_\gamma} |\kappa_\gamma(s_\gamma)|\, ds_\gamma$ and substituting $s_\gamma = \lambda \cdot s_c$, $K_\gamma(L_\gamma) = \int_0^{L_c} \left|\frac{1}{\lambda} \cdot \kappa_c(s_c)\right| \cdot \lambda \cdot ds_c = \int_0^{L_c} |\kappa_c(s_c)|\, ds_c = K_c(L_c)$ hence the integral absolute curvature is invariant to scale changes.

The trapezoidal rule gives the integral absolute curvature in the discrete case:

$$K_q = \sum_{i=1}^{q} \frac{|\kappa_i| + |\kappa_{i-1}|}{2} \cdot (s_i - s_{i-1}) \tag{5}$$

$$K_{p,q} = \sum_{i=p+1}^{q} \frac{|\kappa_i| + |\kappa_{i-1}|}{2} \cdot (s_i - s_{i-1}) = K_q - K_p \tag{6}$$

The last equation shows that, having computed K_p for a given curve, the computation of $K_{p,q}$ of a candidate can be achieved with $O(1)$ complexity.

4.4   Scale-Invariant Gesture Detection Algorithm

The integral absolute curvature may be used in order to design rejection rules for a given candidate marked by indexes $p < q$ on the continuous motion. Given a set of training samples for a gesture pattern, we can compute the integral absolute curvatures and store the interval $[K_{min}, K_{max}]$ for that gesture type. This will lead to a very simple yet efficient rejection rule for the candidate p, q on the Γ curve, in accordance with Theorem 2 above:

Rule #1. Reject candidate (p, q) if $K_{p,q} \notin [K_{min}, K_{max}]$

The second more powerful observation relates to Theorem 1: any integral value K is associated to a unique arc-length interval Δs due to the monotonic ascending

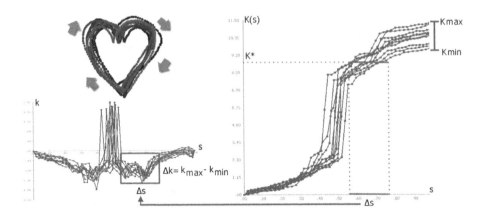

Fig. 5. Left: training set of heart-like gestures and their associated curvature functions. Right: integral absolute curvatures computed for the heart gestures. K_{min} and K_{max} as well as associations between a given K^* value and what the curvature at that s should be in terms of $[\kappa_{min}, \kappa_{max}]$.

property of $K(s)$. By correlating Δs with the curvature function $\kappa(s)$, lower and upper margins for curvature at K are obtained $\Delta k = \kappa_{max} - \kappa_{min}$ from the samples in the training set.

Rule #2. Reject candidate (p, q) if $\kappa_r \notin [\kappa_{min}, \kappa_{max}]$ for $\forall r \in [p, q]$ where κ_{min} and κ_{max} correspond to the value of $K_{p,r} = K_r - K_p$.

The two rules run in $O(1)$ and $O(q - p)$ time. Figure 5 gives a visual illustration.

5   Results and Discussion

In order to test the performance of our gesture detector we used the dataset of Wobbrock et al. [20] composed of 1,600 already segmented gesture samples = 16 types x 10 subjects x 10 executions for each gesture type at normal speed.

The 100 samples available for each gesture type were divided into training and testing giving sets of size $p \cdot 100$ for training and $(1 - p) \cdot 100$ for testing, where $p \in (0..1)$ was the training percentage. The training set was used to generate the rejection rules parameters. Each sample from the testing set was

Fig. 6. The set of 16 gesture types of Wobbrock et al. [20]: triangle, x, rectangle, circle, check, caret, question-mark, arrow, left square bracket, right square bracket, v, delete, left curly brace, right curly brace, star, pigtail

Algorithm 2. SpeedUp-Detection(G, m, Γ, n)

Require: $K[p]$ is the integral absolute curvature at index $0 \leq p < n$
Require: $\kappa_{min}[K]$ and $\kappa_{max}[K]$ are the lower/upper curvatures at integral value K
1: **for** $p = 0$ to $n - 1$ **do**
2:      **for** $q = p + step$ to $n - 1$ **do**
3:          $K_{p,q} \Leftarrow K[q] - K[p]$
4:          **if** $K_{p,q} < K_{min}$ **then**
5:              **continue** with next q, **go to** 2
6:          **end if**
7:          **if** $K_{p,q} > K_{max}$ **then**
8:              **continue** with next p, **go to** 1
9:          **end if**
10:         $k[p..q] \Leftarrow$ compute the scaled curvature of Γ for the $q - p + 1$ scale
11:         **for** $r = p + 1$ to $q - 1$ **do**
12:             $K_{p,r} \Leftarrow K[r] - K[p]$
13:             **if** $\kappa[r] < \kappa_{min}[K_{p,r}]$ or $\kappa[r] > \kappa_{max}[K_{p,r}]$ **then**
14:                 **continue** with next q, **go to** 2
15:             **end if**
16:         **end for**
17:         $distance \Leftarrow Recognizer(G, \Gamma_{[p,q]})$
18:         **if** $min > distance$ **then**
19:             $min \Leftarrow distance, p' \Leftarrow p, q' \Leftarrow q$
20:         **end if**
21:     **end for**
22: **end for**
23: **return** p', q'

---

inserted at a random scale $\in [0.1 - 0.5]$ and at a random location in a randomly generated motion with the scale and location stored as ground truth. When generating random trajectories there is the danger that simple gestures such as v or *check* from Figure 6 are generated by chance at a different location than that of the inserted pattern which would affect the detection rate. To avoid this we proof checked each generated motion by running the naive algorithm in order to test if the pattern can be detected correctly. We varied the training percentage p from 10% to 90% of the available samples with increments of 10% (the smallest training set had 10 samples or 1 sample from each participant). For each testing set we computed the detection rate, start error, scale error, and execution time. The *start error* (e_{start}) represents the difference between the detected start position of a gesture compared with the ground truth (the exact position where the gesture was inserted) expressed as percentage of the motion length. The *scale error* (e_{scale}) is defined similarly. The detection rate equals the percentage of patterns successfully detected (for which $e_{start} < 0.1$ and $e_{scale} < 0.1$ but the average errors were less than 0.04 as we report below). In order to avoid biased results due to random sampling, we repeated 10 times each splitting procedure for a given p and averaged the results. We thus report results obtained from:

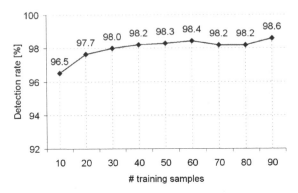

Fig. 7. Detection rate (%) vs. the number of samples in the training set ($p \cdot 100$)

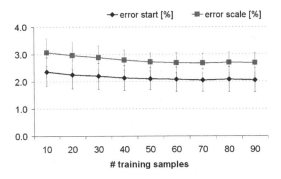

Fig. 8. Error rates (%) vs. the number of samples in the training set ($p \cdot 100$)

16 gesture types ×
10 repetitions ×
9 different testing sets (p = 0.1 to 0.9, increment of 0.1) ×
$(1 - p) \cdot 100$ generated motions per set =

$$= 16 \cdot 10 \cdot \sum_{p=0.1}^{p=0.9} (1 - p) \cdot 100 = 72,000 \text{ continuous motion trajectories.}$$

Figure 7 plots the detection rate vs. the size of the training set $p \cdot 100$. Even with a small training set consisting in only 10 samples (or 1 sample per participant) the detection rate is above 96% and raises up to 98% with a minimum of 3 samples per subject. The starting point error is approximately constant at 2% while the scale error is below 3% of the length of the motion trajectory as Figure 8 illustrates. Figure 9 plots the individual detection rates for each gesture type. Rates were averaged for all the trials $p \in [0.1, 0.9]$ and standard deviation are also presented. Except for the *left curly brace* gesture that averages a 94.1% detection rate, all the other patterns are detected with rates higher than 96.8%.

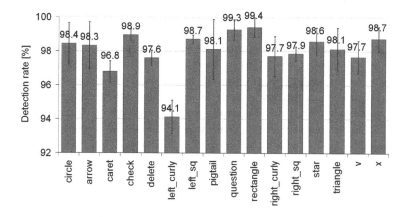

Fig. 9. Detection rate (%) vs. gesture type

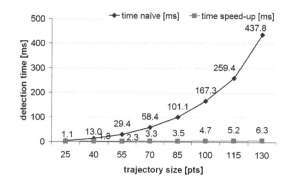

Fig. 10. Detection time (ms) vs. the size of the continuous motion (number of points)

The lower rate of *left curly brace* can be explained by its greater variation in execution: as Wobbrock et al. [20] mention, the participants disliked the curly braces as they felt "clumsy" drawing them. The standard deviation across all p has an average of 0.84% for all gestures with a maximum of 1.77% for *pigtail*.

The great advantage of the technique is presented in Figure 10 which illustrates execution time in ms versus the length of the continuous motion in points. In order to detect the full set of 16 gestures, the naive algorithm becomes impractical at a trajectory size of 70 points with 58.4 ms required per gesture while the speed-up algorithm executes in 3.3 ms. The discrepancy becomes even greater for longer trajectories: 437.8 ms for the naive versus only 6.3 ms for the speed-up at trajectories lengths of 130 sampled points. The measurements were performed on a 2.66 GHz P4 desktop computer.

6 Conclusions

We presented a new technique for the multiscale detection of gesture patterns in 2D continuous motions. The technique is fast due to several rejection rules that filter out most of the weak candidates. Detection rates above 96% were obtained for a large data set of 72,000 samples. We introduced the integral absolute curvature and showed its application in the discrete case. Our technique makes possible automatic segmentation of continuous motions without constraining users to segment their own gestures. As future work, it would be interesting extending the technique to 3D for which torsion next to curvature could be employed.

References

1. Arvo, J., Novins, K.: Fluid Sketches: Continuous Recognition and Morphing of Simple Hand-Drawn Shapes. In: ACM UIST 2000, pp. 73–80 (2000)
2. Arvo, J., Novins, K.: Fluid Sketching of Directed Graphs. In: 7th Australasian User Interface Conference, pp. 81–86. Australian Computer Society (2006)
3. Do Carmo, M.: Differential Geometry of Curves and Surfaces. Prentice-Hall, Englewood Cliffs (1976)
4. Cerlinca, T.I., Pentiuc, S.G., Vatavu, R.D., Cerlinca, M.C.: Hand posture recognition for human-robot interaction. In: WMISI at ICMI 2007, pp. 47–50 (2007)
5. Dong, Q., Wu, Y., Hu, Z.: Gesture Segmentation from a Video Sequence Using Greedy Similarity Measure. In: ICPR 2006, pp. 331–334 (2006)
6. Hershberger, J., Snoeyink, J.: Speeding Up the Douglas-Peucker Line-Simplification Algorithm. In: Proc. of 5th Symposium on Data Handling, pp. 134–143 (1992)
7. LaViola, J.J.: Sketching and gestures 101. In: ACM SIGGRAPH 2007 Courses, p. 2. ACM, New York (2007)
8. Marcel, S.: Hand Posture Recognition in a Body-Face centered space. In: ACM CHI 1999 Extended Abstracts, pp. 302–303. ACM Press, New York (1999)
9. Moeslund, T.B., Hilton, A., Krüger, V.: A survey of advances in vision-based human motion capture and analysis. Computer Vision and Image Understanding 104(2), 90–126 (2006)
10. Pavlovic, V.I., Sharma, R., Huang, T.S.: Visual interpretation of hand gestures for human–computer interaction: A review. IEEE TPAMI 19(7), 677–695 (1997)
11. Poppe, R.: Vision-based human motion analysis: An overview. Computer Vision and Image Understanding 108(1-2), 4–18 (2007)
12. Reng, L., Moeslund, T.B., Granum, E.: Finding Motion Primitives in Human Body Gestures. In: Gibet, S., Courty, N., Kamp, J.-F. (eds.) GW 2005. LNCS (LNAI), vol. 3881, pp. 133–144. Springer, Heidelberg (2006)
13. Rubine, D.: Specifying gestures by example. In: Proc. of SIGGRAPH 1991, pp. 329–337. ACM Press, New York (1991)
14. Sowa, T.: The Recognition and Comprehension of Hand Gestures - A Review and Research Agenda. In: Wachsmuth, I., Knoblich, G. (eds.) ZiF Research Group International Workshop. LNCS (LNAI), vol. 4930, pp. 38–56. Springer, Heidelberg (2008)
15. Schlomer, T., Poppinga, B., Henze, N., Boll, S.: Gesture Recognition with a Wii Controller. In: TEI 2008, Bonn, Germany, pp. 11–14 (2008)

16. Thorne, M., Burke, D., van de Panne, M.: Motion doodles: an interface for sketching character motion. In: ACM SIGGRAPH 2004, pp. 424–431 (2004)
17. Vatavu, R.D., Grisoni, L., Pentiuc, S.G.: Gesture Recognition based on Elastic Deformation Energies. In: Sales Dias, M., Gibet, S., Wanderley, M.M., Bastos, R. (eds.) GW 2007. LNCS (LNAI), vol. 5085, pp. 1–12. Springer, Heidelberg (2009)
18. Vatavu, R.D., Pentiuc, S.G.: Interactive Coffee Tables: Interfacing TV within an Intuitive, Fun and Shared Experience. In: Tscheligi, M., Obrist, M., Lugmayr, A. (eds.) EuroITV 2008. LNCS, vol. 5066, pp. 183–187. Springer, Heidelberg (2008)
19. Wilson, A.D.: Robust computer vision-based detection of pinching for one and two-handed gesture input. In: ACM UIST 2006, pp. 255–258 (2006)
20. Wobbrock, J.O., Wilson, A.D., Li, Y.: Gestures without libraries, toolkits or training: a $1 recognizer for user interface prototypes. In: UIST 2007, pp. 159–168 (2007)

Recognition of Gesture Sequences in Real-Time Flow, Context of Virtual Theater

Ronan Billon, Alexis Nédélec, and Jacques Tisseau

CERV: Centre Européen de Réalité Virtuelle,
Laboratoire d'Informatique des SYstèmes Complexes
{billon,nedelec,tisseau}@enib.fr
http://www.cerv.fr/

Abstract. Our aim is to put on a short play featuring a real actor and a virtual actor, who will communicate through movements and choreography, with mutual synchronization. Gesture recognition in our context of Virtual Theater is mainly based on the ability of a virtual actor to perceive gestures made by a real actor. We present a method for real-time recognition. We use properties from Principal Component Analysis (PCA) to create signature for each gesture and a multiagent system to perform the recognition.

Keywords: motion-capture, gesture recognition, virtual theatre, synthetic actor.

1 Introduction

Our test-bed is "Theater", where actors perform on a stage in front of an audience. Our aim is to integrate virtual actors in the play and make them interact with the real actors. We take our inspiration from the post-production stage of a movie. Constraints appear with our specific context. Indeed, the virtual actor has to perceive the real actor in real-time and react with a good timing, to create believable characters [1]. Our global project goal is to put on a short play featuring a real actor and a virtual actor, who will communicate through movements and choreography with mutual synchronization. We limit our study to the perception of gesture. This work is an improvement of the one done for the paper published in [2].

We will begin with a state of the art about gesture recognition and usage criteria. The next section will describe briefly our method of signature generation and recognition system in real-time flow. We add a little part to describe how our model can help choreographer with gesture sequences. We will conclude with our experiments and public demonstration to define the limitations of our system.

2 Gesture Recognition, Classification of Related Works

Before explaining related works on gesture recognition, it is important to define the scope of our study. In the literature the word gesture has been used to identify

S. Kopp and I. Wachsmuth (Eds.): GW 2009, LNAI 5934, pp. 98–109, 2010.

many types of interactions with computer. To avoid confusion, Cadoz [3] uses functionality to classify gestures: Ergotic, Epistemic, Semiotic. According to our earlier decisions [2], the last category seems to be the right one.

> *Semiotic*: the action of conveying information to the environment (or virtual actor).

Indeed, we limit ourselves to transform the continuous flow of movements to a sequence of symbols.

In an attempt to encompass the field of gesture based interactions, we noted the diversity of approaches. For example, it can be the way to handle an object in a virtual world or, how to change the song on your player, even finger moves on a touch table. Faced with this amount of approaches, Karam [4] propose a taxonomy of gestures in human-computer interaction. This work presents a unique perspective on gesture-based interactions, categorized in terms of four key elements: gesture functions, the application domains they are applied to, input technologies and output technologies used for implementation. We do not detail this entire taxonomy, but we pick up the relevant category. There are four classes:

- gesture functions: 'semaphoric gestures' is a system based on a set of limited and defined gestures. This approach is referenced as a method for communicating symbols;
- scope: 'communication interface' is a system that try to mimic the communication between human;
- system response: 'Directed Command CPU' is a system response that is not directly used, but is stored or interpreted by the application;
- input: we do not want to fix the input technology.

This taxonomy allows us to select studies close to ours, in the gesture recognition field. Briefly, all these works rely heavily on statistical tools such as principal component analysis (PCA), the Hidden Markov Model (HMM), the K-Means or the Gaussian models. All these methods are divided into two stages: learning and recognition. Furthermore, we would like to clearly distinguish the static gesture and the dynamic gestures. There are currently difficulties for the latter style of interaction and we will only work on this one. We create a short classification of these works into three categories as follow.

Exotic Algorithms. "Exotic" means that this set of algorithms are unusual in the field of recognition. Few studies explain how to use these unconventional methods. The gesture can be modeled as a finite state machine where each state is defined by the characteristics of trajectories. Bobick [5] or Hong [6] propose the most typical approach. Also, in this first group we put soft computing approach, like Sandberg [7] or Zhao [8] mainly based on neural networks.

Hidden Markov Model Based Algorithms. Most studies rely on HMM. The gesture is modeled by a Markov process of unknown parameters. The process is a sequence of states whose transitions between states are based on probabilities calculated from a set of examples. The recognition is done according to the probability that a sequence of observation belongs to this model. Yamato [9] was the first to apply the HMM to the gesture recognition. The following works are improvements of this approach. On the recognition side, Lee [10] suggest a method to compute automatically the threshold of recognition by adding a global HMM. Kim [11] solve the real-time issue with a forward spotting scheme that executes gesture segmentation and recognition simultaneously. On the learning side, Rajko [12] and Bevilacqua [13] aim to decrease the number of examples. During the training, they add semantic states on the model and more prior information about probability distribution for each state. To finish with the HMM style, Kahol [14] addresses the problem in a very different way. He uses the events of the movement instead of postures. An event is defined by the stabilization of the data.

Signal Compression Based Algorithms. The class of method is quite different from previous ones because it can't be used alone. Indeed, you must add a system that will make the comparison between current observation and the recorded signal. If the compression is appropriate, the added module can be very simple. The main idea behind compression is the possibility to extract the essence of a movement to keep only relevant information. One of the first work was done by Campbell [15]. The intuition here is that the invariance of a movement can be found in a particular subspace of this movement. The learning stage is the creation of a *predictive curve* that represent the gesture. The recognition is the computation of difference between a *predictive curve* and an observation curve. More recently, Vasilescu [16] or Jenkins [17] work on signal compression with SVD or Isomap. The following papers deal with the search of similar gesture in a database. Although the problematic is different, the tools are very close. For exemple, Forbes [18] uses PCA to compute a compressed database of animations. Another way to represent gesture is to use a "dictionary compression" style, like Muller [19]. They call their method Motion Template. They create 39 simple geometric constraints that encode the spatial and timing data. The movement is described with a boolean feature matrix ($frame \times constraint$).

Conclusion. Various algorithms were discussed here, but we never discuss about the recognition rate. Indeed, this information is irrelevant to discriminate between methods. All these algorithms have a recognition rate between 90% and 100%. In addition, these values are based on different devices, different movements or different contexts. We are more interested on the usage criteria. We create a table (tab. 1) to summarize information from every paper. According to our context of Theater, we choose the following criteria:

- number of recognizable gestures;
- number of repetitions for learning stage;
- is the recognition in real-time ?
- is there automatic segmentation ?
- is there a simple way to expand the database ?

Table 1. Usage criteria (✓: available, X : unavailable, ? : not mention)

method	nb gesture	repetition	real-time	segmentation	expansion
FSM [6]	3	30	?	?	✓
Soft-computing [7]	14	333	?	X	X
HMM [9]	6	30	X	?	✓
HMM real-time [11]	8	30	✓	✓	X
MMC learning [12]	58	3	X	X	X
MMC music [13]	1	1	✓	X	?
Comp dance [15]	9	1	X	weak	✓
Comp devices [5]	2	40 to 70	X	✓	✓
Comp [16]	3	10	?	?	?
Comp template [19]	64	10 to 50	X	✓	✓
Comp index [18]	70sec	1	X	✓	?

These points have particular interest for us. Within the context of Virtual Theater, the ideal situation is as follows: about twenty recognizable gesture, very few repetitions, must be real-time, must be an automatic segmentation system and the database must be expandable. We can note that there is no system that met all these criteria.

3   Gesture Recognition Model

Our system works as follows: the actor performs the action, this action is translated into symbol, with this symbol, the virtual actor can choose his action according to the story. This context creates some constraints. This is the same real actor who records during the rehearsals and who performs on stage. Thus, the gesture can be complicated and personal. The learning phase takes place during rehearsals before the show. The gestures may change day after day according to the artistic mood of the director. We cannot afford to record all actions one time. So, the gesture must be recorded in a dynamic way to be tested by the director and by the actor. We made the choice of a single recording, based on signal compression (PCA). The generation of the signature has already been described in the paper [2], we summarize here the main ideas. After describing the signature generation with PCA (learning step), we report our choice of multiagent system (recognition step), then we end up with the control of gesture sequence.

3.1   Gesture Signature Generation

By definition a gesture is a variation between two rest states. We decided to work on this variation. PCA makes it possible to compute a space from a set of data where the variance is maximal. Our aim is to compute a projection matrix to be used as a data filter. It is like **feature selection** [20]. After applying PCA on the data of **one gesture**, we generate its dedicated space. As stated by Shlens [21], the most interesting dynamics occur only in the first dimensions. To save

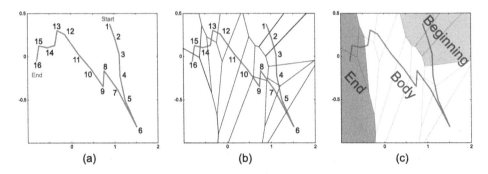

Fig. 1. The three abstraction levels of our representation of the gesture. (a) 16 relevant points gesture. (b) cutting the space into zones of influence. (c) the three areas defining the gesture: beginning, body and end.

computing time and eliminate all the non-impact data due to the exponential drop-off of the variances, we decide to retain only two dimensions. Let $\vec{V_1}$ and $\vec{V_2} \in \mathbb{R}^n$ be the eigen vectors associated with the two greatest eigen values. The projection matrix is $\Pi = (\vec{V_1}, \vec{V_2})$.

To facilitate the recognition step, we create different layers of abstraction. The gesture is a fine-grained curve in the 2D space. We can reduce this curve with polygonal approximation [22]. According to these relevant points (fig. 1-a), we can divide the 2D space using the associated Voronoi diagram (fig. 1-b). This allows us to visualize the zone of influence of each of the relevant points. Then, we make the assumption that the gesture is broken down into three parts as described by the following works: beginning-body-end [23] or preparation-stroke-recall [24]. It is reasonable to assign the first quarter of the overall gesture to the beginning and the last quarter to the end (fig. 1-c). The central part of the gesture should be long enough to capture the effort provided by the user, and it seemed wise to reserve half of all the information. We end up with a gesture composed of the following elements:

- a projection matrix Π, enabling the transition from a list of sensor values to a point in 2D;
- an ordinate list of 2D points representing the gesture;
- the time taken to perform the gesture.

Now that we have a very synthetic representation of the gesture which is designed to simplify the matching system, we can consider how the gesture is perceived.

3.2   Gesture Recognition in Real-Time

With our model, gestures are all independent from one other. We can find similarities with **multiagent systems** where each agent is a gesture (perception of the real-time flow, decision of the similarity recognition and action of sending a recognition event). Figure 2 shows that every gesture has its own projection matrix and is independent from the others.

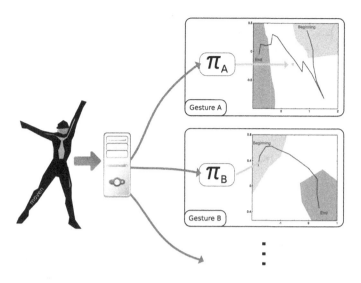

Fig. 2. The same posture from Xsens Moven is mapped in every gesture space

Two main problems are raised by recognition: segmentation (*e.g.* finding the beginning and the end); recognition (*e.g.* fidelity computation between the recorded gesture and the observed one). To solve these problems, we rely on two agents: *Gesture* and *Observer*. The first one is the manager of the gesture representation (fig. 2) and the second one is a structure to segment and stock the real-time flow. The following part focus on the *Observer*. As stated by Kim [11], we use a forward spotting scheme that executes gesture segmentation and recognition simultaneously.

We make the assumption that the gesture is broken down into three parts: beginning, body and end (fig. 1). To detect a hypothetical beginning, it is enough that a posture projected in 2D space with Π is in the beginning area. For each posture detected this way, the *Gesture* instantiates an *Observer*. Its role is to accumulate the following postures in 2D space. Many *Observers* can be running at the same time. The hypothetical end of the gesture is detected in a similar manner. With an end detection, we can stop all the running *Observers* and compare there stored data (*e.g.* list of 2D points) with the signature of the gesture. Not all of these *Observers* are relevant, many of them are old or repetition or wrong detection. The agent *Gesture* select the best *Observers* with the following three criteria:

- the distance between curves (Dynamic Time Warping), which provides the nonlinear difference between the two signals [25]. This measurement is the difference between the shapes of the two curves;
- the difference of characteristic points. This measurement is the number of validated zones;
- the time difference between the recording reference and the observation.

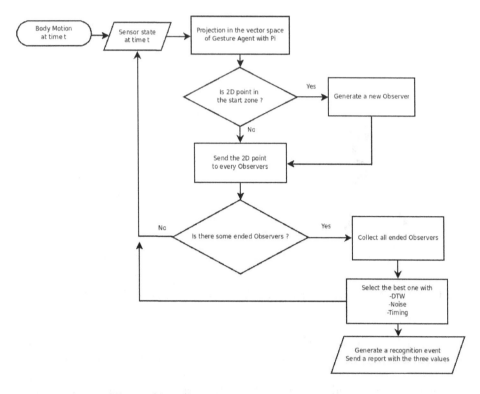

Fig. 3. Algorithm of segmentation and recognition

We note these three values: **fidelity values**. The virtual actor receives these information with the recognition event. They enable him to validate or not the action. Figure 3 summarizes the overall process of segmentation and recognition.

3.3 Gesture Sequence Helper

In practice, semiotic gesture don't follow themselves directly, there is always a pause or recall between execution of movements. But in the particular context of gesture sequence (like short choreography), our representation provides a bonus. Now that we are able to recognize gesture in real-time, we plan to understand a more abstract layer: the syntax. We can compare our work to language analysis with different layers of abstraction as stated by Kendon [24]. Our next step is to analyze the structure or syntax. There are two main advantages to rise up over simple lexicon analysis. First, for the recognition part: even with the multi-freedom degrees of our body, we cannot do all possible movements between two gestures, we can eliminate false-positive recognition. Second, for the context understanding: the same gesture can be repeated at different time during the play, we can distinguish two moments with the current sequence.

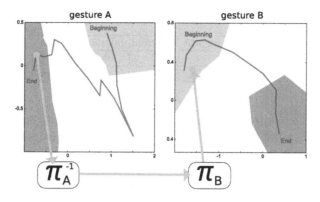

Fig. 4. Check if gesture B can follow gesture A

Technically, our model allows us to check the continuity between two gestures. Indeed, in 2D space, we can see the overlapping of the beginning area and the ending area. To illustrate our point, we want to check if gesture A can be followed by the gesture B. We take the relevant point at the end of gesture A and then we project them in the 2D space of B. If these points are in the beginning of B, then we can assume that the action B can follow the gesture A. The figure 4 shows that we can go from the 2D space of A to the space of B with an inverse-projection Π_A^{-1} and a projection Π_B. It is essential to return in the n-dimension space of sensors before projection in the B dedicated space. It is also possible to directly test this property during recording. On one hand, this property can be used for writing the syntax rules. For example, during the writing of the script, the choreographer can check whether the sequence of movements can be valid during recognition. On the other hand, recognition can eliminate false positives. If a gesture has been recognized, then only a restricted set of gesture will follow.

4   Evaluations and Results

4.1   Experimental Measurements

We decided to improve our experiments started in our previous study [2]. We used two existing databases. The first one comes from a different project experiment [26]. Each gesture involves the same joints and little variation. They are very similar to the others; even a human could be mistaken. But these gestures are easy to reproduce. It consists of 22 gestures (8 gestures repeated 2-3 times). The second one is the set of gesture from a reproducibility experience. With this set, we can check if the reproducibility alter the recognition. It consists of 21 gestures (7 gestures repeated 3 times). These seven gestures are increasingly difficult to be reproduced. All this gestures have an average duration of 2.5 seconds. We considered four cases:

Table 2. Experimentation

DB	nb	foolp.	compr.	disputed	unknow	time
DB1	22	15	4	3	0	-0.533474
DB2	21	14	0	6	1	-0.431683

- foolproof; the gesture can be identified without any doubt. The fidelity values are lower than the $(mean - \frac{variance}{2})$ of the false-positive set;
- comprehensive; the gesture can be identified, but another false-positive gesture may be selected. The fidelity values are lower than the mean of the false-positive, but greater than the $(mean - \frac{variance}{2})$ of the false-positive set;
- disputed; the gesture cannot be easily identified. The fidelity values are greater than the *mean* of the false-positive.
- unknown; the gesture is not recognized.

A disputed gesture is not a problem, it only means that the application has to deal with ambiguous events. Table 2 shows the results. We can see that each gesture is recognized **0.5 seconds** before the effective end of gesture, it is a good point for real-time recognition. 100% of the 22 gestures are recognized, and 68% of these are easily classified without any threshold. With the second database, only one gesture cannot be recognized. The reproducibility does not seem to be a problem.

4.2   A Short Public Play

We have created a short demonstration featuring a fight between a real Capoeira fighter and a virtual one. This demonstration has been produced during the winter 2007/2008 for "Les Antipodes 2008". This festival is a gathering of different fields: dance, theater, visual arts, puppetry ... We tried to produce a lively show with our system. It allows the real actor and the virtual one to synchronize and react depending on the current situation. This demonstration was 15 minutes long, repeated during three hours over seven days. This format allows spectators to ask questions and review important elements at the end of the demonstration. It is still available in our laboratory.

According to the short script, the actor has to perform only six different gestures. Besides this limited number of gesture with a real impact on the script, the recognition system was up during the three hours with a good reaction time. And most of the gestures are difficult to reproduce because they are mainly capoeira kick. We used the motion-capture suit Moven from Xsens[1].

To conclude, in this performance held in 2008 the recognition of gestures was robust enough for this demonstration, the actor felt comfortable and the public was conviced. Since the recognition of this kind of gesture has been demonstrated

---

[1] http://www.moven.com/

Fig. 5. Demonstration at "Les Antipodes 2008"

in real-time environments, we believe that there are no technical obstacles for a more complex and longer play.

5   Conclusion and Future Directions

We developed a model of gesture based on compression signal (PCA). This reduction of the data representation facilitates recognition in real time. Our system, based on a simple multiagent system, allows us to segment, recognize and record dynamically gestures. We can complete the table 1 with our own values:

method	nb gesture	repetition	real-time	segmentation	expansion
GRIF [2]	37	1	✓	✓	✓

We have not used yet the sequences of gesture to their full potential for inter-action between user and virtual actor. This feature of gestures sequence and its meaning will be very helpfull, associated with a script writing software and with the improvement of the virtual actor's behavior. The recognition system is only a part of a continuing work of understanding and developing technology for an interactive virtual actor. Computer Theater, as stated by Pinhanez [27], is a good ground for research on action recognition. Defined context, exagger-ated gestures, known and reliable mappings between symbols and real worlds and explicit translation of intention into physical activities can provide a fertile environment for research on perception of the human.

Acknowledgements. The research described here was supported in part by France Telecom R&D and in part by the Regional Council of Brittany.

References

1. Thomas, F., Johnston, O.: Disney Animation: The Illusion of Life. Abbeville Press, New York (1981)
2. Billon, R., Nédélec, A., Tisseau, J.: Gesture recognition in flow based on pca analysis using multiagent system. In: ACE 2008: Proceedings of the 2008 International Conference on Advances in Computer Entertainment Technology, pp. 139–146. ACM, New York (2008)
3. Cadoz, C.: Les réalités virtuelles. In: DOMINOS, Flammarion, Paris (1994)
4. Karam, M., Schraefel, M.C.: A taxonomy of gestures in human computer interactions. Technical report, Electronics and Computer Science, University of Southampton (2005)
5. Bobick, A., Wilson, A.: A state-based technique for the summarization and recognition of gesture. ICCV 00, 382 (1995)
6. Hong, P., Turk, M., Huang, T.S.: Constructing finite state machines for fast gesture recognition. In: Proc. 15th ICPR, pp. 691–694 (2000)
7. Sandberg, A.: Gesture recognition using neural networks. Technical report, KTH University, Sweden (1997)
8. Zhao, L.: Synthesis and Acquisition of Laban Movement Analysis Qualitative Parameters for Communicative Gestures. PhD thesis, University of Pennsylvania, USA (2001)
9. Yamato, J., Ohya, J., Ishii, K.: Recognizing human action in time-sequential images using hidden markov model. In: Computer Vision and Pattern Recognition, Proceedings CVPR 1992, June 15-18, pp. 379–385 (1992)
10. Lee, H.K., Kim, J.: An hmm-based threshold model approach for gesture recognition. IEEE Transactions on Pattern Analysis and Machine Intelligence 21(10), 961–973 (1999)
11. Kim, D., Song, J., Kim, D.: Simultaneous gesture segmentation and recognition based on forward spotting accumulative hmms. Pattern Recogn. 40(11), 3012–3026 (2007)
12. Rajko, S., Qian, G., Ingalls, T., James, J.: Real-time gesture recognition with minimal training requirements and on-line learning. In: IEEE Conference on Computer Vision and Pattern Recognition. CVPR 2007, June 2007, pp. 1–8 (2007)
13. Bevilacqua, F., Guédy, F., Schnell, N., Fléty, E., Leroy, N.: Wireless sensor interface and gesture-follower for music pedagogy. In: NIME 2007: Proceedings of the 7th international conference on New interfaces for musical expression, pp. 124–129. ACM, New York (2007)
14. Kahol, K., Tripathi, P., Panchanathan, S.: Documenting motion sequences with a personalized annotation system. IEEE MultiMedia 13(1), 37–45 (2006)
15. Campbell, L.W., Bobick, A.: Recognition of human body motion using phase space constraints. In: Proceedings of Fifth International Conference on Computer Vision, pp. 624–630 (1995)
16. Vasilescu, M.A.O.: Human motion signatures: Analysis, synthesis, recognition. In: ICPR 2002: Proceedings of the 16 th International Conference on Pattern Recognition (ICPR 2002), Washington, DC, USA, vol. 3, p. 30456. IEEE Computer Society, Los Alamitos (2002)
17. Jenkins, O.C., Mataric, M.J.: Automated derivation of behavior vocabularies for autonomous humanoid motion. In: AAMAS 2003: Proceedings of the second international joint conference on Autonomous agents and multiagent systems, pp. 225–232. ACM, New York (2003)

18. Forbes, K., Fiume, E.: An efficient search algorithm for motion data using weighted pca. In: SCA 2005: Proceedings of the 2005 ACM SIGGRAPH/Eurographics symposium on Computer animation, pp. 67–76. ACM, New York (2005)
19. Müller, M., Röder, T.: Motion templates for automatic classification and retrieval of motion capture data. In: SCA 2006: Proceedings of the 2006 ACM SIGGRAPH/Eurographics symposium on Computer animation, Aire-la-Ville, Switzerland, Switzerland, Eurographics Association, pp. 137–146 (2006)
20. Guyon, I., Elisseeff, A.: An introduction to variable and feature selection. J. Mach. Learn. Res. 3, 1157–1182 (2003)
21. Shlens, J.: A tutorial on principal component analysis. Systems Neurobiology Laboratory, University of California at San Diego (2005)
22. Dunham, J.G.: Optimum uniform piecewise linear approximation of planar curves. IEEE Transactions on Pattern Analysis and Machine Intelligence PAMI-8(1), 67–75 (1986)
23. Wilson, A., Bobick, A., Cassell, J.: Recovering the temporal structure of natural gesture. In: Proceedings of the Second International Conference on Automatic Face and Gesture Recognition, October 1996, pp. 66–71 (1996)
24. Kendon, A.: How gestures can become like words. In: Cross-Cultural Perspectives in Nonverbal Communication, pp. 131–141. F. Poyatos Publishers (1988)
25. Berndt, D.J., Clifford, J.: Finding patterns in time series: a dynamic programming approach, pp. 229–248 (1996)
26. Aubry, M., Julliard, F., Gibet, S.: Apprentissage des paramètres d'un contrôleur pour la synthèse de mouvements réalistes. LISyC, rapport interne, Journées l'Aber Wrac'h des 29 et 30 mai 2008 (June 2008)
27. Pinhanez, C.: Computer theater. In: International Symposium of Electronic Arts (ISEA 1997), Chicago, Illinois (September 1997)

Deictic Gestures with a Time-of-Flight Camera

Martin Haker, Martin Böhme, Thomas Martinetz, and Erhardt Barth

Institute for Neuro- and Bioinformatics, University of Lübeck,
Ratzeburger Allee 160, 23538 Lübeck, Germany
{haker, boehme, martinetz, barth}@inb.uni-luebeck.de
http://www.inb.uni-luebeck.de

Abstract. We present a robust detector for deictic gestures based on
a time-of-flight (TOF) camera, a combined range and intensity image
sensor. Pointing direction is used to determine whether the gesture is
intended for the system at all and to assign different meanings to the
same gesture depending on pointing direction. We use the gestures to
control a slideshow presentation: Making a "thumbs-up" gesture while
pointing to the left or right of the screen switches to the previous or next
slide. Pointing at the screen causes a "virtual laser pointer" to appear.
Since the pointing direction is estimated in 3D, the user can move freely
within the field of view of the camera after the system was calibrated.
The pointing direction is measured with an absolute accuracy of 0.6
degrees and a measurement noise of 0.9 degrees near the center of the
screen.

1 Introduction

We use a novel type of sensor, the time-of-flight (TOF) camera, to implement
simple and robust gesture recognition. The TOF camera [1] provides a range map
that is perfectly registered with an intensity image at 20 frames per second or
more, depending on the integration time. The camera works by emitting infrared
light and measuring the time taken by the light to travel to a point in the scene
and back to the camera; the time taken is proportional to the distance of the
point from the camera, allowing a range measurement to be made at each pixel.

In this paper, we use gestures recognized using the TOF camera to control a
slideshow presentation, similar to [2] where, however, a data glove was used to
recognize the gestures. Another idea we adapt from [2] is to recognize only gestures made towards an "active area"; valid gestures made with the hand pointing
elsewhere are ignored. This solves the problem (also known as the "immersion
syndrome") that unintentional hand movements or gestures made towards other
people may erroneously be interpreted as commands.

We expand this idea by allowing the same gesture to mean different things
when made towards different active areas. Specifically, the slideshow is controlled
in the following way: To go to the next slide, point to the right of the screen and
make a thumbs-up gesture with the hand; to go to the previous slide, point to
the left of the screen and make a thumbs-up gesture. Point at the screen and a

S. Kopp and I. Wachsmuth (Eds.): GW 2009, LNAI 5934, pp. 110–121, 2010.

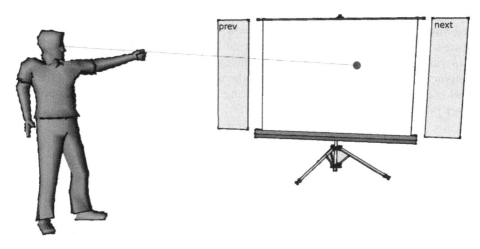

Fig. 1. The application scenario where a user controls a slideshow presentation using deictic gestures. The gestures include switching between the slides and pointing at the screen using a virtual laser pointer.

dot appears at the location you are pointing to, allowing you to highlight certain elements of the slide. This scenario is depicted in Fig. 1.

To determine where the user is pointing on the screen, we need to know its position relative to the camera. This is determined in a calibration procedure where the user points at the four corners of the screen from two different locations; this information is sufficient to compute the position of the screen. After calibration the user is allowed to move freely within the field of view of the camera, as the system estimates both the screen and the pointing direction in 3D with respect to the camera coordinate system.

The "thumbs-up" gesture is recognized using a simple heuristic on the silhouette of the hand. This simple technique is sufficient because hand gestures are only recognized when the user is pointing at one of the two active regions; when pointing elsewhere, the user need not be concerned that hand movements might be misinterpreted as gestures.

One important advantage of the TOF camera in this setting is that it directly measures the three-dimensional position of objects in space, so that the pointing direction can easily and robustly be obtained as a vector in space. This is much more difficult for approaches that attempt to infer pointing direction using a single conventional camera. One solution is to restrict oneself to pointing directions within the camera plane (see e.g. [3,4]), but this places restrictions on the camera position and type of gestures that can be recognized. A physical arm model with kinematic constraints (see e.g. [5]) allows arm pose to be estimated from a single camera image, but the depth estimation can be unreliable for some poses of the arm. In contrast, the approach we will present here is simple but at the same time accurate and robust.

In the remainder of the paper we will first discuss the detection of the pointing and the "thumbs-up" gesture. We will then describe the calibration of the system. Finally, the accuracy of the virtual laser pointer will be evaluated in an experimental setup where users had to point at given targets. This evaluation is conducted in two scenarios: One, where the user does not receive visual feedback, and another, where the estimated pointing position is indicated by the virtual laser pointer.

2   Method

Our method can be divided into three individual components: (i) the detection of the pointing gesture, (ii) the detection of the thumbs-up gesture used for navigating between slides, and (iii) the calibration of the system. This section will cover each component in the order mentioned above. For simplicity, we assume that the user always points towards the left as seen from the camera throughout this section although this is not a restriction of the system.

2.1   Pointing Gesture

The algorithm for detecting pointing gestures can be subdivided into four main stages. The first stage segments the person in front of the camera from the background. The second stage uses the segmented image to identify both the head and the extended hand that is used for pointing. During the third stage, the 3D coordinates of head and hand in space are estimated, which are then used to determine the location on the screen the user is pointing to during the fourth stage. In the following, we will discuss each step of this procedure individually in more detail.

Stage 1: The segmentation of the person in front of the camera uses combined information from both the range and intensity data of the TOF camera. Previous work [6,7] has shown that the combined use of both range and intensity data can significantly improve results in a number of different computer vision tasks. We determine adaptive thresholds for range and intensity based on histograms. In case of the intensity data the threshold discards dark pixels. This has two effects: Firstly, the amount of light that is reflected back into the camera decays proportionally to the squared distance of the object from the camera, thus the background generally appears significantly darker than the foreground. Secondly, this procedure discards unreliable pixels from the range measurement, because the intensity can be considered a confidence measure for the depth estimation as it is related to the signal-to-noise-ratio. In case of the range data, peaks in the histogram can be assumed to correspond to objects at different distances in front of the camera. The threshold is determined as the one that separates the peak of the closest object from the remaining range values. The final segmented image is composed of those pixels that were classified as foreground pixels with respect to both types of data. To ensure that only a single object is considered, only the largest connected component of foreground pixels is retained, all other

Fig. 2. Sample image taken with a MESA SR4000 TOF camera. The leftmost image shows the intensity data. The range image is given in the center, and the resulting segmentation is shown on the right.

objects are considered background. A sample TOF image showing both range and intensity with the resulting segmented foreground is given in Fig. 2.

Stage 2: In the second stage, the segmented image is used to determine an initial guess for the location of the head and hand in the image. We employ a simple heuristic based on the number of foreground pixels in each column of the segmented image. The initial guess for the hand is the topmost pixel in the leftmost pixel column of the silhouette; the head is the topmost pixel in the tallest pixel column. This procedure is extremely simple to implement, yet reliable. We use a single parameter θ to determine whether we have a valid initial estimate, i.e. whether the hand is actually extended and the person is performing a pointing gesture:

$$|i_{\text{head}} - i_{\text{hand}}| \geq \theta \qquad (1)$$

Here, i_{head} and i_{hand} denote the indices of the pixel columns corresponding to the initial guess for the head and hand, respectively, where indices of pixel columns increase from left to right.

Stage 3: During the third stage of the method, the initial guesses are refined to more accurate pixel positions in the image. Once these positions are determined, the corresponding range values are estimated, and finally the coordinates of both the head and hand can be computed in 3D by inverting the camera projection using the known intrinsic camera parameters.

In order to refine the pixel positions of the head and hand in the image, we define rectangular regions of interest (ROIs) around the initial guesses and compute the centroids of the foreground pixels in the ROIs to find the centers of the head and hand blobs; these refined positions are marked by crosses in Figure 3.

To invert the camera projection we require the actual distance of the head and hand from the camera. Again, we define ROIs around the estimated pixel coordinates and take the average range value of the foreground pixels within the ROI to obtain estimates for the two range values. Finally, from the pixel coordinates (x, y), the distance from the camera r, and the intrinsic parameters

Fig. 3. Segmented image of the user with the detected locations of the head and hand marked by crosses. The time-of-flight camera measures the three-dimensional positions of these points, which are then used to compute the pointing direction.

of the camera one can infer the 3D coordinates of the corresponding point x in camera coordinates using the following formula:

$$x = r \frac{((c_x - x) \cdot s_x, (c_y - y) \cdot s_y, f)^T}{\|((c_x - x) \cdot s_x, (c_y - y) \cdot s_y, f)^T\|_2} \tag{2}$$

Here, (c_x, c_y) denotes the principal point, i.e. the pixel coordinates of the point where the optical axis intersects the image sensor. The width and height of a pixel are defined by s_x and s_y, and the focal length is given by f. To obtain a more stable estimate, a Kalman filter [8] tracks the 3D coordinates of the head and hand from frame to frame.

Stage 4: Because the TOF camera allows us to determine the position of the head and hand in space, we directly obtain an estimate for the pointing direction from the ray that emanates from the head and passes through the hand. (As Nickel and Stiefelhagen [9] show, the line connecting the head and hand is a good estimate for pointing direction.) This ray can be represented in camera coordinates by the following line equation:

$$r = o + \lambda d \tag{3}$$

Here, o denotes the origin of the ray and corresponds to the 3D position of the head. The direction of the ray is given by $d = p - o$, where p denotes the position of the hand. The parameter $\lambda \geq 0$ defines a point r in front of the person along the pointing direction.

We now intersect this ray with the screen used for projecting the slides. To this end we represent the screen by its center c and the normal n of the screen plane. Assuming that both c and n are also given in camera coordinates, the intersection x of the ray and the screen is given by:

$$x = o + \frac{\langle c - o, n \rangle}{\langle d, n \rangle} d \tag{4}$$

The intersection is only valid if the scalar product $\langle c-o,\ n \rangle$ is positive, otherwise the user is pointing away from the screen plane.

What remains to determine is if the intersection lies within the limits of the screen. In that case, the intersection can be converted to pixel coordinates on the screen in order to display the virtual laser pointer.

The location and size of the screen are determined by the calibration procedure introduced in Sect. 2.3. Since the procedure determines the 3D position of the four corners of the screen independently, the screen is generally not represented by a perfect rectangle. Thus, we determine the intersection by considering two triangles that are obtained by dividing the screen diagonally along the line from the bottom left corner to the top right corner. Assume that the triangles are defined by their three corners a, b, and c in counter-clockwise order such that either the top left or the bottom right corner are represented by a. For both triangles one can solve the following equation under the constraint that $d_1 = 1$:

$$x = \begin{pmatrix} a_1 & b_1 - a_1 & c_1 - a_1 \\ a_2 & b_2 - a_2 & c_2 - a_2 \\ a_3 & b_3 - a_3 & c_3 - a_3 \end{pmatrix} \begin{pmatrix} d_1 \\ d_2 \\ d_3 \end{pmatrix} \tag{5}$$

Intuitively, we check if the intersection x, represented as a linear combination of the two sides of the triangle given by $b - a$ and $c - a$, lies within the bounds of the triangle. Thus, if $d_2 + d_3 \leq 1$ holds for the upper triangle, the intersection x lies above the diagonal through the screen. Correspondingly, x lies below the diagonal if $d_2 + d_3 \leq 1$ holds for the lower triangle.

We now convert the coefficients d_2 and d_3 to coordinates x and y on the screen in such a way that the top left corner corresponds to $(x, y) = (0, 0)$ and the bottom right corner corresponds to $(x, y) = (1, 1)$. This is achieved by setting $(x, y) = (d_2, d_3)$ if x was above the diagonal through the screen and setting $(x, y) = (1 - d_2, 1 - d_3)$ otherwise. As a result one obtains for example the four different interpretations of the pointing gesture listed in Tab. 1. These interpretations correspond to the scenario depicted in Fig. 1.

In the "on screen" case, the virtual laser pointer is displayed on the screen at the location (x, y) the user is pointing to. If the user is pointing to one of the two active areas "left of screen" or "right of screen", a small triangle is displayed at the corresponding edge of the screen to indicate that the system is now expecting input in form of the "thumbs-up" gesture to navigate between the slides of the presentation. In all other cases, any detected pointing gesture is ignored, which avoids the so-called immersion syndrome [2].

Table 1. Interpretation of pointing gesture

on screen	$0.0 \leq x \leq 1.0$	$\wedge$	$0.0 \leq y \leq 1.0$
left of screen	$-0.05 \leq x < 0.0$	$\wedge$	$0.0 \leq y \leq 1.0$
right of screen	$1.0 < x \leq 1.05$	$\wedge$	$0.0 \leq y \leq 1.0$
off screen	otherwise		

Despite the fact that the estimation of the head and hand is quite robust and we apply a Kalman filter to the approximated 3D coordinates for temporal smoothing, the estimated intersection of the pointing direction and the screen in the "on screen" case is not entirely free of noise. This is dealt with by applying a smoothing filter with an exponential impulse response. The strength of the smoothing is adaptive and depends on the amount by which the pointing position changed: The greater the change, the less smoothing is applied. In this way, we suppress "jitter" in the virtual laser pointer when the user's hand is stationary but allow the pointer to follow large hand movements without the lag that would be caused by a non-adaptive smoothing filter.

2.2 Thumbs-Up Gesture

The detection of the thumbs-up gesture is only triggered when a pointing gesture made towards one of the two active areas was detected for the current frame according to the procedure described above.

The thumbs-up detector uses the segmented image and the pixel coordinates that were estimated for the hand. The main idea of the algorithm is that the silhouette of an extended thumb that points upwards is significantly narrower along the horizontal axis than a fist.

Thus, we define an ROI around the position of the hand and count the number of foreground pixels in each row. Next, we estimate w_{fist}, which denotes the width of the fist, by taking the maximum number of foreground pixels counted per row. The parameter w_{fist} is then used to determine the presence of both the fist and the thumb. We count the number c_{fist} of rows containing at least $0.8 \cdot w_{fist}$ foreground pixels and the number c_{thumb} of rows containing at least one and at most $0.3 \cdot w_{fist}$ foreground pixels. A thumb is detected in the current frame if both c_{fist} and c_{thumb} exceed a threshold of two. Due to the fact that the thresholds for detecting the fist and thumb depend on the estimated width of the fist w_{fist} in the current image, the procedure is relatively independent of the distance of the user from the camera, i.e. the algorithm is scale-invariant.

To avoid misdetections due to noise, we keep track of the detections of the thumb per frame over a certain time window, i.e. the command for switching to the next slide is only issued if the thumbs-up gesture was detected in four out of six consecutive frames. At the same time, we want to avoid multiple activations of the command for switching to the next slide if the above criterion is fulfilled in a number of consecutive frames. Otherwise, the user would not be able to go from one slide to the next in a controlled fashion without unintentionally skipping slides. Thus, we ignore any detections of the gesture for a total of 50 frames once a switch-to-next-slide command was issued. Since our system operates at roughly 25 Hz, a new command can only be issued every two seconds. This gives the user sufficient time to end the thumbs-up gesture once the gesture takes effect in order to prevent the system from switching directly to the next slide.

2.3   System Calibration

The third component of our method deals with the calibration of the system. To determine where the user is pointing on the screen, we need to know its position relative to the camera. This is determined in a calibration procedure where the user points at the four corners of the screen from two different locations; this information is sufficient to compute the position of the screen, as we will demonstrate in more detail in the following.

During calibration the user is asked to point continuously at one of the four corners of the screen for a total of 50 frames. This allows us to obtain a robust estimate for the position of the head and hand for the given pointing direction. Again, the pointing direction can be represented by a ray $r = o + \lambda d$ that emanates from the head and passes through the hand. We can assume that this ray passes through the corner the user was pointing at. However, we do not know the exact location of the corner along the ray.

To obtain this information, the user is asked to move to a different position in the field of view of the camera and to point again at the same corner for a total of 50 frames. By this procedure we estimate a second ray that should also pass through the corner of the screen. Ideally, the two rays intersect at the position of the corner; however, this assumption does generally not hold due to measurement noise. Nevertheless, a good estimate for the position of the corner can be obtained from the point that is closest to both rays in 3D space.

Assuming that the two estimated pointing directions are represented by rays $r_i = o_i + \lambda_i d_i$ where $i \in \{1, 2\}$, one can obtain this point by minimizing the squared distance $(o_1 + \lambda_1 d_1 - o_2 - \lambda_2 d_2)^2$ between the two rays with respect to λ_1 and λ_2. This leads to the following linear system of equations where we assume $\|d_i\| = 1$ without loss of generality:

$$\begin{pmatrix} 1 & \langle d_1, d_2 \rangle \\ -\langle d_1, d_2 \rangle & -1 \end{pmatrix} \begin{pmatrix} \lambda_1 \\ \lambda_2 \end{pmatrix} = \begin{pmatrix} -\langle o_1 - o_2, d_1 \rangle \\ -\langle o_1 - o_2, d_2 \rangle \end{pmatrix} \tag{6}$$

Solving Eq. (6) yields the parameters λ_1 and λ_2, which specify the closest point on one ray with respect to the other, respectively. Taking the arithmetic mean of both solutions as specified by Eq. (7) yields the approximation of the intersection of both rays and, thus, an estimate for the position of the corner in camera coordinates:

$$x = 0.5 \cdot (o_1 + \lambda_1 d_1 + o_2 + \lambda_2 d_2) \tag{7}$$

This procedure can be repeated for the remaining three corners of the screen. The approach does not guarantee, however, that all four corners lie in one plane. Thus, we fit a plane through the four corners by least squares and project the corners onto this plane to obtain their final estimates. The normal to this plane and the four corners are used to determine where the user is pointing on the screen, as described in Sect. 2.1. Obviously, this calibration procedure does not generally yield a screen that resembles a perfect rectangle in 3D space. How this problem can be treated by dividing the screen into two triangles along its diagonal was also discussed in Sect. 2.1.

We consider the procedure of not enforcing the screen to be rectangular an advantage, because it provides an implicit way of correcting systematic errors. Such errors may for example be caused by measurement errors or a simplified approximation of the camera parameters. The former can e.g. be due to multiple reflections of the scene [10]. The latter can occur if the optical system is not modelled accurately in the process of inverting the camera projection, e.g. if radial distortions of the lens or other effects are not taken into account.

3   Results

The method was implemented in C++ under the Windows operating system. On a 2 GHz Intel Core 2 Duo, it requires 40 ms per frame, achieving a frame rate of 25 frames per second.

To assess the accuracy with which the pointing direction is measured, we performed a test with 10 users. Each user was first given a few minutes to practice using the system. We then presented a sequence of nine targets at predefined positions on the screen; users were instructed to point at a target as soon as it appeared. Once a pointing gesture towards the screen was detected, each target was presented for a total of 50 frames, which corresponds to a time interval of roughly two seconds, before it disappeared. Users were asked to return to a normal standing position after the target had disappeared. Before presenting the next target, the system waited for four seconds to allow the user to rest the arm. The order in which the targets appeared was chosen in such a way that the average distance between successive targets on the screen was maximized.

For each user, we performed this test under two different conditions: Under the first condition, the virtual laser pointer was switched off, i.e. the users did not receive any feedback about the measured pointing direction. This gives an impression of the overall accuracy of the system. For the second test condition, the virtual laser pointer was switched on, allowing users to compensate for systematic calibration and measurement errors. This test condition therefore gives an impression of the residual measurement noise after the temporal smoothing described in Sect. 2.1.

Fig. 4a shows the results of the first test condition (without visual feedback) to assess the overall accuracy of the system. Here, measured error in pointing direction can have two sources: (i) Systematic errors due to measurement noise and inaccurate calibration and (ii) errors induced by the assumption that the ray emanating from the eyes across the hand corresponds to the natural human pointing direction [11]. The horizontal axis plots the frame number after the pointing gesture was detected, and the vertical axis plots the distance between the target and the measured pointing position in pixels. In the test setup the screen had a size of 1.71 m × 1.29 m and the user was standing at a distance of roughly 3.2 m from the screen. As a result, an offset of 20 pixels corresponds to approximately one degree. The solid line gives the mean distance, averaged over all users and pointing targets, and the shaded area indicates an interval of two standard deviations above and below the mean, i.e. 95% of the errors fell within this range.

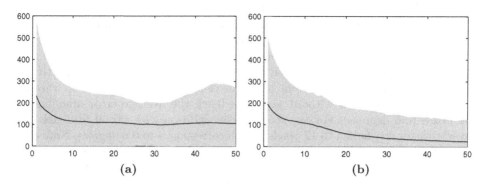

Fig. 4. Measurement error in pointing direction (a) without visual feedback (the virtual laser pointer was switched off) and (b) with visual feedback (virtual laser pointer switched on). The horizontal axis plots the time in seconds after the target appeared, and the vertical axis plots the distance between the target and the measured pointing position.

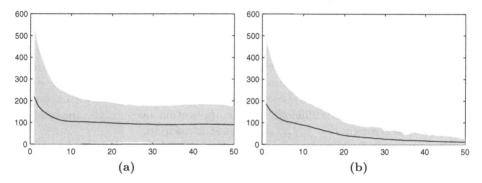

Fig. 5. Measurement error in pointing direction (a) without visual feedback (the virtual laser pointer was switched off) and (b) with visual feedback (virtual laser pointer switched on). Only targets near the center of the screen where considered.

From the plot, we can see that users took around 10 frames or 400 ms to point at a target; after this time, the average error stabilizes at around 106 pixels (or 5.3 degrees), with 95% of error falling between 0 and 271 pixels.

Fig. 4b shows the results of the second test condition (with visual feedback). As expected, the error stabilizes at a lower value of 23 pixels (or 1.2 degrees) on average but also takes a longer time to do so – around 1600 ms. This is because, after pointing at the target as in the first test, users need to correct their hand position to compensate for the systematic measurement error and bring the virtual laser pointer onto the target.

A closer look at the data reveals that the largest measurement errors occur for targets that are close to the corners of the screen. This is mainly due to shortcomings of the rather simple calibration procedure. However, the system is well calibrated for the center of the screen where most of the content of a presentation is likely to be placed. Thus, the impact of calibration errors near the corners on the usability is rather low. This becomes clear by looking at Fig. 5a and Fig. 5b. Again, the plots show the distance between the target and the measured pointing position without and with visual feedback, respectively. This time however, only targets near the center were considered. In case of the first test condition without visual feedback the average error amounts to 91 pixels (4.6 degrees). For the second test condition with visual feedback the average error was halfed to 12 pixels, which corresponds to 0.6 degrees. Note also that the standard deviation decreased significantly to 17 pixels (0.9 degrees) in the test with visual feedback, which indicates that the system is very robust and hence intuitive to use near the center of the screen.

4   Discussion

We have presented a framework that implements simple and robust gesture recognition in the context of a slideshow presentation. The system is based on a TOF camera that allows us to detect and interpret pointing gestures in an intuitive and effective way, because the provided range data facilitates the localization of the user in front of the camera and allows the estimation of the pointing direction in 3D space once the head and hand have been identified.

We believe pointing is a powerful way to determine whether a gesture is intended for the system at all and to assign different meanings to the same gesture depending on where the user is pointing. A simple gesture with a simple recognition procedure is sufficient for our application because the meaning of the gesture is strongly tied to the direction it is made in.

Thus, we have developed an intuitive system that allows the user to control a slideshow by switching between slides through a simple thumbs-up gesture that is made towards one of the sides of the screen. Alternatively, we could have implemented an additional thumbs-down gesture using a single active area, but our intention here was to demonstrate the use of multiple active areas, i.e. the number of active areas multiply the number of actions that can be triggered with a given set of gestures. Finally, the user may highlight certain details on the slides simply by pointing at them; a virtual laser pointer is displayed at the location the user is pointing to. This virtual laser pointer has two advantages: First, the size and appearance can be chosen depending on the context. Second, the build-in smoothing of the pointer can veil a tremor of the users hand that may originate from an impairment or excitement.

Acknowledgment

This work was developed within the ARTTS project (www.artts.eu), which is funded by the European Commission (contract no. IST-34107) within the Information Society Technologies (IST) priority of the 6th Framework Programme. This publication reflects the views only of the authors, and the Commission cannot be held responsible for any use which may be made of the information contained therein.

References

1. Oggier, T., Büttgen, B., Lustenberger, F., Becker, G., Rüegg, B., Hodac, A.: SwissRanger^{TM} SR3000 and first experiences based on miniaturized 3D-TOF cameras. In: Ingensand, K. (ed.) Proc. 1st Range Imaging Research Day, Zurich, pp. 97–108 (2005)
2. Baudel, T., Beaudouin-Lafon, M.: CHARADE: Remote control of objects using free-hand gestures. Communications of the ACM 36, 28–35 (1993)
3. Hofemann, N., Fritsch, J., Sagerer, G.: Recognition of deictic gestures with context. In: Rasmussen, C.E., Bülthoff, H.H., Schölkopf, B., Giese, M.A. (eds.) DAGM 2004. LNCS, vol. 3175, pp. 334–341. Springer, Heidelberg (2004)
4. Moeslund, T.B., Nøregaard, L.: Recognition of deictic gestures for wearable computing. In: Gibet, S., Courty, N., Kamp, J.-F. (eds.) GW 2005. LNCS (LNAI), vol. 3881, pp. 112–123. Springer, Heidelberg (2006)
5. Moeslund, T.B., Granum, E.: Modelling and estimating the pose of a human arm. Machine Vision and Applications 14, 237–247 (2003)
6. Haker, M., Böhme, M., Martinetz, T., Barth, E.: Geometric invariants for facial feature tracking with 3D TOF cameras. In: Proceedings of the IEEE International Symposium on Signals, Circuits & Systems (ISSCS), Iasi, Romania, vol. 1, pp. 109–112 (2007)
7. Haker, M., Martinetz, T., Barth, E.: Multimodal sparse features for object detection. In: Alippi, C., Polycarpou, M., Panayiotou, C., Ellinas, G. (eds.) ICANN 2009. LNCS, vol. 5769, pp. 923–932. Springer, Heidelberg (2009)
8. Kalman, R.E.: A new approach to linear filtering and prediction problems. Transactions of the ASME, Series D, Journal of Basic Engineering 82, 35–45 (1960)
9. Nickel, K., Stiefelhagen, R.: Pointing gesture recognition based on 3D-tracking of face, hands and head orientation. In: International Conference on Multimodal Interfaces, pp. 140–146 (2003)
10. Gudmundsson, S.A., Aanæs, H., Larsen, R.: Effects on measurement uncertainties of time-of-flight cameras. In: Proceedings of the IEEE International Symposium on Signals, Circuits & Systems (ISSCS), vol. 1, pp. 1–4 (2007)
11. Kranstedt, A., Lücking, A., Pfeiffer, T., Rieser, H., Wachsmuth, I.: Deixis: How to Determine Demonstrated Objects Using a Pointing Cone. In: Gibet, S., Courty, N., Kamp, J.-F. (eds.) GW 2005. LNCS (LNAI), vol. 3881, pp. 300–311. Springer, Heidelberg (2006)

Towards Analysis of Expressive Gesture in Groups of Users: Computational Models of Expressive Social Interaction

Antonio Camurri, Giovanna Varni, and Gualtiero Volpe

Casa Paganini – InfoMus Lab, DIST – University of Genova,
Viale F. Causa 13, 16145 Genova, Italy
antonio.camurri@unige.it, giovanna@infomus.org,
gualtiero.volpe@unige.it
www.infomus.org, www.casapaganini.org

Abstract. In this paper we present a survey of our research on analysis of expressive gesture and how it is evolving towards the analysis of expressive social interaction in groups of users. Social interaction and its expressive implications (e.g., emotional contagion, empathy) is an extremely relevant component for analysis of expressive gesture, since it provides significant information on the context expressive gestures are performed in. However, most of the current systems analyze expressive gestures according to basic emotion categories or simple dimensional approaches. Moreover, almost all of them are intended for a single user, whereas social interaction is often neglected. After briefly recalling our pioneering studies on collaborative robot-human interaction, this paper presents two steps in the direction of novel computational models and techniques for measuring social interaction: (i) the interactive installation *Mappe per Affetti Erranti* for active listening to sound and music content, and (ii) the techniques we developed for explicitly measuring synchronization within a group of users. We conclude with the research challenges we will face in the near future.

Keywords: expressive gesture analysis and processing, analysis of social interaction in small groups, multimodal interactive systems.

1 Introduction

This paper presents a survey of our research on analysis of expressive gesture and how it is evolving towards the analysis of social interaction in (small) groups of users.

Research on *expressive gesture* became particularly relevant in recent years (e.g., see the post-proceedings of Gesture Workshops 2003, 2005, and 2007). Psychological studies have been a fundamental source for automatic analysis of expressive gesture since they identified which features are most significant (e.g., De Meijer, 1989; Wallbott, 1998; Boone and Cunningham, 1998). A further relevant source has been research in the humanistic tradition, in particular choreography. As a major example, in his Theory of Effort, the choreographer Rudolf Laban (1947)

S. Kopp and I. Wachsmuth (Eds.): GW 2009, LNAI 5934, pp. 122–133, 2010.

describes the most significant qualities of movement. Starting from these sources, several systems for analysis of expressive gesture were developed (e.g., Camurri et al., 2003, 2005; Kapur et al., 2005; Bernhardt et al., 2007).

However, most of such systems classify gestures according to basic emotion categories or simple dimensional approaches. Moreover, almost all of the existing systems are intended for a single user, whereas social interaction is neglected.

Nevertheless, social interaction is an extremely relevant component for analysis of expressive gesture, since it provides significant information on the context expressive gestures are performed in. *Social intelligence* or social competencies, understood as the ability to deal effectively in interpersonal contexts, is a paradigmatic human ability, widely studied in psychology and more recently in neurophysiology, which is receiving a growing interest from the ICT communities. Research in experimental psychology and neurosciences has shown that nonverbal communication, and in particular expressive gesture, is a key aspect of social interaction.

Current research on social interaction, however, does not focus on the high-level emotional aspects, but rather on group cohesion and decision-making. In this framework, pioneering studies by Pentland (2007) investigated techniques to measure social signals in scenarios like salary negotiation and friendship. Particular attention was also directed to the recognition of functional roles (e.g., most dominant people) played during small-group meetings (e.g., Dong et al., 2007). These works are often based on laboratory experiments and do not address the more subtle aspects of social interaction such as emotional contagion and empathy. Empathy, in fact, has been studied mainly in the framework of synthesis of (verbal) dialogues by virtual characters and embodied conversational agents (see for example de Rosis et al., 2005; McQuiggan and Lester, 2007). The EU-ICT project SAME (www.sameproject.eu) has recently developed techniques for social active listening to music by mobile devices, i.e., for allowing a (small) group of users to mould collaboratively a pre-recorded music piece they are listening to (e.g., see Varni et al., 2009, for the description of an application presented at Agora Festival, Ircam, Paris, in June 2009).

The major research challenge in our work consists of analyzing even the subtlest and most significant emotional expressions conveyed by expressive gesture in a social framework, such as empathy and emotional contagion. After recalling our pioneering studies on collaborative robot-human interaction, carried out in the late Nineties, this paper presents two steps in the direction of novel computational models and techniques for measuring social interaction: (i) the interactive installation *Mappe per Affetti Erranti*, where we first investigated social interaction in a small group of users and explored how to use this information in a multi-user multimodal interactive system for active listening of sound and music content, and (ii) the techniques we developed for explicitly measuring synchronization within a group of users. Such techniques are based on the analysis of complex systems, where each user is modelled as a component of a complex system, and which have been applied both in experiments and applications in the framework of the SAME Project.

Finally, starting from this experience, we conclude with the research challenges we will face in the near future. These are in the direction of a deeper understanding of the mechanisms underlying phenomena such as empathy and emotional contagion, that are studied by considering ensemble music performance (e.g., a string quartet) as an ideal test-bed for experiments and proof-of-concepts.

2 Pioneering Studies: Collaborative Human-Robot Interaction

Our pioneering studies on analysis of expressive gesture in social interaction date back to the beginning of our Lab in 1984. In particular, in the late Nineties, such studies were carried out in the framework of human-robot interaction (e.g., Camurri et al., 2000). A major goal was (and partially still is) to explore paradigms of expressive social interaction between humans and robots in the framework of multimodal environments in music, theatre, museum exhibitions, and art installations.

In one of such works (Suzuki et al., 1998), we experimented with a small mobile robot on wheels (a Pioneer 1 from Stanford Research Institute) as a semi-autonomous agent capable of communicating with the visitors of a museum exhibit on contemporary art (*Arti Visive 2*, Palazzo Ducale, Genova, October 1998) by means of several channels, including sound and music, visual media, and style of movement (e.g., fast/slow, smooth/nervous, tail-wagging). The robot wandered in the museum exhibit as one of the visitors, a sort of medium between humans and machines inhabiting the exhibit area. Sensors allowed it to avoid collisions with the surrounding people and to observe artworks and visitors. The goal was to generate a musical and visual feedback for visitors and to interact with them (see Figure 1a). Feedback depended on a model of artificial emotions, simulating the internal emotional state of the robot. A basic idea for the visual output was to take the images the robot captured and to transform them in real time by "virtual mirrors" reflecting the internal state of the robot. For example, if the robot could not follow its path – one of its goal was to visit the exhibit – a mirror deformation in a sort of pulsing spiral emerged (see Figure 1b), accompanied by faster rhythmic music textures. More details on the models and the architecture we used can be found in (Suzuki et al., 1998; Camurri and Coglio, 1998, Camurri and Ferrentino, 1999).

In another experimental set-up, we developed a "theatrical machine" for the performance of the music piece *Spiral*, by K. Stockhausen, for one singer or player (in this performance, one trombone) endowed with a short wave radio. The radio, audio amplifier, and loudspeakers were installed on board of a robot navigating on the stage, thus creating effects of physical spatialization of sound due to the movement of the

(a)   (b)

Fig. 1. Social interaction between a robot and a group of visitors at the art exhibition *Arti Visive 2* (Genova, Italy, October 1998): (a) the robot interacting with visitors, (b) an example of visual output.

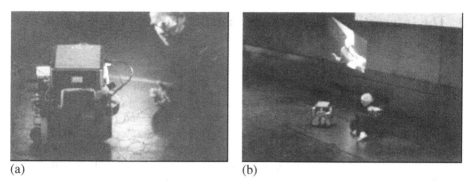

(a)   (b)

Fig. 2. Collaborative human-robot interaction in the framework of the multimedia performance *L'Ala dei Sensi* (Ferrara, Italy, November 1998): (a) robot/dancer interaction, (b) an example of visual feedback

robot during the performance (trombone: Michele Lo Muto, live electronics: Giovanni Cospito, Civica Scuola di Musica, Sezione Musica Contemporanea, Milano, June 1996). The movements of the robot were influenced by sound parameters and by the gesture of the trombone performer: for example, a high "energy" content by the trombonist's gesture and a high sound spectral energy were stimuli for the robot to move away from the performer. Smooth and calm phrasing and movements were stimuli attracting the robot near and around the performer. Further, the robot sound and music output were part of the interaction process, i.e., the expressive gesture nuances and the sound produced by the performer influenced the robot, and vice-versa.

For *L'Ala dei Sensi* (see Figures 2a and 2b), a multimedia performance about human perception (Director: Ezio Cuoghi; Choreographer and dancer: Virgilio Sieni, Ferrara, Italy, November 1998), we contributed two episodes involving interactive dance/music performance, making use of a small mobile robotic platform (a Pioneer 2 from Stanford Research Institute). The robot was equipped with sensors, an on-board video projector and a video-camera. Sensors allowed the robot to avoid collisions with the scenery and the dancers. In the main episode, initially the on-board video projector and the video-camera were directly controlled in real-time by the director (off-stage). He also used the images coming from the robot (the robot's point of view) to mix them in real time on a large screen. The director controlled the movements of the robot too. That is, the robot was a sort of passive companion of the dancer. At a certain point, the dancer plugged off the electric power cable of the robot. This was a specially important gesture: the robot came to life and a deeper dialogue with the dancer started. The dancer was equipped with two sensors on the palms of the hands. By acting on the first one, he was allowed to influence the robot towards one between two different styles of movement: a kind of "ordered" movement (aiming at a direct, constant speed movement) and a "disordered" type of movement. Through the second sensor the movement could be stopped and restarted. The dancer was also observed by a video-camera and his expressive gestures were a further stimulus for the robot, which was able to react by changing (morphing) its style of moving.

3   The Interactive Collaborative Installation *Mappe Per Affetti Erranti*

More recently, we studied expressive gesture in social interaction in the framework of collaborative and active listening to sound and music content. With *active listening* we mean that listeners are enabled to interactively operate on (pre-recorded) music content through their movement and gesture, by modifying and moulding it in real-time while listening. Active listening is investigated in the framework of the EU-ICT Project SAME (www.sameproject.eu). *Mappe per Affetti Erranti* is a collaborative multi-user multimodal interactive system, where four users collectively collaborate in the active listening to a music piece, by their expressive movement and gesture.

Mappe per Affetti Erranti – literally "maps for wandering affects" – (Camurri et al., 2008) reworks and extends the concept of navigation and exploration of a virtual orchestra by introducing multiple levels: from the navigation in a physical space populated by virtual objects or subjects up to the virtual navigation in emotional spaces populated by different expressive performances of the same music piece. Users can navigate such emotional spaces by their expressive movement and gesture. Only social interaction and collaboration leads to a correct reconstruction of the music piece. In other words, while users explore the physical space, the (expressive) way in which they move and the degree of collaboration between them allow them to explore at the same time an emotional space, by means of transformations in real-time of the interpretation of the music content.

At the physical level, space is divided in several areas. A voice of a polyphonic music piece is associated to each area. The music content is coded as multiple independent audio channels. The presence of a user (even a single user, who can vary from a non-expert user to a dancer) triggers the reproduction of the music piece. By exploring the space, the user walks through several areas and listens to the single voices separately. If the user stays in a single area, she listens to the voice associated to that area only. If she does not move for a given time interval, music fades out and turns off. The user can mould the voice she is listening to in several ways. At a low level, she can intervene on parameters such as loudness, density, amount of reverberation, and spatial position. At a higher level, she can intervene on the expressive features of the music performance, i.e., change the interpretation. This is done through the navigation of an emotional space. The system analyzes the expressive intention the user conveys with her expressive gesture and translates it in a position (or a trajectory) in an emotional space. Like the physical space, such emotional space is also divided in several areas, each corresponding to a different performance of the same voice with a different expressive intention. Several examples of such emotional spaces are available in the literature, for example the spaces used in dimensional theories of emotion (e.g., Russell, 1980; Tellegen et al., 1999) or those especially developed for analysis and synthesis of expressive music performance (e.g., Juslin, 2000; Vines et al., 2005). Users can thus explore the music piece in a twofold perspective: navigating the physical space they explore the polyphonic musical structure; navigating the emotional space they explore music interpretation. A single user, however, can only listen to and intervene on a single voice at time: she cannot listen to the whole polyphonic piece.

Only a group of users can fully experience *Mappe per Affetti Erranti*. In particular, the music piece can be listened to in its whole polyphony only if a number of users at least equal to the number of voices is interacting with the installation. Each user controls the interpretation of the performance of the voice associated to the area she occupies: e.g., a shy, hesitant behavior causes the corresponding voice interpretation to be whispering, soft; if a user is moving aggressively and with sudden impulsive gesture, the corresponding voice becomes interpreted correspondingly (louder, with sudden peaks, etc.). The whole piece is performed coherently, that is with the same expressive intention, only if all the users are moving with the same expressive intention. Thus, the more users move with different, conflicting expressive intentions, the more the musical output is incoherent and chaotic. But the more users move with similar expressive intentions and in a collaborative way, the more the musical output is coherent and the music piece is listened to in one of its different expressive interpretations.

In the current instance of the system of *Mappe per Affetti Erranti* (Figure 3), the physical map is composed by four areas. Tenore and soprano voices are associated to the central areas and contralto and basso to the lateral ones. Four expressive performances of the same music piece are available: Happy/Joyful, Solemn, Intimate/Shy, and Angry/Aggressive. These are associated to the same four expressive intentions classified from users expressive gestures. Analysis of expressive gesture is performed by means of twelve expressive features: Quantity of Motion, computed on the overall body movement and on translational movement only; Impulsiveness, vertical and horizontal components of velocity of peripheral upper parts of the body; speed of the barycentre; variation of the Contraction Index; Space Occupation Area; Directness Index (inspired by the Space dimension of Laban's Effort Theory), Space Allure (inspired by the Pierre Schaeffer's Morphology), Amount of Periodic Movement, and Symmetry Index. Such descriptors are computed in real-time for each user. Further descriptors are computed also on the whole group of users: e.g., the contraction/expansion of the group and its cohesion. This perspective corresponds to Rudolf Laban's *General Space* (Laban, 1947). Classification is performed following a fuzzy-logic like approach. Such approach has the advantage that it does not need a training set of recorded movement and it is also flexible enough to be applied to the movement of different kinds of users (e.g., adults, children, elder people).

Fig. 3. *Mappe per Affetti Erranti* experienced by a group of four users (left) and by two dancers during a dance performance (right)

In *Mappe per Affetti Erranti*, synchronization has a particular importance. Only synchronization in the expressive intentions conveyed by the users allows the correct reconstruction of the music piece.

Techniques for the real-time management of the synchronization of the four musical voices have been developed. At the audio level, each audio file is manually or semi-automatically segmented in phrases and sub-phrases. Changes in the expressive intention detected from movement trigger a switch to the corresponding audio file at a position, which is coherent to the position reached by that expressive interpretation as a result of the movement of the users. In such a way, we obtain a continuous resynchronization of the single voices depending on the expressive intentions conveyed by the users.

The system analyzes the expressive gesture of each single user. Synchronization emerges as the result of the collective behavior of the users. As for the audio processing and real-time synchronization of the several voices, we developed a series of techniques to align the audio channels following the phrasing, the changing of interpretation of the recorded voices, and the mutual behavior of the users. For example, when a user imitates the expressive behavior of another, her associated voice changes to the same interpretation as the other one (the leader, at this moment): the two voices then synchronize, by aligning in real-time the second voice to the leader's voice, keeping into account the phrasing for having naturalness and continuity in the perceived audio. The synchronization is therefore modeled at a "sub-phrasing" level. A sudden, musically unrelated synchronization of two voices just at the time instant in which the system detects a change of behavior would be perceived unnatural. Let us consider the two-user example mentioned above. The first is moving joyful/happy and the second shy/intimate/hesitant, with the corresponding rendering of the music interpretations joyful and soft/whispering, respectively. The music results not synchronized: an intimate performance is usually slower than a joyful one. If the second user changes her behavior from shy to joyful, her corresponding voice, once concluded the current musical sub-phrase, will shift from the shy to the joyful audio file, and the time instant where it continues to play the audio will be the same of the other (leading) voice. This synchronization driven by the expressive gesture and by the semantics of the musical content causes a short delay (a few hundreds of ms, corresponding to sub-phrase average duration), but proved to be the best strategy: it is perceived as natural by users, and it also follows the natural motor task strategy that would be adopted by a singer to manage sudden changes in interpretation (the most natural way is to change interpretation at the starting of the next sub-phrase, allowing a preparation and re-programming of the next motor task of singing). We considered other synchronization strategies, e.g., time-warping of voice music signals, but these demonstrated to be unnatural both from the singer and listener perspective. Further, they destroy the naturalness of expressive interpretation, and are computationally much more intensive.

The next step, still missing in *Mappe per Affetti Erranti*, is to explicitly measure the synchronization of the group.

4 Measuring Synchronization in a Group of Users

Starting from the results obtained in *Mappe per Affetti Erranti*, the focus of our research is shifted to the development of methodological frameworks, computational models, and algorithms for the analysis of creative communication within groups of users in terms of synchronization.

Synchronization can be broadly referred to as a phenomenon occurring when "two or many systems adjust a given property of their motion to a common behaviour, due to coupling or forcing" (Boccaletti et al., 2002). This definition covers different kinds of synchronization: from Phase Synchronization (PS), in which only the phases of the trajectories described from the systems in the phase space are locked, to Complete Synchronization (CS) in which the trajectories are almost identical.

To date, notwithstanding the large number of works on synchronization in many research fields (e.g., electronics, physics, medicine, psychology), there is a lack of studies focusing on this phenomenon in non stereotyped and non laboratory conditions and taking into account non-verbal expressive communication.

Our approach considers all interacting users as a complex system having as basic units the single users. It is well known that interacting units of a complex system are able to auto-organize and exhibit global properties, which are not obviously derived from their individual dynamics: synchronization is one of these properties. Each user is described by means of the time evolution of a N-dimensional state vector of behavioral expressive features. The state vector components may include, for example, coordinates and velocity of joints or other body parts (e.g., center of mass of head or limbs), energy and amount of motion, or audio and physiological features. We refer to such multimodal features as *expressive Movement, Audio, Physiological* (eMAP) features. eMAP features are extracted using real-time, synchronized, multi-modal feature extraction techniques and are the inputs to the computational models explaining the processes underlying interpersonal creative communication.

We chose PS as one of the baseline low-level signals to indirectly measure more complex phenomena like empathy and dominance in small groups of subjects. Our hypothesis is that empathy occurs when synchronization of specific expressive features emerge. Nonetheless, our hypothesis considers this a necessary, but not sufficient, condition: synchronization may emerge also in cases where empathy does not occur. Our work addresses PS exploiting the concepts of Recurrence (Poincaré, 1890), Recurrence Plots (RP) (Eckmann et al., 1987) and Cross-Recurrence Plot (CRP), and their quantification by means of Recurrence Quantification Analysis (RQA) (Marwan et al., 2007, Zbilut et al., 1992). RP/CRP and RQA give qualitative and quantitative information on systems' dynamics and their interrelations in terms of trajectories in the phase space, whereas RQA allows to quantify small-scale patterns in RP/CRP and provides quantitative information on the systems dynamics. We think that changes in the number of occurrences and strength of PS among users can be considered useful features toward evaluation of empathy.

In our research, we focused on joint music performance, an ideal test-bed for the development of models and techniques for measuring creative social interaction in an ecologically valid framework. Music is widely regarded as the medium of emotional expression par excellence. Moreover, ensemble performance is one of the most closely synchronized activities that human beings engage in: it is believed that this

Fig. 4. Experiments on joint music performance: (a) music duo performance in which the two musicians can communicate, also exchanging visual information, (b) the famous string quartet Quartetto di Cremona during the experiment. Each musician wears a white hat including a green passive marker and a 3-axis accelerometer, plus a 3-axis accelerometer on the back, and physiological sensors for heart rate, breath, ocular movements, and face muscles.

ability from individuals and groups to entrain to music is unique only to humans and that, unlike speech, musical performance is one of the few expressive activities allowing simultaneous participation.

During the last three years, we focused on the analysis of famous string quartets and on duos of violin players. The ensembles Cuarteto Casal, Quartetto di Cremona, Quartetto Prometeo have been involved initially in feasibility studies (e.g., to study and understand which multimodal features can explain their expressive social behavior) and in experiments at our Centre and in occasion of their concerts at the Opera House of Genova. In addition, in collaboration with Ben Knapp (SARC, University of Belfast) and Carol Krumhansl (Cornell University) we carried out measurements of duos of violinists participating in the International Violin Competition Premio Paganini in 2006, in the framework of the EU Summer School of the HUMAINE Network of Excellence. More recently, again in collaboration with the SARC colleagues, we performed multimodal synchronized recordings of the Quartetto di Cremona. Figure 4 shows snapshots from the experiments.

Using the PS approach described above, several results emerged: for example, in the case of a music duo performance, it was possible to evaluate how the visual and acoustic channels affect the exchange of expressive information during the performance and how positive emotion can affect the emergence of synchronization (Varni et al., 2008). Moreover, foundations for a criterion to distinguish between parallel and reactive empathic outcomes have been defined. Furthermore, measures of the direction of PS confirmed the hypothesis on egalitarian distribution of dominance in a duo performance . Further, preliminary results from the analysis of string quartets highlighted how the induction of a positive emotion in one of the musicians of the group resulted in an increased synchronization among musicians (in terms of heads movement), with respect to no emotion induction condition. In the same experiment, the SARC colleagues found high physiological synchronization with the structural changes in the music. Moreover, measures relating to performer mistakes, and the perceived difficulty of the music were found, which also strongly affect both intra- and inter-personal synchronization. This effect of emotion on synchronization (emotional synchronization) is an important issue that will be further explored in our research.

We developed a real-time implementation of these techniques, resulting in the EyesWeb XMI Social Signal Processing Library (Varni et al., 2009a), which is employed in the framework of the SAME Project to develop applications for social active music listening experiences. In particular, the *Sync'n'Move* application prototype, based on EyesWeb XMI and its extensions to Nokia S60 mobile phones, enables users to experience novel form of social interaction based on music and gesture (Varni et al., 2009b). Users move rhythmically (e.g., dance) while wearing their mobiles. Their PS is extracted from their gesture (e.g., using the accelerometers data from the mobiles) and used to modify in real-time the performance of a pre-recorded music. More specifically, every time users are successful in synchronizing among themselves, music orchestration and rendering is enhanced; while in cases of low synchronization, i.e., poor collaborative interaction, the music gradually corrupts, looses sections and rendering features, until it becomes a very poor audio signal.

5 Conclusion

This paper presented a survey of our research on analysis of expressive gesture and how it is evolving towards the analysis of social interaction in (small) groups of users. However, to date, research on measuring quantitative and qualitative interpersonal communication in groups and on supporting models and tools is still a broadly unexplored field. In this scenario, our future research directions include: investigation on the key factors driving interpersonal synchronization in a group and determining the feeling of group cohesion; how emotional, physical, and social contexts can affect interpersonal and intrapersonal synchronization in one or more modalities; the identification of specific functional roles inside a group. Further, another recent research project concerns the social active experience of audiovisual content, in the framework of museum and cultural projects: it is an extension of the concept of active music listening, and we are exploring directions to enhance the visiting experience of museum visitors.

Acknowledgements. This research is partially supported by the EU 7FP ICT SAME Project (www.sameproject.eu). We thank our colleagues at InfoMus – Casa Paganini Corrado Canepa, Paolo Coletta, Donald Glowinski, Maurizio Mancini, Alberto Massari, and Barbara Mazzarino for their important contributes to research. We are grateful to Ipke Wachsmuth and Stefan Kopp for the precious suggestions.

References

Bernhardt, D., Robinson, P.: Detecting Affect from Non-stylised Body Motions. In: Paiva, A.C.R., Prada, R., Picard, R.W. (eds.) ACII 2007. LNCS, vol. 4738, pp. 59–70. Springer, Heidelberg (2007)

Boccaletti, S., Kurths, J., Osipov, G., Valladeres, D.L., Zhou, C.S.: The Synchronization of Cahotic Systems. Phys. Rep. 366(1-2), 1–101 (2002)

Boone, R.T., Cunningham, J.G.: Children's decoding of emotion in expressive body movement: The development of cue attunement. Developmental Psychology 34, 1007–1016 (1998)

Camurri, A., Coglio, A.: An Architecture for Emotional Agents. In: IEEE Multimedia, October-December 1998, pp. 24–33. IEEE CS Press, Los Alamitos (1998)

Camurri, A., Ferrentino, P.: Interactive environments for music and multimedia. Multimedia Systems 7, 32–47 (1999)

Camurri, A., Coletta, P., Ricchetti, M., Volpe, G.: Expressiveness and Physicality in Interaction. Journal of New Music Research 29(3), 187–198 (2000)

Camurri, A., Lagerlöf, I., Volpe, G.: Recognizing emotion from dance movement: Comparison of spectator recognition and automated techniques. Intl. J. Human-Computer Studies 59, 213–225 (2003)

Camurri, A., De Poli, G., Leman, M., Volpe, G.: Toward Communicating Expressiveness and Affect in Multimodal Interactive Systems for Performing Art and Cultural Applications. IEEE Multimedia 12(1), 43–53 (2005)

Camurri, A., Canepa, C., Coletta, P., Ferrari, N., Mazzarino, B., Volpe, G.: The Interactive Piece The Bow is bent and drawn. In: Proc. 3rd ACM Intl. Conf. on Digital Interactive Media in Entertainment and Arts (DIMEA 2008), Athens, Greece, pp. 376–383 (2008)

De Meijer, M.: The contribution of general features of body movement to the attribution of emotions. J. of Nonverbal Behavior 13, 247–268 (1989)

De Rosis, F., Cavalluzzi, A., Mazzotta, I., Novielli, N.: Can embodied conversational agents induce empathy in users? In: Proceedings of AISB 2005, Virtual Social Character Symposium (2005)

Dong, W., Lepri, B., Cappelletti, A., Pentland, A., Pianesi, F., Zancanaro, M.: Using the influence model to recognize functional roles in meetings. In: Proc. 9th Intl. ACM Conf. on Multimodal Interfaces, pp. 271–278 (2007)

Eckmann, J.P., Kamphorst, S.O., Ruelle, D.: Recurrence plots of dynamical system. Eurpph. Lett. 5, 973–977 (1987)

Juslin, P.N.: Cue utilization in communication of emotion in music performance: relating performance to perception. Journal of Experimental Psychology: Human Perception and Performance 26(6), 1797–1813 (2000)

Kapur, A., Kapur, A., Virji-Babul, N., Tzanetakis, G., Driessen, P.F.: Gesture-Based Affective Computing on Motion Capture Data. In: Tao, J., Tan, T., Picard, R.W. (eds.) ACII 2005. LNCS, vol. 3784, pp. 1–7. Springer, Heidelberg (2005)

Laban, R., Lawrence, F.C.: Effort. Macdonald&Evans Ltd., London (1947)

Marwan, N., Romano, M.C., Thiel, M., Kurths, J.: Recurrence plots for the analysis of complex systems. Phsysics Reports 438, 237–329 (2007)

McQuiggan, S.W., Lester, J.C.: Modeling and evaluating empathy in embodied companion agents. Intl. J. Human-Computer Studies 65(4), 348–360 (2007)

Pentland, A.: Social signal processing. IEEE Signal Processing Magazine 24(4), 108–111 (2007)

Poincaré, H.: Sur la problèmedes trois corps et les equations de la dynamique. Acta Math 13, 1–271 (1890)

Russell, J.A.: A circumplex model of affect. J. of Personality and Social Psychology 39, 1161–1178 (1980)

Suzuki, K., Camurri, A., Hashimoto, S., Ferrentino, P.: Intelligent Agent System for Human-Robot Interaction through Artificial Emotion. In: Proc. IEEE Intl. Conf. on Systems Man and Cybernetics SMC 1998, San Diego, USA (1998)

Tellegen, A., Watson, D., Clark, L.A.: On the dimensional and hierarchical structure of affect. Psychological Science 10(4), 297–303 (1999)

Varni, G., Camurri, A., Coletta, P., Volpe, G.: Emotional entrainment in music performance. In: Proc. of 8th Intl. Conf. on Automatic Face and Gesture Recognition FG 2008 (2008)

Varni, G., Camurri, A., Coletta, P., Volpe, G.: Toward Real-time Automated Measure of Empathy and Dominance. In: Proc. 2009 IEEE Intl. Conf. on Social Computing SocialCom, Vancouver, Canada (2009a)

Varni, G., Mancini, M., Volpe, G., Camurri, A.: Sync'n'Move: social interaction based on music and gesture. In: Proc. 1st Intl. ICST Conference on User Centric Media, Venice, Italy, December 2009 (2009b)

Vines, B.W., Krumhansl, C.L., Wanderley, M.M., Ioana, M.D., Levitin, D.J.: Dimensions of Emotion in Expressive Musical Performance. Ann. N.Y. Acad. Sci. 1060, 462–466 (2005)

Wallbott, H.G.: Bodily expression of emotion. Eur. J. Soc. Psychol. 28, 879–896 (1998)

Zbilut, J., Webber Jr., C.L.: Embeddings and delays as derived from quantification of recurrence plots. Phys. Lett. A 5, 199–203 (1992)

On Gestural Variation and Coarticulation Effects in Sound Control

Tommaso Bianco, Vincent Freour, Nicolas Rasamimanana, Frederic Bevilaqua, and René Caussé

IRCAM UMR STMS,
1 Place Igor Stravinsky Paris, France
{tommaso.bianco,vincent.freour,nicolas.rasamimanana,
frederic.bevilacqua,rene.causse}@ircam.fr

Abstract. In this paper we focus on the analysis of sound producing gestures in the musical domain. We investigate the behavior of intraoral pressure exerted by a trumpet performer in the production of single and concatenated notes. Investigation is carried out with functional data analysis techniques. Results show that different variation patterns occur for single note production, which depend on dynamic level, suggesting the hypothesis that two different motor control programs are available. Results from analysis on consecutive notes give evidence that the coarticulation between two gesture curves cannot be modelled by linear superposition, and that local coarticulation is affected by contiguous units.

Keywords: coarticulation, music performance, gesture synthesis, anticipation, motor program, functional statistical analysis.

1 Introduction

In music performance, sound production is always linked to continuous gesture processes. Thus, the subtle variations of these processes must be taken into account to study how the musicians actually control expressively their sound. Moreover, the variation in the execution of a gesture depends on the musical context. When embedded into a continuous stream of units, each gesture segment undergoes influences from the surrounding segments, a contextual modification usually called, from phonetics literature, coarticulation.

In this paper we focus on the analysis of gestures for the production of sound in trumpet performance. Our analysis concentrates on two main types of variability: intrinsic, that is related to the gesture for a single note execution, and extrinsic, that is variability caused by coarticulation effects between adjacent gesture events. We apply functional data analysis techniques in order to identify specificities among different playing techniques.

Our aim is to give more evidence for the understanding of the underlying process related to the sound control in trumpet performance. The results of our analysis might be of help for recognition as well as for synthesis purposes in the general domain of control of sound synthesis.

S. Kopp and I. Wachsmuth (Eds.): GW 2009, LNAI 5934, pp. 134–145, 2010.
© Springer-Verlag Berlin Heidelberg 2010

2   Related Works

The subject of coarticulation has been widely studied in phonetics [1]. Nevertheless, it is still a central and challenging theme both for automatic speech and sign recognition [2]. Among few theories elaborated for the modeling of this phenomenon (see Farnetani for a review [3]), the co-production theory of Fowler is of particular interest for the present account. The co-production theory explains the coarticulation between two segments as the result of their overlapping activity. The boundaries of the two segments thus extend onto each other, instead of a common "perpendicular to the time axis" frontier [4].

There is, however, a fundamental difference between natural speech and music performance. For the latter, in fact, the timing of gesture units is subjected to an exogenous temporal scheduling, usually dictated by the score tempo mark, or by the global cadence of the performers ensemble. Moreover, an expressive taxonomy - technically referred as "articulation" and explicitly formalized in the score notation - intervenes on the units transitions. Due to its intrinsic multiplicity and to the strict temporal scheduling of events, the coarticulation in the musical domain is also related to anticipation. This refers to the adjustments made to units of motor action in order to accommodate the instantiation of the next units in the sequence.

Anticipation in music performance has been studied in the performance of piano [5] [6], drums [7], and violin [8], whereas coarticulation in relation to chunking has been tackled in [9]. To our knowledge, no work on the subject has been done for the trumpet.

The majority of literature on trumpet performance, and on wind-instrument in general, has focused on the analysis of steady values, such as sound dynamic level, sound spectrum, and blowing pressure thresholds [10], and connected to human respiratory mechanics [11]. Transient analysis has been investigated for the relationship between mouthpiece and instrument's bell pressures [12], and for the tonguing and muscular synergy, with EMG [13][14] and cinefluoric techniques [15]. We are not aware of studies of temporal behavior of intraoral pressure, for single note as well as for coarticulation between notes.

3   Experimental Methods

Protocol. A professional trumpet player was asked to perform a combination of C5 and B4 quarter notes with specific dynamic level and articulatory indications, at a fixed 120 bpm tempo throughout all the recordings. An example of the score is shown in Fig.1. A first set of measurements focused on the execution of a single C5 quarter note with three different dynamical levels (*pp*, *mf* and *ff*), and with a staccato mark and *mf* dynamics. In a second set of measurements, the performer was asked to play a sequence of quarter notes (concatenation of C5 notes and of alternating B4-C5 notes) with *mf* dynamics. The last part of the experiment involved a sequence of alternating C5 and B4 notes with fixed *mf* dynamics. Two consecutive groups of four notes formed the entire sequence.

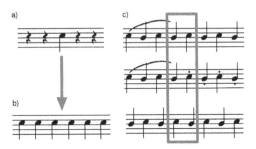

Fig. 1. A subset of the tasks executed by the performer, for the first (a), second (b) and third (c) set of measurements

Each group was assigned a type of articulation: *non-legato*, *legato*, and *staccato*. In all cases no measure bar was presented in the score, so as to avoid any possible dynamic accentuation on the first note of each measure, possiblly due to cognitive rhythmic grouping [16].

Materials and Recording. Intraoral pressure was measured with a catheter tube of approximately 15 cm. The pressure was sensed with a SCX Pressure Sensor, which can afford a 100 microseconds of response time. Pressure and sound were recorded with a NI acquisition card with sampling rate set to 48 kHz. The performer was asked to keep one extremity of the tube proximal to the soft palate, behind the lingua-alveolar place of occlusion for /t/ and /d/ consonants. Each measurement was checked after each take in order to detect possible artifacts in the measurements. The closing of the extremity of the tube by the contact with the internal mouth surfaces or tongue could, indeed, lead to "locks" in pressure, which remains constant during the closing period. Thus, such cases were excluded from the analysis.

4   Analysis Methods

Filtering. The initial 2 seconds long sequences were filtered by a lowpass 6th order Butterwort filter with cutoff frequency equal to 300 Hz. This process removed possible sensor noise as well as the frequency of oscillation of the lips. A comparison between the original and the filtered curves is shown in Fig.2.

Segmentation. For the analysis of single notes, the transition of the intraoral pressure over a background threshold level determined the start and the end of each sequence. The threshold level corresponded to the physical configuration in which the mouth is closed onto the instrument mouthpiece, but neither an airflow, nor a pressure potential are present. We partitioned the single note curves into four zones (as displayed in Fig.2a), each of them corresponding to a different phase in the sound production. In zone 1, the performer starts increasing the pressure in the oral cavity; its tongue closes onto the alveolar ridge, obstructing

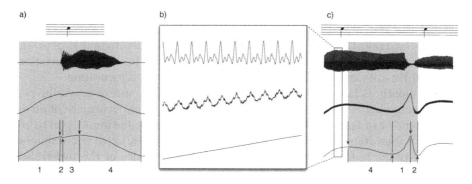

Fig. 2. Segments of recorded data used in the analysis. Detail of sound, original pressure and filtered pressure (a); windows used for coarticulation (b), and single note (c) analysis.

the airflow in the vocal tract. The beginning of zone 2 marks the opening - the detaching of the tongue from the alveolar ridge - of the vocal tract to the airflow. The pressure instantly drops, and the lips begin to oscillate, marking the onset of the note. This process is usually called alveolar stop in phonetics, and it characterizes voiceless plosive consonants such as /t/ and /d/, which are usually used as example in trumpet teaching. Zone 3 encloses the second pressure increase, during which the performer brings the note sound to the sustain phase. Finally, the pressure decreases all along zone 4 for the note closure.

This functional partition helped to identify similar zones in the recordings of concatenated notes. Hence, the coarticulation window built upon a combination of these four zones. The criteria based on the background level to distinguish the end of zone 4 and the beginning of zone 1 for the single note case, has here been substituted by a criteria based on the curve between the two notes. An example of the resulting segment for the transition of two non-legato notes is presented in Fig.2c. For the last part of the experiment the zone 3 of the incoming note has been excluded from the window of analysis. Indeed, as a staccato mark imposes the note to be played with shorter duration, a right boundary on the peak of sustain would have shortened the segment, hence allowing an external factor to interfere on the coarticulation study.

Length Reduction. Last, in order to obtain sequences with an equal number of samples, and to reduce computation time in the analysis process, we extracted 1000 points from each segment, equally spaced in time from the start to the end of the segment.

Functional Data Analysis. The curves were processed with functional analysis techniques provided by the R package of Ramsay and colleagues[1] [17] [18]. Each time-series was converted into a linear combination of 200 equally spaced 6-order B-spline basis functions. Approximation to the original data points is obtained by a combined least squares and roughness penalty, with a λ weighing

---

[1] http://r-forge.r-project.org/projects/fda/

coefficient equal $10^{-0.5}$ on the second derivative, as delivered by the generalized cross validation criterion [17]. The smoothing process with 200 spline basis functions for trajectories of 1000 points, in relation to the original lengths and sampling rates, assures - according to the relation formula in [19] - that variations up to 500 Hz are preserved in the functional smoothed representation.

Subsequently, a landmark registration synchronized the set of curves by performing nonlinear time stretching, ensuring the concurrent occurrence of an arbitrary number of key points among instances. A higher value for λ equal to 10^5 in the previous step was used to register velocities to guarantee equal number of valleys-peaks in the curves, required for the convergence of the registration process.

To investigate the primary modes of variation in the data, we recurred to functional principal component analysis. Roughly, the functional version of PCA replaces variable values with function values, converting the search for eigenvectors of the covariance matrix with the search for orthonormal eigenfunctions of the bivariate covariance function. Each eigenfunction ξ_j represents a form of variation around the mean curve $\bar{x}(t)$, participating in each instance curve $x_i(t)$ with a score given by the integral $\int \xi_t(t)[x_i(t) - \bar{x}(t)]dt$.

5   Results

Single Note. We registered the curves of each class separately, so as to obtain a representative mean curve for each articulation. The resulting means and standard deviations are presented in Fig.3.

A close examination of the plots show that the variability distribution among conditions can be classified into two groups according to shape. In the first case

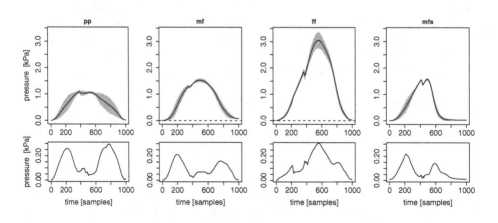

Fig. 3. Mean curves with confidence intervals (upper), and standard deviations (lower) for Pianissimo (pp), Mezzo forte (mf), Fortissimo (ff), and Mezzo forte staccato (mfs) articulations

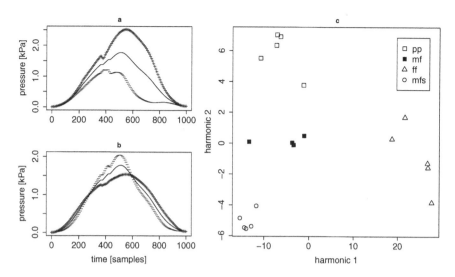

Fig. 4. Mean pressure curve with addition ($++$) and subtraction ($--$) of a suitable multiple of the first (a) and second (b) principal components. Scores of the first two principal components for each original instance.

there is an intensification for the main transitions, for *pp*, *mf*, and *mfs* cases, where pressure is raising before the initiation of the air flow, and is subsequently decreasing for the note closure. In the second case, for *ff* dynamics, the variability increases in the sustain stage of the note.

Absolute variability also changes quantitatively among cases. Values of global coefficients of variation (average values over the curves) for *pp*, *mf*, *mfs* and *ff* are respectively 0.23, 0.12, 0.13 and 0.09, whereas maxima in standard deviation fall at roughly 10% of the pressure maxima for *mf*, *ff*, and *mfs* cases and at 20% for *pp*. Assuming that variability may increase with task demands [20], it seems that *pp* performance represents a higher demanding task compared to the other dynamics, a principle already established for vocal performance [21].

In order to better discriminate the differences of each case, we explored the major modes of variability in the data by means of functional PCA. Fig.4 reports the results for the first two components, which account for 97.4% of the overall variability among the curves. In Fig.4 a) and b), the mean curve is presented, in conjunction with the addition and subtraction of a suitable multiple of the principal components. Plot c) reports the scores of the two principal components for each instance, which distinctly cluster into four groups.

The results of the analysis indicate that the variation in the data, with this set of components, is roughly two-dimensional. The first component, which dominates with 90.6% of the variation, incorporates different typologies of variation: the amplitude of the curve, which operates on the loudness of the note, the curve span, the dynamics of the pressure decrease. However, this component only helps to distinguish the *ff* instances from the other articulations. In order to

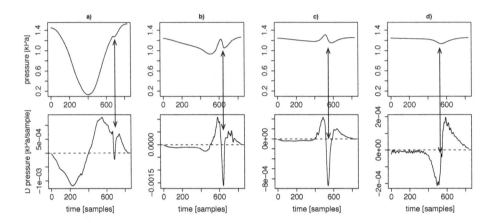

Fig. 5. Pressure curves (upper) and first derivatives (lower) for coarticulation. Synthesized case (a), non-legato transition between two C5 notes (b), non-legato transition between C5 and B4 notes (c), legato transition between C5 and B4 notes (d). Double arrows indicate the sound onsets of the incoming notes.

differentiate the remaining classes, one needs to consider the second component, which accounts for 6.8% of the variation, and which represents variation on the curve narrowness. A positive contribution of the second component on the mean compresses the curve peak, widening and lowering its shape, and spans uniformly the *pp*, *mf*, and *mfs* examples.

Coarticulation. The concurrent activation of primitives in the muscular force field has been shown to be the result of roughly linear vectorial superposition [22][23]. Under the assumption that intraoral pressure approximates to a uniform scalar field inside the oral cavity, the transposition of this principle to our case would resolve into a scalar superposition. We would expect that, in zones of pressure overlap, the overall curve should be approximated by a direct sum of two single note curves.

We therefore compared the recorded coarticulation segments - which comprised zones 4,1,2,3 as of Fig.2 - to a simulated coarticulation profile, obtained by linearly superposing the real recordings of two isolated notes. The superposition was built upon the mean curve of *mf* C5 single note as follows: the curve was first resized, in order for the corresponding sound envelope length to match between the single and concatenated occurrences; it was then segmented into two pieces at the pressure maximum, where the decrease in pressure begins - start of zone 4. A shifted version of the first segment has been linearly superposed to the second one, so as to build a max-to-max window of the same length as the one segmented from the real recordings. The cut-and-paste operation has been performed by adjusting the spline coefficients level, to maintain continuity in derivatives for the resulting curve, and therefore to assure a maximal smooth

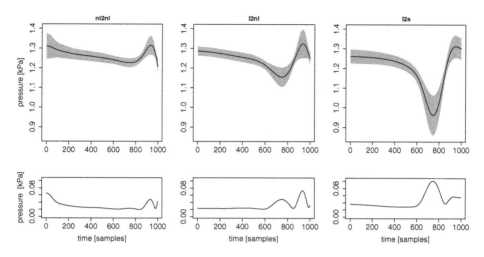

Fig. 6. Mean curves with confidence intervals (upper), and standard deviations (lower) for non-legato to non-legato (nl2nl), non-legato to legato (nl2l), and legato to staccato (l2s) coarticulations

transition. The resulting curve and the real coarticulation recordings are shown in Fig.5. The figure shows that the synthesized curve (case a) is significantly different from the real curves (b,c and d). First, the pressure minimum is lower in the synthesized curve. Second, the first part of the pressure's first derivative is relatively constant in the real cases, whereas this is not the case in the synthesized curve. And third, the intermediate pressure peak is almost absent in the synthesized curve. In a dynamical perspective, the musician appears to hold further the previous note, delaying to the very last instants the instantiation of the new note.

In what follows we will show that coarticulation between two units is also affected by preceding or following units. The segments analyzed correspond to the grey window of Fig.2c (sequential union of zones 4,1 and 2), extrapolated from the transition between the fourth and fifth notes during the performances of the scores in Fig.1c. According to the notation in the scores, the transition in the three occurrences should be performed in a similar fashion. Indeed, the legato mark enclosing the outgoing note only regulates the transition with its predecessor, and such transition is not considered in our segment. And the staccato mark on the incoming note only behaves on its last part, which also is omitted from our segment.

The registered mean curves and their standard deviation, synchronized by a collective landmark registration process, are reported in Fig.6. The three cases manifest a clear individual profile, with an increasing (relatively for *nl2nl*, *l2nl*, and *l2s*) negative spurt just before the instantiation of the incoming note. The peak's amplitudes correlate with the peaks in standard deviation, which attain between 20% and 30% of the peak amplitude. A minimum level in standard

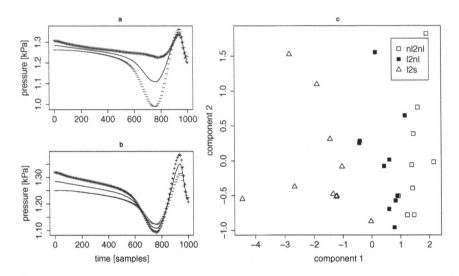

Fig. 7. Mean pressure curve with addition $(++)$ and subtraction $(--)$ of a suitable multiple of the first (a) and second (b) principal components, for coarticulation records. Scores of the first two principal components for each original instance.

deviation equal to 2% of the average pressure level, and common to all records, suggests inconsistency in the level when playing *mf* among executions.

In order to analytically locate the principal modes of variation, we again turned to functional PCA, whose results are presented in Fig.7. The first component (a), which accounts for 74.5% of the variation, represents the amount of pressure valley, while the second (b), which accounts for 16.5% of the variation, represents variability in the steady level and slightly in spurt over/undershoot. The plot for components' scores (c) tells us that the first component suffices for classification purposes, giving evidence that the amount in pressure valley can explain the different coarticulation behaviors.

Principal curve analysis for higher order derivatives did not improve the clustering results.

6   Conclusions

Functional data modeling represents a promising tool for synthesis purposes. First, the spline basis representation allows to easily smoothly join consecutive curves. An arbitrary long sequence of gesture units can then be built by connecting single note and coarticulation segments. The presence of end-point level differences between segments could be eliminated by using a dual representation as in [24], so to preserve the same pressure (and therefore sound output) level among notes repetitions. Second, as shown by the low dimensional set of eigenfunctions, functional PCA allows for the storage of a reduced set of curves (means and dominant eigenfunctions), but with the possibility to span the set of original real recordings, or unrecorded but plausible instances, via their linear combination. Further investigation have to be done on the verification of original curves reconstruction trough principal functions, and on the relation between components' scores and task practice [25].

In the analysis of single notes, we showed how a single gesture unit exhibits systematically different behaviors, depending on the dynamic level required for the sound outcome. On the basis of a twofold shape for variability distribution, we hypothesize that two motor control programs may be available for the completion of the task: a continuous feed-back guided control for the production of *pp*, *mf*, and *mfs* notes, and a pre-planned movement control for the *ff* performance. The first movement strategy is employed to target a value with a maximal accuracy in the endpoint, that is with minimum steady-state error and overshoot issues. In practice, the oral and respiratory systems have to raise the pressure at the minimum level necessary to instantiate the oscillation of the lips. The performer's skill resides in the organization of the muscles synergy, in order to reach the target level at a specific time instant, and starting from different initial configurations. He continuously adjusts the forces applied to the muscles - this is confirmed as well by a higher number of acceleration zero crossings - transferring variability from the endpoint trajectory outcome to the whole movement pattern. Variability as a result of compensation has been defined as "adaptive variability" [26], and it has been found in more general motor tasks [27]. The second control strategy - the one which underlies the ff performance - draws similarities with ballistic movement theory: a fast, preprogrammed and impulsive movement, which lacks of on-line control, and whose purpose is to reach a target in the shortest time. This motor program would explain the higher variability in the sustain stage, for the occurrence of target undershoot/overshoot. In order to validate these hypothesis, however, one should also consider the relation between intraoral pressure variability and sound variability on a perceptive scale, for the performer regulates expiratory airflow rate according to auditory feedback [28].

In the second part of this work, we provided evidence that further complexity is added when individual gestures are interconnected or overlap each other in a continuous sequence of units. At a local level, we gave evidence of the inappropriateness of linear superposition for the simulation of coarticulation between two notes. The transition revealed a compund interaction between the two units, by lenghtening the end of the first and adding extra movement (the increase for the pressure peak) to the beginning of the second. At a contextual level, results establish the hypothesis that the surrounding units exert influence on the local coarticulation. Anticipatory behavior and memory effects are the most plausible cause for regulating differently the three conditions. On one hand, anticipation in the preparation of a staccato note before its instantiation, as shown by the difference between *l2nl* and *l2s* curves. On the other hand, memory effects for the use of previous legato when switching to non-legato articulations, as evident from the comparison between *nl2nl* and *l2nl* curves. Performance memory has proved to transfer between consecutive tasks [29]. Here, however, the performer seems to "overreact" to a possible transfer of performance skill, emphasizing the abruptness in transition when departing from a legato context, and performing what would behave as non-legato transition with increased overshoot.

Acknowledgments. We would like to thank Fabien Norbert, Gérard Bertrand and "Instrumental Acoustics" team for their help in this study.

References

1. Hardcastle, W.J., Hewlett, N.: Coarticulation: theory, data, and techniques. Cambridge University Press, Cambridge (1999)
2. Gineke, T.H., Hendriks, P., Andringa, T.: Why don't you see what i mean? prospects and limitations of current automatic sign recognition research. Sign Language Studies 6(4), 416–437 (2006)
3. Farnetani, E.: Coarticulation and connected speech process (1999)
4. Fowler, C.: Coarticulation and theories of extrinsic timing control. Journal of Phonetics 8, 113–133 (1980)
5. Engel, K., Flanders, M., Soechting, J.: Anticipatory and sequential motor control in piano playing. Experimental brain research 113(2), 189–199 (1997)
6. Loehr, J., Palmer, C.: Cognitive and biomechanical influences in pianists' finger tapping. Experimental brain research 178(4), 518–528 (2007)
7. Dahl, S.: The playing of an accent - preliminary observations from temporal and kinematic analysis of percussionists. Journal of New Music Research 29(3), 225–234 (2000)
8. Rasamimanana, N.H., Bevilacqua, F.: Effort-based analysis of bowing movements: evidence of anticipation effects. The Journal of New Music Research (2009) (in press)
9. Gody, R., Jensenius, A., Nymoen, K.: Production and perception of goal-points and coarticulations in music. In: Proceedings of Acoustics 2008 (2008)
10. Fletcher, N.H., Tarnopolsky, A.: Blowing pressure, power, and spectrum in trumpet playing. Journal of Acoutical Society of America 105(2), 874–881 (1999)
11. Bouhuys, A.: Lung volumes and breathing patterns in wind-instrument players. Journal of Applied Physiology 19(1), 967–975 (1964)
12. Campbell, M., Bromage, S., Chick, J.: Attack transients on lip reed instruments. Journal of Acoustical Society of America 117(4), 2477 (2005)
13. White, E., Basmajian, J.: Electromyography of lip muscles and their role in trumpet playing. Journal of Applied Physiology 35(6), 892–897 (1973)
14. Berger, K.: Electromyographic recording during wind instrument performance. Annals of the New York Academy of Sciences 155(1), 297–302 (1968)
15. Merriman, L.C., Meidt, J.A.: A cinefluorographic investigation of brass instrument performance. Journal of Research in Music Education 16(1), 31–38 (1968)
16. Cooper, G., Meyer, L.B.: The Rhythmic Structure of Music. University of Chicago Press, Chicago (1960)
17. Ramsay, J.O., Silverman, B.W.: Functional Data Analysis. Springer, Heidelberg (2005)
18. Ramsay, J., Hooker, G., Graves, S.: Functional Data Analysis with R and MATLAB. Springer, Heidelberg (2009)
19. Koenig, L.L., Lucero, J.C., Perlman, E.: Speech production variability in fricatives of children and adults: results of functional data analysis. The Journal of the Acoustical Society of America 124(5), 3158–3170 (2008)

20. Yan, J.H., Thomas, J.R., Stelmach, G.E., Thomas, K.T.: Developmental features of rapid aiming arm movements across the lifespan. Journal of Motor Behavior 32(2), 121–140 (2000)
21. Coward, H.: Choral Technique and Interpretation. H.W. Gray (1914)
22. Bizzi, E., Giszterb, S.F., Loeba, E., Mussa Ivaldi, F.A., Saltiela, P.: Modular organization of motor behavior in the frog's spinal cord. Trends in Neurosciences 18(10), 442–446 (1995)
23. Bizzi, E., d Avella, A., Saltiel, P., Tresch, M.: Modular organization of spinal motor systems. The Neuroscientist 8(5), 437–442 (2002)
24. Ramsay, J.O., Munhall, K.G., Gracco, V.L., Ostry, D.J.: Functional data analyses of lip motion. Journal of Acoustical Society of America 99(6), 3718–3727 (1996)
25. Sanger, T.D.: Human arm movements described by a low-dimensional superposition of principal component. The Journal of Neuroscience 20, 1066–1072 (2000)
26. Kazutoshi, K., Tatsuyuki, O.: Adaptive variability in skilled human movements. Information and Media Technologies 3(2), 409–420 (2008)
27. Darling, W., Cooke, W.G.: Movement related emgs become more variable during learning of fast accurate movements. Journal of Motor Behavior 19(3), 311–331 (1987)
28. Bouhuys, A.: Airflow control by auditory feedback: Respiratory mechanics and wind instruments. Science 154(750), 797–799 (1966)
29. Palmer, C.: Nature of memory for music performance skills, pp. 39–53 (2006)

Gesture Saliency: A Context-Aware Analysis

Matei Mancas[1], Donald Glowinski[2], Gualtiero Volpe[2],
Paolo Coletta[2], and Antonio Camurri[2]

[1] University of Mons, F.P.Ms/IT Research Center/TCTS Lab,
31, Bd. Dolez, 7000 Mons, Belgium
Matei.Mancas@umons.ac.be
[2] University of Genoa, INFOMUS Lab, Italy
{Donald.Glowinski, Gualtiero.Volpe, Antonio.Camurri,
Paolo.Coletta}@unige.it

Abstract. This paper presents a motion attention model that aims at analyzing gesture saliency using context-related information at three different levels. At the first level, motion features are compared in the spatial context of the current video frame; at the intermediate level, salient behavior is analyzed on a short temporal context; at the third level, computation of saliency is extended to longer time windows. An attention/saliency index is computed at the three levels based on an information theory approach. This model can be considered as a preliminary step towards context-aware expressive gesture analysis.

Keywords: Visual attention, expressive gesture, context-aware analysis.

1 Introduction

Objects and situations can lead our attention because of their emotional values. Neuroimaging and behavioral studies suggest that emotional signals may affect the allocation of attentional resources either to facilitate performance in a current task or to interrupt an ongoing activity and redirect attention towards a more relevant event [17]. In the context of social communication, body gestures appear to be a relevant channel in the human judgment of affective behavior. Discrete emotions like anger or attitudinal states like boredom can be communicated through full-body or body-parts movements such as the hands and head's ones. These types of gesture that convey an emotional message are called expressive gestures [4].

A better understanding of bodily communication processes can actually lead to the development of intelligent/affective computing that could anticipate people intention without request of explicit instructions by considering the spatial or temporal context of their behavior [16]. Affective gestural analysis, however, often applies to a single user which is manually selected (e.g., at the start-up of the system or when the user enters the area the system is operating on). In addition, the dynamics of the expressive gesture features is rarely considered. The naturalness of the human-computer interaction could highly benefit from the possibility to dynamically select the person to carry analysis on or from the possibility to adapt and personalize analysis to the context and to the current behavior of a user. We hypothesize that a system which

S. Kopp and I. Wachsmuth (Eds.): GW 2009, LNAI 5934, pp. 146–157, 2010.

aims to recognize emotions on the basis of expressive gesture could be enhanced and applied in multi-user scenarios if it reproduces some of the attentional mechanisms present in humans. The goal of this paper is to investigate the relationship between part of the human attention, which is here computationally modeled, and the way to automatically extract expressive cues from human gestures.

After a state of the art of computational attention models, we recall the notion of expressive gesture. A second section will describe how an automatic saliency index is modeled and implemented to highlight which movements may be the most salient for a human observer. In a third section, the application of motion attention is achieved on several scenarios that exemplify the three contexts of the analysis (spatial, short and long-term). Finally, we conclude by the findings on the relationship between gestures expressivity analysis and computational attention algorithms.

2   State of the Art

2.1   Computational Attention or Automatic Modeling of Human Attention

The aim of computational attention is to automatically predict human attention on multimodal data such as sounds, images, video sequences, smell or taste, etc... The term *attention* refers to the whole attentional process that allows one to focus on some stimuli at the expense of others. Human attention mainly consists of two processes: a bottom-up and a top-down one. Bottom-up attention uses low-level signal features to find the most salient or outstanding objects. Top-down attention uses a priori knowledge about the scene or task-oriented knowledge in order to modify (inhibit or enhance) the bottom-up saliency. While numerous models were provided for attention on still images, time-evolving two-dimensional signals such as videos have been less investigated. Nevertheless, some of the authors providing static attention approaches generalized their models to videos, but very few to audio or time-evolving feature signals (for a detailed review, see [11]). Most of these methods provide bottom-up attention approaches. To our knowledge, a majority of these computational models focuses on low-level motion features (e.g., displacement of people). We suggest in this paper that computational models would gain considering higher-level motion features related to full-body movements to better capture the expressive gestures that characterize the communication of an emotion. Our approach is able to easily adapt to different spatial, short and long temporal contexts.

2.2   Gesture Expressivity and Attention

According to Kurtenbach and Hulteen gesture can be defined as "a movement of the body that contains information" [8]. Thus, gestures can be named expressive since the information they carry is an expressive content, i.e., content related to the emotional sphere. A multilayered framework for automatic expressive gesture analysis was proposed by Camurri et al. [4]. In this framework, expressive gestures are described with a set of motion features that specify how the expressive content is encoded. Different attempts can be found in literature to map a set of expressive gesture features with one of the emotional dimensions that are considered to describe the entire space of conscious emotional experience [18] which are valence and activation.

For example activation dimension has been mapped to expressive features such as the amount of energy of a person [3]. However, the main shortcoming of expressive gesture analysis is the scarce consideration of the context in which expressive gestures take place. The context we focus on has to be considered both related to the temporal dynamics of a motion feature and to the spatial context of this feature if the behavior analysis of more than one user is performed.

First studies related to the context-aware analysis of expressivity which established a relationship between the arousal level of an emotion and the uncertainty of a visual stimulus can be found in [2]. Mehrabian and Russell formulated the information rate-arousal hypothesis and confirmed a linear correlation between information rates of a real environment and emotion arousal [15]. These studies put in evidence that the saliency of an event can be related to the novelty of an expressive content.

3   The Model of Motion Attention

3.1   A Rarity-Based Approach

As we already stated in [9] and [14] a feature does not attract attention by itself: bright and dark, locally contrasted areas or not, red or blue can equally attract human attention depending on their context. In the same way, motion can be as interesting as the lack of motion depending on the context. The main cue which involves bottom-up attention is the rarity and contrast of a feature in a given context. The features considered in this paper are speed, and the motion and contraction indexes. They are described in the presentation of the experiments in the next section.

A low-computational-cost quantification of rarity was achieved referring to the notion of self-information. Let us note m_i a message containing an amount of information. This message is part of a message set M. The bottom-up attention attracted by m_i is quantified by its self-information $I(m_i)$ which will be called here *saliency index*:

$$I(m_i) = -\log(p(m_i)) \tag{1}$$

where $p(m_i)$ is the occurrence likelihood of the message m_i within the message set M. We estimate $p(m_i)$ as a combination of the global rarity of m_i within M and its global contrast compared to the other messages from M. Mathematically, $p(mi)$ is the result of a two-terms combination:

$$p(m_i) = A(m_i) \times B(m_i) \tag{2}$$

The $A(m_i)$ term is the direct use of a histogram to compute the occurrence probability of the message m_i in the context M:

$$A(m_i) = \frac{H(m_i)}{Card(M)} \tag{3}$$

where $H(m_i)$ is the value of the histogram H for message m_i and $Card(M)$ the cardinality of M. The M set quantification provides the sensibility of $A(m_i)$: a smaller quantification value will let messages close to each others to be seen as the same.

$B(m_i)$ quantifies the global contrast of a message m_i on the context M:

$$B(m_i) = 1 - \frac{\sum_{j=1}^{Card(M)} |m_i - m_j|}{(Card(M) - 1) \times Max(M)} \qquad (4)$$

If a message is very different from all the others, $B(m_i)$ will be low so the occurrence likelihood $p(m_i)$ will be lower and the message attention will be higher. $B(m_i)$ was introduced to avoid the cases where two messages have the same occurrence value, hence the same attention value using $A(m_i)$ but in fact one of the two is very different from the others while the other one is just a little different. The saliency index (or motion attention index, $I(m_i)$) operates at three levels corresponding to three different time scales: up to 1s (instantaneous motion attention), from 1s to 3s (short-term motion attention), more than 3s (long-term motion attention).

3.2 Instantaneous Level

Let us consider a collective context, e.g., a group with interacting people. Motion features (e.g., speed, direction) characterizing each moving person are compared at each instant. Salient motion behavior (e.g., one person speed very different from the others) immediately pops-out and attracts attention. This refers to pre-attentive human processes, usually faster than 200 milliseconds. In our approach, motion saliency detection at instantaneous level is computed over time intervals of 200ms – 1s.

3.3 Short-Term Level

Each participant selected in the previous instantaneous level may have his motion features analyzed over short-term time intervals from 2 to 3 seconds. This level refers to the human sensory memory (SM), in the range of 2 - 3 seconds [1]. This stage goal is to ensure that the selected object remains outstanding compared to its past behavior or not. Information from SM goes then to the short-term memory (STM). The capacity of STM, in terms of tracked objects, is limited to about 4 simultaneous occurrences of instantaneous rarity [5].

3.4 Long-Term Attention Modulation

The long-term memory (LTM) [1] component of the model processes the saliency index in a time interval from several seconds to much longer periods (related to the application time scale). The output is a modification of the instantaneous attention indexes in such interval according to their considered recurrence. The attention amplitude map in the different locations of the observed scene along time is progressively built. This leads to the definition of areas, which capture attention more than others: e.g., a street accumulates more attention than a grassy area. The scene can thus be segmented into several areas of *attention accumulation* and the motion in these areas can be summarized by only one motion vector per area. If a moving object passes through one of these areas and it has a motion vector similar to the one summarizing this area, its attention is inhibited (usual motion). If this object is outside those segmented attention areas or its motion vector is different from the one summarizing the area where it passes through, the moving object will be assigned with high attention (novel motion).

4 Application to Analysis of Expressive Gesture

4.1 Instantaneous Motion Attention

We tested the motion attention model and the saliency index it provides during a dance master-class to consider the emergence of a salient behavior in the components of a group. The feature taken into account here was Motion Index. This index is a measure of the overall amount of motion detected by a video camera and is obtained by integrating in time the variations of the body silhouette (called Silhouette Motion Images - SMI). In this dance application, the value of the saliency index was computed for each dancer and compared in the spatial context of the current video frame. This salient index value controlled the transparency of the silhouette of the dancer, which was extracted from the live video from an infra-red video-camera using a multi-blob tracking technique. The higher was the dancer's saliency index, the more opaque was its silhouette. Figure 1 shows some results. On the left image, the dancer located in the middle stays still whereas the two others are running: his behavior is salient relatively to the others. On the right image, the dancer, located in the right, is moving at a higher speed than the two others, thus having the most salient behavior. A following discussion with dancers put in evidence that this algorithm provide telltale signs of the onset or progression of their movements and forced them to be aware of the other's motion pattern. A saliency index based feedback may foster a higher interaction in social and collective behaviors. Moreover, from a psychological point of view, in a collective context all the participants naturally tend to reach the dominant emotion through emotional contagion processes [7].

If a minority of participants exhibit a different, salient behavior, this is worthy of attention because it shows at least a higher perseverance in delivering their expressive message.

Fig. 1. Two snapshots of two situations observed during the dance master-class. In both situations the silhouette which appears on the video in the background is the one of the dancer which has the rarest behavior with respect to the two others.

4.2 Short-Term Motion Attention

The saliency index was tested over short temporal periods on expressive features such as the motion index (MI) and the contraction index (CI) related to individual full-body movements. The CI measures the amount of contraction of the body with respect to its baricenter (i.e., contraction is high when the posture is such that limbs are kept near to the baricenter, e.g., arms along the body). An actor performing two sequences of movements was recorded. Each one of these sequences emphasizes a particular gestural characteristics: (i) movement activity (MI-performance: figure 2, right box) and (ii) arms' extension with respect to the body (CI-performance: figure 2, left box).

The two videos were presented to 16 participants (six males and 10 females, with a mean age of 26) who pointed out moments of novelty in the sequence of movements by pressing the space bar of a computer keyboard. Stimuli were displayed and participants' responses were recorded and time-logged to the video using the EyesWeb-Mobile platform [6]. Participant's motion sequence segmentations were collected and then compared with the automatic segmentation obtained with the saliency index algorithm. More details about the experiment can be found in [13].

As proposed in [12] and [13], the mono-dimensional signal that characterizes saliency over time was computed on the spectrogram of each expressive feature (CI and MI). The following procedure was applied:

- computation of the signal Fourier transform on a 50 ms sliding temporal window
- division of the resulting spectrogram into 128 frequency bands
- quantification of each frequency band into 16 bins
- selection of a time window on which applying the saliency index (Eq. 1): 128 saliency indexes corresponding to each band are obtained
- integration on the lower frequency bands in order to neglect the effect of noise and to obtain a mono-dimensional signal characterizing feature signal saliency

A preliminary analysis presented in [13] showed that for both expressive gestural features (MI and CI) the automatic saliency index with a temporal window of 2 s and a bin number of 16 provided a segmentation close to the human's one.

A comparison between the human observers' segmentation variability (figure 3, bottom row, dotted red line) and the one provided by the saliency index (figure 3, bottom row, blue line) showed a very high correlation with 100% of precision (a measure of fidelity) and recall (a measure of completeness) for the MI feature and 100% and 95% of precision and recall respectively for the CI feature.

Fig. 2. Snapshots of the CI (left box) and MI (right box) performance

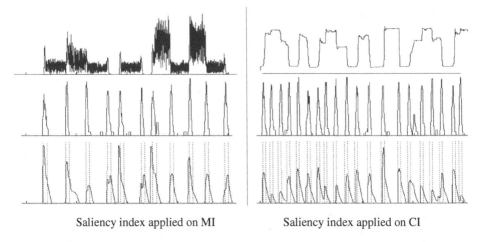

|Saliency index applied on MI|Saliency index applied on CI|

Fig. 3. From top to bottom: initial feature measures (top images), participants' mean segmentation (middle images) automatic saliency index segmentation (in blue) and participants' mean variability in dotted red line (bottom images)

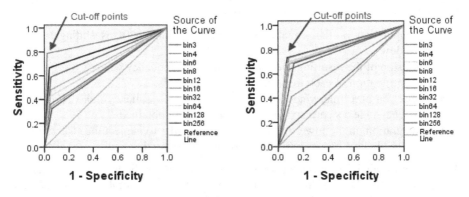

Fig. 4. ROC curve of the saliency index implemented with ten different bin values (MI feature)

Fig. 5. ROC curve of the saliency index implemented with ten different bin values (CI feature)

In this paper, we completed the evaluation of the algorithm segmentation with an in-depth statistical analysis. We wanted in particular to observe how the performance can be related to the bin number used for quantifying the frequency bands in the algorithm. This bin number specifies the sensibility of the algorithm to distinguish between different events. Receiver operating characteristics (ROC) curve were employed to assess the saliency index algorithm performance with respect to human segmentation (*ground truth*).

The saliency index was tested with 10 different bin number values from 3 to 256. Analysis of the ROC curves (figures 4 and 5) shows that changing the bin number considerably affect the resulting classification on both MI and CI features (i.e., the distinction between rare/non-rare events). Considering in particular the area under the curve (AUC), the algorithm with a bin number of 16 (bin16) can be considered a good compromise as it shows the best performance in MI (AUC=0.88 ± 0.01 (95% C.I. (*confidence interval*) 0.86-0.91), *p*=0.000) and the second best performance (but very close to the best performance) in the CI (Contraction Index feature) case (AUC=0.83± 0.008 (95% C.I. (*confidence interval*) 0.80-0.84), *p*=0.000).

At the cut-off points for the MI feature (figure 4) the algorithm correctly identified 95.4 % of the rare event indicated by subjects (accuracy). Sensitivity (true positive rate or the rate of salient events which are detected as so by the saliency index) is of 78.8 % and the specificity (true negative rate or the rate of non salient events which are labeled as non-salient by the saliency index) is of 97.6 %. At the cut-off points for the CI feature (figure 5), the algorithm correctly identified 87.5 % of the rare event indicated by subjects (accuracy). The sensitivity is of 70.9% and the specificity of 92.4 %.

4.3 Long-Term Motion Attention

For long-term motion attention, preliminary techniques were developed to compute the rarity for the direction and speed of participants observed in different regions of the space. Generalizing the work started in [10], motion history images (MHI) were used to compute the position, the direction and the velocity of participants over long-time scales (e.g., 4 minutes). The saliency index computed over these features allowed to build a model of the scene highlighting the regions where rare behaviors were observed. The model is obtained using an increment and a decrement function so that at each frame, when a participant is observed with a certain speed and direction which is already dominant for the considered region, the saliency index for the pixels in the region is decreased, otherwise, it is increased.

If current motion has the same features as the model at the same locations, the motion detection will be inhibited: it is an already seen one, it is not rare, and thus it is not worthy of attention. If motion occurs with different features as those from the corresponding model, the motion detection will not be inhibited: it is a novel movement which is rare and which should attract attention. Figure 6 shows snapshots of a recording session in a class room where most of the participants were asked to move along predetermined paths while few others moved with different velocities, directions or positions as the majority.

A quantitative validation of the long-term attention model was achieved with a dancer who walked along a 6x4 meters space in various directions and at different speeds. As shown in figures 7 and 8, the dancer performed six different paths. Three models (containing information about position, motion direction, and velocity) were computed for the first three more regular paths (see figure 7). An inhibition rate (*IR*) was computed to describe how much of the initial detected motion of the dancer was inhibited by the long term attention model.

IR values ranged from 0 (the detected motion is inhibited because it is similar to the model) to 1 (the detected motion is different from the model and it can be considered as salient). The procedure is detailed in the following pseudo-code:

Fig. 6. Left column, the images show the detected motion of the participants (in red), the motion vector of the model (in green) and the current motion vector of the frame (in blue). Right column: salient motion of the participants (in red) detected after the model was applied (participants have different motion directions, different velocities or they are located in positions where few motion was detected).

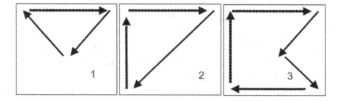

Fig. 7. The three regular paths followed by the dancer were used as models (model 1, 2 and 3)

```
a= 0.6, Eps = 10^-5
Nb_frames_salient_motion=0, Nb_frames_detected_motion=0
if sum(moving_pixels_after_inhibition)/sum(initial_moving_pixels)>a
        Nb_frames_salient_motion = Nb_frames_salient_motion+1
if sum(initial_moving_pixels)>0
        Nb_frames_detected_motion = Nb_frames_detected_motion+1
IR = Nb_frames_salient_motion /(Nb_frames_detected_motion+Eps)
```

Table 1 presents the inhibition rate (IR) values obtained through the application of the long-term attention models 1, 2 and 3 when the dancer moved along the paths 1, 2 and 3 (see figure 7). When the performed trajectory is close to the model used to analyze it (e.g., model 1 applied to path 1), the inhibition rate (IR) values tend to 0. On the opposite, IR values tend to 1 when the performed path differs from the model (e.g., model 1 applied to path 2).

Table 1. The comparison of the referent three models (1, 2, 3) with the three corresponding paths (1, 2, 3) shows a low inhibition rate (IR) value when matching between model and path is high and a high IR values in the opposite case

	Path 1	Path 2	Path 3
Model 1	**0.03**	0.35	0.35
Model 2	0.15	**0.01**	0.20
Model 3	0.11	0.13	**0.07**

Table 2 shows the inhibition rate was very low for the portions of the paths 5, 6 and 7 (see figure 8), that correspond to trajectories learnt by the model (see figure 8, blue lines). The inhibition rate was on the opposite very high for novel/salient motion that was not considered by the models (see figure 8, red lines).

Table 2. IR values of paths 5, 6 and 7 when motion is already detected (see figure 8, blue line) and when motion is salient (see figure 8, red line)

	Path 5	Path 6	Path 7
Already detected motion	**0.04**	**0.03**	**0.05**
Novel/Salient motion	0.57	0.68	0.34

Top-down information let us pointing out the novel motion on one side, but it is also interesting in detecting already seen motion patterns. This second, long-term approach is related to task-driven top-down attention.

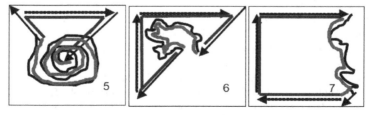

Fig. 8. In black: trajectories 5, 6 and 7. In blue: already detected motion of the models 1, 2 and 3 from figure 7. In red: novel/salient motion.

5 Conclusion

Context-related information is naturally captured by humans through attentional mechanisms and help to focus limited visual resources on the most salient aspects of the visual scene. Our saliency index draws upon these human bottom-up attentional processes. It relieves on the saliency of user's behavior by computing the probability of occurrence and contrast of the expressive features values during instantaneous, short-term, and long-term time periods. We demonstrated that human attention related algorithms are able to set attention focus on the person with a different behavior compared to the others, to a person who exhibits changes regarding his own behavior history, but also to people whose behavior is different from the one of the majority of the people passing in the same areas. Our algorithm has been successfully tested in applications dealing with one or several participants simultaneously. The saliency index algorithm can be considered as a first step to provide real-time multimodal interfaces with context-aware abilities and to adapt them efficiently to multi-user scenarios.

We plan to further investigate the potentialities of the saliency index as a descriptor of human expressivity in three directions: (i) by applying it to a more sophisticated set of expressive features (e.g., fluidity, impulsiveness) (ii) by selecting the relevant expressive features according to their rarity score (iii) by analyzing how a visual feedback computed on the saliency index can affect user behavior (e.g., whether it fosters expressive behavior).

Acknowledgements

This work was partially supported by the Numediart project (www.numediart.org) funded by the Walloon region, Belgium. The authors thank to Loïc Reboursière and André Serre-Milan for the dancer video acquisition. Finally, this work has also been partially supported by the Walloon region with projects BIRADAR, ECLIPSE, and DREAMS, and by the EU-ICT Project SAME (Sound And Music for Everyone Everyday Everywhere Every way, www.sameproject.eu).

References

[1] Atkinson, R.C., Shiffrin, R.M.: Human memory: A proposed system and its control processes. The psychology of learning and motivation: Advances in research and theory 2, 89–195 (1968)
[2] Berlyne, D.E., Berlyne, D.E.: Studies in the new experimental aesthetics (1974)
[3] Camurri, A., Lagerlöf, I., Volpe, G.: Recognizing emotion from dance movement: Comparison of spectator recognition and automated techniques. International Journal of Human-Computer Studies 59, 213–225 (2003)
[4] Camurri, A., Volpe, G., De Poli, G., Leman, M.: Communicating Expressiveness and Affect in Multimodal Interactive Systems. IEEE Multimedia, pp. 43–53 (2005)
[5] Cowan, N.: The magical number 4 in short-term memory: A reconsideration of mental storage capacity. Behavioral and Brain Sciences 24(01), 87–114 (2001)

[6] Glowinski, D., Bracco, F., Chiorri, C., Atkinson, A., Coletta, P., Camurri, A.: An investigation of the minimal visual cues required to recognize emotions from human upper-body movements. In: Proceedings of ACM International Conference on Multimodal Interfaces (ICMI), Workshop on Affective Interaction in Natural Environments (AFFINE). ACM, New York (2008)

[7] Hatfield, E., Cacioppo, J.T., Rapson, R.L.: Emotional contagion Studies in emotion and social interaction. Editions de la Maison des sciences de l'homme (1994)

[8] Kurtenbach, G., Hulteen, E.A.: Gestures in Human-Computer Communication. The Art of Human-Computer Interface Design, 309–317 (1992)

[9] Mancas, M.: Computational attention: Towards attentive computers. Similar edition (2007); CIACO University Distributors

[10] Mancas, M.: Image perception: Relative influence of bottom-up and top-down attention (2008)

[11] Mancas, M.: Relative influence of bottom-up and top-down attention. In: Paletta, L., Tsotsos, J.K. (eds.) WAPCV 2009. LNCS, vol. 5395, pp. 212–226. Springer, Heidelberg (2009)

[12] Mancas, M., Couvreur, L., Gosselin, B., Macq, B.: Computational attention for event detection. In: Proceedings of ICVS Workshop on Computational Attention & Applications, WCAA 2007 (2007)

[13] Mancas, M., Glowinski, D., Volpe, G., Camurri, A., Breteche, J., Demeyer, P.: Real-time motion attention and expressive gesture interfaces. Journal On Multimodal User Interfaces, JMUI (2009)

[14] Mancas, M., Mancas-Thillou, C., Gosselin, B., Macq, B.: A rarity-based visual attention map–application to texture description. In: Proceedings of IEEE International Conference on Image Processing, pp. 445–448 (2007)

[15] Mehrabian, A., Russell, J.A.: An approach to environmental psychology (1974)

[16] Picard, R.W.: Affective Computing. MIT Press, Cambridge (1997)

[17] Vuilleumier, P., Armony, J., Dolan, R.: Reciprocal links between emotion and attention. In: Friston, K.J., Frith, C.D., Dolan, R.J., Price, C., Ashburner, J., Penny, W., Zeki, S., Frackowiak, R.S.J. (eds.) Human brain functions, pp. 419–444 (2003)

[18] Watson, D., Clark, L.A., Tellegen, A.: Development and validation of brief measures of positive and negative affect: The PANAS scales. Journal of Personality and Social Psychology 54(6), 1063–1070 (1988)

Towards a Gesture-Sound Cross-Modal Analysis

Baptiste Caramiaux, Frédéric Bevilacqua, and Norbert Schnell

Real Time Musical Interactions Team,
IRCAM, CNRS - STMS,
1 Place Igor Stravinsky, 75004 PARIS, France
{baptiste.caramiaux,frederic.bevilacqua,norbert.schnell}@ircam.fr

Abstract. This article reports on the exploration of a method based on canonical correlation analysis (CCA) for the analysis of the relationship between gesture and sound in the context of music performance and listening. This method is a first step in the design of an analysis tool for gesture-sound relationships. In this exploration we used motion capture data recorded from subjects performing free hand movements while listening to short sound examples. We assume that even though the relationship between gesture and sound might be more complex, at least part of it can be revealed and quantified by linear multivariate regression applied to the motion capture data and audio descriptors extracted from the sound examples. After outlining the theoretical background, the article shows how the method allows for pertinent reasoning about the relationship between gesture and sound by analysing the data sets recorded from multiple and individual subjects.

Keywords: Gesture analysis, Gesture-Sound Relationship, Sound Perception, Canonical Correlation Analysis.

1 Introduction

Recently, there has been an increasing interest in the multimodal analysis of the expression of emotion as well as expressivity in music. Several works reveal that motor expression components like body gestures are always accompanying other modalities [23]. For instance, human face-to-face communication often combines speech with non-verbal modalities like gestures. In this context, multimodal analysis reveals co-expressive elements that play an important role for the communication of emotions. In a similar way, we'd like to explore the relationship between gestures and sound in the context of music performance and listening.

We are particularly interested in the relationship between sound and the movements of an individual or a group in a listening situation as well as the movements of a music performer that are related primarily to the production of sound, in addition to the musical intention and the expression of emotion ([16]).

In our current project, we develop a set of methods for the analysis of the relationship between different aspects of gestures and sound. We would like to

S. Kopp and I. Wachsmuth (Eds.): GW 2009, LNAI 5934, pp. 158–170, 2010.
© Springer-Verlag Berlin Heidelberg 2010

be able to apply these methods to a variety of contexts, covering the performance of traditional and electronic (virtual) instruments as well as different music listening scenarios. The goal of this work reaches the creation of tools for the study of gesture in musical expression and perception. In a greater context, these tools contribute to the development of novel paradigms within the intersection between music performance and music listening technologies.

In this paper, we present a new approach to the quantitative analysis of the relationship between gesture and sound. The article is organized as follows. We first present a review of related works. Then we introduce in section 3 the multivariate analysis method called canonical correlation analysis. In section 4 we present the experimental context including our data capture methods and we show results on feature selection and correlation analysis of collected data. We discuss these results in 5. Finally, we conclude and give the implications on further works in section 6.

2   Related Work

The concept of embodied cognition has been adopted by a wide community of researchers. In this context, the relationship between gesture and sound has come into interest to interdisciplinary research on human communication and expression.

Some recent researches in neurosciences ([13], [25]) and others in perception ([2], [18], [26]) have shown that action plays a predominant role in perception insisting on the inherently multimodal nature of perception. In [1], [12], [14] the authors show that gesture and speech are to some extent complementary co-expressive elements in human communication.

Research in the domain of music and dance has studied the embodiment of emotion and expressivity in movement and gesture. Leman ([16]) has widely explored various aspects of music embodiment based on the correlation between physical measurements and corporeal articulations in respect to musical intention. Camurri et al. in [4] show that emotion can be recognized in a dancing movement following dynamic features such as *quantity of motion* extracted from motion capture data. Dahl et al. in [5] show to what extent emotional intentions can be conveyed through musicians' body movements. Moreover, Nusseck and Wanderley in [19] show that music experience is multimodal and is less depend on the players' particular body movements than the player's overall motion characteristics.

Several recent works have studied gestures performed while listening to music revealing how an individual perceives and imagines sound and sound production as well as music and music performance. In [6], [10] and [7] the authors explore the relationship between gesture and musical sound using qualitative analysis of the gestural imitation of musical instrument performance (*air-instruments*) as well as free dance and drawing movements associated with sounds (*sound-tracing*). For instance, [6] shows that air-instrument performance can reflect how people perceive and imagine music highly depending on their musical skills.

On the other hand, only a few works have taken a quantitative approach and are mostly focussing on the synchronisation between gestures and music. In [15], Large proposes a pattern-forming dynamical system modelling the perception of beat and meter that allows for studying the synchronisation and rhythmic correspondence of movement and music. Experiments in which subjects were asked to tap along with the musical tempo have revealed other pertinent characteristics of the temporal relationship between movement and music ([17], [22], [24]) such as negative asynchrony, variability, and rate limits. In [17], the authors give a quantitative analysis of the ensemble musicians' synchronization with the conductor's gestures. The authors have used cross-correlation analysis on motion capture data and beat patterns extracted from the audio signal to study the correspondence between the conductor's gestures and the musical performance of the ensemble. Lastly, Styns ([24]) has studied how music influences the way humans walk analysing the correspondence between kinematic features of walking movements and beat patterns including the comparison of movement speed and walking tempo in addition to the analysis of rhythmic synchronicity. He shows that walking to music can be modelled as a resonance phenomenon (with resonance frequency at 2Hz).

In our work we attempt to introduce a method for the quantitative multimodal analysis of movement and sound that allows for the selection and analysis of continuous perceptively pertinent features and the exploration of their relationship. It focuses on free body movements performed while listening to recorded sounds. The mathematical approach is a general multivariate analysis method that has not been used yet in gesture-sound analysis, but that has given promising results in the analysis of multimedia data and information retrieval ([11]).

3   Canonical Correlation Analysis: An Overview

Proposed by Hotelling in [9], Canonical Correlation Analysis (CCA) can be seen as the problem of measuring the linear relationship between two sets of variables. Indeed, it finds basis vectors for two sets of variables such that the correlations between the projections of the variables onto these basis vectors are mutually maximised. Thus, respective projected variables are a new representation of the variables in directions where variance and co-variance are the most explained.

Let us introduce some notations: bold type will be used for matrices ($\mathbf{X}$, $\mathbf{Y}$, etc...) and vectors ($\mathbf{u}$, $\mathbf{v}$, etc...). The matrix transpose of $\mathbf{X}$ will be written as $\mathbf{X}^T$. Finally, an observation of a random variable $\mathbf{v}$ will be written as v_i at time i.

Consider two matrices $\mathbf{X}$ and $\mathbf{Y}$ where the rows (resp. columns) are the observations (resp. variables). $\mathbf{X}$, $\mathbf{Y}$ must have the same number of observations, denoted m, but can have different numbers of variables, denoted n_x resp. n_y. Then, CCA has to find two projection matrices, $\mathbf{A}$ and $\mathbf{B}$, such as

$$\max_{\mathbf{A},\mathbf{B}} \left[\mathrm{corr}\left(\mathbf{XA}, \mathbf{YB}\right) \right] \tag{1}$$

Here *corr* denotes the correlation operator between two matrices. Usually, the correlation matrix of a matrix $\mathbf{M}$ of dimension $m \times n$ is the correlation matrix of n random variables (the matrix columns $\mathbf{m}_1, ..., \mathbf{m}_n$) and is defined as a $n \times n$ matrix whose (i, j) entry is corr $(\mathbf{m}_i, \mathbf{m}_j)$. The correlation between two matrices is the correlation between the respective indexed columns. Therefore $\mathbf{XA}$ and $\mathbf{YB}$ must have the same number of variables. $\mathbf{A}$ and $\mathbf{B}$ are $n_x \times \min(n_x, n_y)$ and $n_y \times \min(n_x, n_y)$ matrices. Let h be one arbitrary variable index in $\mathbf{XA}$ (as in $\mathbf{YB}$), equation (1) can be written as finding $\mathbf{a}_h$ and $\mathbf{b}_h$, $\forall h = 1...\min(n_x, n_y)$, that maximize:

$$\text{corr}(\mathbf{Xa}_h, \mathbf{Yb}_h) \tag{2}$$

We remind the reader that the correlation coefficient between two random variables is computed as the quotient between the covariance of these two random variables and the square root of the product of their variance. Let denote $\mathbf{C}(\mathbf{X}, \mathbf{Y})$ the covariance matrix. It is a positive semi-definite matrix and can be written as

$$\mathbf{C}(\mathbf{X}, \mathbf{Y}) = \hat{\mathbb{E}}\left[\begin{pmatrix} \mathbf{X} \\ \mathbf{Y} \end{pmatrix}^T \begin{pmatrix} \mathbf{X} \\ \mathbf{Y} \end{pmatrix} \right] = \begin{bmatrix} \mathbf{C}_{xx} & \mathbf{C}_{xy} \\ \mathbf{C}_{yx} & \mathbf{C}_{yy} \end{bmatrix}$$

Thus we can formulate the problem from equation (2) using the previous notations: find $\mathbf{A}, \mathbf{B}$ such that the following quotient is maximized

$$\text{corr}(\mathbf{Xa}_h, \mathbf{Yb}_h) = \frac{\text{cov}(\mathbf{Xa}_h, \mathbf{Yb}_h)}{\sqrt{\text{var}(\mathbf{Xa}_h)\,\text{var}(\mathbf{Yb}_h)}} = \frac{\mathbf{a}_h^T \mathbf{C}_{xy} \mathbf{b}_h}{\sqrt{\mathbf{a}_h^T \mathbf{C}_{xx} \mathbf{a}_h \mathbf{b}_h^T \mathbf{C}_{yy} \mathbf{b}_h}} \tag{3}$$

One can show that equation (3) leads to a generalized eigenproblem of the form (see [8]):

$$\mathbf{M}_1 \mathbf{v} = \lambda \mathbf{M}_2 \mathbf{v}$$

Efficient methods can be implemented to find interesting projection matrices. The key terms for an understanding of CCA are: *canonical weights* (coefficients in $\mathbf{A}$ and $\mathbf{B}$); *canonical variates* (projected variables, $\mathbf{XA}$ and $\mathbf{YB}$); *canonical function* (relationship between two canonical variates whose strength is given by the canonical correlation).

Interpreting canonical correlation analysis involves examining the canonical functions to determine the relative importance of each of the original variables in the canonical relationships. Precise statistics have not yet been developed to interpret canonical analysis, but several methods exist and we have to rely on these measures. The widely used interpretation methods are: canonical weights, canonical loadings and canonical cross-loadings. In this paper we use the second one because of its efficiency and simplicity. Canonical Loadings measure the simple correlation between variables in each set and its corresponding canonical variates, i.e. the variance that variables share with their canonical variates. Canonical Loadings are computed as:

$$\textit{Gesture loadings}: \mathbf{L}_G = \text{corr}(\mathbf{X}, \mathbf{U})$$
$$\textit{Sound loadings}: \mathbf{L}_S = \text{corr}(\mathbf{Y}, \mathbf{V})$$

4   Cross-Modal Analysis

We applied the method based on CCA to some examples of data collected in an experiment with subjects performing free body movements while listening to sound recordings imagining themselves producing the sound. Given the setup of the experiment, gesture and sound can be assumed as highly correlated without knowing their exact relationship that may be related to the subjects' sound perception, their intention of musical control, and their musical and motor skills. In this sense, the collected data sets have been a perfect context to explore the developed method and its capability to support reasoning about the relationship between gesture and sound.

4.1   Collected Data

The data has been collected in May 2008 in the University of Music in Graz. For the experiment 20 subjects were invited to perform gestures while listening to a sequence of 18 different recorded sound extracts of a duration between 2.05 and 37.53 seconds with a mean of 9.45 seconds. Most of the sound extracts were of short duration. Since the experience was explorative, the sound corpus included a wide variety of sounds: environmental and musical of different styles (classical, rock, contemporary).

For each sound, a subject had to imagine a gesture that he or she performed three times after an arbitrary number of rehearsals. The gestures were performed with a small hand-held device that included markers for a camera-based motion capture system recording its position in Cartesian coordinates. A foot-pedal allowed to synchronise the beginning of the movement with the beginning of the playback of the sound extract in the rehearsal as well as for the recording of the final three performances.

4.2   Gesture Data

As input of the analysis method, a gesture is a multi-dimensional signal stream corresponding to a set of observations. The most basic kinematic features are the position coordinates x, y, z, velocity coordinates v_x, v_y, v_z and acceleration coordinates a_x, a_y, a_z derived from the motion capture data. These features give a basic and efficient representation of postures and body movements describing their geometry and dynamics. For instance, Rasamimanana in [21] shows that three types of bow strokes considered in the paper are efficiently characterized by the features (a_{min}, a_{max}). In order to abstract from absolute position and movement direction, we calculate vector norms for position, velocity, and acceleration. To also consider movement trajectories, we additionally represent the gestures in an adapted basis using Frenet-Serret formulas giving *curvature* and *torsion* in the coordinate system $(\mathbf{t}, \mathbf{n}, \mathbf{b})$. In the same coordinate system, we add *normal* and *tangential accelerations* denoted by acc_N and acc_T (that replace previous acceleration).

Finally, at the input of the method a gesture is represented by a finite sequence of observations of the following variables:

$$\{position, velocity, acc_N, acc_T, curvature, radius, torsion\}$$

The CCA here permits to select the most pertinent features used in further calculations eliminating non-significant parameters.

4.3   Sound Features

The perception of sound has been studied intensively since one century and it is now largely accepted that sounds can be described in terms of their pitch, loudness, subjective duration and "timbre". For our exploration, we extract a set of audio descriptors from the audio files used in the experiment that have been shown to be perceptively relevant (see [20]). While we easily can rely on loudness and pitch the perceptual relevance of audio descriptors for timbre and its temporal evolution is less assured. Nevertheless, we have chosen to use *sharpness* corresponding to the perceptual equivalent to the spectral centroïd. Pitch has been discarded since in musical performance it generally requires high precision control associated to expert instrumental gestures (defined as *selection gestures* in [3]).

At the input of the method a sound is represented by a finite sequence of observations of the following variables:

$$\{loudness, sharpness\}$$

Their perceptual characteristic allows the easy interpretation of gesture-sound relationship analysis.

4.4   Results

For free body movements performed while listening to recorded sound extracts, we are interested in investigating how gesture can explain sound through sound features and how sound can highlight important gesture characteristics. Among the whole set of sounds we chose two: the sound of an ocean wave and a solo flute playing a single note with strong timbre modulation (extract from *Sequenza I* for flute (1958), by Luciano Berio). These two sounds appeared to be the most pertinent extracts given the selection of audio descriptors discussed in 4.3. The set of two perceptual audio descriptors computed on each sound can be seen in figure 1.

The wave sound is characterized by a spectral distribution similar to a white noise passing through a specific filter. It leads to a sharpness feature highly correlated with the loudness (correlation coefficient of 0.814). Since the flute example characteristic resides in a continuous transformation of its spectrum without significatively changing the fundamental frequency, its computed loudness and sharpness are less correlated (its correlation coefficient is -0.61).

First, gesture parameters considered as pertinent in the context cannot be chosen arbitrarily. Our analysis method can be applied to select a subset of pertinent gesture parameters using one gesture and many audio descriptors. In this

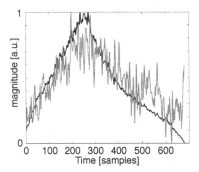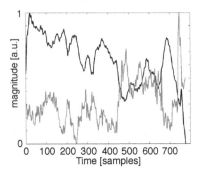

Fig. 1. Loudness and Sharpness. On the left, feature values are plotted for the wave sound. The line corresponds to loudness, and the gray line sharpness. The same features for the flute timbre example are plotted on the right.

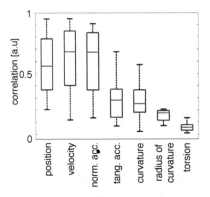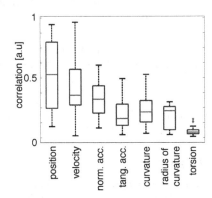

Fig. 2. Relevant gesture parameters. Each parameter is analysed together with the audio descriptors using CCA for 42 gestures. Results for the wave sound are plotted on the left side while flute results can be seen on the right.

way, the method operates as a multiple regression: the gesture parameter is predicted from audio descriptors. Each analysis returns one correlation coefficient corresponding to the canonical function strength between the current gesture parameter and the audio canonical component. 42 gestures are considered landing 42 canonical analysis iterations for each gesture parameter and each sound. Figure 2 shows two box plots corresponding to this process as applied to the wave and flute sounds. Three principal features are emphasized: position (index 1), velocity (index 2), and normal acceleration (index 3). Since these features have the highest correlation means among those in the set of gesture parameters, they constitute a set of pertinent parameters related to the wave and flute sounds.

Nevertheless, selection based on correlation means returns more significant results for the wave sound. For both cases, torsion has been discarded because the data derived from the motion capture recordings were very noisy.

Therefore, the selected subset of gesture parameters is $\{position, velocity, acc_N\}$. Canonical correlation analysis has been used as a selection tool; now we apply this method in our search for the intrinsic relationships between the two sets of data. In the first step, we discard outliers related to the first and the second canonical component. This leads to two subsets: 14 gestures among 42 for the wave example and 10 gestures for the flute example. Following the previous notations, CCA returns two projection matrices $\mathbf{A}$, $\mathbf{B}$ whose dimensions are 3×2 and 2×2 for each gesture, respectively. Loadings are computed at each step; figure 3 and 4 illustrate their statistics. The figures show the variance shared by each original variable with its canonical component for all gestures. Canonical gesture loadings are on the left side of the figures while audio descriptors respective canonical loadings are on the right. The first component is placed above the second one.

The wave case is illustrated by figure 3 and can be interpreted as follows. Gesture parameter velocity and normal acceleration are the most represented in the first canonical component: around 90% of their variance is explained. In the audio space, one original variable is clearly highlighted: the loudness (at the top of figure 3). In other words, the first canonical function correlates $\{velocity, acc_N\}$ to $\{loudness\}$.

Position contributes the most to the second canonical component in the gesture space while the sharpness descriptor is predominant in this case. So second canonical function correlates $\{position\}$ to $\{sharpness\}$ (at the bottom of figure 3).

One can remark that analysis reveals that loudness and sharpness descriptors can be separated when considering sound with gesture while they were highly correlated (figure 1).

A similar interpretation can be given for the flute timbre sound showed in figure 4. In this case, we have:

$$\text{first function :} \quad \{position\} \rightarrow \{loudness\}$$
$$\text{second function :} \{velocity, acc_N\} \rightarrow \{sharpness\}$$

5   Discussion

To analyse the cross-modal relationship between gesture and sound, a multivariate analysis method is used in two ways: first for the selection of pertinent gesture features, then for the analysis of the correlation between the selected features with the audio descriptors. In the first step, the selection yields a subset of movement features that best correlate with the audio descriptors. The low correlations obtained for some of the features have been discarded for further exploration. This seems to be coherent with kinematic studies of human gestures:

- Tangential acceleration is the acceleration component which is collinear to the velocity vector. If we consider the two-thirds power law by Viviani and

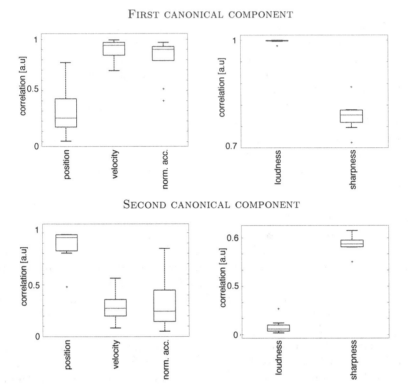

Fig. 3. Canonical loadings for the wave sound. Each row is a canonical component. Gesture parameter loadings are plotted on the left while audio descriptors can be seen on the right. Top: *velocity* and acc_N are correlated to *loudness*. Bottom: *position* is correlated to *sharpness*.

Flash ($A = K.C^{2/3}$ where A is the angular velocity, C the curvature and K a constant), normal acceleration is related to curvature by $acc_N = K'.C^{1/3}$, where K' is a constant. In this case, tangential acceleration does not convey relevant information.

– The fact that curvature is no longer pertinent means there is no linear relation either between curvature and the audio descriptors or between the curvature and other gesture parameters. This result is in agreement with the previous kinematic law and can be also applied to the radius of curvature.

The next step of the analysis explores the correlation of selected movement features with the audio descriptors. The results of this analysis are correlations highlighting pertinent aspects of the gesture-sound relationship. Without surprise the subjects seem to favour gestures correlating with perceptual audio energy (*loudness*).

FIRST CANONICAL COMPONENT

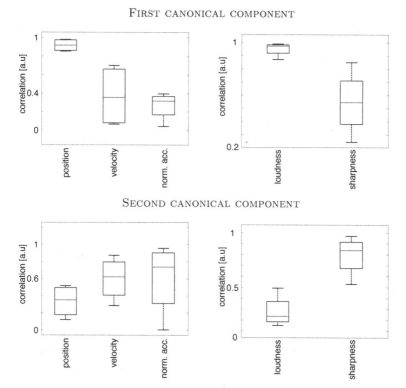

SECOND CANONICAL COMPONENT

Fig. 4. Canonical loadings for the flute sound. Each row is a canonical component. Gesture parameter loadings are plotted on the left while audio descriptors can be seen on the right. Top: *position* is correlated to *loudness*. Bottom: *velocity* and *acc_N* are correlated to *sharpness*.

In the case of the wave sound, velocity or normal acceleration are highly correlated to loudness. Confronting this result with performance videos, one can see that the subjects are concerned about sonic dynamics and continuity. Increasing audio energy implies increasing velocity, i.e. increasing kinetic energy. Here the analysis reveals that the subjects tend to embody sound energy through the energy of their movement.

On the other hand, for the gestures performed on the flute sound we observe a high correlation between the norm of the position and the loudness. Instead of embodying the sound dynamic the subjects rather tend to transcribe its temporal evolution tracing the modulation of the sound feature over time. As the variation of audio energy in the flute example is rather subtle compared to the wave sound, the subjects seem to adapt their strategy for the imagined sound control.

At last, we have started to inspect data of particular subjects that may reveal individual strategies and skills. For instance, considering the velocity feature, defined as $velocity^2 = v_x^2 + v_y^2 + v_z^2$, one can bring directional information to the analysis splitting $velocity^2$ into three specific variables: v_x^2, v_y^2, v_z^2. Canonical correlation analysis is no longer constrained to a uniform weight equal to 1 in the resulting linear combination but finds an optimal set of weights favouring directions. In other words, the analysis method takes into account the movement asymmetries. For the selection of movement parameters among a redundant set of extracted features, a trade-off has to be found between achieving a complete description of the movement and avoiding redundancies.

6   Conclusion and Future Works

Our goal was to study the relationship between gesture and sound. Gesture was considered as a set of kinematic parameters representing a free movement performed on a recorded sound. The sound was considered as a signal of feature observations. The method used in the paper arises from multivariate analysis research and offers a powerful tool to investigate the mutual shared variance between two sets of features. Objective results inferred from the application of CCA as a selection tool was presented. In addition, more subjective conclusions concerning mapping from the gesture parameter space to the audio descriptor space was highlighted. Thereby, we saw in this paper that gestural expression when relating to sounds can be retrieved considering gesture-sound as a pair instead of as individual entities.

However, the method suffers from some restrictive limitations. First of all, canonical functions correspond to linear relations so CCA cannot exhibit non-linear relations between variables. Besides, since we must restrict the variable sets to finite sets that encode only a part of the information contained in both gestures and sounds, the correlation (i.e. variance) as an objective function is not always relevant when real signals are analysed. The correlation involved in CCA could be replaced by the mutual information. By arising the statistical order of the multivariate relation, the main idea is to find canonical variates that are maximally dependent. It should lead to a more complete semantic interpretation of gesture-sound relationships in a musical context. To summarize, the method presented in this paper has given promising results and further works will consist in refining the method using information theory.

Acknowledgments

This work was supported by the ANR project 2PIM/MI3. Moreover, we would like to thank the COST IC0601 Action on Sonic Interaction Design (SID) for their support in the short-term scientific mission in Graz.

References

1. Bergmann, K., Kopp, S.: Co-expressivity of speech and gesture: Lessons for models of aligned speech and gesture production. In: Symposium at the AISB Annual Convention: Language, Speech and Gesture for Expressive Characters, December 2007, pp. 153–158 (2007)

2. Berthoz, A.: Le Sens du mouvement. Odile Jacob, Paris (1997)
3. Cadoz, C., Wanderley, M.M.: Gesture-music. In: Trends in Gestural Control of Music, pp. 1–55. Ircam, Paris (2000)
4. Camurri, A., Lagerlöf, I., Volpe, G.: Recognizing emotion from dance movement: comparison of spectator recognition and automated techniques. International Journal of Human-Computer Studies 59(1-2), 213–225 (2003)
5. Dahl, S., Friberg, A.: Expressiveness of musician's body movements in performances on marimba. In: Camurri, A., Volpe, G. (eds.) GW 2003. LNCS (LNAI), vol. 2915, pp. 479–486. Springer, Heidelberg (2004)
6. Godøy, R.I., Haga, E., Jensenius, A.R.: Playing "Air instruments": Mimicry of sound-producing gestures by novices and experts. In: Gibet, S., Courty, N., Kamp, J.-F. (eds.) GW 2005. LNCS (LNAI), vol. 3881, pp. 256–267. Springer, Heidelberg (2006)
7. Haga, E.: Correspondences between music and body movement. PhD thesis, University of Oslo, Department of Musicology (2008)
8. Hair, J.F., Black, W.C., Babin, B.J., Anderson, R.E.: Multivariate Data Analysis, 7th edn. Prentice Hall, New Jersey (2009)
9. Hotelling, H.: Relations between two sets of variates. Biometrika 28(3/4), 321–377 (1936)
10. Jensenius, A.R.: Action-Sound, Developing Methods and Tools to Study Music-Related Body Movement. PhD thesis, University of Oslo, Department of Musicology (2007)
11. Kidron, E., Schechner, Y.Y., Elad, M.: Pixels that sound. IEEE Computer Vision & Pattern Recognition (CVPR 2005) 1, 88–95 (2005)
12. Kita, S., Asli, Ö.: What does cross-linguistic variation in semantic coordination of speech and gesture reveal?: Evidence for an interface representation of spatial thinking and speaking. Journal of Memory and Language 48, 16–32 (2003)
13. Kohler, E., Keysers, C., Umiltà, A., Fogassi, L., Gallese, V., Rizzolatti, G.: Hearing sounds, understanding actions: Actions representation in mirror neurons. Science 297, 846–848 (2002)
14. Kopp, S., Wachsmuth, I.: Synthesizing multimodal utterances for conversational agents. Computer Animation and Virtual Worlds 15(1), 39–52 (2004)
15. Large, E.W.: On synchronizing movements to music. Human Movement Science 19(4), 527–566 (2000)
16. Leman, M.: Embodied Music Cognition and Mediation Technology. Massachusetts Institute of Technology Press, Cambridge (2008)
17. Luck, G., Toiviainen, P.: Ensemble musicians' synchronization with conductors' gestures: An automated feature-extraction analysis. Music Perception 24(2), 189–200 (2006)
18. Noë, A.: Action in Perception. Massachusetts Institute of Technology Press, Cambridge (2005)
19. Nusseck, M., Wanderley, M.M.: Music and motion - how music-related ancillary body movements contribute to the experience of music. Music Perception 26, 335–353 (2009)
20. Peeters, G.: A large set of audio features for sound description. CUIDADO Project (2004)
21. Rasamimanana, N., Fléty, E., Bévilacqua, F.: Gesture analysis of violin bow strokes. In: Gibet, S., Courty, N., Kamp, J.-F. (eds.) GW 2005. LNCS (LNAI), vol. 3881, pp. 144–155. Springer, Heidelberg (2006)

22. Repp, B.H.: Musical Synchronization. In: Altenmüller, E., Wiesendanger, M., Kesselring, J. (eds.) Music, motor control and the brain, pp. 55–76. Oxford University Press, Oxford (2006)
23. Scherer, K.R., Ellgring, H.: Multimodal expression of emotion: Affect programs or componential appraisal patterns? Emotion 7(1), 158–171 (2007)
24. Styns, F., van Noorden, L., Moelants, D., Leman, M.: Walking on music. Human Movement Science 26(5), 769–785 (2007)
25. Thomas, M., Vittorio, G.: The emergence of a shared action ontology: Building blocks for a theory. Consciousness and Cognition 12(4), 549–571 (2003)
26. Varela, F., Thompson, E., Rosch, E.: The Embodied Mind: Cognitive Science and Human Experience. Massachusetts Institute of Technology Press, Cambridge (1991)

Methods for Effective Sonification of Clarinetists' Ancillary Gestures

Florian Grond[1], Thomas Hermann[1],
Vincent Verfaille[2], and Marcelo M. Wanderley[2]

[1] Ambient Intelligence Group, CITEC, Bielefeld University
http://www.techfak.uni-bielefeld.de/ags/ami
[2] IDMIL, CIRMMT, McGill University
http://www.idmil.org

Abstract. We present the implementation of two different sonifications methods of ancillary gestures from clarinetists. The sonifications are data driven from the clarinetist's posture which is captured with a VICON motion tracking system. The first sonification method is based on the velocities of the tracking markers, the second method involves a principal component analysis as a data preprocessing step. Further we develop a simple complementary visual display with a similar information content to match the sonification. The effect of the two sonifications with respect to the movement perception is studied in an experiment where test subjects annotate the clarinetists performance represented by various combinations of the resulting uni- and multimodal displays.

Keywords: sonification, 3D movement data, ancillary gestures, multimodal displays.

1 Introduction

Through advanced recording and simulation possibilities the amount of 3D movement data is constantly growing. The standard technique to investigate such data is the scientific 3D visualization of moving points or models, a self evident approach, since the human visual and cognitive system seems highly adapted to perceive and interpret human motion. However, the rather young research field of sonification offers novel inspection techniques that complement visual analysis by transforming data into audible sound. This perception mode is beneficial for several reasons: Firstly, sonification is ideal for representing dynamic patterns in multivariate data sets with complex information such as fast transient motions. Secondly, sound requires neither a particular orientation of the user nor directed attention. Thirdly, in many applications the eyes are already occupied with a specific task and have therefore limited capacity to focus on additional information. In this case however, the intricate interplay of multimodal displays, specifically the one of sound and moving image has to be taken into account. These benefits are of potential interest for the study of ancillary gestures of instrumentalists, in our case clarinetists.

S. Kopp and I. Wachsmuth (Eds.): GW 2009, LNAI 5934, pp. 171–181, 2010.
© Springer-Verlag Berlin Heidelberg 2010

Ancillary gestures are those body movements which are not directly involved in the sound production [1] [2] but are omnipresent in musical performance. For clarinet players, lip and finger motions are effective gestures, whereas motions like weight transfer and body curvature for instance are ancillary gestures. Their importance is due to the fact that they tend to align with musical motives in the score [2] and are therefore an integral part of the player's performance as these movement patterns show consistency even for various levels of expressiveness [3].

In this paper, we develop two different sonification strategies of ancillary gestures. The first is a direct mapping of marker velocities to sound, the second involves a principal component analysis as a data preprocessing step. Specific sonifications for this purpose have already been developed to some extent by the authors [4] [5] [6] [7] and others [8] [9] but there is still a lack of understanding, how sonification influences multimodal displays. and if different sonification strategies have noticeably different effects on how we perceive data in a in multimodal displays. Besides the development of sonification techniques, we put our focus on assessing the effects in a psychophysical experiment, in which we ask test subjects to identify self-chosen events and consistently detect their selection in repeated presentations.

2   The Vicon Motion Tracking Data

The motion capturing sessions were conducted in previous projects at the IDMIL. All performers were advanced instrumentalists playing an excerpt of Brahms' Sonata for clarinet op. 120 no 1. The movement data of the clarinetist were recorded with a VICON system 460 system using the standard plug-in-gait model [10], which provides 38 marker positions and gives a global description of the body posture. We removed from the resulting data redundant channels and decided to apply sonification to the posture information in terms of marker positions each with x, y and z Cartesian coordinates and its derivatives. This choice was motivated by that fact that we wanted to apply sonification to aspects of the data which could also be seen in a simple visual representation. The remaining set consisted of 18 markers, some of them were computed as combinations of originally measured data c.f. Table 1.

Table 1. On the left: the reduced dataset of 18 markers. On the right: clarinetists in the VICON motion capturing system.

body part	left	middle	right
head	front	back of the head	front
spine		neck C7	
		T10	
		end of spine	
arms	shoulder		shoulder
	Elbow		Elbow
	arm wrist		arm wrist
legs	hip		hip
	knee		knee
	ankle		ankle

The marker in the middle on the backside of the head corresponding to the two on the front, was computed as the mean of two left and right markers in the back. The marker at the end of the spine was the mean vector of the left right backside of the hips. The markers on the hips are the average of two markers back/front of each side respectively.

3   Data Preparation and Preprocessing

Before reducing the data as described above, we centered them between both feet. This was done such that for each time frame the center of origin of the coordinate system was moved to the middle between the left and right toe. In general, the clarinetists left their toes in one place during the whole performance (except one recording). Therefore, there was not much dynamics in the marker on the toe.

The left and right as well as the back and forth movements (weight transfer, WT) of most of the subjects dominated the whole dataset. For the PCA transform this lead to the fact that the first and second components consisted of the WT movement. In the velocity sonification approach, the WT was dominating in a similar way, when mapping velocity to sound. Therefore we removed this component from the data set. The WT can be understood as the moving center of mass (COM) of the performer, like a reversed pendulum pointing up, which is anchored between both feet of the performer and oscillates around the basis vector z $(0,0,1)$ in the x,y plane. After removing this motion, the COM vector always remained parallel to $(0,0,1)$.

4   Sound Synthesis and Mapping

4.1   Sound Synthesis

According to the Design Space Map [11] a recording rate of 100 Hz, suggested a continuous parameter mapping sonification as an appropriate strategy. The following two considerations were guiding us during the sonification design: The continuous sonification should automatically lead to acoustic articulations which segment the audio in a perceptually meaningful way according to the movement patterns. Further, the sonification should allow to distinguish movements from different parts of the body. Yet in order to know, what the test subjects would be listening to, if they directed their attention towards the sonification, we decided to design a single auditory stream. Therefore we constructed as the simplest sonification unit a source filter model. using white noise filtered through a resonant filter.

$$s(t) = \sum_{i=1}^{n} H_{Resonz}(\eta_i(t); f_i, rq, g) \tag{1}$$

Where H_{Resonz} is the resonant filter with the resonant frequency f_i, the gain g, the bandwidth is specified with the filter's reciprocal q -value rq and $\eta_i(t)$ is a white noise source. Motion data are mapped to these parameters as follows. The resulting sonification as $s(t)$ is the sum over all n sonified data-features. To address the frequency loudness dependency we used basic psychoacoustic amplitude compensation.[1]

These sounds of filtered noise integrated nicely into one sound stream where the varying amplitude of the different resonant frequencies f_i could be distinguish.

4.2 Mapping

As mentioned two different mappings of the the data features to the sonification units have been applied.

Velocity Sonification: The first was a direct mapping of the velocities of all 18 data points to the sound parameters described above. Due to the noise in the data the derived velocity was smoothed with a rectangular window of 5 samples. Frequencies between 150 and 4000 Hz were assigned to each marker. The gain corresponded to the velocity exponentially mapped between 0.001 and 1. The velocity of each data point modulated the center-frequencies with ±5% and additionally the rq of each resonant filter was mapped exponentially between 0.001 and 0.1.

PCA Sonification: For the second mapping, we computed the principal components of the data set consisting of $3 * 18 = 54$ features over a complete performance.[2] Since the COM corresponding to the 54d vector of the mean posture has been subtracted before computing the data set covariance matrix $C = \frac{1}{N} \sum_\alpha x^\alpha x^{\alpha T}$ the principal components describe axis along coordinated activity. Then we took the first 6 coefficients corresponding to the largest eigenvalues of C that that cover approx. 85 % of the data set variance. It turned out, that taking components after the first 6, which described minute movement details could not be distinguish acoustically to our experience and were hard to identify visually too. The coefficients of the principal components were exponetially mapped between 300 - 2000 Hz.[3] The velocities of the coefficients were exponentially mapped to gain between 0.001 and 1. Frequency modulation corresponded to ±5% around the assigned frequency controlled by the time coefficients. The rq of the resonant filters corresponded to the principal components exponentially mapped between 0.001 and 0.1 In both approaches the resulting sound was the sum over all sonified data features as in eq. 1.

Data Selection for the Experiment: In order to cover different ancillary gesture patterns these sonifications were applied onto the data of the complete performance of 3 clarinetists, which have been selected since they exhibited noticeably

---

[1] For the details of the resonant filter and the amplitude compensation we refer to the implementation details of the **Resonz** and **AmpComp** class in **SuperCollider3**.

[2] PCA was computed via pythonSC [12].

[3] Frequencies and range were chosen to yield an acoustically rich result.

different movement patterns. Clarinetist 1 and 3 exhibited very pronounced ancillary gestures with lots of weight transfer movements, whereas clarinetist 2 was only occasionally moving the whole body, but instead made rapid movements with the elbows and the arm wrist.

5   Considerations on Sound and Image

For the design of multi modal displays it is important to consider that human perception is not merely a superposition of moving image plus sound. The fact that sound can give an added value to the image has already been extensively studied by Chion [13] and Flueckiger [14] for the cinema. Some findings from these works are particularly instructive for the design of sonifications for multi modal displays. One is that we always look for a visual cause that explains our acoustic impressions. Therefore the sound always seems to come from the image and is together with a visual representation not perceived in isolation. On the contrary, if no cause can be found in the visual display, no integrated perception emerges. This implies in turn that complementarity receives a particular meaning for multi modal displays. Sonification can most effectively be used when it emphasizes information that is already in the visual display and can be more precisely identified there. Unfortunately this "searching" for a visual cause can also lead to unwanted results as the following experience shows: In [7] a framework for ancillary gestures sonifications for clarinetists was developed, where in a first trial sonifications were combined with videos from the clarinet players clearly showing the finger movements. The effect was that some test subjects asked if the finger movements (effective gesture) caused the sound, where in fact the sonification was representing only ancillary gestures such as weight transfer and body curvature, which were less visible.

Given these considerations about the interplay of sound and image, the main focus was if different sonifications of ancillary gestures change the way how we perceive them and if both modalities can be efficiently integrated. By giving the test subjects an open task we investigated if sonifications can contribute towards a more unanimous interpretation of perceived movements amongst test subjects.

5.1   The Visual Display of Body Movements

Because of the aforementioned considerations we developed a visual display which only shows ancillary gestures[4]. Figure 1 shows an abstract stick figure in profile and from the front omitting details such as finger movements. In small preliminary tests we received a good feedback for this display design in terms of a consistency between sonification and image, yet people still reported difficulties to identify which part of the body was responsible for a certain sound. Therefore we added, at least for the velocity sonification, a red glyph to each sonified joint, which changed in size and color (by varying the alpha channel) according to the velocity. This provided visually similar information, as mapped to sound in the velocity sonification.

---

[4] The visualization in `SuperCollider3` was implemented in `SCgraph` [15].

Fig. 1. Visualization of the clarinetists: (a) simple stickman (b) enhanced stickman where the velocities of joints are additionally highlighted with red glyphs

6   Experiment

6.1   Task

Given the diverse background of the test-subjects, we designed an open task for the experiment, which consisted of identification and detection of events in stimuli for selected sequences of movements of the three clarinetists. All stimuli represented the same musical phrase consisting of 4 distinct melodic units. The test subjects were asked to look and listen to each stimulus 9 times and to identify events that they encountered and to mark their choice in real time by mouse clicks. The test subjects were told to consider the first two runs as test runs and to try to repeat their selection of events consistently in the subsequent 7 runs. At the end of all trials the test subjects were asked to fill out a questionnaire about the different stimuli and about their musical experience.

6.2   Setup

The combination of the two visual representations and the two sonifications resulted in 7 different stimuli, which were presented to the test subjects.

id	sonification	vizualization	acronym
1	direct	-	A1 V0
2	direct	stickman	A1 V1
3	direct	stickman + glyphs	A1 V2
4	-	stickman	A0 V1
5	-	stickman + glyphs	A0 V2
6	PCA	-	A2 V0
7	PCA	stickman	A2 V1

In the case of the PCA based sonification we omitted the highlighting red glyphs since those aspects were not sonified. For each test subject the order of the stimuli was randomized ensuring that the 3 clarinetists were interleaved. For clarinetists 1 and 3 the velocity sonification resulted in a very structured sound that was easy to connect with the visual representation. The PCA sonification for the selected region appeared less structured and was therefore more difficult to connect with the visualization. This was reversed for clarinetist 2, where the PCA sonification lead to more structured sounds.

7   Experimental Data Evaluation

We recorded and analyzed data for 12 test subjects aged from 22 - 33, 11 male, 1 female, 7 of them playing an instrument. Since the movement patterns are very different for each clarinetist, resulting in very different direct and PCA sonifications, the analysis was made for each clarinetist individually.

Average Click Frequency: At first we are interested in the average number of clicks given for each stimuli. The results are compiled in Figure 2. In all the subsequent figures the results for the different stimuli are represented showing the audio only condition on the left (A1V0, A2V0) and the visual only condition on the right (A0V1, A0V2) , leaving the middle for the combined stimuli (A1V1, A1V2, A2V1).

Although the click-frequency does not vary significantly across the conditions, it is interesting to note that the highest click frequency was obtained with stimuli that at least included a visual representation. The lowest click-frequency always appeared with stimuli that contained an audio only condition. For clarinetist 3, who had a very structured performance with pronounced ancillary gestures, the standard-deviation is much smaller for most of the conditions comparing it with the other two clarinetists. This suggests that the intersubjective convergence in the perception of ancillary gestures is first and foremost influenced by how pronounced the ancillary gestures themselves appear.

Kernel Estimated Click Density: In order to compare the different stimuli along the performance of the clarinetists we visualized the results by computing a kernel estimated click density. Selected intervals of the click densities are depicted in figure 3.[5] The three selections (a, b, c) from figure 3 are examples for patterns we noticed in the plots. Selection a shows that in some cases multimodal conditions led to a noticeable delay in the reaction of the participants (we also found a case where visualization only, V2A0, was triggering clicks faster, than in the multimodal case V2A1). We hypothesize that integrating two perceptual streams increases the cognitive load and therefore causes the delay. Selection b shows that the velocity sonification seemed to dominate in clarinetist 2 and made the test-subjects ignore an event that was selected in A0V1 and A2V1. The last two conditions are very similar in the click-profile (except the multimodal delay in A2V1), the sonification of A2 therefore seemed not to overrule the visualization. Around second 6 in selection b we found that A1V1 made the test-subjects clearly differentiate two events which we could identify as two quick arm-wrist movements. Selection c clearly shows a peak at sec. 3 for the stimulus A1V2. At this moment clarinetist 3 made a step, which was interestingly not noticeably marked by clicks in any V1 or V2 only condition.

In Table 2 you find the results of the Kolmogorov Smirnov test over the click trains comparing different stimuli. An interesting because most general

---

[5] For an overview about all kernel estimated click densities please follow this URL: http://www.techfak.uni-bielefeld.de/~fgrond/GW2009/

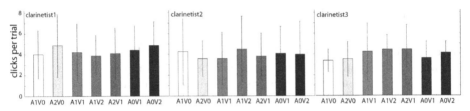

Fig. 2. Average number of clicks per trial

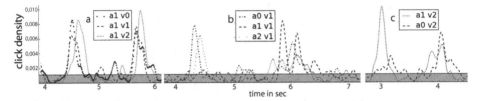

Fig. 3. Kernel estimated click densities. a,b and c are selected intervals of clarinetist 1, 2 and 3 respectively. The grey horizontal bar indicates the average click density $\int = 1$.

Table 2. comparing the clicktrains by the Kolmogorov Smirnov test. Values below 5% are indicated. The first block of 3 stimuli pairs (line 1-3) compares A1 in combination with V0 V1 V2. The second block of 3 stimuli pairs (line 6-9) compares V1 in combination with A0 A1 A2.

compared stimuli	clarinetist 1	clarinetist 2	clarinetist 3
A1V0 — A1V1	0.233	**0.032**	**0.011**
A1V1 — A1V2	**0.010**	0.493	0.302
A1V2 — A1V0	0.180	**0.010**	0.078
A2V0 — A2V1	0.226	0.086	0.248
A0V1 — A0V2	0.144	0.105	0.441
A0V1 — A1V1	0.618	**0.018**	0.127
A1V1 — A2V1	0.223	**0.007**	0.360
A2V1 — A0V1	0.487	0.508	0.368
A1V0 — A2V0	0.086	**0.001**	**0.012**
A1V2 — A0V2	**0.006**	**0.006**	0.104

result (last row) is that adding the velocity sonification to V2 made a significant difference for clarinetists 1 and 2, even for clarinetist 3 the value of 10% is low. Particularly for clarinetist 2 the click distribution of many stimuli pairs were significantly different accepting a threshold of 5%. A qualitative analysis as done for figure 3 reveals however that also for clarinetist 1 and particularly for 3 different choices were made by the test-subjects depending on the modality of the stimuli. In order to illustrate those differences we plotted the click time versus the click number as shown in figure 4. Comparing the conditions A1V0, A1V2, A0V2 shows how adding the velocity sonification A1 to an already enhanced visualization V2 led to a smaller distribution around the diagonal of succeeding clicks. The condition A1V0 on the left shows the most pronounced diagonal with

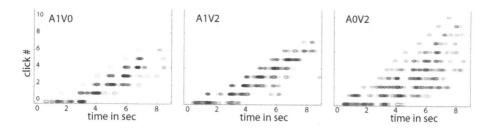

Fig. 4. Clarinetist 3, click time versus click number

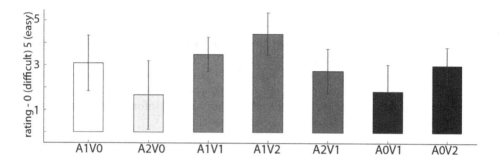

Fig. 5. Self rating of test subjects. x shows the stimuli, y the mean ± standard error.

few outliers, in the condition A0V2 we find less coherence, the plot in the middle A1V2 lies in between, this can be interpreted as intersubjective convergence, which is that velocity sonification alone or together with a visual display forced the test-subjects to select similar events in a similar order.

Self Rating: At the end of the experiment the participants were asked to rate all the stimuli between 1 (difficult) and 5 (easy) with respect to how much they helped them in achieving the given task of consistently selecting events in the display. The results are compiled in figure 5. The multimodal conditions involving velocity sonification A1V2 A1V1 were first and second rated. Interestingly less preference was given to the PCA sonification, which is consistent with the findings in analyzing selection *b* in figure 3.

8   Conclusion

In this paper we implemented a velocity and a PCA based sonification for ancillary gestures and studied them as a stand alone as well as in combination with a visual displays. Sonification as a stand alone display directed the focus on similar events. These events were marked in their timely order in a more unanimous way amongst test subjects. The velocity sonification seemed to be more efficient in highlighting otherwise overseen aspects of the gestures and was preferred by the test-subjects. We hypothesize that the coordinated directions of movement as extracted through the PCA do not necessarily correspond to what we perceive in a visual display and we encounter therefore difficulties in connecting these two display modes. The fact that the PCA extracts for each clarinetist different coordinated directions of movement depending on their idiosyncratic patterns means that the "meaning" of the PCA, i.e. how it connects with the visual display, has to be learned by the test subjects for each clarinetist anew. For clarinetist 3 we found that, even if the visualized information was similar to the sonification, displaying ancillary gestures visually made the subjects select different events compared to the unanimous choice in the A1V0 and A1V2 case. Although we set up a very open task without testing reaction time, we found evidence that multimodal displays are processed slower by the user. Further we found evidence that sonification has the potential to effectively guide attention to information that is present in the visual display, but not necessarily in the focus of attention. This might be of particular interest for annotation tools in gesture analysis. We therefore see the main purpose of sonification in this particular setting in guiding attention rather than adding information that is not present in the visual display or not perceivable there.

Acknowledgments. This work was supported through a Short-Term Scientific Mission at IDMIL CIRMMT McGill University by the COST Action IC0601 on Sonic Interaction Design and later by an NSERC Discovery grant. For interesting discussions and various support we like to thank Alexandre Savard, Ulf Grosskatehöfer, Till Bovermann and Florian Paul Schmidt.

References

1. Cadoz, C., Wanderley, M.M.: Gesture - Music. In: Wanderley, M.M., Battier, M. (eds.) Trends in Gestural Control of Music. Ircam – Centre Pompidou (2000)
2. Wanderley, M.M., Vines, B.W., Middleton, N., McKay, C., Hatch, W.: The musical significance of clarinetists' ancillary gestures: an exploration of the field. Journal of New Music Research 34(1), 97–113 (2005)
3. Wanderley, M.M.: Quantitative analysis of non-obvious performer gestures. In: Gesture and Sign Language in Human-Computer Interaction, pp. 241–253 (2002)
4. Hermann, T., Höner, O., Ritter, H.: Acoumotion - an interactive sonification system for acoustic motion control. In: Gibet, S., Courty, N., Kamp, J.-F. (eds.) GW 2005. LNCS (LNAI), vol. 3881, pp. 312–323. Springer, Heidelberg (2006)
5. Nusseck, M., Wanderley, M.M.: Music and motion—how music related ancillary body movements contribute to the experience of music. Music Perception 26(4) (2009)
6. Verfaille, V., Quek, O., Wanderley, M.M.: Sonification of musicians' ancillary gestures. In: Proceedings of the 12th International Conference on Auditory Display, London, UK, June 20 -23 (2006)
7. Savard, A.: When gestures are perceived through sounds: A framework for sonification of musicians' ancillary gestures. Master's thesis, IDMIL CIRMMT McGill University (August 2008)

8. Effenberg, A.O.: Movement sonification: Effects on perception and action. IEEE Multim. 12(2), 56–69 (2005)

9. Goina, P., Polotti, M.: Elementary gestalts for gesture sonification. In: NIME 2008, pp. 150–153 (2009)

10. Ferrari, A., Benedetti, M.G., Pavan, E., Frigo, C., Bettinelli, D., Rabuffetti, M., Crenna, P., Leardini, A.: Quantitative comparison of five current protocols in gait analysis. GAIT POSTURE (2008)

11. de Campo, A.: Toward a data soni cation design space map. In: Scavone, G.P. (ed.) ICAD 2007, Schulich School of Music, McGill University, Schulich School of Music, McGill University, Montreal, Canada, pp. 342–347 (2007), http://www.icad.org/Proceedings/2007/deCampo2007.pdf

12. Hermann, T.: PythonSC, http://www.sonification.de/projects/sc3

13. Chion, M.: Un art sonore, le cinéma, le phrasé audio visuelle. Cahiers du cinéma, pp. 541–561 (2003)

14. Flückiger, B.: Sound Design Die virtuelle Klangwelt des Films. Schüren, Marburg (2001)

15. Schmidt, F.P.: Design and implementation of a realtime 3d graphics server. Master's thesis, Bielefeld University, Germany (April 2007)

Systematicity and Idiosyncrasy in Iconic Gesture Use: Empirical Analysis and Computational Modeling

Kirsten Bergmann and Stefan Kopp

SFB 673 Alignment in Communication, Bielefeld University,
Sociable Agents Group, CITEC, Bielefeld University,
P.O. Box 100 131, D-33615 Bielefeld, Germany
{kbergman,skopp}@techfak.uni-bielefeld.de

Abstract. Why an iconic gesture takes its particular form is a largely open question, given the variations one finds across both situations and speakers. We present results of an empirical study that analyzes correlations between contextual factors (referent features, discourse) and gesture features, and tests whether they are *systematic* (shared among speakers) or *idiosyncratic* (inter-individually different). Based on this, a computational model of gesture formation is presented that combines data-based, probabilistic and model-based decision making.

Keywords: Iconic gesture, meaning-form mapping, systematicity, idiosyncrasy.

1 Introduction

The use of speech-accompanying iconic gestures is ubiquitous in human-human communication, especially when spatial information is expressed. Current literature on gesture research states that the question *"why different gestures take the particular physical form they do is one of the most important yet largely unaddressed questions in gesture research"* [2, p. 499]. This holds especially for iconic gestures, for which information is mapped from some mental image into (at least partly) resembling gestural form. Although their physical form, hence, corresponds to object or event features like shape or spatial properties, empirical studies have revealed that similarity with the referent cannot fully account for all occurrences of iconic gestures [19]. Rather, recent findings indicate that a gesture's form is influenced by specific contextual constraints or the use of more general gestural representation techniques such as shaping, drawing, or placing [17,4]. In addition to those *systematic* patterns in gesture use, human speakers are of course unique and inter-subjective differences in gesturing also hold (cf. [12]). For example, while some people rarely make use of their hands while speaking, others gesture almost without interruption. Similarly, individual variations are seen in preferences for particular representation techniques or low-level morphological features such as handshape [4]. Such inter-subjective differences in gesture behaviour are common and reflect an *idiosyncrasy* of iconic gestures – gestures are created locally by speakers while speaking, without adhering to any conventionalized standards of good form. McNeill & Duncan [25, p. 143] conclude that, by this idiosyncracy, *"gestures open a 'window' onto thinking that is otherwise curtained"*.

S. Kopp and I. Wachsmuth (Eds.): GW 2009, LNAI 5934, pp. 182–194, 2010.

In this paper, we look at how systematic and idiosyncratic aspects appear and inter-relate with each other in iconic gesture production. We start with empirically analyzing their influence in the formation of gestures, given certain visuo-spatial features of the referent and an overall discourse context. Section 2 introduces the experimental setting and the data coding methodology, Section 3 presents results from the corpus analysis. Based on these findings, we describe in Section 4 a computational modeling account that goes beyond previous systems, which either rely on generalized rule-based models that disregard idiosyncrasy in gesture use [6,18], or employ data-based methods that approximate single speakers but have difficulties with extracting systematicities of gesture use. These data-based approaches are typically (and successfully) employed to generate gesturing behavior which has no particular meaning-carrying function, e.g., discourse gestures [27] or beat gestures (Theune & Brandhorst, this volume). We propose to combine probabilistic and rule-based decision-making. Embedded into an integrated production architecture, this approach allows for generic, yet speaker-attunded gesture production, which is driven by iconicity as well as the overall discourse context. We conclude with modeling results from a prototype implementation.

2   Empirical Study

We aim at identifying systematic and idiosyncratic patterns in the formation of gestures. In our experimental setup, two interlocutors engage in a spatial communication task of direction-giving and sight description, in which they are to convey the shape of objects and spatial relations between them (Fig. 1).

Fig. 1. Experiment setting: VR stimulus presentation (left) and dialog phase with the speaker uttering "the left church has two towers" (right)

2.1   Data Coding

We collected a dialog corpus of 25 dyads (~5000 gestures). In the scope of the work reported here, we concentrate on descriptions of four different landmarks from 5 dyads (489 noun phrases, 290 gestures). Multimodal annotation has been carried out on several different levels as described in the following (see Table 1).

Gesture Form. All coverbal gestures have been segmented and coded for their *representation techniques* for transforming perceived object information into a gesture. Representation techniques capture the aspect that iconic gesturing does not seem to entirely

Table 1. Coding scheme for gestures and their discourse context

	Variable	Annotation Primitives	Agreement Coefficient
Gesture	Representation Technique	indexing, placing, shaping, drawing, posturing	$AC_1 = .784$[1]
	Handedness	rh, lh, 2h	$\kappa = .924$
Discourse Context	Thematization	theme, rheme	$\kappa = .917$
	Information State	private, shared	$\kappa = .802$
	Communicative Goal	lm, lmDescrProp, lmDescrConstr, lmDescrPos	$\kappa = .847$
Referent Features	Subparts	1 or more, none	
	Symmetry	sym, none	
	Main Axis	x-axis, y-axis, z-axis, none	$\kappa = .91$
	Position	3D vector (left, middle, right)	

follow the goal to maximize similarity with the referent model, but also brings into play conventions, experiences, and habituations, which people seem to have acquired and apply in their multimodal deliveries (cf. [26,15,32]) According to our focus on object descriptions we distinguish the following five categories: (1) Indexing: pointing to a position within the gesture space; (2) Placing: an object is placed or set down within gesture space; (3) Shaping: an object's shape is contoured or sculpted in the air; (4) Drawing: the hands trace the outline of an object's shape; and (5) Posturing: the hands form a static configuration to stand as a model for the object itself.

In addition, each gesture has been coded for its morphology in terms of handedness, handshape, hand position, palm and finger orientation, and movement features (cf. Rieser, this volume). For the scope of this paper, however, we will consider only one of these features, namely *handedness*: each gesture is either performed with the right hand (rh), with the left hand (lh) or with both hands (2h).

Discourse Context. The transcription of the interlocutor's words is enriched with further information about the overall discourse context. For this purpose, the utterance is broken down into clauses, each of which holding to represent a proposition. For each clause we annotated its communicative goal. Denis [8] developed several categories of communicative goals that can be distinguished in route directions. As we were mainly interested in object descriptions, we revised and refined these for this case into four categories: (1) Landmark (*lm*): a landmark is mentioned without further exploration, e.g., 'there is a chapel'; (2) Landmark property description (*lmDescrProp*): the properties of an object are described as in 'the town hall is u-shaped'; (3) Landmark construction description (*lmDescrConstr*): an object's construction is described, e.g., 'the church has two towers'; and (4) Landmark Position Description (*lmDescrPos*): the description localizes the object as in 'there is a tree in front of the building'.

Clauses are further divided into two smaller units of thematization partitioning of the content of a sentence according to its relation to the discourse context. The structuring of utterances into a topic part and a comment part is a pervasive phenomenon in human language and there are numerous theoretical approaches describing thematization and

---

[1] We employ the *first order agreement coefficient AC* since the gestural representation techniques are data of type II according to [10].

its semantics (cf. [21]). Following Halliday [11] we distinguish between thematization in terms of *theme* and *rheme* on the one hand, and information focus in terms of *given* and *new* on the other hand. According to the former, a sentence's theme is what the sentence is about. The rheme is defined as what is being said about the theme. For example, in the utterance "the church has two towers" the first noun phrase ("the church") is the theme and the second noun phrase is the rheme. Focussing on noun phrases and their accompanying gestures, to which we restrict our annotation, we annotate information focus following Stone et al. [31] in using the terms 'information state' and distinguish straight-forward between 'private' and 'shared' knowledge: a referent (or referent feature) already mentioned in the previous discourse is 'shared' between interlocutors, whereas a discourse referent which lacks an antecedent in the previous discourse, is not part of the discourse situation is assumed to be 'private'. For instance, in the utterance "the church has a dome-shaped roof" the first noun phrase ("the church") is shared since the must haven been introduced into the discourse before (use of definite article). The second noun phrase ("a dome-shaped roof"), on the contrary, is private because the object (feature) is discourse-new. As suggested in [28], thematization and information focus are annotated independently as different dimensions of information structure, assuming no prior relation between them. In particular, rhematic information is not always private as for instance when content is repeated for better comprehension or in reply to interposed questions.

Referent Features. All gestures used in the object descriptions have further been coded for their referent and some of its spatio-geometrical properties. These object features are drawn from an imagistic representation built for the VR stimulus of the study (e.g., houses, trees, streets). This hierarchical representation is called *Imagistic Description Trees* (IDT) [29], and is designed to cover all decisive visuo-spatial features of objects one finds in iconic gestures. Each node in an IDT contains an Imagistic Description (IMD) which holds a schema representing the shape of an object or object part. Object schemas contain up to three axes representing spatial extents in terms of a numerical measure and an assignment value like 'max' or 'sub', classifying this axis' extent relative to the other axes. Each axis can cover up to three spatial dimensions to account for rotation symmetries (becoming a so-called 'integrated axis'). The boundary of an object can be defined by a profile vector that states symmetry, size, and edge properties for each object axis or pair of axes. Links in the tree structure represent spatial

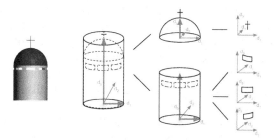

Fig. 2. A church tower (from the VR stimulus) and IDT representation of its shape

relations between parts and wholes, and are defined by transformation matrices. Fig. 2 illustrates how imagery can be operationalized with the IDT model. The spatio-geometrical features entered in the corpus are drawn from these visuo-spatial representations (see Table 1).

3   Results—Systematicities and Idiosyncracies

As reported in [4] individuals differ significantly in the surface level of their gestural behavior, i.e., in their gesture rate and their preferences for particular representation techniques or morphological gesture features. Our corpus analysis here investigates whether such aspects of iconic gesture production seem to be rather systematic, i.e. common among speakers in the same situation, or idiosyncratic, i.e. perculiar to a certain individual. We focus on the following two generation decisions: (1) whether or not a gesture will be produced, and (2) which hand(s) will be used. Since we are dealing with data measured on a nominal scale, we employ Pearson's chi-square test to to judge whether paired observations on two variables, expressed in a contingency table, are independent of each other.

One important question arising is whether the individual differences are due to the fact that different speakers follow different subsets of (possibly shared) dependencies between contextual factors and gestural features? Or do they rather select different features for the same factors, i.e. do individuals diverge from the general tendencies found in the data? We employ two different kinds of measure to investigate these questions. First, we assessed for each individual if the particular (significant) correlation found in the whole data is also significant for the individual. Second, as a measure for individual divergence from the significant common correlations, we assessed for each speaker if her/his joint distributions coincide with the general distribution. Notably, we only considered those cells in the contingency tables in which there is at least a significant difference between observed and expected number of occurrences ($p < .05$).

3.1   To Gesture or Not to Gesture?

The question whether or not a gesture is produced for a particular object seems to be highly idiosyncratic. In the whole corpus (N=25) gesture rates differ from a minimum of 2.34 to a maximum of 32.83 gestures per minute. The mean gesture rate is 15.64 gestures per minute (SD = 7.06). For the five dyads which are analyzed in detail here, the gesture rates vary between 12.5 to 25.0 gestures per minute. The a priori probability for gesture occurrence during a noun phrase in speech is 58.0%. This distribution varies inter-subjectively between a minimum of 44.4% and a maximum of 74.5%.

The choice to produce a gesture is decisively influenced by several other variables, as displayed in Table 2. For the discourse context we found the thematization to be decisive insofar as rhematic information is significantly more likely to be accompanied by a gesture ($\chi^2 = 66.396, df = 1, p < 0.001$). Individuals share this relationship: although the relation is not significant for one of the speakers, all five speakers agree on the distribution, i.e. they tend to use gestures for rhematic information whereas for thematic information gestures are less likely to occur. Regarding the information state, people are more likely to produce gestures for entities whose information state is private

Table 2. Interrelation of gesture occurrence and influencing variables. Parenthetical values are expected occurrences (*p<.05, **p<.01, ***p<.001).

		Gesture (y/n)		Individuals	
		no gesture	gesture	significance	similar distr.
Thematization	rheme	103 (142.8) ***	248 (208.2) **	4/5	5/5
	theme	96 (56.2) ***	42 (81.8) ***		
InfoState	private	83 (102.1)	168 (148.9)	2/5	5/5
	shared	116 (96.9)	122 (141.1)		
CommGoal	lm	17 (10.6) *	9 (15.4)		
	lmDescrProp	67 (65.1)	93 (94.9)	2/5	5/5
	lmDescrConstr	54 (49.6)	68 (72.4)		
	lmDescrPos	61 (73.7)	120 (107.3)		
MainAxis	none	44 (47.2)	72 (68.8)		
	width	44 (43.5)	63 (63.5)	3/5	4/5
	height	100 (87.9)	116 (128.1)		
	depth	11 (20.3) *	39 (29.7)		
Subparts	none	68 (92.8)**	160 (135.2)*	2/5	5/5
	1 or more	131 (106.2) *	130 (154.8) *		
SymAxes	none	97 (74.5) **	86 (108.5) *	2/5	5/5
	sym	102 (124.5) *	204 (181.5)		

($\chi^2 = 12.432, df = 1, p < 0.001$). This is in line with the view that new information is introduced into the discourse by gesture [24]. Again, all individuals share the same distribution, although the relation is only significant for two of them. So it seems as if this link between information state and gesture occurrence is not as strong as the link between thematization and gesture occurrence. Moreover, the communicative goal has an impact on the question whether or not to gesture ($\chi^2 = 10.970, df = 3, p = 0.012$). When a landmark is just mentioned (lm), this utterance is not very likely to be accompanied by a gesture. This dependence between variables, however, is only significant for two individuals, although all five agree on the distribution by trend. That is, they use less gestures than expected for landmarks which are just mentioned without further elaboration of any kind.

As concerns the influence of referent features, three features appear to be decisive. First, there is a significant relationship between the choice to gesture and the referent's main axis: if from the speaker's point of view the main axis of an object is its depth (e.g. a tunnel into which one is looking) a gesture is more likely to be produced than in other cases ($\chi^2 = 10.424, df = 3, p = 0.015$). For three of the five speakers this relation is significant, and only one speaker does not share the trend. Moreover, the complexity of the object (part) is influential. Utterances which refer to leaf nodes of the IDT representation are more often accompanied by gestures than utterances referring to inner nodes of the tree representation ($\chi^2 = 20.916, df = 1, p < 0.001$). All individuals share this kind of distribution, however, it is only significant for two of them. Furthermore, for objects which have at least one symmetry axis, gestures are more likely to occur than for objects which do not have any symmetry ($\chi^2 = 18.363, df = 1, p < 0.001$). Again, all speakers share this kind of distribution, but it is only significant for two of them.

In summary, the decision[2] to gesture is influenced by two kinds of variables, the discourse context and referent features. As concerns the former, gestures are predominantly produced for rhematic and private information. Regarding the latter, gestures

---

[2] The term 'decision' is not meant to imply a conscious process here.

occur more often for less complex (parts of) objects in the sense that they are symmetrical to some degree and have no subparts in the IDT representation. These two findings are rather systematic, i.e., uncontroversial among the five speakers we looked at. However, a significance of the very correlation is not given for all individuals. In other words, speakers vary particularly in how strong the link between particular variables is.

3.2   Which Hand to Use?

A further analysis concerned another fundamental choice in the generation of gestures: the question which hand(s) to use when referring to an entity. The general distribution of handedness in our data (in which all speaker describe exactly the same spatial scenes) is as follows: with 56.6% the majority of gestures is performed two-handed, while right-handed gestures occur in 28.6% of the cases and left-handed gestures in 14.8%. Again, this distribution is not shared by all speakers. To illustrate this we contrast two particular speakers, P7 and P15. P7 prefers two-handed gestures (65.8%). Accordingly, the number of right-handed gestures (20.5%) and left-handed gestures (13.7%) is reduced. In contrast, P7 has a strong preference for one-handed gestures: 45.1% of this speakers' gestures are performed with the right hand and 25.5% are performed with the left hand. The number of two-handed gestures is accordingly low (29.4%).

Again, we found several correlations in the data constraining this decision (see Table 3). First, there is a significant relationship between the gestural representation technique and the handedness ($\chi^2 = 50.476, df = 8, p < 0.001$). This positive correlation is due to the fact that indexing gestures are hardly ever performed with both hands. On the contrary, shaping gestures are more likely to be performed two-handed. This distribution is shared among all five speakers, whereas significance is only given in four speakers.

Second, there is a significant relationship between the referent's main axis and the gesture's handedness ($\chi^2 = 54.645, df = 6, p < 0.001$): for objects whose major extent is oriented horizontally, two-handed gestures are likely to occur, whereas left- and right-handed gestures occur less often than expected. On the contrary, objects with a main vertical axis are predominantly accompanied by left- or right-handed gestures. The number of two-handed gestures is decreased in these cases. Here we have four speakers sharing this kind of distribution in a significant way.

And finally, as one would expect, the referent's position is influential for handedness ($\chi^2 = 50.893, df = 4, p < .001$). Referents which are on the right from the speaker's point of view are more likely to be accompanied by right-handed gestures and referents which are on the speaker's left tend to be referred to by left-handed gestures. Additionally, for referents which are centered, the number of two-handed gestures is increased compared to expectation. Four of the five individuals agree on the distribution which is significant in three speakers.

In conclusion, we found that a gesture's handedness is not independent from the representation technique used as well as the referent's main axis and position. Individual differences, as we measured them, are not very strong in these relations. As we have already seen in the previous section, individuals tend to agree on the general distribution, but may differ in how strong the links are.

Table 3. Interrelation of handedness and influencing variables. Parenthetical values are expected occurrences (*p<.05, **p<.01, ***p<.001).

		Handedness			Individuals	
		2H	LH	RH	significance	similar distr.
Technique	indexing	3 (20.4) ***	12 (5.3) **	21 (10.3) ***		
	placing	41 (38.5)	12 (10.1)	15 (19.5)		
	shaping	81 (65.0) *	13 (17.1)	21 (32.9) *	4/5	5/5
	drawing	27 (25.4)	2 (6.7)	16 (12.9)		
	posturing	12 (14.7)	4 (3.9)	10 (7.4)		
MainAxis	none	47 (40.7)	8 (10.7)	17 (20.6)		
	width	56 (43.6) ***	1 (9.3) **	6 (18.0) **		
	height	39 (65.6) ***	27 (17.2) **	50 (33.2) **	4/5	4/5
	depth	22 (22.1)	7 (5.8)	10 (11.2)		
Position	left	42 (44.1)	16 (11.6)	20 (22.3)		
	right	32 (56.0) ***	21 (14.7)	46 (28.3)***	3/5	4/5
	middle	90 (63.9) ***	6 (16.8) **	17 (32.3) **		

3.3 Which Representation Technique?

Another interesting question in gesture generation is the choice of representation techniques. The distribution of representation techniques in our data is as follows: shaping (39.7%), placing (23.4%), drawing (15.5%), indexing (12.4%) and posturing (9.0%). As described in [4], the choice of representation technique is influenced by the communicative goal of the utterance: descriptions (lmDescrProp) come along with significantly more depicting gestures (shaping, drawing, posturing), while the spatial arrangement of entities is accompanied by indexing and placing gestures in the majority of cases. Moreover, complex objects (without symmetry, or with further subparts) are likely to be positioned gesturally, while less complex objects are more likely to be depicted by gesture. Individuals tend to agree on this general distribution for the most part, but differ in how strong the relations between correlated variables are. Fore a more detailed analysis of the interrelation between use of gestural representation techniques and correlated variables see [4].

4 Computational Modeling

In the previous section we have shown that decisions in the generation of iconic gestures are influenced by a number of variables. Most of the correlations are shared among individuals, whereas for some there is considerable variance among individuals. For a computational model of speech and iconic gesture production three major conclusions can be drawn: first, iconic gestures are not solely implied by the object they are referring to. Rather, 'thematization' as a variable characterizing (part of) the linguistic context into which a gesture is embedded is decisive. This correlation goes with empirical findings that speech and gesture production mutually influence each other. On the one hand, information packaging for iconic gestures parallels linguistic packaging (cf. [16,9,3]); on the other hand, representational gesturing can have a significant impact on conceptualization as well as lexical access for language (cf. [1,13]). An adequate model for speech and gesture production, therefore, should allow for a close interaction between content planning and formulation of speech and gesture. Second, generation decisions are influenced by the overall discourse context. For a computational model this means that a discourse record is necessary to distinguish between private and shared knowledge about a referent. Such a discourse record is indispensable for speech formulation to, e.g., decide for the adequate type of determiner (definite or indefinite), and it must be accessible for gesture formulation too. Third, an adequate model of how speakers produce iconic gestures must account for both types of influential patterns, general and individual ones. Previous modeling attempts either ignored idiosyncrasy coming up with generalized model-based approaches [18], or they employ statistical data-driven techniques which have problems with identifying and explicating systematicities from corpora of managable size [27].

We have proposed and described elsewhere [17,4] a production architecture that is inspired by psycholinguistic models [16,7] and accounts for our first two requirements. As outlined in Fig. 3 (right) it consists of interacting, modality-specific modules at each of three stages: (1) an *Image Generator* and a *Preverbal Message Generator* are concerned with content planning; (2) a *Speech Formulator* and a *Gesture Formulator* compose and specify, on-the-fly, natural language sentences and gesture morphologies; (3) *Motor Control* and *Phonation* turn them into synchronized speech and gesture animations. This production model adopts a dual-coding approach to multimodal content representation in that an imagistic description (IDT), propositional knowledge, and an interfacing representation out of so-called multimodal concepts are composed and maintained simultaneously. These semantic representations are also utilized for a multimodal discourse model that is available to both speech- and gesture-specific content planning modules, thus meeting the second requirement.

Accounting for the third requirement, the challenge of considering general and individual patterns in gesture formulation, we employ Bayesian decision networks (BDN) which supplement standard Bayesian networks by decision nodes [14]. This formalism suitably provides a representation of a finite sequential decision problem, combining probabilistic and rule-based decision-making. Each decision to be made in the

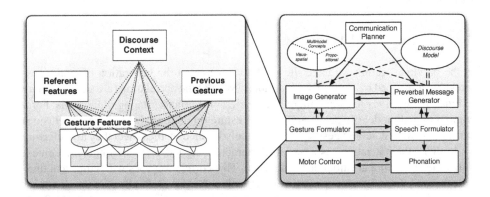

Fig. 3. Overview of the speech and gesture generation model (right), and a zoom in onto the Bayesian decision network for gesture formulation (left)

formation of an iconic gesture, e.g., whether or not to gesture or which representation technique to use, is represented in the network either as a decision node or as a 'chance node with a probability distribution. All factors which potentially contribute to these choices are also entered in the model.

Bayesian networks can be built from the corpus data, both for the whole data corpus, or, for each individual speaker seperately. In either case, the structure of the Bayesian network is learned using the Necessary Path Condition (NPC) algorithm [30]. The NPC algorithm is a constraint-based structure learning algorithm that identifies the structure of the underlying graph by performing a set of statistical tests for pairwise independence between each pair of variables. That is, the independence of any pair of variables given any subset of other variables is tested. The result of structure learning is a network containing all links between variables that are significant for the modeled individual. Once the structure of the network has been found, its maximum likelihood estimates of parameters are computed employing the EM (Estimation-Maximization) algorithm [22]. However, not all variables of a complete gesture specification can be learned from the data. This is due to the large set of values some of the variables have. Variables specifying a gesture's morphology, e.g., values for palm and finger orientation, are combined out of six basic values which can moreover be concatenated into sequences to describe dynamic gestures. It is therefore necessary to formulate additional rules and constraints in decision nodes of the network to specify these values adequately.

A resulting decision network is illustrated in the left of Fig. 3. Influences of three types of variables manifest themselves in dependencies (edges) between the large groups of respective chance nodes (drawn as ovals): (1) referent features, (2) discourse context, and (3) the previously performed gesture. Although not in the scope of the current paper, some generation decisions are related to the previous gesture context, i.e., whether the hands have been in a rest position before, and, if already gesturing, which gesture features were found in that gesture (handedness, representation technique). The network is supplemented with decision nodes (drawn as rectangles) which are defined universally, i.e., they do not vary in the individual networks. Nevertheless, each decision node has chance nodes as predecessors so that these rule-based decisions depend on chance variables whose (individual) values have been determined previously. BDNs are suitable for gesture formation since they provide a way to combine probabilistic (data-driven) and model-based decision-making. Moreover, two sources of individual differences are explicated: first, individual 'local preferences for certain aspects are reflected in the respective conditional probability distributions. Second, individuals that do not share significant correlations between variables have a different link structure in their respective networks .

4.1 Modeling Results

A prototype of the previously described generation model has been realized using a multi-agent system toolkit, a Prolog implementation of SPUD [31], the Hugin toolkit for Bayesian inference [23], and the ACE realization engine [20]. In this prototype implementation a virtual agent explains the same virtual reality buildings that we already used in the previously described empirical study. Being equipped with proper knowledge sources, i.e., communicative plans, lexicon, grammar, propositional and imagistic

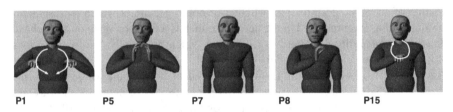

Fig. 4. Example gestures simulating different speakers, each of which produced for the same referent (a round window of a church) in the same initial situation

knowledge about the world, the agent randomly picks a landmark and a certain spatial perspective towards it, and then creates his explanations autonomously. Currently, the system has the ability to simulate five different speakers by switching between the respective decision networks built as described above. The resulting gesturing behavior for a particular referent in a respective discourse context varies in dependence of the decision network which is used for gesture formulation. In Figure 4, examples are given from five different simulations, each of which based on exactly the same initial situation. All gestures are referring to the same round window of a church and are generated in exactly the same discourse context ('lmDescrConstr', 'rheme', 'private'). The resulting gesture hence varies depending only on the employed decision network.

In a first evaluation, we measured the model's prediction accuracy by computing how often the models assessment agreed with the empirically observed gesturing behavior. To evaluate the decisions for those four variables we currently assess as chance nodes, we divided the corpus into training data (80%) and test data (20%) and used the training set for structure learning and parameter estimation of the decision networks. In total, we achieved a mean of 62.4% (SD=11.0) highly accurate predictions with the individual networks. The mean accuracy for the rule-based choices made in the network's decision nodes is 57.8% (SD=15.5) (see [5] for details). A perception-based evaluation study is underway to investigate how the generated behavior is judged by human observers.

5   Conclusion

Our objective in this paper was to shed light on the question how systematic (inter-individual) and idiosyncratic patterns interrelate with each other in iconic gesture production. Our empirical corpus analysis has shown that major decisions in the formation of speech-accompanying gestures are influenced by a number of variables, either referent-features or variables characterizing the overall discourse context.

Some of the correlations are found among individuals, suggesting systematicity, whereas for others there is considerable variance among individuals, hence suggesting a more idiosyncratic nature. Note, however, that these latter patterns may well be the result of the very dialog situation (including, e.g., the recipient), rather than being hard-wired in the individual speaker. Nevertheless, the reason that different speakers overlap in some features of iconic gestures while they tend to differ in others, suggests that the use of iconic gestures is governed by a number of rather stable systematicities and, at the same time, allows for flexible attunements that may result from a personal or context-sensitive use of iconic gesture by the speaker. A computational model has been developed and the results from a prototype implementation are promising, so that we are confident that our approach is a step forward towards a comprehensive account of iconic gesture generation. Future work in this direction will need to look at a larger spectrum of factors: from individual cognitive skills (as suggested in [12]) to features of the current state between interlocutors. Furthermore, the limitation to five individuals and a set of 290 gestures has to be lifted. Nevertheless, this data suffices to get a first impression of the interrelation of systematic and idiosyncratic patterns and provided a proof of concept for our modeling approach.

Acknowledgements

This research is partially supported by the Deutsche Forschungsgemeinschaft (DFG) in the SFB 673 "Alignment in Communication" and the Center of Excellence in "Cognitive Interaction Technology" (CITEC).

References

1. Alibali, M., Kita, S., Young, A.: Gesture and the process of speech production: We think, therefore we gesture. Language and cognitive processes 15, 593–613 (2000)
2. Bavelas, J., Gerwing, J., Sutton, C., Prevost, D.: Gesturing on the telephone: Independent effects of dialogue and visibility. Journal of Memory and Language 58, 495–520 (2008)
3. Bavelas, J., Kenwood, C., Johnson, T., Philips, B.: An experimental study of when and how speakers use gestures to communicate. Gesture 1, 1–17 (2002)
4. Bergmann, K., Kopp, S.: Increasing expressiveness for virtual agents–Autonomous generation of speech and gesture for spatial description tasks. In: Decker, K., Sichman, J., Sierra, C., Castelfranchi, C. (eds.) Proceedings of the 8th International Conference on Autonomous Agents and Multiagent Systems, pp. 361–368 (2009)
5. Bergmann, K., Kopp, S.: GNetIc – using bayesian decision networks for iconic gesture generation. In: Ruttkay, Z., Kipp, M., Nijholt, A., Vilhjálmsson, H.H. (eds.) IVA 2009. LNCS, vol. 5773, pp. 76–89. Springer, Heidelberg (2009)
6. Cassell, J., Stone, M., Yan, H.: Coordination and context-dependence in the generation of embodied conversation. In: Proceedings of the First International Conference on Natural Language Generation (2000)
7. de Ruiter, J.: The production of gesture and speech. In: McNeill, D. (ed.) Language and gesture. Cambridge University Press, Cambridge (2000)
8. Denis, M.: The description of routes: A cognitive approach to the production of spatial discourse. Current Psychology of Cognition 16, 409–458 (1997)
9. Gullberg, M., Hendriks, H., Hickmann, M.: Learning to talk and gesture about motion in french. First Language 28(2), 200–236 (2008)
10. Gwet, K.: Handbook of Inter-Rater Reliability. STATAXIS Publishing Company (2001)
11. Halliday, M.: Notes on transitivity and theme in english (part 2). Journal of Linguistics 3, 199–247 (1967)
12. Hostetter, A., Alibali, M.: Raise your hand if you're spatial–Relations between verbal and spatial skills and gesture production. Gesture 7(1), 73–95 (2007)

13. Hostetter, A., Alibali, M., Kita, S.: I see it in my hands' eye: Representational gestures reflect conceptual demands. Language and Cogn. Processes 22, 313–336 (2007)
14. Howard, R., Matheson, J.: Influence diagrams. Decision Analysis 2(3), 127–143 (2005)
15. Kendon, A.: Gesture–Visible Action as Utterance. Cambridge University Press, Cambridge (2004)
16. Kita, S., Özyürek, A.: What does cross-linguistic variation in semantic coordination of speech and gesture reveal?: Evidence for an interface representation of spatial thinking and speaking. Journal of Memory and Language 48, 16–32 (2003)
17. Kopp, S., Bergmann, K., Wachsmuth, I.: Multimodal communication from multimodal thinking–Towards an integrated model of speech and gesture production. International Journal of Semantic Computing 2(1), 115–136 (2008)
18. Kopp, S., Tepper, P., Cassell, J.: Towards integrated microplanning of language and iconic gesture for multimodal output. In: Proc. Intern. Conf. on Multimodal Interfaces, pp. 97–104. ACM Press, New York (2004)
19. Kopp, S., Tepper, P., Ferriman, K., Striegnitz, K., Cassell, J.: Trading spaces: How humans and humanoids use speech and gesture to give directions. In: Nishida, T. (ed.) Conversational Informatics, pp. 133–160. John Wiley, New York (2007)
20. Kopp, S., Wachsmuth, I.: Synthesizing multimodal utterances for conversational agents. Computer Animation and Virtual Worlds 15(1), 39–52 (2004)
21. Kruijff-Korbayova, I., Steedman, M.: Discourse and information structure. Journal of Logic, Language and Information 12, 249–259 (2003)
22. Lauritzen, S.L.: The EM algorithm for graphical association models with missing data. Computational Statistics and Data Analysis 19, 191–201 (1995)
23. Madsen, A., Jensen, F., Kjærulff, U., Lang, M.: HUGIN–The tool for bayesian networks and influence diagrams. International Journal of Artificial Intelligence Tools 14(3), 507–543 (2005)
24. McNeill, D.: Hand and Mind - What Gestures Reveal about Thought. University of Chicago Press, Chicago (1992)
25. McNeill, D., Duncan, S.: Growth points in thinking-for-speaking. In: Language and gesture. Cambridge Univ. Press, Cambridge (2000)
26. Müller, C.: Redebegleitende Gesten: Kulturgeschichte–Theorie–Sprachvergleich. Berlin Verlag, Berlin (1998)
27. Neff, M., Kipp, M., Albrecht, I., Seidel, H.-P.: Gesture modeling and animation based on a probabilistic re-creation of speaker style. ACM Transactions on Graphics 27(1), 1–24 (2008)
28. Ritz, J., Dipper, S., Götze, M.: Annotation of information structure: An evaluation across different types of texts. In: Proceedings of the 6th LREC conference, pp. 2137–2142 (2008)
29. Sowa, T., Wachsmuth, I.: A model for the representation and processing of shape in coverbal iconic gestures. In: Proc. KogWis 2005, pp. 183–188 (2005)
30. Steck, H., Tresp, V.: Bayesian belief networks for data mining. In: Proceedings of the 2nd Workshop on Data Mining and Data Warehousing (1999)
31. Stone, M., Doran, C., Webber, B., Bleam, T., Palmer, M.: Microplanning with Communicative Intentions: The SPUD System. Comput. Intelligence 19(4), 311–381 (2003)
32. Streeck, J.: Depicting by gesture. Gesture 8(3), 285–301 (2008)

To Beat or Not to Beat:
Beat Gestures in Direction Giving

Mariët Theune and Chris J. Brandhorst

Human Media Interaction,
University of Twente,
P.O. Box 217, 7500 AE Enschede,
The Netherlands
m.theune@ewi.utwente.nl, c.j.brandhorst@alumnus.utwente.nl

Abstract. Research on gesture generation for embodied conversational agents (ECA's) mostly focuses on gesture types such as pointing and iconic gestures, while ignoring another gesture type frequently used by human speakers: beat gestures. Analysis of a corpus of route descriptions showed that although annotators show very low agreement in applying a 'beat filter' aimed at identifying physical features of beat gestures, they are capable of reliably distinguishing beats from other gestures in a more intuitive manner. Beat gestures made up more than 30% of the gestures in our corpus, and they were sometimes used when expressing concepts for which other gesture types seemed a more obvious choice. Based on these findings we propose a simple, probabilistic model of beat production for ECA's. However, it is clear that more research is needed to determine why direction givers in some cases use beats when other gestures seem more appropriate, and vice versa.

Keywords: gesture and speech, gesture analysis, beats, direction giving.

1 Introduction

When humans speak, they use gestures that "are not random but convey to listeners information that can complement or even supplement the information relayed in speech" [1], p. 228. One type of discourse in which this relation is undoubtedly present is direction giving. To illustrate this, consider two of the main gesture types distinguished by gesture researcher David McNeill [2]. *Deictic gestures* are pointing movements indicating the location of items being referred to. In direction giving, such gestures are often used to indicate the location of landmarks along a route [3]. *Iconic gestures* depict a physical aspect of what is spoken about, such as the shape of an object or the trajectory of a movement. Such gestures are often used to illustrate the shape of landmarks [4].

For another important type of gestures, however, the link with direction giving is less obvious. *Beat gestures* do not convey any semantic content, but reflect discourse structure by marking important words and phrases. Unlike other gestures, they tend to have the same shape regardless of the speech content. McNeill describes their shape as follows:

S. Kopp and I. Wachsmuth (Eds.): GW 2009, LNAI 5934, pp. 195–206, 2010.

The hand moves along with the rhythmical pulsation of speech. [...] The typical beat is a simple flick of the hand or fingers up and down, or back and forth; the movement is short and quick and the space may be the periphery of the gesture space (the lap, an armrest of the chair, etc.). The critical thing that distinguishes the beat from other types of gesture is that it has just two movement phases – in/out, up/down, etc. [2], p. 15

In a video corpus of people narrating the events from a Tweety cartoon, McNeill found that beats made up 44,7% of all gestures [2], p. 93. Though the beat ratio may be different for other types of discourse, McNeill's finding shows that beats are frequently used by human speakers, and therefore should not be overlooked when developing gesture models for embodied conversational agents (ECA's): human-like computer characters that can employ gestures and speech to carry out conversations with human users.

In our department we have developed an ECA that can give directions to visitors in a virtual environment [5]. This ECA, called the Virtual Guide, can generate deictic and (simple) iconic gestures, but it has only very limited support for beat gestures. To improve this, we analysed the use of beat gestures in a video corpus of human route descriptions, with the aim of using the results for a simple beat usage model for the Virtual Guide. First, however, we needed to determine which of the gestures in our corpus were beats and which were not.

The research questions addressed in this paper are the following:

1. How can beat gestures be distinguished from other gesture types?
2. At which points in route descriptions do people use beat gestures?
3. Knowing when to use beats, how can this be modelled for the Virtual Guide?

The remainder of the paper is structured as follows. First, in Section 2 we discuss related work on gesture generation for (direction giving) ECA's. In Section 3 we describe our route description corpus. Then, in Section 4 we examine whether beats can be distinguished from non-beats based on their physical properties. In Section 5 we investigate when beat gestures are used during route giving discourse. In Section 6 we propose a simple probabilistic model for the generation of beat gestures, and in Section 7 we end with conclusions and future work.

2   Related Work

NUMACK (the Northwestern University Multimodal Autonomous Conversational Kiosk) is an ECA that can give directions to locations on the Northwestern University campus, using a sophisticated 'multimodal microplanner' for integrated language and gesture generation. The generation of iconic gestures is based on a model by Kopp et al. that links visual properties of objects to gesture features such as hand shape and trajectory [4]. Using this model, new iconic gestures that appropriately reflect the shape of landmarks can be assembled on the fly, instead of using fixed gesture animations as is done by most ECA's (including our Virtual Guide). NUMACK can also generate gestures indicating the location of landmarks, as described by Striegnitz et al. [3]. However, beat gestures do not appear to be included in NUMACK's gesture repertoire.

A well-known framework for automatic gesture and speech generation for animated characters is BEAT, the Behavior Expression Animation Toolkit [6]. It can be used to animate an ECA based on an input text that is automatically analysed and augmented with suggestions for nonverbal behaviour. This augmentation is done in a "liberal and all-inclusive" fashion: any gesture that is deemed appropriate is suggested and given a priority. Beats are used when introducing new material or when contrasting items and are always given the lowest priority. They are only selected when no higher-priority gestures are available to express the same information (unless they can be overlaid on top of the other gesture). Similar approaches to gesture generation, in which the use of more specific gestures is preferred over beat gestures, include [7,8,9].

A completely different approach to gesture generation is that by Neff et al. [10], who create statistical models that capture the gesture style of individual speakers based on annotated video material. In their system, gesture choice is based on speaker profiles: probabilistic mappings from semantic tags (capturing aspects of the semantics and communicative function of the verbal message) to gesture types. In this approach, the probability of generating a beat gesture is based on the frequency with which the modelled speaker used beat gestures in combination with a particular semantic tag, as encoded in the speaker's profile.

Most recently, Bergmann and Kopp proposed a data-driven model for integrated language and gesture generation that can still account for systematic meaning-form mappings, where speaker preferences are learned from corpus data [11]. However, like [4], this model is restricted to iconic gestures.

3   Route Description Corpus

Our corpus comprises 16 short movie clips with an average duration of 38 seconds. Each clip shows a person giving an indoor route description in Dutch. All descriptions start from the same point in the building (the point where the direction giver is standing). The movie clips differ in a number of respects:

- Route: two different routes are described. They have the same starting point but a different destination within the same building.
- Camera viewpoint: in 8 movie clips, the direction giver explains the route to the route seeker in a face-to-face dialogue. In the other 8 clips, the route is described to the camera.
- Direction giver: four direction givers were filmed. All were male students or employees in our department, and native speakers of Dutch. Each of them explained both routes twice: first to the route seeker and then to the camera (see the previous point). This resulted in four movie clips for each speaker.

The movie clips were transcribed and segmented into gesture clips using Transana,[1] resulting in a data set of 162 gestures.

---

[1] www.transana.org

4 Distinguishing Beats from Other Gestures

In this section it is examined whether beat gestures can reliably be distinguished using physical properties only. To this end, we annotated the gestures in our video corpus with Beat Filter scores and gesture types.

4.1 The Beat Filter

McNeill's Beat Filter[2] is a method for distinguishing imagistic gestures such as iconics from non-imagistic gestures, i.e., beats [2]. It is a purely formal scoring system, without reference to content or function. It only looks at the kinetics of the gestures. Applying the beat filter to a gesture means giving it a score by adding 1 for each positive answer to the following questions (except question 2). The higher the resulting score, the less likely the gesture is a beat.

1. Does the gesture have more than two movement phases?[3]
2. How many times does wrist/finger movement OR tensed stasis appear in any movement phase not ending in a rest position? (ignore retraction phase, add the number of times to the score)
3. If the first movement is in non-central space: is any other movement performed in central space?[4]
4. If there are exactly two movement phases: is the first phase in a different place as the second phase?

The beat filter was applied by two annotators (the authors) to 154 of the 162 gestures in the corpus. The other 8 gestures were not clearly visible, for example because the speaker turned his back to the camera, and could not be annotated.

4.2 Gesture Types

The Beat Filter does not explicitly group gestures into beats or non-beats; the resulting score only represents the (un)likeliness of a gesture being a beat. To determine the relation between Beat Filter scores and gesture type, all 154 visible gestures from the corpus were independently annotated for gesture type by three annotators: the authors plus a third annotator. The gesture types used were those from McNeill [2]: beats, deictic gestures, iconic gestures, and metaphoric gestures. The latter are like iconics, but describe non-physical, abstract entities, for example shaping the hands like a bowl to illustrate the concept 'group'.

Many gestures do not neatly fit into one of the four above-mentioned gesture categories; they may have features of more than one gesture type, for example because a beat is superimposed on another gesture [2]. Therefore we included the possibility of annotating gestures as belonging to more than one type. In

---

[2] Originally developed by Bill Eilfort.

[3] Movement phases are preparation, stroke and retraction. Beats have no stroke.

[4] The *central space* is the part of the gesture space directly in front of the torso, excluding the hip area and lower [2].

cases when no one dominant type could be established for a particular gesture, it was annotated as a mixed type, e.g., beat/iconic.

In general, the gesture type annotations were based on the gestures' global shape in combination with the speech context, i.e., the words spoken while the speaker was gesturing. For example, if the hands were moved forward in parallel, mimicking a tunnel-like shape when talking about a "hallway", the gesture was annotated as iconic. If the speaker pointed in a certain direction in combination with words such as "left", "right" or "there" this was annotated as a deictic gesture. Beat gestures formed an exception to this: since they have no inherent meaning, they were classified on the basis of their shape alone.

Beat gestures and deictic gestures, which can be somewhat similar in shape, were distinguished based on the amount of extension of the arms (the larger this extension, the more probably it is a deictic gesture), hand shape (extension of the index finger indicates a deictic gesture), and directional aspect in combination with the speech context. Concerning the latter property, we assume that beats are in principle 'directionless', meaning that when making a beat gesture, the hand does not move in the horizontal plane but only in the vertical plane. This is in line with McNeill's characterisation of beats as low-energy gestures with the lowest kinetic complexity [2]. So, if a speaker mentioned a specific direction or landmark while making a somewhat beat-like gesture in the corresponding direction, this was annotated as a deictic gesture, not a beat.

Note this means that gestures were classified as beats only when they had the right shape and there were no indications (e.g., from the speech context) that they were of another type. This 'classification by negation' approach may have led to an underestimation of the number of beats in our data.

4.3   Results

When analysing the results, our first step was to analyse the reliability of the annotations by computing the level of agreement between annotators in terms of the Kappa coefficient. When considering all possible gesture types, agreement between pairs of annotators was quite low (Kappa values ranging between .41 and .44). However, when only considering the distinction between beat gestures and other types of gesture, i.e., when classifying all non-beat gestures as 'other', agreement between annotators was much better with Kappa values of .68, .60 and .57 between annotator pairs. Though not all good according to the strictest scale for evaluating Kappa significance, according to more lenient scales these values indicate at least moderate agreement [12]. In the remainder of this paper, we therefore classify the gestures in our corpus as either beats or 'other' gestures, referring to more specific types only when necessary. For the final type classification we used the type assigned by the majority of the annotators. This resulted in 52 gestures being classified as beats, which amounts to 32,1% of all gestures in our corpus (33,8% of all annotated gestures).[5] This set includes 7 beats that were

---

[5] The actual percentage of beats in our corpus may be slightly higher, because some of the 8 unannotated gestures could be beats.

Table 1. Gesture use of individual direction givers

	Gestures	Beats	Gestures/word
Speaker 1	23	10 (43,5%)	.06
Speaker 2	61	24 (39,3%)	.12
Speaker 3	40	12 (30,0%)	.10
Speaker 4	38	6 (15,8%)	.14
Total	162	52 (32,1%)	

classified as beat/other, and 2 what we termed 'multibeats': quick sequences of beats that could not be separated into individual beat gestures.

We found large differences in beat usage between individual speakers. Table 1 shows the total number of gestures per speaker, the number of beats, and also the average number of gestures per word. Note the striking contrast between speakers 1 and 4: the former used few gestures, many of which were beats, while the latter used many gestures, few of which were beats.

For the Beat Filter, agreement on the filter questions was unfortunately very low. The highest agreement between the two annotators was .34 for the answers to question 1. This means that the Beat Filter scores assigned to the gestures in our corpus are very unreliable. Nevertheless, as illustrated by Fig. 1, the Beat Filter does give some indication of the probability that a gesture is a beat: for both annotators, gestures with a low score are more likely to be beats than not. In Fig. 1, the multibeats are shown separately from the other beats. This is because the former are always assigned a relatively high score by the Beat Filter, since these successions of beat moves are seen as one gesture ([2], p. 381).

As can be seen in Fig. 1, several gestures were assigned a low Beat Filter score despite not having been classified as beats. Most of the non-beat gestures with a score of 0 or 1 were annotated (by the majority of annotators) as deictic gestures: 13 out of 19 (68%) for annotator A and 11 out of 20 (55%) for annotator B. This is not surprising, since deictic gestures are fairly similar in shape to beat gestures, as discussed in Section 4.2.

4.4   Discussion

As shown above, human annotators can fairly reliably distinguish beats from other gestures based on a global impression of their shape, but they cannot reliably apply the Beat Filter that was designed to make the same distinction in a more formal way. Moreover, Fig. 1 shows that although lower Beat Filter scores do tend to correspond to higher relative numbers of beat gestures, many gestures with a low beat score are not beats. In most cases these 'other' low scoring gestures turn out to be deictic gestures, which can be very similar in shape to beats. This holds in particular for what we call 'weak' deictic gestures, i.e., deictic gestures on which the speaker did not spend much energy. They are small and quick: the hand only moves a short distance into the direction that is indicated, staying inside the periphery of the gesture space, and there is no

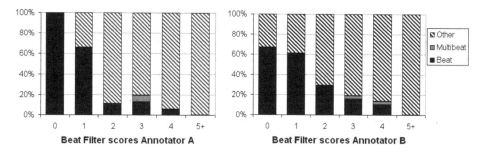

Fig. 1. Beat Filter scores and gesture types

tensed stasis or finger movement. Both characteristics are shared by beats and earn zero Beat Filter points for questions 2 and 3. Moreover, other features that do distinguish deictic gestures from beats (arm extension and the presence of a directional component) are not checked by the Beat Filter. In other words, the Beat Filter is not well-suited to distinguish beats from deictic gestures. This can be explained by the fact that the Beat Filter was only designed to distinguish imagistic gestures (iconic/metaphoric) from non-imagistic gestures (beats), and deictic gestures are somewhere in between the two.

To make the Beat Filter better suited for distinguishing between beats and all other gestures it needs to be extended with additional questions that are specifically aimed at filtering out deictic gestures, by checking for directional aspects and arm extension. However, even then it will remain difficult to distinguish beats from 'weak' deictic gestures. In addition, the description of the Beat Filter will have to be improved so the questions cannot give rise to different interpretations by individual annotators, which we assume was one of the causes for the low agreement found in our study.

5   When Are Beat Gestures Used?

This section takes a closer look at the speech context in which beat gestures are used. We identified some important route description concepts and examined by which type of gestures (beats or other) they were accompanied in our data.

5.1   Route Description Concepts

Conceptually, the basic elements of route descriptions are **paths**, instructions to move along some pathway, **turns**, instructions to change direction at a choice point, and **landmarks**, mentions of objects along the route that help with navigation, in particular by signalling where turns are to be made [13]. A fourth category distinguished in [13] is that of **location** information, indicating the spatial location of the destination. For our purposes, we have replaced this concept with two new categories: the more general **spatial information** indicating the spatial location of all route objects (not just the destination) and **destination**, which are direct references to the destination. Additional concept categories we distinguish are **deictic references**, situationally dependent references to points in time and space, and **hesitations**. These are not specific to route descriptions, but they occurred frequently in our corpus in combination with gestures.

Below, we list all concept categories used in our analysis, together with some examples of how these concepts were verbally expressed in our corpus.[6] In some examples, multiple concepts are mentioned in one phrase. Here, the words that were accompanied by a gesture are given in italics, to indicate which concept was marked by the gesture:

- **Paths**: "*through* the corridor, "*past* the lavatories", "*all the way* to the end"
- **Turns**: "turn left", "walk downstairs", "go in that direction".
- **Landmarks**: "very long corridor", "spiral staircase", "windows"
- **Spatial information**: "then you are *near*", "*behind* it we see lots of computers", "the tunnel *on the right*"
- **Destination**: "the East Hall", "the practicum rooms"
- **Deictic references**: "now", "here", "over there", "*that* corridor"
- **Hesitations**: "ehm", "maybe", "I don't know"

For each of the 162 gestures in our corpus, we annotated which concept it accompanied. If the speech context of the gesture did not match any of the categories given above, the concept was classified as **other**.

5.2 Results

Figure 2 shows the results of our analysis, where the 8 'unknown' gestures are those of which the type could not be determined (see Section 4). In our corpus, some concepts are more often accompanied by beats than any other gestures. In the first place we find **destinations**: 85,7% of all gestures accompanying the mention of a destination are beats. Beats are also prevalent during **hesitations**. Here, 53.5% of accompanying gestures are beats. Finally, almost all (81,8%) of the gestures accompanying **other** concepts are beats. This category is mainly made up of various discourse structure markers ("*and* because", "*so* I'd say", "which *also* says") and abstract actions ("what you want to *do* is", "then you *see*"). For the remaining concepts, other gestures were used more frequently than beats, with beat frequencies ranging from 36,8% (**paths**) to 15% (**landmarks**).

5.3 Discussion

In our corpus, references to the route **destination** are predominantly accompanied by beats. Presumably this is because these references mostly had the form of proper names rather than descriptions referring to shape or location, meaning that the use of an iconic or deictic gesture was not appropriate in these cases.

We also found a relatively high number of beats accompanying *hesitations*.[7] One possible explanation for this is Krauss' hypothesis that gesturing aids lexical

---

[6] All examples have been translated from Dutch to English.

[7] The beat ratio for hesitations in our corpus may be relatively high because one speaker uttered relatively many hesitations, mostly accompanied by beat gestures.

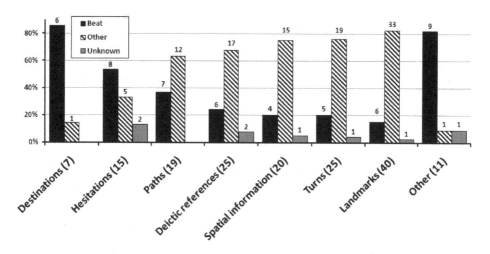

Fig. 2. Concept categories and gesture types for all 162 gestures in the corpus. For 8 gestures the type could not be determined; these are labeled as 'unknown'.

access [14]. Interestingly, Krauss' hypothesis was explicitly limited to 'lexical gestures', i.e., non-beats, while our findings suggest that beats might play a similar role. An alternative explanation is that the beats serve as 'attempt-suppressing signals' indicating that the speaker intends to hold the turn, thus suppressing any interruption attempts by the conversation partner while the speaker is searching for words [15].

For the other categories besides the rest category **other**, beats are in a clear minority. References to spatial locations, directions and landmarks lend themselves well to being illustrated by deictic or iconic gestures, which may explain why beat gestures are only rarely used when expressing these concepts. Still, the fact that beats are used at all, when seemingly more appropriate gestures are available, is somewhat surprising. To shed more light on this issue, we take a closer look within some of the concept categories, inspecting the specific cases in which beats are used. For **deictic references**, it turns out that most beats accompany references to the "here" and "now" of the speaker (4 beats out of 5 gestures) rather than references to concrete, visible locations (2 beats out of 20 gestures). This make sense, since for concrete spatial references beats are less useful than deictic gestures (17 of 20), as the latter may help the hearer to identify the referent. On the other hand, pointing does not have much added value in case of 'here and now' references, which are quite unambiguous. Gestures accompanying these references only seem to be used for marking them as new or otherwise important, and this discourse function can be fulfilled with the least effort by a beat gesture.

On a smaller scale, this 'principle of least effort' also seems to apply to **spatial information**. If we split this category into references to *topological* information and references to *projective* information, cf. [16], we see that beats are used more often for topological information (3 beats out of 10 gestures) than for projective information (1 beat out of 10 gestures). Again, a possible explanation is that deictic gestures have less added value for topological information (references to a region proximal to some object, e.g., "near", "behind") than for projective information (references to a particular direction relative to an object, e.g, "to the left of"), so for topological information speakers are more likely to use the less effortful beat gestures instead. However, in both this and the previous case, our data are too sparse to draw any strong conclusions from them.

Another explanation for the use of beats with 'less obvious' concept categories lies in the notion of information structure. McNeill claims that less informative discourse elements are more likely to be accompanied by beats than by other gestures [2]. This holds for example for anaphoric references to discourse elements that have been previously mentioned. When inspecting the **landmarks** category, we see that our corpus contains 8 anaphoric references to landmarks (within the same route description) that are accompanied by a gesture, and for these the 'beat ratio' is 3 beats out of 8 gestures (37,5%) as opposed to 3 beats out of 32 gestures (9,4%) for first mentions. Though again these data are too low in number to allow any strong conclusions, they do support the information structure explanation for the use of beats in references to landmarks. Another finding that points in this direction is the fact that most beats were found in the second versions of the route descriptions in our corpus. On average, the second versions had about twice as many beats as the first.

6   A Simple Model of Beat Gesture Use

Some gesture generation models for ECA's only select beat gestures when no other gestures are available [8,9]. In contrast, we propose to give beat gestures the same basic priority as other gesture types. Given the results of statistical corpus analysis, along with the notion that the use of beat gestures also depends on personal style of the individual speakers, the probability that a beat gesture is generated in a certain context can be given by the following formula:

$$P(B|u) = P(B|c_u)m_s$$

where B is the generation of a beat gesture, u is the speech context (a word or phrase to be uttered), c_u is the concept being expressed by the utterance, and m_s is a multiplier for a specific speaker.

This probability function can also be used for other gesture types. It can be easily applied in the Virtual Guide, which already uses a weighted randomization algorithm for gesture selection [5]. It would also be applicable in other frameworks such as BEAT [6] that assign priorities to possible gestures, which is something a probability can be used for. Note that our proposed data-driven approach is similar in spirit to that of Neff et al. [10], though their model is far more sophisticated. Whether this sophistication also leads to better results than our simple approach or is overly complex for a merely marginally better result is a question that can only be answered when our model has been implemented and tested in practice. To this end, more data have to be gathered to feed the model.

7   Conclusions and Future Work

Our corpus analysis has shown that beat gestures are frequently used within route descriptions. We found that, in line with the literature [2], beats are most often used to mark important concepts in the discourse. In the case of direction giving discourse, the concepts marked by beats tend to be the ones that cannot be easily visualised using other gestures, such as (named) route destinations and topological spatial information. However, beats are also used - albeit much less frequently - with concepts for which other gestures seem a more obvious choice, for example turn directions. These findings can be at least partially explained in terms of information structure: information which is 'discourse-old' is more likely to be accompanied by a beat than by another type of gesture (if a gesture is used at all).

We applied McNeill's Beat Filter on our corpus, to see if we could reliably distinguish beats from other gestures on purely formal grounds [2]. We found that very low agreement between annotators, probably due to different interpretations of the filter questions. To avoid this a more detailed coding manual will be required, defining exactly what counts as movement phases etc. and how borderline cases should be handled. Probably, thorough annotator training will be needed as well. In addition, to make the Beat Filter more useful it should have additional questions to distinguish between beats and deictic gestures.

We have proposed a probabilistic model of beat gesture use in direction giving in which the likelihood of using a beat gesture to mark certain concepts is derived from corpus data, similar to the approach of Neff et al. [10]. Though this is a step forward compared to the way beats are currently handled in the Virtual Guide, as well as those ECA models where beats have a lower priority than other gestures [6,7,8,9], we are aware that the model is still far too simple. In the current version of the model, gesture choice only depends on the concept being expressed, optionally weighted to take speaker preferences into account. In reality, gesture choice is also influenced by other factors, including the newness of the presented information. Nevertheless, we expect that implementing our current model will already increase the perceived naturalness of our direction giving ECA. Before we can test this, however, we need more – and more reliably annotated – corpus data to derive the gesture probabilities needed by the model. Having more data available may also help uncover additional factors influencing direction givers' choice to use beat gestures in certain contexts.

Acknowledgements. We thank Renate ten Ham for segmenting the video corpus, Pieter van Veelen for annotating the corpus with gesture types, and Rieks op den Akker for his help with computing the Kappa values. We also thank our reviewers for their useful comments on an earlier version of this paper. This work has been supported in part by the European Community's Seventh Framework Programme (FP7/2007-2013) under grant agreement 231287 (SSPNet).

References

1. Iverson, J., Goldin-Meadow, S.: Why people gesture when they speak. Nature 396, 228 (1998)
2. McNeill, D.: Hand and Mind: What Gestures Reveal about Thought. The University of Chicago Press, Chicago (1992)
3. Striegnitz, K., Tepper, P., Lovett, A., Cassell, J.: Knowledge representation for generating locating gestures in route directions. In: Coventry, K., Tenbrink, T., Bateman, J. (eds.) Spatial Language in Dialogue, pp. 147–166. Oxford University Press, Oxford (2009)
4. Kopp, S., Tepper, P., Striegnitz, K., Ferriman, K., Cassell, J.: Trading spaces: How humans and humanoids use speech and gesture to give directions. In: Nishida, T. (ed.) Engineering Approaches to Conversational Informatics, pp. 133–160. John Wiley & Sons, Chichester (2007)
5. Theune, M., Hofs, D., van Kessel, M.: The Virtual Guide: A direction giving embodied conversational agent. In: Proceedings of Interspeech, pp. 2197–2200 (2007)
6. Cassell, J., Vilhjálmsson, H., Bickmore, T.: BEAT: the Behavior Expression Animation Toolkit. In: Proceedings of SIGGRAPH, pp. 477–486 (2001)
7. Hartmann, B., Mancini, M., Pelachaud, C.: Formational parameters and adaptive prototype instantiation for MPEG-4 compliant gesture synthesis. In: Proceedings of Computer Animation 2002, pp. 111–119. IEEE Computer Society, Los Alamitos (2002)
8. Nakano, Y.I., Okamoto, M., Nishida, T.: Enriching agent animations with gestures and highlighting effects. In: Intelligent Media Technology for Communicative Intelligence, pp. 91–98 (2004)
9. Olivier, P., Jackson, D., Wiggins, C.: A real-world architecture for the synthesis of spontaneous gesture. In: Proceedings of the 19th annual conference on Computer Animation and Social Agents, CASA (2006)
10. Neff, M., Kipp, M., Albrecht, I., Seidel, H.P.: Gesture modeling and animation based on a probabilistic re-creation of speaker style. ACM Transactions on Graphics 27(5), 1–24 (2008)
11. Bergmann, K., Kopp, S.: Increasing the expressiveness of virtual agents – autonomous generation of speech and gesture for spatial description tasks. In: Proceedings of AAMAS, pp. 361–368 (2009)
12. DiEugenio, B.: In the usage of Kappa to evaluate agreement on coding tasks. In: Proceedings LREC, pp. 441–444 (2000)
13. Williams, S., Watson, C.: A profile of the discourse and intonational structure of route descriptions. In: Proceedings of Eurospeech, pp. 1659–1662 (1999)
14. Krauss, R.M.: Why do we gesture when we speak? Current Directions in Psychological Science 7, 54–59 (1998)
15. Duncan, S.: Some signals and rules for taking speaking turns in conversation. Journal of Personality and Social Psychology 23(2), 161–180 (1972)
16. Kelleher, J.D., Costello, F.J.: Applying computational models of spatial prepositions to visually situated dialog. Computational Linguistics 35(2), 271–306 (2009)

Requirements for a Gesture Specification Language
A Comparison of Two Representation Formalisms

Alexis Heloir and Michael Kipp

DFKI, Embodied Agents Research Group,
Campus D3 2, 66123 Saarbrücken, Germany
`firstname.surname@dfki.de`

Abstract. We present a comparative study of two gesture specification languages. Our aim is to derive requirements for a new, optimal specification language that can be used to extend the emerging BML standard. We compare MURML, which has been designed to specify coverbal gestures, and a language we call LV, originally designed to describe French Sign Language utterances. As a first step toward a new gesture specification language we created EMBRScript, a low-level animation language capable of describing multi-channel animations, that can be used as a foundation for future BML extensions.

Keywords: embodied conversational agents, gesture description language, comparative study.

1 Introduction

Describing human movement is a challenging task, given the many degrees of freedom of the human body. When using embodied agents in a human-computer interface context, a formal description of gestures is needed to ensure a faithful rendering by the underlying character animation engine. The design of a gesture description language is determined by three factors: the producer (human author or generation module) of the language wants it to be expressive and easy to use, the consumer (animation module) requires it to be complete, precise and convenient to interpret and, finally, there is usually an underlying theory that directs the language design. The behavior markup language (BML) [1,2] offers such a specification. However, the current version of BML focuses on the problem of temporal synchronization between modalities, whereas the question of how to describe the surface form of a gesture is still open. In order to get a better understanding for how BML must be extended toward a complete specification of gestural form, we compare in this paper two existing formalisms for specifying human gestures. The first one, MURML, has been designed to specify coverbal gestures for an embodied conversational agent [3]. The second one has been designed to describe French sign language [4] and will be called LV in the further discourse. Both models have a similar theoretical background: sign language

S. Kopp and I. Wachsmuth (Eds.): GW 2009, LNAI 5934, pp. 207–218, 2010.

phonology. MURML bases some gesture description elements on HamNoSys [5]. LV is based on the Movement-Hold model by Liddel et Johnson [6]. The insights provided by this comparison will drive the design of a future BML extension. This extension does not yet exist, but its specification will be supported by EMBRScript, an intermediate animation language whose concepts can be used as building blocks to formally describe the future BML extension.

2   Related Work

Recent research has identified three fundamental layers of processing which facilitates the creation of generic software components [1,2] for ECA applications: intent planner, behavior planner and surface realizer, as depicted in Fig. 1. In this framework called SAIBA[7], users work on the level of intent planning and behavior planning and then dispatch high-level behavior descriptions in the behavior markup language (BML) to the realizer which transforms it into an animation. Because the behavior description is abstract, many characteristics of the output animation are left for the realizer to decide.

As depicted in Fig. 1, the realizer itself can be decomposed into three components: the motion resolver, the motion planner and the animation engine. The role of the motion resolver is to select the motion segments that best convey the abstract behavior specified in the BML input. If needed, the user may override the motion resolver by embedding the description of a desired motion segment in the BML input using an higher *level of description* [2]. For instance, MURML can be directly integrated into BML on level 1. The motion segment description is then sent to the motion planner. Its role is to timestamp every motion segment in order to guarantee inter-channel synchronization (e.g. between prominent syllable in speech and a particular point in a motion segment) and ensure realistic velocity profiles for the character's limbs. This results in a time-stamped motion description which can be processed by the animation engine. Finally, the animation engine computes a geometrical description (angles, morph targets etc.) of the characters's animation that can be rendered by a 3D graphics engine.

Any sign language/gesture generation system based on a behavioral definition needs to map its input data to trajectories and postures. Researchers have developed form-based description languages allowing to specify a wide range of gestures by symbolically composing form and movement primitives in a structured way.

A language aimed at providing an intermediate representation of motion segments should fulfill the following requirements:

– for the user: expressive and easy to use,
– for the animation engine: complete, precise and convenient to interpret

Researchers have focused on the development of representation systems for multimodal utterances [3,4,8,9]. Although such languages where initially developed independently from the behavioral layers, it is possible to integrate them as animation-centered description languages as extensions to existing higher-level behavior description languages like BML.

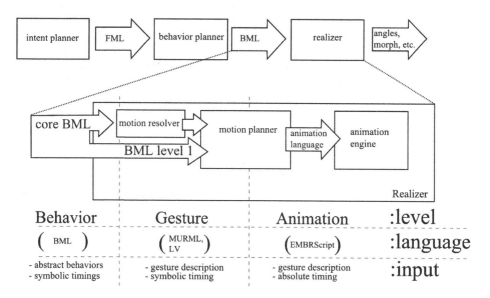

Fig. 1. Processing pipeline for producing human behaviors according to the SAIBA framework

Early formal attempts to encode multimodal utterances for animated virtual characters were motivated by the need of automatic sign language production like the GESSYCA system [8]. In GESSYCA, simple gestures involving the arms and the hands can be described as an arrangement of formational parameters (hand shape, hand position and hand orientation) inspired by early studies dedicated to sign language phonology [10]. This pioneering work has been followed by the Signing Gesture Markup Language (SigML [9]), which itself stems from the HamNoSys linguistic notation system [5]. SigML can be described as mediating between a behavioral and a physical/anatomical sign description for the automatic production of sign language sequences. In 2001, Losson and Vannobel proposed a formal description language which we will call LV [4] in the further discourse. This language takes into account gestures and facial expression as well as the different gesture phases (preparation, stroke, hold and retraction) as described by Kendon [11]. More recently, Huenerfauth introduced a multi-channel coding system for sign language called the Partition/Constitute (PC) formalism [12]. The system uses a two-dimensional grammar (one dimension representing time, the other representing channels) and introduces an explicit representation of coordination and non-coordination for a multichannel animation stream. However, the described concepts have not been formalized into a syntactic description to the best of our knowledge.

In parallel, many interactive applications featured virtual characters as a new human-machine interaction metaphor. Early attempts did not need elaborate multimodal specification models, as they mainly relied on pre-recorded or pre-specified animations, either obtained using motion capture or key-framed by a skilled animator [13,14,15,16]. These approaches used speech as the dominant modality to which all other modalities (gesture, facial expression etc.) would refer for temporal synchronization. Synchrony was achieved by starting the animation pieces simultaneously with the correlated verbal phrase. The nonverbal behaviors are referred to by unique identifiers and are drawn from a behavior database. In these systems, it is impossible to create nonverbal behaviors from atomic elements and to adapt their structure in the synchronization process.

The MURML gesture description language [3] starts from straightforward descriptions of the multimodal utterance in a XML-based specification language. Such a description contains the verbal utterance augmented by nonverbal behaviors including gestures. In MURML, the desired gesture can be described explicitly in terms of spatiotemporal features. In addition to gestures, further behaviors can be incorporated such as arbitrary body movement and facial animations given as sequences of face muscle values.

To sum up, it seems that so far both LV and MURML are the most elaborate description languages providing an implementable grammar. However, even if they share similar goals, there are significant differences in both their structure and expressiveness. We thus present in the following a comparison between the two languages.

3   Comparison of MURML and LV

We base our comparative study on a sample iconic gesture. This gesture, depicted in Fig. 2 may be used to describe a square-shaped structure like a fireplace frame or the structure of a bridge and we will call it **BRIDGE** in the following. The **BRIDGE** gesture conveys two changes in wrist position (one where the wrists follow a horizontal straight path and a one where they follow a vertical straight path) and one change in hand orientation (the back of the hand changes form pointing upward to pointing toward the sides) which occur before the second wrist position's change.

Both LV and MURML can describe multimodal gestures including hand-arms configurations and trajectories as well as facial expressions. In both systems, gesture timing is expressed symbolically and are resolved later on by the animation

Fig. 2. Iconic **BRIDGE** gesture

engine. Both systems limit their descriptions to the meaningful phases of the described gestures (stroke or independent hold). In an architecture like the one outlined in Fig. 1, the timing of non-meaningful surrounding phases such as retraction, preparation and dependent hold are left to the motion planner engine while the final realization is left to the animation engine.

3.1   MURML

MURML describes gestures in a tree structure of constraints and features, each of which specifies either a sub-gesture (atomic gesture) or a set of feature conveying the configuration of one or more modalities (facial animation parameter, hand shape, hand position, hand orientation). In MURML, two different types of movement constraints are provided in order to specify a feature over a certain period of time: A static constraint, which defines a postural feature that is to be held for a certain period of time and a dynamic constraint which specifies a significant submovement within a feature that is fluently connected with adjacent movement phases. The relationships between the feature constraints can be denoted by specific MURML elements like *parallel, sequence, repetition and symmetry*. Such constraints can be arranged in a flexible fashion.

The lower part of Fig. 3 shows a MURML description of the **BRIDGE** gesture presented in Fig. 2. In our example gesture, the hands are kept in the same configuration through the entire gesture, hand configuration is thus expressed in a separate branch under a *parallel* element. The remaining constraints describing the gesture are assembled in a *sequence* element. Features are located under a *static* or *dynamic* constraint depending on whether they are kept static or change during each sequential sub-motion. At the upper end of the tree, a *symmetry* constraint expresses the fact that the gesture is symmetrical, i.e. the description applies to both hands.

The structure of MURML encourages feature factorization through hierarchical arrangement of constraints and features. On the one hand, by allowing arrangements of arbitrary complexity between constraints and features, MURML can be viewed as a concise language which prevents duplication, but, on the other hand, because no restriction is imposed on how constraints can be arranged, MURML allows multiple (syntactically) valid descriptions for a single gesture. For instance, the tree depicted on the upper side of Fig. 3 shows a MURML description of the **BRIDGE** gesture which is valid, but against MURML's philosophy (the handshape feature is, for instance, redundant between the three atomic gestures).

We believe that the non-uniqueness of MURML descriptions for certain gestures and the a-priori arbitrary complexity of a gesture description is a challenging aspect both for an author and for implementing a realizer based on MURML. Furthermore, MURML does not introduce a *contact* constraint (see Sec. 3.2). Finally, we believe that although very expressive, the complex tree structures required to describe the gestures may be challenging for users.

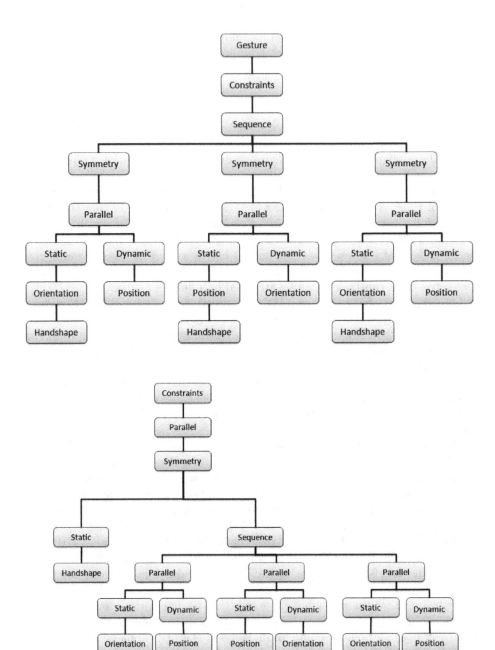

Fig. 3. MURML representation

3.2 LV

LV follows the *movement-hold theory* which describes a gesture in terms of postures and transitions. The illustration in Fig. 4 shows the LV description of **BRIDGE**.

Like MURML, LV describes a gesture as a combination of features organized in a tree. However, as opposed to MURML, the feature arrangement is fixed and follows the following organization: a gesture (*sign*) is described as a succession of *shifts*. The *shifts* are bundles of hand features at the beginning and end of the sign and of the movement itself. Depending on its complexity, a *shift* can be described as one of the following three options:

− single hand shift primitive
− dominant hand shift primitive plus a specification for the weak hand and a spatial relationship (as it is the case for the description in Fig. 4)
− two shift primitives, one for each hand

The drawback of specifying hand configuration at the beginning and end of the *shift* is the redundancy between the end of one *shift* and the beginning of the following *shift* when a gesture is described as a sequence. The tree depicted on the right side of Fig. 4 highlights this redundancy problem.

In LV, the constraints conveying relationships between features are considered as attributes belonging to specific nodes. For instance, the repetition constraint is a feature of the *shift* element and all features under a shift are realized in parallel. For instance, shift elements belonging to the tree depicted in Fig. 4 aggregate the simultaneous movement of both weak hand and strong hand. Finally, LV offers a feature to represent *contact gestures*, i.e. gestures that touch a part of the body (expressed using landmarks) somewhere along their trajectory.

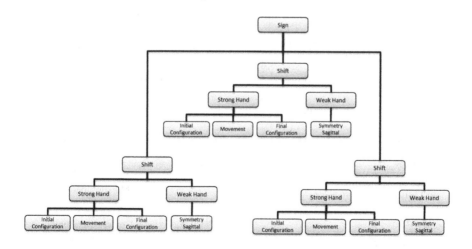

Fig. 4. LV Representation

First, LV leads to unique description of gestures. Second, because LV uses assumptions about human modalities (e.g. symmetry is only related to arm/hands, the default hand is strong hand), it appears that its gesture description scripts have a comparatively flat tree structure. The following script presents the textual version of our example gesture.

```
Sign %BRIDGE.
  Manual:
  (Shift from: (HandSpec config: #C point: #ThumbRoot
           at: [Shoulders FrontProx Sagittal] ori: [f f & u])
           to: [Shoulders FrontProx IpsiSide]
         move: #Linear
     weakMove: #Symmetrical ),
  (Shift ...),
  (Shift ...).
```

We believe that a flat description is a desirable feature for a gesture description language, because it provides the user with a more intuitive way to specify the character's configuration using sets of constraints. However, the variety of modalities LV can address are rather limited (hand and basic face). Furthermore, LV uses a terminology and contains some elements that are too dependent on its underlying theory (e.g. sign language modifiers, grammatical modifier element).

3.3   Discussion

Based on the gesture description we presented in the sections above, we now draw a comparison between MURML and LV based on the complexity of their structure, the way dynamic elements are described, the presence of convenience features like arm-swivel or contact specification and the ability to specify co-occurring movements in the main animation. Our comparison is summarized in Table 1.

Although both LV and MURML use tree structures, we found descriptions provided by LV to be flatter. We believe that flat structures are more desirable for a high-level language dedicated to the specification of human gestures for

Table 1. Summary of limitations of MURML and LV

Aspect	LV	MURML	Conclusion
Complexity of representation	Relatively flat structure	Deep, nested structure	Use flat structure
Redundancy	Start/end poses	None	Move to a pose-based representation
Arm swivel	---	Featured	Add feature for hand-arm configuration
Contact	Featured for start and end poses	---	Add static contact constraints
Secondary movement	Predefined set of secondary motions	Generic way to define e.g. hand shape changes	Allow both

two reasons: first, we believe that a flat structure is easier to author and leads to unique less ambiguous descriptions, second, although one could argue a flat structure narrows the range of expressiveness of the language, we believe that this limitation can be overcome using certain assumptions on human modalities (two hands, symmetry only applies on arms/hands, etc.).

Another issue is the redundancy introduced when describing dynamic features that are occurring sequentially in both LV and MURML. As described in paragraph 3.2 LV implies a duplication between the end pose of an atomic gesture and the start pose of the subsequent atomic gesture. in MURML, this problem can be avoided if the user carefully factorizes static and dynamic constraints. We believe high-level features conveying contact and arm swivel are particularly convenient for authors. LV provides a feature to describe contacts, MURML does not. MURML takes arm swivel into account, LV does not. Finally, both LV and MURML permit the specification of movement co-occurring with a main gesture (e.g. fingers wriggling while tracing the **BRIDGE** gesture). LV uses a set of pre-defined secondary movements as a parameter of a shift (e.g. wriggling, rubbing, counting). MURML can define such movements in a generic fashion using a subtree that is a sibling of the tree depicting the main gesture, both trees grouped under a *parallel* constraint.

4   The Animation Layer and EMBRScript

Having compared MURML and LV, we found that MURML was very expressive but probably too complicated for easy authoring and that LV is an elegant formalism for specifying gestures but may have limitations when it comes to multi-channel coordination. But how can we devise a powerful language without overloading the syntax in terms of structure and lexicon? We decided to start by first creating another layer of abstraction *underneath* the BML layer. We call this layer the *animation layer* and argue that this layer should have maximum expressivity without regard to the question whether it is easy to author and easy to read by humans. It should provide an abstract interface to character animation engines and form a basis for the future development of the BML layer which can then be built on top of it. This strategy allows us to more systematically define the BML layer using clearly defined building blocks. In this section we will outline the animation layer, using a concrete language we call EMBRScript.

4.1   Overview

In the processing pipeline depicted in Fig. 1 the animation engine is the last element which creates the animations sent to the graphics renderer. This animation engine can involve multiple motion generation mechanisms acting on different parts (channels) of the character to be animated. Because of the heterogeneity of the different motion generation mechanisms, we argue that a new layer of control, the *animation layer*, is necessary to keep the higher-level control layers (behavioral/functional) consistent and slim, while allowing a unified and

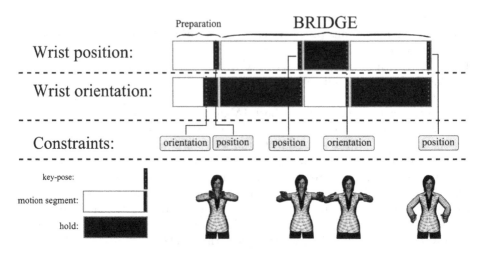

Fig. 5. This illustration displays an EMBRScript based description of the **BRIDGE** gesture. The description is spread over two channels, synchronization is done using key poses which can span several channels.

abstract access to the animation engine, e.g. for the procedural animation of nonverbal behavior. EMBRScript is the language that provides this interface.

EMBRscript is a channel-oriented, pose-based gesture description language. Every animation is described as a succession of *key poses* timestamped with absolute times and spanning multiple channels. Contrary to LV and MURML which only depict meaningful phases of the gestures, EMBRScript does not make distinguish between gestures phases. Fig. 5 depicts a EMBRScript description of the **BRIDGE** gesture.

4.2   Description

A *key pose* describes the state of part of an animated character at a specific point in time using a set of constraints. A *key pose* spans over at least one channel, a channel represents one of the character's modalities. When spanned over multiple channels, the *key pose* expresses synchronization between them. A pose can be specified using a combination of four principal methods, each acting on a separate channel: skeletal configuration (e.g. reaching for a point in space, bending forward), morph targets (e.g. smiling and blinking with one eye), shaders (e.g. blushing or paling) or autonomous behaviors (e.g. breathing). In the example we show in Fig. 5, only the skeletal configuration is specified using spatial constraints (wrist position and wrist orientation). The skeletal configurations satisfying the constraints are computed in the animation engine using inverse kinematics.

For instance, in the EMBRScript description of the **BRIDGE** gesture in Fig. 3, two channels are depicted: The *wrist position* channel and the *wrist orientation* channel. The two first motion segments in both channels represent the preparation phase. They are both bounded by a different *key pose* which means that there are independent in time, in this case, the preparation phase corresponding to the wrist orientation channel is achieved before the preparation phase corresponding to the wrist position channel.

The subsequent key poses are bundling both the wrist position and the wrist orientation. The first key pose specifies the wrist's position change while its orientation is kept still, the second key pose expresses the wrist's orientation change while the wrist's position is kept still, the last key pose specifies the last wrist's position change while the wrist orientation is kept still.

5   Conclusion

In order to identify and highlight the requirements for a high-level gesture specification language that could be integrated as a BML level of description, we conducted a comparative study over two gesture specification languages: MURML, designed to specify coverbal gestures and LV, designed to describe French Sign Language utterances. The study gave us insights regarding the desired structure and the level of expressivity of this new language. We found that it should have a flat structure and take advantage of the assumptions that can be made regarding the modalities of a human being. The language should take into account the multichannel nature of gestures while being able to express both synchronization and temporal independence between channels. The design of such a language is a work in progress which will build on the EMBRScript animation language. EMBRScript provides an interface to the animation layer which gives to users the possibility to describe fine-grained output animations without requiring a deep understanding of computer animation techniques [17]. In future work, the concepts of EMBRScript will be used as building blocks to formally describe fine-grained behaviors on the BML layer.

References

1. Kopp, S., Krenn, B., Marsella, S., Marshall, A.N., Pelachaud, C., Pirker, H., Thórisson, K.R., Vilhjálmsson, H.: Towards a common framework for multimodal generation: The behavior markup language. In: Gratch, J., Young, M., Aylett, R.S., Ballin, D., Olivier, P. (eds.) IVA 2006. LNCS (LNAI), vol. 4133, pp. 205–217. Springer, Heidelberg (2006)
2. Vilhjalmsson, H., Cantelmo, N., Cassell, J., Chafai, N.E., Kipp, M., Kopp, S., Mancini, M., Marsella, S., Marshall, A.N., Pelachaud, C., Ruttkay, Z., Thórisson, K.R., van Welbergen, H., van der Werf, R.J.: The behavior markup language: Recent developments and challenges. In: Pelachaud, C., Martin, J.-C., André, E., Chollet, G., Karpouzis, K., Pelé, D. (eds.) IVA 2007. LNCS (LNAI), vol. 4722, pp. 99–111. Springer, Heidelberg (2007)
3. Kranstedt, A., Kopp, S., Wachsmuth, I.: Murml: A multimodal utterance representation markup language for conversational agents. In: Proceedings of the Workshop Embodied Conversational Agents, Autonomous Agents and Multi-Agent Systems (AAMAS 2002), Bologna, Italy (2002)

4. Losson, O., Vannobel, J.M.: Sign specification and synthesis. In: Proc. of Gesture Workshop (1999)
5. Prillwitz, S.L., Leven, R., Zienert, H., Zienert, R., Hanke, T., Henning, J.: Ham-NoSys. Version 2.0. International Studies on Sign Language and Communication of the Deaf (1989)
6. Liddell, S.: American sign language: The phonological base. Sign language studies 64, 195–278 (1989)
7. Vilhjálmsson, H., Thórisson, K.R.: A brief history of function representation from gandalf to saiba. In: Proceedings of the 1st Function Markup Language Workshop at AAMAS (2008)
8. Lebourque, T., Gibet, S.: High level specification and control of communicative gestures: the gessyca system. In: Proceedings of Computer Animation, May 26-29, pp. 24–35 (1999)
9. Kennaway, R.: Synthetic animation of deaf signing gestures. In: Wachsmuth, I., Sowa, T. (eds.) GW 2001. LNCS (LNAI), vol. 2298, pp. 146–157. Springer, Heidelberg (2002)
10. Stokoe, W.: Sign language structure: An outline of the visual communication systems of the american deaf. In: Studies in Linguistic, Occasional Papers, vol. 8 (1960)
11. Kendon, A.: Some relationships between body motion and speech: an analysis of an example. In: Siegman, A., Pope, B. (eds.) Studies in Dyadic Communication, pp. 177–210. Pergamon Press, New York (1972)
12. Huenerfauth, M.: Representing coordination and non-coordination in an american sign language animation. In: Assets 2005: Proceedings of the 7th international ACM SIGACCESS conference on Computers and accessibility, pp. 44–51. ACM, New York (2005)
13. Cassell, J., Vilhjalmsson, H., Bickmore, T.: BEAT: The behavior expression animation toolkit. In: Fiume, E. (ed.) SIGGRAPH 2001, Computer Graphics Proceedings, pp. 477–486 (2001)
14. Stone, M., DeCarlo, D., Oh, I., Rodriguez, C., Stere, A., Less, A., Bregler, C.: Speaking with hands: Creating animated conversational characters from recordings of human performance. In: Proc. ACM/EUROGRAPHICS Symposium on Computer Animation (2004)
15. Kipp, M., Neff, M., Kipp, K.H., Albrecht, I.: Toward Natural Gesture Synthesis: Evaluating gesture units in a data-driven approach. In: Pelachaud, C., Martin, J.-C., André, E., Chollet, G., Karpouzis, K., Pelé, D. (eds.) IVA 2007. LNCS (LNAI), vol. 4722, pp. 15–28. Springer, Heidelberg (2007)
16. Hartmann, B., Mancini, M., Pelachaud, C.: Implementing Expressive Gesture Synthesis for Embodied Conversational Agents. In: Gesture in Human-Computer Interaction and Simulation (2006)
17. Heloir, A., Kipp, M.: EMBR – A realtime animation engine for interactive embodied agents. In: Ruttkay, Z., Kipp, M., Nijholt, A., Vilhjálmsson, H.H. (eds.) IVA 2009. LNCS, vol. 5773, pp. 393–404. Springer, Heidelberg (2009)

Statistical Gesture Models for 3D Motion Capture from a Library of Gestures with Variants

Zhenbo Li[1], Patrick Horain[1], André-Marie Pez[2], and Catherine Pelachaud[2,3]

[1] Institut Telecom, Telecom SudParis, 9 rue Charles Fourier, 91011 Evry Cedex, France
[2] Institut Telecom, Telecom ParisTech, 46 rue Barrault, 75634 Paris Cedex 13, France
[3] CNRS, LTCI, 46 rue Barrault, 75634 Paris Cedex 13, France
zhenboli@gmail.com, Patrick.Horain@Telecom-SudParis.eu,
andremarie.pez@telecom-paristech.fr,
catherine.pelachaud@telecom-paristech.fr

Abstract. A challenge for 3D motion capture by monocular vision is 3D-2D projection ambiguities that may bring incorrect poses during tracking. In this paper, we propose improving 3D motion capture by learning human gesture models from a library of gestures with variants. This library has been created with virtual human animations. Gestures are described as Gaussian Process Dynamic Models (GPDM) and are used as constraints for motion tracking. Given the raw input poses from the tracker, the gesture model helps to correct ambiguous poses. The benefit of the proposed method is demonstrated with results.

Keywords: Gaussian Process, 3D motion capture, gesture model, gesture library.

1 Introduction

Avatars are virtual self representations. They evolve in a 3D world and interact with other virtual entities on our behalf. Avatars are animated by their human counterpart. One difficulty is the control of their behaviors. Selecting behaviors from a menu or by using icons is tedious. Moreover the avatar animation is not lively as it moves only on command. Some attempts have been made to alleviate the user's role and endow avatars with some autonomy [1]. These approaches are promising but require intensive computation to parse what the user aims to say and derive an appropriate nonverbal behaviors that accompany this text. In our project we aim at letting the user fully control his avatar [2]. 3D user motion is captured through a plain webcam using computer vision algorithms, and rendered by his avatar.

Vision-based human body tracking allows inexpensive, non-obtrusive marker-less motion capture [3]. Research in this field has been motivated by numerous target applications: human-computer interfaces, animation, interaction with virtual environments, video surveillance, games, etc. Monocular vision based markerless 3D motion capture is a difficult problem because of the ambiguities resulting of the lack of depth information, partial occlusion of human body parts, high number of degrees

S. Kopp and I. Wachsmuth (Eds.): GW 2009, LNAI 5934, pp. 219–230, 2010.

of freedom, variations in the proportions of the human body and various clothing [3,4,26]. It has an intrinsic limitation of poor precision and robustness.

In this paper, we address the issue of improving motion capture with statistical gesture models. These models require training on some relevant gesture databases. Most existing databases as CMU Graphics Lab Motion Capture Database (http://mocap.cs.cmu.edu/) and HumanEva (http://vision.cs.brown.edu/humaneva/) gather data on human actions such as running, jumping and the like, but very few include communicative gestures. The variety of communicative gestures is a challenge by itself. Even though some gestures with a defined shape can be linked to a precise meaning, most of the communicative gestures are creative [5] that is they are created on the spot. Thus, gesture shape can vary a lot depending on their meaning and discourse context. Building a library of such gestures is a tremendous enterprise.

To avoid this problem, we have selected the context of a recruiting interview and we have gathered video data from 4 interviews, each about 30 minutes. We have generated gesture by mimicking real user motion and their variations using the Greta expressive conversational agent [6]. The resulting library of gestures has then been described with a statistical model suitable for constraining tracking and disambiguating monocular 3D people tracking.

The rest of the paper is organized as follows. Section 2 introduces the related works about gesture modeling in a low-dimensional space. In section 3, we present our real-time monocular motion capture system. Then, we present our work toward building a library of communicative gestures in section 4. We describe also how we encompass user's communicative distinctiveness in our library. In section 5, we propose using Gaussian Process Dynamic Models (GPDM) [7] to statistically describe gesture models and use them as guides for motion tracking. The interest of this approach is demonstrated with results.

2 Related Work

Although people can perform very large variation of complex motions, their movements can be represented in a low-dimensional space. Pullen et al. [8] observed human motions have certain cooperative relationships especially when people do some specific movements like walking, swimming, etc. This relationship can be used to reduce the parameter space dimensionality while performing human motion analysis. Safonova et al. [9] have demonstrated that many dynamic human motions can be adequately represented with only five to ten parameters. Elgammal et al. [10] and Grochow et al. [11] observed that human activities can be described in a latent space. So, human motion can be modeled in a low-dimensional latent space.

Building the latent motion space from existing motion data consists in defining a subspace with a lower dimension than the full motion capture data. Because human motion is non-linear, basic dimensionality reduction methods such as principal component analysis (PCA) are inadequate to describe non-linear human motion [4]. Other methods such as Locally Linear Embedding (LLE) [27] and Isomap[28] either do not provide invertible mapping from the low dimensional latent space to the original pose space or do not provide probability distribution over data in latent space. They are not suitable to build low dimensional gesture models [7].

Locally Linear Coordination (LLC) [12], Gaussian Process Latent Variable Models (GPLVM) [13] and later appeared approaches like Gaussian Process Dynamic Models (GPDM) [7] and Laplacian Eigenmaps Latent Variable Model (LELVM) [14] can learn a non-linear mapping between the human motion parameter space and a latent space and they provide an inverse mapping. They allow describing human motion in a low-dimensional latent space.

Recently, latent gesture models have been used as prior constraints to help 3D human motion tracking. Urtasun [15, 16] used GPLVM and GPDM to learn prior models for tracking 3D human walking. She achieved good results even in case of serious occlusion. Raskin et al. [17] presented an approach to combine annealed particle filter tracker with GPDM that allows reducing the state vector and that enhances tracking stability. Moon and Pavlovic [19] investigated the effect of dynamics in dimensionality reduction problems on human motion tracking. Lu et al. [20] used LELVM as constraints in the probabilistic sigma point mixture tracker for robust operation with missing data, noisy and ambiguous image measurements. In these approaches, gesture models were combined with the image-based likelihood in the tracker to reduce the number of state sampling particles [21].

3 Real-Time 3D Motion Capture with a Webcam

Our baseline is a real-time webcam-based system for 3D motion capture that was previously developed in our team [18]. It works by registering an articulated 3D model of the human body on a video stream (Fig. 1).

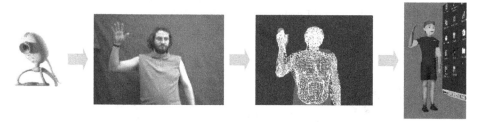

Fig. 1. Real time motion capture by monoscopic computer vision and virtual rendering

Our 3D human model has 3 global position parameters and 20 joint angles of the upper-body (bust, arms, forearms, hands, neck and head), so a body-pose is represented by a vector of 23 parameters. For each input image we search for the model pose that best matches the image. Image features (color regions, edges) are extracted and matched with model features (colored limbs, occluding edges) projected in the candidate pose. For each captured image, optimal registration is searched with respect to the pose parameters by iteratively maximizing the color region overlap and by minimizing the distance between the image edges and the projected occluding edges of the model (Fig. 2) [18].

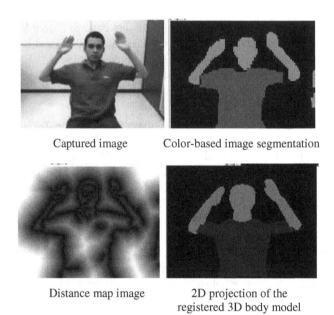

Captured image   Color-based image segmentation

Distance map image   2D projection of the
                            registered 3D body model

Fig. 2. The captured image, the color-segmented image, distance map image edges in the foreground mask and finally the projection of the 3D human body model in the optimal matching pose [18]

Joint angles are then output in real-time over the network as low bandwidth MPEG-4 body animation parameters (BAPs). The captured motion is rendered remotely by animating the user avatar in the virtual space (Fig. 3).

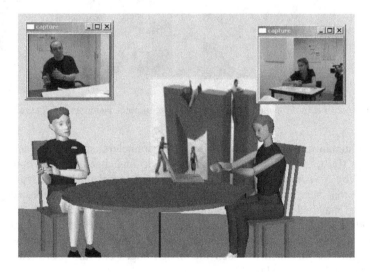

Fig. 3. Real-time motion capture using a single camera for each user and virtual rendering. Demonstration videos are available at *http://MyBlog3D.com*.

4 Creating a Library of Gestures

Several dictionaries of emblematic gestures have been gathered in our project. They are bound to a given culture. These dictionaries provide detailed information about the gesture shape and its associated meaning. Other attempts have looked to describe gesture shape in association with their physical meaning [22]. Raised hand with palm facing one's interlocutor carries the meaning to stop something or somebody to do something. It can be viewed as symbolizing a wall between both interlocutors.

In our work we are interested at all types of gestures as we aim to track any hand and arm movements done while communicating. We do not aim to recognize gestures or to interpret them. We are interested in detecting their shape and following their movement in view in reproducing them by the avatar. This reproduction does not require understanding the meaning of the gestures. With such an aim we decided to consider only one feature of the gestures: their shape.

Most of the existing databases of motion capture data gather data on action movements such as walking, jumping or running. Almost no databases are centered on communicative gestures. In our work, our aim is to track people gesturing while conversing. To be able to train our tracking algorithm, we need to gather data on nonverbal gestures. Rather than creating a database of motion capture data, we have decided to use virtual agent technology as it is cheaper. We have created a database with the animation of the synthetic character. It is difficult to select which gestures to consider. Communicative gestures are often 'creative'. It is not possible to create an extensive library of communicative gestures. At a first step of our work, we have decided to focus on one conversational domain: recruiting interviews. We have gathered data of real people going through job interview and we have searched for the gestures shapes that are the most frequent. The agent was made to replay those gestures. To ensure to gather gesturing variability of users, we have applied a set of expressivity parameters that modulate the animation of the virtual agent.

4.1 Gesture Variability

While communicating, people show large variability not only in their intentions but also in their way of expressing them. One can be characterized by a signature, a style one carries along in, basically, all circumstances [23].

We have developed a model of distinctive agent that encompasses variability in the modality preference used to communicate a given intention and on the behavior expressivity [24]. In particular when modulating the last set of parameters, the agent can display gestures more or less extent, more or less fast and powerful, etc. These variations occur at the level of execution of behaviors and not on the type of behaviors to be displayed.

4.2 Gesture Clustering

In our corpus we have gathered data from 8 interlocutors. The data was annotated using ANVIL [25]. Around 800 communicative gestures were found in the data. We gathered them into classes of gestures looking alike in their shape and movement.

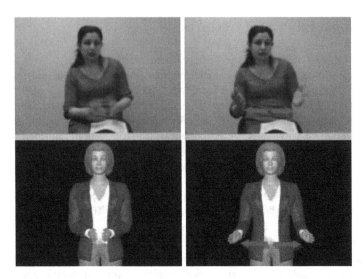

Fig. 4. Rendering by the virtual agent of a gesture belonging to a gesture class

Our aim is to create a library to train our gesture tracking algorithm [2]. To ensure robustness of our tracking algorithm over a large population of users, we have enhanced the library of gestures of the training phase with gesture variability using the model of distinctive agent [24]. The gesture of each class found in our corpus is reproduced by a virtual agent (Fig. 4). The library contains the reproduced gesture as well as the same gesture with different expressivities. Thus each gesture in a class and its variations are present.

5 Gesture Modeling and 3D Motion Capture

5.1 Gaussian Process Dynamical Models

Gaussian Process Dynamic Models (GPDMs) are a powerful approach for probabilistically modeling high dimensional time related data through dimension reduction that make it possible to learn probability gesture models from small training data sets [7]. We propose hereafter a brief introduction to GPDMs.

A GPDM consists of 1) a continuous mapping between the full-dimensional data space (joint angles) and a low-dimensional latent space and 2) a dynamical model in the latent space. It is obtained by marginalizing out the parameters of the two mappings, and optimizing the latent coordinates of training data.

GPDMs aim at modeling the probability density of a sequence of vector-valued states $y_1 ..., y_t, ..., y_N$ with discrete-time index t and $y_t \in R^D$ where D is the number of parameters that define a body pose in the full dimensional parameters space. These two mapping can be expressed as:

$$x_t = f(x_{t-1}; A) + n_{x,t} \tag{1}$$

$$y_t = g(x_t; B) + n_{y,t} \tag{2}$$

where $x_t \in R^d$ denotes the d dimensional latent coordinates at time t. $n_{x,t}$ and $n_{y,t}$ are zero-mean white Gaussian noise processes. f and g are (nonlinear) mappings defined as linear combinations of basis functions ϕ_i and φ_i with weight vectors A and B:

$$f(x; A) = \sum_i a_i \phi_i(x) \tag{3}$$

$$g(x; B) = \sum_j b_j \varphi_j(x) \tag{4}$$

where $A = [a_1, a_2, ...]$, $B = [b_1, b_2, ...]$.

The specific forms of f and g will be marginalized out in GPDM. With an isotropic Gaussian prior on each b_j, we can marginalizing over B in closed form [29] to yield a multivariate Gaussian data likelihood:

$$p(Y / X, \bar{\beta}) = \frac{|W|^N}{\sqrt{(2\pi)^{ND} |K_Y|^D}} \exp(-\frac{1}{2} tr(K_Y^{-1} Y W^2 Y^T)) \tag{5}$$

where $Y = [y_1, ... y_N]^T$ is a matrix of training poses, $X = [x_1, ..., x_N]^T$ is a matrix of latent positions, K_Y is a kernel matrix, and $\bar{\beta} = \{\beta 1, \beta 2, ..., W\}$ comprises the kernel hyperparameters. $W \equiv diag(w_1, ..., w_D)$ is a scaling matrix used to account for the different variances in the different data dimensions. The kernel matrix elements are defined by a kernel function $(K_Y)_{i,j} = K_Y(x_i, x_j)$. For the latent mapping, $X \rightarrow Y$, the Radial Basis Function (RBF) kernel is used.

$$k_Y(x, x') = \beta_1 \exp(-\frac{\beta_2}{2} \|x - x'\|^2) + \beta_3^{-1} \delta_{x,x'} \tag{6}$$

Hyperparameter β_1 represents the overall scale of the output function, while β_2 corresponds to the inverse width of the RBFs. The variance of the noise term $n_{y,t}$ is given by β_3^{-1}.

The dynamic mapping on the latent coordinates X is:

$$p(X / \bar{\alpha}) = p(x_1) \frac{1}{\sqrt{(2\pi)^{(N-1)d} |K_X|^d}} \exp(-\frac{1}{2} tr(K_X^{-1} X_{out} X_{out}^T)) \tag{7}$$

Where $X_{out} = [x_2, ..., x_N]^T$, K_X is the $(N-1) \times (N-1)$ kernel matrix constructed from $\{x_1, ..., x_{N-1}\}$, and x_1 is assumed to be have an isotropic Gaussian prior. Where $\bar{\alpha}$ is a vector of kernel hyperparameters. The dynamics can be modeled using the following "Linear + RBF" kernel:

$$k_X(x, x') = \alpha_1 \exp(-\frac{\alpha_2}{2} \|x - x'\|^2) + \alpha_3 x^T x' + \alpha_4^{-1} \delta_{x,x'} \qquad (8)$$

Hyperparameters α_1, α_2 represent the output scale and the inverse width of the RBF terms, and α_3 represents the output scale of the linear term. Together, they control the relative weighting between the terms, while α_4^{-1} represents the variance of the noise term $n_{x,t}$.

Learning the GPDM from measurements $Y = [y_1, ..., y_N]^T$ entails minimizing the negative log-posterior:

$$\ell = -\ln p(X, \bar{\alpha}, \bar{\beta} / Y)$$

$$= \frac{d}{2} \ln |K_X| + \frac{1}{2} tr(K_X^{-1} X_{out} X_{out}^T) + \sum_j \ln a_j \qquad (9)$$

$$- N \ln |W| + \frac{D}{2} \ln |K_Y| + \frac{1}{2} tr(K_Y^{-1} Y W^2 Y^T) + \sum_j \ln \beta_j$$

5.2   Gesture Modeling

Gesture models are learnt offline from the gesture library using GPDM. Here we use a 3D latent space as this appears to be the lowest dimension for robustly learning complex motions with stylistic variability [16]. We select gestures from each subject for training in order to get the mean trajectories and variances of gestures in the latent space. The input matrix for GPDM learning is pose parameters, which are 20 joint angles of the upper-body (bust: 3DOFs, left shoulder: 3DOFs, right shoulder: 3DOFs, left forearm: 1DOFs, right forearm: 1DOFs, left hand: 3DOFs, right hand: 3DOFs, neck and head: 3DOFs). Fig. 5 shows two conversational gestures from our library and their description as trajectories in a 3D latent space.

5.3   Gesture Modeling for 3D Motion Capture

In our model-based approach, tracking relies on evaluating how well some synthesized appearance of the human body model matches the input image, i.e. how well some model instantiation explains the input image. However, because we only use a single camera, depth ambiguities can occur. Furthermore, because real-time processing implies limited computation power, only a limited subset of the human body degrees of freedom can be processed, so the hand pose cannot be captured, and

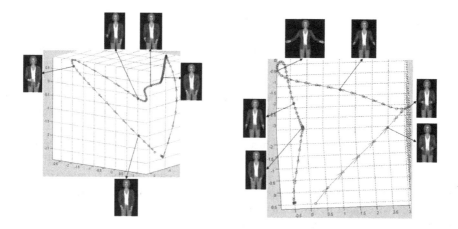

Fig. 5. Conversational gestures described in a 3D latent space. Each circle on the trajectories represents a body pose.

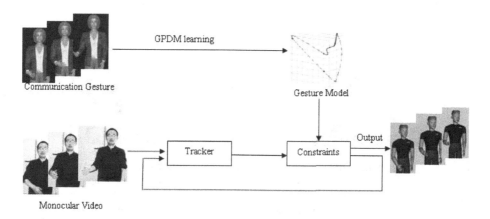

Fig. 6. Gesture model working as constraints in tracking

image size may even be limited. We use the gesture model as a constraint to raise ambiguities and augment the captured motion with details (Fig. 6).

For each iteration, the motion tracker outputs a candidate pose to be constrained with the gesture model. That pose is projected from the full motion parameter space to the 3D latent model space and then replaced with the closest point on the latent motion trajectory. Since GPDM mapping is continuous, poses that are close in the full motion parameter space remain close in the latent space. The output constrained pose at each time step is the pose reconstructed into the full motion space. The point used for pose reconstruction is the closest point from the projected point on the model trajectory in the latent space. The resulting pose is then used as the initial pose for tracking at the next image.

5.4 Experiments

We used those gesture models as constraints while tracking communicative gestures and actions gestures from videos. As we only using one webcam, the tracker can not always distinguish poses correctly due to lacking depth information (for example, hands orientation are sometimes incorrectness). In the gesture models based tracking, each candidate pose is projected into the latent gesture model space, so enforcing the captured motion regularity.

We tested our approach on 4 subjects of communication gestures (each test video is about 90 frames). Because the output poses lay on the gesture model internal trajectory, most of the monocular vision ambiguities can be solved. Impossible poses will not happen in the gesture model space, so heuristic biomechanical constraints, which otherwise must be used for pruning the pose space, can be replaced with the gesture model that constrain the output poses to be on the learnt motion trajectory (fig.7). Another benefit of this approach is that the poses reconstructed in the latent space include motion details that cannot be captured from the input video sequence (such as hand shapes) (fig.8).

Fig. 7. Motion tracking with biomechanical constraints *vs.* gesture model. **Left:** An input image where the left hand orientation can hardly be distinguished. **Middle:** Motion capture result with heuristic biomechanical constraints: the unlikely pose of the left hand is biomechanically possible, so it is accepted. **Right:** Tracking with gesture model instead of biomechanical constraints: the gesture model avoids the awkward pose.

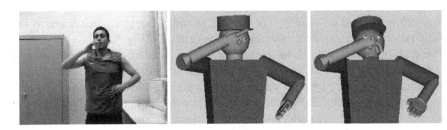

Fig. 8. Augmenting motion capture with gesture models. **Left:** Input image. **Middle:** Tracking without gesture model: the hand shape is not captured to meet real-time computation constraints. **Right:** The gesture model augments the motion capture with fingers movements.

6 Discussion and Future Work

We have created a library of communication gestures with variants and used it to learn gesture models with a GPDM statistical approach. These models allow both non-linear mapping for reconstruction and dimension reduction between the motion parameters space and a low-dimensional latent space, while being simple to learn from small training data. The main contribution of this work is used the low-dimensional gesture models as prior constraints for monocular motion capture while tracking communicative gestures. These gesture models help track ambiguous poses and render some motion details.

Our approach works on specific gestures. Future work is still required to be done to support broader classes of gestures.

Acknowledgement

The computer vision motion capture we used was widely developed by David Antonio Gómez Jáuregui.

References

1. Vilhjálmsson, H.: Avatar Augmented Online Conversation, Ph.D. thesis, Media Arts and Sciences, Massachusetts Institute of Technology, Media Laboratory, Cambridge, MA (2003)
2. Horain, P., Marques Soares, J., Rai, P.K., Bideau, A.: Virtually enhancing the perception of user actions. In: 15th International Conference on Artificial Reality and Telexistence (ICAT 2005), Christchurch, New Zealand, pp. 245–246 (2005), doi:10.1145/1152399.1152446
3. Moeslund, T., Hilton, A., Kruger, V.: A survey of advances in vision-based human motion capture and analysis. Computer vision and image understanding 104(2-3), 90–126 (2006)
4. Poppe, R.W.: Vision-based human motion analysis: An overview. Computer Vision and Image Understanding 108(1-2), 4–18 (2007)
5. Poggi, I.: Mind, Hands, Face and Body. In: A Goal and Belief View of Multimodal Communication, vol. 19. Weidler Verlag, Körper (2007)
6. Bevacqua, E., Mancini, M., Niewiadomski, R., Pelachaud, C.: An expressive ECA showing complex emotions. In: AISB 2007 Annual convention, workshop Language, Speech and Gesture for Expressive Characters, Newcastle, UK, pp. 208–216 (2007)
7. Wang, J.M., Fleet, D.J., Hertzmann, A.: Gaussian Process Dynamical Models for Human Motion. IEEE Transactions on PAMI 30(2), 283–298 (2008)
8. Pullen, K., Bregler, C.: Motion capture assisted animation: Texturing and synthesis. In: SIGGRAPH 2002, pp. 501–508 (2002)
9. Safonova, A., Hodgins, J.K., Pollard, N.S.: Synthesizing physically realistic human motion in low-dimensional, behavior-specific spaces. ACM Transactions on Graphics 23(3), 524–521 (2004)
10. Elgammal, A.M., Lee, C.-S.: Inferring 3D body pose from silhouettes using activity manifold learning. In: Conference on Computer Vision and Pattern Recognition (CVPR 2004), vol. 2, pp. 681–688 (2004)

11. Grochow, K., Martin, S.L., Hertzmann, A., Popovic, Z.: Style-based inverse kinematics. ACM Transactions on Graphics 23(3), 522–531 (2004)
12. Teh, Y.W., Roweis, S.T.: Automatic alignment of local representations. In: Neural Information Processing Systems 15 (NIPS 2002), pp. 841–848 (2003)
13. Lawrence, N.D.: Gaussian process latent variable models for visualisation of high dimensional data. In: Thrun, S., Saul, L., Schölkopf, B. (eds.) Advances in Neural Information Processing Systems, pp. 329–336. MIT Press, Cambridge (2004)
14. Carreira-Perpiñán, M.Á., Lu, Z.: The Laplacian Eigenmaps Latent Variable Model. In: 11th International Conference on Artificial Intelligence and Statistics (AISTATS), Puerto Rico (2007)
15. Urtasun, R., Fleet, D.J., Hertzmann, A., Fua, P.: Priors for people tracking from small training sets. In: International Conference On Computer Vision (ICCV 2005), Beijing, China, vol. 1, pp. 403–410 (2005)
16. Urtasun, R., Fleet, D.J., Fua, P.: 3D people tracking with Gaussian process dynamical models. In: Conference on Computer Vision and Pattern Recognition (CVPR 2006), New York, NY, vol. 1, pp. 238–245 (2006)
17. Raskin, L., Rivlin, E., Rudzsky, M.: Dimensionality Reduction for Articulated Body Tracking. In: 3DTV 2007, pp. 1–4 (2007)
18. Gómez Jáuregui, D.A., Horain, P.: Region-based vs. edge-based registration for 3D motion capture by real time monoscopic vision. In: Gagalowicz, A., Philips, W. (eds.) MIRAGE 2009. LNCS, vol. 5496, pp. 344–355. Springer, Heidelberg (2009)
19. Moon, K., Pavlovic, V.I.: Impact of dynamics on subspace embedding and tracking of sequences. In: Proceedings of the Conference on Computer Vision and Pattern Recognition (CVPR 2006), June 2006, New York, NY, vol. 1, pp. 198–205 (2006)
20. Lu, Z., Carreira-Perpiñán, M.Á., Sminchisescu, C.: People Tracking with the Laplacian Eigenmaps Latent Variable Model. In: Advances in Neural Information Processing Systems, NIPS, vol. 21 (2007)
21. Isard, M., Blake, A.: Condensation-conditional density propagation for visual tracking. Int. J. Computer Vision 29(1), 5–28 (1998)
22. Calbris, G.: The semiotics of French gestures. University Press, Bloomington (1990)
23. Gallaher, P.E.: Individual differences in nonverbal behavior: Dimensions of style. Journal of Personality and Social Psychology 63(1), 133–145 (1992)
24. Mancini, M., Pelachaud, C.: Distinctiveness in multimodal behaviors. In: 7th International Joint Conference on Autonomous Agents and Multi-Agent Systems, AAMAS 2008, Estoril Portugal (May 2008)
25. Kipp, M.: Anvil - A Generic Annotation Tool for Multimodal Dialogue. In: 7th European Conference on Speech Communication and Technology (Eurospeech), Aalborg, pp. 1367–1370 (2001)
26. Davis, J., Agrawala, M., Chuang, E., Popovic, Z., Salesin, D.: A Sketching Interface for Articulated Figure Animation. In: Eurographics/SIGGRAPH Symposium on Computer Animation, SCA (2003)
27. Sam, R., Lawrence, S.: Nonlinear dimensionality reduction by locally linear embedding. Science 290(5500), 2323–2326 (2000)
28. Tenenbaum, J.B., de Silva, V., Langford, J.C.: A Global Geometric Framework for Nonlinear Dimensionality Reduction. Science 290(5500), 2319–2323 (2000)
29. Neal, R.M.: Bayesian Learning for Neural Networks. Lecture Notes in Statistics, vol. 118. Springer, Heidelberg (1996)

Modeling Joint Synergies to Synthesize Realistic Movements

Matthieu Aubry[1], Frédéric Julliard[1], and Sylvie Gibet[2,3]

[1] Université Européenne de Bretagne, LISyC/ENIB
{aubry, julliard}@enib.fr
[2] Université de Bretagne Sud, Valoria
[3] Centre INRIA Rennes Bretagne Atlantique
sylvie.gibet@univ-ubs.fr

Abstract. This paper presents a new method to generate arm gestures which reproduces the dynamical properties of human movements. We describe a model of synergy, defined as a coordinative structure responsible for the flexible organization of joints over time when performing a movement. We propose a generic method which incorporates this synergy model into a motion controller system based on any iterative inverse kinematics technique. We show that this method is independent of the task and can be parametrized to suit an individual using a novel learning algorithm based on a motion capture database. The method yields different models of synergies for reaching tasks that are confronted to the same set of example motions. The quantitative results obtained allow us to select the best model of synergies for reaching movements and prove that our method is independent of the inverse kinematic technique used for the motion controller.

Keywords: Virtual Humanoids, Movement Synthesis, Synergy, Reaching Gesture, Joint Synergies, Movement Learning.

1 Introduction

Designing virtual characters that generate human-like gestures is still a major challenge, the research domain ranging from interactive ergonomics or virtual entertainment, to human gesture studies for different tasks (sport, motor disabilities, *etc*). One of the main issues that researchers are trying to solve is how the human performer coordinates and controls a complex musculo-skeleton system, with many degrees of freedom (DoFs). The rotations applied by the muscles on the DoFs controlling the different joints - shoulder, elbow, wrist - are combined in order to perform a smooth movement. When groups of muscles, corresponding to one or several DoFs, cooperate in this way, they form a synergy [1,2].

We follow here the assumption that synergies can be modeled in a flexible and dynamic fashion in order to produce a reaching movement, according to the task to perform (reaching different target points) and to physical characteristics of the

S. Kopp and I. Wachsmuth (Eds.): GW 2009, LNAI 5934, pp. 231–242, 2010.

individual. One of the basic problems underlying this notion of synergy, from a kinematic point of view, is the influence of use of each DoF within the formation of a movement [2]. Moreover, we may consider that synergies dynamically evolve through time. Therefore the temporal characteristics of the synergies along the movement are a key issue that need to be investigated.

In this paper, we present a new approach to imitate human reaching gestures, based on the modeling of these synergies. Here, the notion of synergy expresses both the spatial interrelation between joints and the dynamical patterns acting on each joint during the course of the movement. Our synergy model can be included into any inverse kinematics (IK) technique, which iteratively computes the posture of the arm system from the specification of goals defined as reaching targets in the 3D space. The originality of our approach relies in the incorporation into the sensorimotor model of an explicit joint synergy function which can be parametrized from captured movements. The goal is to finely reproduce the gesture while preserving the natural characteristics of the real movements. This approach is compared to other classical IK methods, and quantitatively analyzed for a set of reaching movements.

The rest of this paper is organized as follows: in section 2, we briefly discuss related works, and then continue with the mainstay of this paper; in section 3, we describe our method for controlling motion and modeling joint synergies; experiments and results are presented in section 5 for a set of reaching movements; and lastly we conclude by a discussion and give future perspectives for this type of work.

2   Related Work

Over the years, different methods aiming at producing natural gestures reproducing characteristics of real movements have been proposed. We try to highlight how these works may explain the underlying synergies when performing movements.

Learning models of motion from examples has been an active and productive area of research. In these approaches, the main objective consists of synthesizing new sequences of movements from existing ones. Some approaches use Hidden Markov models [3], or use a Linear Dynamic System to learn the style of training motions [4]. Gibet et al. [5] use the Nadarada Watson estimate to learn local transformations of the Jacobian. Rose et al. [6] and Grochow et al. [7] propose respectively a Radial Basis Function model and a Scaled Gaussian Process Latent Variable model to learn inverse kinematics from human poses. Wang et al. [8] learn a probabilistic mapping between poses and style variables, using a parametric Gaussian mixture model. Ong et al. [9] propose a novel modular neural network architecture for learning inverse kinematics. Other approaches determine physical constraints by using Non Linear optimization techniques [10], or clustering models [11], learned from captured motion. Chai et al. [12] learn a statistical dynamical model from motion capture data and use this model to generate new motions from a variety of user-defined constraints. These approaches produce natural-looking and physically plausible motions, and have proven to be effective for a large variety of human motions. Some of them result in the generation of new motions by interpolating or extrapolating the learned parameters. But, for these new motions, the physical laws of motion are not necessarily guaranteed. Moreover, these learning models do not explicitly incorporate the modeling of synergies.

Numerous inverse kinematics (IK) techniques have also been developed to produce realistic motions from the specification of geometrical user-defined constraints. Among these techniques, traditional IK solvers use numerical optimization methods, such as Jacobian pseudo inverse, which implicitly capture the correlation between joints when performing a movement. In order to avoid non realistic situations, constraints may be introduced, such as physical-based constraints [13], shape constraints [14], or ergonomic constraints [15]. These methods rely on the validity of the constraints for a given task and usually do not take into account features specific to an individual.

In order to take advantage of both methods, example-based IK methods are an effective alternative. They combine goal-directed and data-driven methods, thus relying on real motions with an explicit model for solving IK. Komura et al. [16] extract joints' weights from captured data and re-use them during synthesis to reproduce the synergies. Some recent studies perform inverse kinematics in low-dimensional space, such as latent spaces [17], and [18], thus including within the solver the linear combination between the DoF. In these cases, synergies are explicitly specified within the motion. However, these methods make the asumption that the inter-relation between the joints within the synergies may be represented by linear functions. Moreover, they require the passage of one posture to another, and do not take into account the dynamical effect of the synergies over time when performing a movement.

Our approach is also related to example-based IK methods. But in contrast to the above methods, we propose to model the dynamical effect of synergies over time. In the line of previous work [19], based on a sensorimotor optimization loop, we propose a novel approach which uses a motion capture database and a learning technique that automatically computes the parameters of the synergy model.

3   Proposed Model

3.1   Inverse Kinematics Formulation

In this section, we consider the control of a kinematic chain $\mathcal{C}$ composed of n joints linking segments of different lengths, each segment representing a bone of the virtual character. Each joint is characterized by 1, 2 or 3 rotations, defining several DoFs. The set of rotations can be represented by the state vector $\Theta = \{\theta_1, \ldots, \theta_n\}$.

We define the forward kinematic operator $\mathcal{H}$ which computes the end effector location $\mathcal{X}$ of the chain $\mathcal{C}$, given its state Θ. Usually, the location is determined by a position and an orientation.

$$\mathcal{X} = \mathcal{H}(\Theta)$$

The IK problem can be defined as a method that determines a vector Θ so that the end effector is in the desired situation $\mathcal{X}_d$.

$$\Theta = \mathcal{H}^{-1}(\mathcal{X}_d)$$

As the human arm is a complex and redundant system, the kinematic chain $\mathcal{C}$ cannot be inverted in general. Most of previous work solves the IK problem with local linearization methods. In this case, the IK formulation determines small variations of the posture from small variations of the end effector situation, thus trying to converge towards the desired situation.

Different iterative methods can be used to solve IK. Whereas the pseudo-inverse methods can be expressed as:

$$\Delta\Theta = \lambda J(\Theta)^+ \Delta X$$

where $J(\Theta)^+$ is the pseudo-inverse of the Jacobian of $\mathcal{C}$ corresponding to the state Θ, and λ is a scalar changing the rate of convergence. This pseudo-inverse can be obtained, for example, using the Singular Value Decomposition (SVD) of the Jacobian.

Another method: J^T, uses the transpose of the Jacobian $J(\Theta)$:

$$\Delta\Theta = \lambda J^T(\Theta)\Delta X$$

which, while being easier to compute, presents smaller convergence rates on multiple effectors. In our study, we also define a slightly derived method of the J^T (called NJ^T) which computes the normalized variations of the rotations. The iterative algorithm resulting from the numerical solutions of IK can be represented in fig. 1, where $\mathcal{O}$ is the optimized function (J^+, SVD, J^T, NJ^T), $\mathcal{I}$ the integration function, and $\mathcal{H}$ the forward kinematic transformation. The $\mathcal{S}$ block, usually unavailable in conventional methods, allows us to introduce synergies in the loop and is detailed further.

Other optimization functions may be used, thus improving the convergence rate towards the solution, and avoiding singularities [13,20]. Whereas these methods propose optimized solutions to the problem of IK, their common use is to

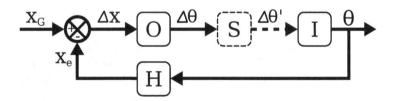

Fig. 1. Optimal feedback control to reach goal $\mathcal{X}_G$ with $\mathcal{O}$ an optimization function, $\mathcal{S}$ the model of synergy introduced by this work (optional), $\mathcal{I}$ the integration block of the command $\Delta\theta$ to the configuration θ and $\mathcal{H}$ the forward kinematic model

drop intermediate postures, thus having to apply the loop for each point of the effector's trajectory. On the other side, one can use intermediate postures as part of the motion, so that he only need the location of the target. However, one has to keep in mind that they do not guarantee the natural quality of the movement through time. We will introduce below a synergy model which is compatible with the use of intermediate postures as a motion, and dynamically modifies the temporal evolution of the synthesized motion, according to characteristics of human movements.

3.2   Modeling Synergies

In our approach, synergies can be represented by dynamical functions interacting within a set of joints. More precisely, we define synergies as a combination of gains applied to each of the n DoFs and a temporal function. By modifying the level of involvement of the DoFs along the motion, we may completely control the velocity and the shape of the motion.

We define a synergy transformation as a function $\mathcal{S}(t, \Theta)$ of time and joint angular values. The calculation of the synergy gains is achieved according to the following equation:

$$\Delta\Theta'_i = \mathcal{S}(t, \Theta).\Delta\Theta = \phi_i(t).(M[\Theta].\Delta\Theta)_i$$

where the function $\phi_i(t)$ and the matrix $M[\Theta]$ represent respectively the temporal part and the spatial part of the synergy function.

The synergy function $\mathcal{S}(t, \Theta)$ is thus parametrized, the parameters depending on the subject physical characteristics, as well as on the task. We will consider in our simulation a parameter vector p with a dimension m which may vary with $\mathcal{S}$; its values are constant over the movement and is noted:

$$p = \{p_1, \ldots, p_m\}$$

By using a global learning approach, based on the comparison between simulated movements and captured ones, our methodology consists in determining the generic synergy model for specific tasks and the set of parameters corresponding to an individual.

3.3   Learning Joint Synergies Parameters

We define a meta-heuristic based on simulated annealing which requires an optimization function $\mathcal{O}$, a synergy model $\mathcal{S}$ and captured movements as training reference. A pseudo-code version of our meta-heuristic is given in algorithm 1. The principle of our meta-heuristic is to generate a random population of parameters (l. 1): $population = \{p_1, \ldots, p_u\}$ and to make them evolve randomly by applying small variations (l. 4) on each parameter. The parameters are then evaluated for each training motion (l. 6-10), by setting the controller in the same initial posture and by simulating the motion for a task similar to the training motion's one. The distance between the training and the synthesized motion is then computed. If the evolutionary algorithm reduces this distance, the vector of parameters is kept otherwise previous values are restored (l. 11-16). These steps are repeated until the average score of the population is stabilized (l. 18) and finally the best parameter's vector is returned (l. 19).

Algorithm 1. Meta-heuristic for determining the best parameters p

---

 1: $population \leftarrow GenerateRandom()$
 2: **repeat**
 3:    **for all** $parameters \in population$ **do**
 4:        $parameters.evolve()$
 5:        **for all** $mocap \in Trainings$ **do**
 6:            $simulatedMotion = controller.synthesize(mocap.task)$
 7:            $score \leftarrow score + distance(simulatedMotion, mocap.motion)$
 8:        **end for**
 9:        $deltaScore \leftarrow parameters.previousScore - score$
10:        **if** $deltaScore >= 0$ **then**
11:            $parameters.restore()$
12:        **end if**
13:    **end for**
14: **until** $population.isStabilized()$
15: $result \leftarrow population.findBest()$

3.4 Metric for Evaluating Synthesized Movements

The naturality of the synthesized motion is evaluated by superposing two virtual characters and playing captured and synthesized movements for the same task and comparing the two motions over time. In this case an error metric is computed by defining a distance between the two motions, based on the mean distance between postures along the motion. The calculation is stopped at the end of the shortest motion:

$$d(\mathcal{M}_A, \mathcal{M}_B) = \sum_{i=1}^{mini} \frac{dist(\mathcal{P}_{A,i}, \mathcal{P}_{B,i})}{mini}, mini = min(length(\mathcal{M}_A), length(\mathcal{M}_B))$$

with $\mathcal{M}_A$ motion A, $\mathcal{P}_{A,i}$ posture from motion A at frame i and $length(\mathcal{M}_A)$ the number of frames in motion A.

Such a distance gives a measure which takes into account both the velocity and the shape of the movement. First of all, by using the frame by frame comparison over time, we ensure that the movements' velocities can be compared. If both movements have a different frame rate, one of the movements has to be interpolated to match the other's frame rate. Secondly, the deformed shape of the movements is computed by using the average Cartesian distance between joints. This distance between two postures $\mathcal{P}_A$ and $\mathcal{P}_B$ is given by equation:

$$dist(\mathcal{P}_A, \mathcal{P}_B) = \left(\sum_{j=1}^{l} \frac{||\mathcal{X}_{A,j} - \mathcal{X}_{B,j}||}{l+1} \right) + \frac{||\mathcal{X}_{A,e} - \mathcal{X}_{B,e}||}{l+1}$$

where the kinematic chain $\mathcal{C}$ is composed of l joints, the position of the j-th joint in global space for the posture $\mathcal{P}_A$ is noted $\mathcal{X}_{A,i}$ and the position of the end effector is noted $\mathcal{X}_{A,e}$. Note that all distances obtained are relative to the environment scale, in this article humanoïd's arm has a size of 5.97 (shoulder to wrist) in this space and length from wrist to finger's end is 2.0.

4   Experiments and Results

In our experiments, 14 reaching movements have been recorded for one subject. This one is seated on a chair and targets from different colors are uniformly distributed in front of him (cf fig. 2). He has been asked, from the rest posture, to reach a specific target and then come back to the same rest posture. To avoid the bias of finding the target, he has to locate the target before starting the motion. The rest posture has been chosen by the subject and is used as the starting position for each motion.

It should be noted that a Cartesian distance instead of an angular one allowed us to use two characters with the same joints but different DoFs. In fact, captured motions are recorded on 4 joints with a total of 12 DoFs, while the synthesis model has 4 joints but only 7 DoFs.

Three different analysis are performed. First, we test different models of synergies to find the best compromise between the number of parameters and the quality of the synthesized motions. Next, different optimization functions are implemented in order to evaluate the genericity of our model. And finally, some characteristics of the synthesized motion are compared to captured motions.

First of all, we define different gains models and compare their performances. These models used for reaching tasks are composed of gains and sigmoids as temporal functions. In particular we evaluate the influence of using same or different gains and sigmoids functions for each DoFs.

For the gains, we use diagonal matrix, one with the same gain for each DoF (M_A) and one with a different gain for each DoF (M_B). While M_A requires only

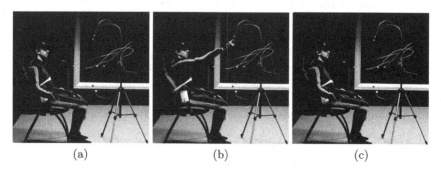

(a)	(b)	(c)

Fig. 2. A subject is seated, his back supported by the chair. Color targets are located in front of him. From its rest posture (a), he is asked to reach a specific target (b) and then come back to the same rest posture (c).

one parameter, M_B will require as many parameters as DoFs. Those matrix are defined by:

$$M_A = \begin{pmatrix} g_1 & & 0 \\ & \ddots & \\ 0 & & g_1 \end{pmatrix}, M_B = \begin{pmatrix} g_1 & & 0 \\ & \ddots & \\ 0 & & g_n \end{pmatrix}$$

We also defined three different time functions inspired from work of Gibet et al. [19]: one neutral and two using sigmoids $sig(t) = \frac{1}{1+e^t}$. These time functions are defined for each DoF by:

$$\phi_{A,i} = 1, \quad \phi_{B,i} = sig(-s.t + o), \quad \phi_{C,i} = sig(-s_i.t + o_i)$$

where ϕ_B uses the same parameters s (slope) and o (offset) for each DoF while ϕ_C uses one for each DoFs.

Therefore, four synergy functions are distinguished:

- $\mathcal{S}_A(t, \Theta)$ using M_A and ϕ_A; $p = \{g_1\}$
- $\mathcal{S}_B(t, \Theta)$ using M_B and ϕ_A; $p = \{g_1, \ldots, g_n\}$
- $\mathcal{S}_C(t, \Theta)$ using M_B and ϕ_B; $p = \{g_1, \ldots, g_n, o, s\}$
- $\mathcal{S}_D(t, \Theta)$ using M_B and ϕ_C; $p = \{g_1, \ldots, g_n, o_1, \ldots, o_n, s_1, \ldots, s_n\}$

Taking one by one the 14 training motions, we obtained 14 sets of parameters associated to 14 distances for each model. To reduce the field of exploration of the meta-heuristic, we used $g_i \in [-5; 5]$, $s_i \in [1; 10]$ and $o_i \in [0; 20]$. These values, obtained by experimentation, also reduced the computational cost. The results in figure 3 show the average, minimum and maximum distances obtained for each model.

These results clearly show the necessity to separate the gains applied to the DoFs. In fact, a reduction of 55% of the average distance is obtained if we move from $\mathcal{S}_A$ to $\mathcal{S}_B$. Next, the insertion of a sigmoid in $\mathcal{S}_C$ allows us to reduce of 13% more, and separating the sigmoid on each DoF gives another reduction of 10%. In addition, whereas $\mathcal{S}_D$ gives the best results over the whole set of motions (1.35), $\mathcal{S}_C$ gives the minimum distance between two motions (0.90). This can be explained by the number of parameters used by $\mathcal{S}_D$ (21) which is more than twice $\mathcal{S}_C$'s one (9). In fact, our meta-heuristic is more efficient on a smaller number of parameters.

For the rest of our experiments, we decide to choose the model $\mathcal{S}_C$, which is a compromise between obtaining a good average result and the number of parameters.

In order to test the genericity of our model according to optimization functions, we have implemented three IK algorithms: the transposed Jacobian (J^T), the normalized transposed Jacobian (NJ^T) and the pseudoinverse Jacobian using SVD. Each optimization function is tested for each of the 14 motions, once with $\mathcal{S}_A$ (raw controller) and once using $\mathcal{S}_C$ (model selected from previous experiment). This experiment allowed us to compare the average distance between motion synthesized with the raw controller and with the controller enhanced by our synergy model.

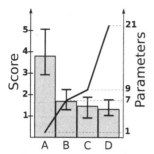

Model	$dim(p)$	Distance		
		avg.	min.	max.
$\mathcal{S}_A$	1	**3.83**	2.92	5.10
$\mathcal{S}_B$	7	**1.71**	1.28	2.28
$\mathcal{S}_C$	9	**1.49**	0.90	1.93
$\mathcal{S}_D$	21	**1.35**	1.02	1.81

Fig. 3. Average, minimum and maximum distance for the different synergy functions $\mathcal{S}_A$, $\mathcal{S}_B$, $\mathcal{S}_C$, and $\mathcal{S}_D$

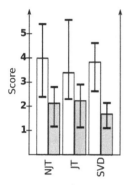

Function	Distance		
	avg.	min.	max.
NJ^T	**4.02**	2.38	5.45
J^T	**3.42**	2.32	5.65
SVD	**3.86**	2.62	4.66

With $\mathcal{S}_A$ (in white)

Function	Distance		
	avg.	min.	max.
NJ^T	**2.15**	1.15	2.84
J^T	**2.26**	1.12	2.95
SVD	**1.71**	1.09	2.18

Using $\mathcal{S}_C$ (in yellow)

Fig. 4. Average, minimum and maximum distance between training motion and synthesized motion with $\mathcal{S}_A$ (in white) or with $\mathcal{S}_C$ (in gray)

Results are displayed in figure 4. They show that for each optimization function, our synergy model decreases the distance between synthesized and captured motions. In fact, incorporating $\mathcal{S}_C$, we improve the results of 34% for J^T, of 66% for SVD, and of 47% for NJ^T. Furthermore, the average distance is lower when using the SVD method (1.71 versus 2.15 and 2.26), but we can observe that results achieved with J^T and NJ^T can be as good as the SVD's ones (only 6% difference between the minimum values).

Finally, the realism of the movements is evaluated for the different synergy models. As many researchers have demonstrated that the velocity profiles of simple reaching arm movements are approximatively bell-shaped [19], we compare the velocities of synthesized and captured trajectories during the movement execution.

The hand velocities for recorded and synthesized movements, using a raw controller $\mathcal{S}_A$ and a $\mathcal{S}_C$ controller is diplayed in figure 5. These curves clearly highlight the improvement made by the synergy model. Practically, the trajectories of the synthesized movements produced with $\mathcal{S}_C$ are very close to the captured ones, whereas trajectories produced by the raw controllers do not match at all the bell-shaped curve.

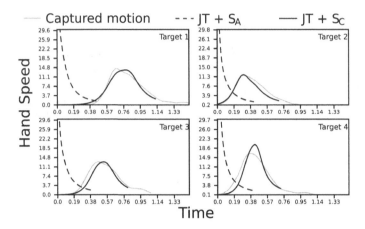

Fig. 5. Hand speed through time for captured motion (plain gray), synthesized motion with a raw controller (dotted black), and synthesized motion with the synergy model $\mathcal{S}_C$ (plain black) for four different targets

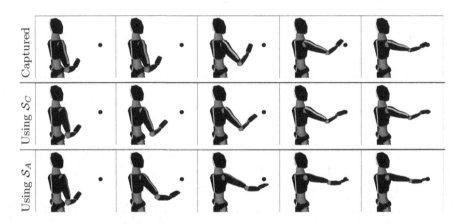

Fig. 6. Superposition of captured motion and synthesized motions both with $\mathcal{S}_A$ and with $\mathcal{S}_C$ as a synergy model. Motion synthesized with $\mathcal{S}_C$ match the captured one while motion synthesized with $\mathcal{S}_A$ does not (motion is quicker and elbow is moved too high).

We also produced videos[1] that make possible to compare a recorded task with the corresponding synthesized task with and without the synergy model (cf. fig. 6). While we can see that the use of $\mathcal{S}_C$ instead of $\mathcal{S}_A$ allowed to the synthesized motion to match the captured one both in speed and shape, these animations still need to be perceptually evaluated.

---

[1] Videos are available on author's website: http://www.enib.fr/~aubry/

5   Discussion and Perspectives

In this paper, we present a novel approach to finely reproduce reaching gestures by preserving natural human characteristics for an individual. The originality of the approach relies on the notion of joint synergy which is explicitly included into the model as a spatio-temporal function, parametrized from motion capture training data.

In order to precisely tune up our synergetic model, we used a preliminary database built from 14 motions obtained from a single person. We then tried to find a sufficiently small relevant set of synergetic parameters able to maximize the naturality of motions. For estimating this naturality, a motion metric is defined as an average Cartesian distance between joint positions, computed on the whole movement. This study reveals that pointing gestures can be naturally synthesized by the use of only one constant gain per DoF and one shared sigmoid.

The interchangeability of the optimization function, regardless of the synergetic function, has then been carried out by testing different numerical inversion methods as optimization functions. A quantitative analysis of the synthesized motions has been performed. Generated motions reveal that the specific hand's velocity bell-shaped profile is close to the velocity of real motions, only when the synergetic function is employed.

Our experience has been successfully extended to a largest set of captured motions (192) from two different persons. Results highlight the ability of the model to learn individual joint synergies regardless of the number of captured data. Due to the genericity of our approach, we may incorporate synergy mechanisms into a wide range of inverse kinematics motor controllers. The meta-heuritic also proves to be fully independent of the task, of the synergetic function, and of the number of training data.

The main limitation of the current model concerns its generalization to the synthesis of any objective in the task space: parameters are learned motion by motion and it is obviously inconceivable to learn parameters for each point of the accessible space. However, we observed that for a given set of parameters learned from a particular original target, it is possible to synthesize new motions, from nearby targets, whose characteristics are relatively close to the features of the original motion. The parameters' space thus contains continuous regions that we still have to identify in order to define the applicability domain for a set of parameters. Moreover, this perspective should highlight the possibility to efficiently map each partition of the accessible space with a valid set of parameters, thus lowering the number of required training motions.

References

1. Bernstein, N.A.: The co-ordination and regulation of movements. Pergamon Press, Oxford (1967)
2. Latash, M.L.: Synergy. Oxford University Press, Oxford (2008)
3. Brand, M., Hertzmann, A.: Style machines. In: SIGGRAPH 2000: Proceedings of the 27th annual conference on Computer graphics and interactive techniques, pp. 183–192. ACM Press/Addison-Wesley Publishing Co. (2000)

4. Li, Y., Wang, T., Shum, H.-Y.: Motion texture: a two-level statistical model for character motion synthesis. In: SIGGRAPH 2002: Proceedings of the 29th annual conference on Computer graphics and interactive techniques, pp. 465–472. ACM, New York (2002)

5. Gibet, S., Marteau, P.F.: Expressive gesture animation based on non parametric learning of sensory-motor models. In: Computer Animation and Social Agents, pp. 465–472. ACM, New York (2003)

6. Rose, C.F., Sloan, P.-P.J., Cohen, M.F.: Artist-directed inverse-kinematics using radial basis function interpolation. Computer Graphics Forum 20, 239–250 (2001)

7. Grochow, K., Martin, S.L., Hertzmann, A., Popović, Z.: Style-based inverse kinematics. ACM Trans. Graph. 23(3), 522–531 (2004)

8. Wang, Y., Liu, Z., Zhou, L.: Key-styling: learning motion style for real-time synthesis of 3d animation. Computer Animation and Virtual Worlds 17(3-4), 229–237 (2006)

9. Ong, E.-J., Hilton, A.: Learnt inverse kinematics for animation synthesis. Graphical Models 68(5-6), 472–483 (2006)

10. Liu, C.K., Hertzmann, A., Popović, Z.: Learning physics-based motion style with nonlinear inverse optimization. ACM Trans. Graph. 24(3), 1071–1081 (2005)

11. Oyama, E., Agah, A., MacDorman, K.F., Maeda, T., Tachi, S.: A modular neural network architecture for inverse kinematics model learning. Neurocomputing 38-40, 797–805 (2001)

12. Chai, J., Hodgins, J.K.: Constraint-based motion optimization using a statistical dynamic model. In: SIGGRAPH 2007: ACM SIGGRAPH 2007 papers, p. 8. ACM, New York (2007)

13. Baerlocher, P., Boulic, R.: An inverse kinematic architecture enforcing an arbitrary number of strict priority levels. The Visual Computer 20(6), 402–417 (2004)

14. Le Callennec, B., Boulic, R.: Interactive motion deformation with prioritized constraints. Graphical Models 68(2), 175–193 (2006)

15. Yang, F., Ding, L., Yang, C., Yuan, X.: An algorithm for simulating human arm movement considering the comfort level. Simulation Modelling Practice and Theory 13(5), 437–449 (2005)

16. Komura, T., Kuroda, A., Kudoh, S., Tai, C.-L., Shinagawa, Y.: An inverse kinematics method for 3d figures with motion data. In: Computer Graphics International, pp. 266–271 (2003)

17. Raunhardt, D., Boulic, R.: Motion constraint. The Visual Computer 25(5), 509–518 (2009)

18. Tournier, M., Wu, X., Courty, N., Arnaud, E., Reveret, L.: Motion compression using principal geodesics analysis. Eurographics 28(2) (April 2009) (to appear)

19. Gibet, S., Marteau, P.F.: A self-organized model for the control, planning and learning of nonlinear multi-dimensional systems using a sensory feedback. Applied Intelligence 4(4), 337–349 (1994)

20. Buss, S.R., Kim, J.-S.: Selectively damped least squares for inverse kinematics. Journal of Graphics Tools 10(3), 37–49 (2005)

Multimodal Interfaces in Support of Human-Human Interaction

Alex Waibel

Interactive Systems Laboratories,
Carnegie Mellon University, USA
and
University of Karlsruhe, Germany
waibel@cs.cmu.edu
http://www.cs.cmu.edu/%7Eahw/

1 Extended Abstract

After building computers that paid no intention to communicating with humans, the computer science community has devoted significant effort over the years to more sophisticated interfaces that put the "human in the loop" of computers. These interfaces have improved usability by providing more appealing output (graphics, animations), more easy to use input methods (mouse, pointing, clicking, dragging) and more natural interaction modes (speech, vision, gesture, etc.). Yet all these interaction modes have still mostly been restricted to human-machine interaction and made severely limiting assumptions on sensor setup and expected human behavior. (For example, a gesture might be presented clearly in front of the camera and have a clear start and end time). Such assumptions, however, are unrealistic and have, consequently, limited the potential productivity gains, as the machine still operates in a passive mode, requiring the user to pay considerable attention to the technological artifact.

As a departure from such classical user interfaces, we have turned our attention to developing user interface for use in computing services that place Computers in the midst of Humans, i.e. in the Human Interaction Loop (CHIL), rather than the other way round. CHIL services aim to provide assistance implicitly and proactively, while causing minimal interference. They operate in environments, where humans interact with humans and computers hover in the background providing assistance wherever needed. Providing such services in real life situations, however, presents formidable technical challenges. Computers must be made aware of the activities, locations, interactions, and cognitive states of the humans that they are to serve and they must become socially responsive. Services must be delivered and provided in a private, secure, and socially acceptable manner.

CHIL services require perceptual technology that provides a complete description of human activities and interactions to derive and infer user needs, i.e., they must describe the WHO, WHERE, HOW, TO WHOM, WHY, WHEN of human interaction and engagement. Describing human-human interaction in open, natural and unconstrained environments is further complicated by robustness issues, when noise, illumination, occlusion, interference, suboptimal sensor positioning, perspective, localization and segmentation all introduce uncertainty. Relevant perceptual cues

S. Kopp and I. Wachsmuth (Eds.): GW 2009, LNAI 5934, pp. 243–244, 2010.

therefore must be gathered, accumulated and fused across modalities and along time opportunistically, i.e., whenever and wherever such cues can be determined and merged reliably. And finally, gathering of such multimodal cues, should involve a proactive participation of the interface to seek out such cues, as the interface may move (Humanoid Robots), coordinate (multiple sensors), and calibrate its own sensors and data gathering.

In this talk, ongoing work and results were presented from perceptual interfaces under development in realistic human-human interaction environments, using data from smart rooms and humanoid robot interaction.

Gestures for Large Display Control

Wim Fikkert*, Paul van der Vet, Gerrit van der Veer, and Anton Nijholt

Human Media Interaction, University of Twente,
P.O. Box 217, 7500 AE Enschede, The Netherlands
{f.w.fikkert, p.e.vandervet, g.c.vanderveer, a.nijholt}@utwente.nl
http://hmi.ewi.utwente.nl

Abstract. The hands are highly suited to interact with large public displays. It is, however, not apparent which gestures come naturally for easy and robust use of the interface. We first explored how uninstructed users gesture when asked to perform basic tasks. Our subjects gestured with great similarity and readily produced gestures they had seen before; not necessarily in a human-computer interface. In a second investigation these and other gestures were rated by a hundred subjects. A gesture set for explicit command-giving to large displays emerged from these ratings. It is notable that for a selection task, tapping the index finger in mid-air, like with a traditional mouse, scored highest by far. It seems that the mouse has become a metaphor in everyday life.

Keywords: Human-centered computing, user interfaces, input devices and strategies, intuitive hand gestures, large display interaction.

1 Introduction

Physically large, digital surfaces can supply richly detailed yet diverse content in our everyday environments, whether it is at home, at the office or in a public space [1]. Such surfaces can be embedded in walls, floors, furniture and other physical objects. Ubiquity characterizes the availability of these large digital surfaces in future environments. A wide range of sensors enable us users to interact with such surfaces through very diverse modalities, resulting in an interactive exchange of information between human and computer. Depending on the settings, not all modalities will be suited for interacting with the digital surfaces, also known as 'displays'. For example, (parts of) the displays are not always within reach of the user; preventing touch input. Likewise, speech input is not always desirable, for example, in shopping malls or during conversations.

In this paper, we focus on large display interaction through hands gesturing from beyond arm's length [2]. The goal of interaction is to extract information from the display by navigating through its digital contents, not through a strictly menu-based approach per se [3]. The large display interaction may be obtaining the latest fashion trends in a shopping mall to supporting discussions with detailed results in project-based teamwork to entertainment and games [4]. The

---

* Corresponding author.

S. Kopp and I. Wachsmuth (Eds.): GW 2009, LNAI 5934, pp. 245–256, 2010.
© Springer-Verlag Berlin Heidelberg 2010

common denominator for such large display interfaces as we address them is that they offer diverse, detailed and structured information for comprehensive access and that they require explicit command-giving. Communicative modalities in proactive displays such as body posture or eye-contact are beyond our scope [2].

The contribution of this work is a gesture set that comes naturally and with which commands can be issued to a large interactive display with ease [5]. A typical way to interact with large displays through gesturing is to introduce a gesture set that is designed to accommodate the sensors used [6]. Such a gesture set can be difficult for users to learn and use [7]. We consider gestures that come naturally to be intuitive but we recognize that this may have very diverse causes ranging from strong metaphors in everyday life and work, which, we feel, by now includes the indoctrination by decades of mouse-based interfaces.

This work is structured as follows. Section 2 starts with a categorization of the commands that are present in an interactive system. In Section 3 we describe an initial study aimed to discover which gestures are made by uninstructed users. Section 4 then describes how we consulted an international population on gesture representations for issuing specific commands. We discuss our findings in Section 5 where we also describe future work for validating this gesture set.

2   Commands to Issue with Gesturing

Explicit command-giving is the basis for the large display interfaces that we focus on. Our aim is not to design new interaction paradigms but to discover how existing large display interfaces might be controlled with the hands. However, it is not clear which elementary commands are at the basis of this interface.

Navigation, selection and manipulation have been mentioned as the elementary tasks in an interface [9]. However, such tasks are often formed by chunking together more fundamental tasks [10]. Buxton argues that human-computer interaction should be regarded from a more human perspective rather than from the device or system [8]. This approach can describe interface tasks at a more generic level. Buxton proposed a three-state model to represent the interactions such as point, select and drag for indirect devices such as the mouse, see Figure 1. For instance, a one-button mouse can be represented to be out-of-range (state #0) when the user is not touching it, tracking (state #1) when the user is moving it and dragging (state #2) when pressing the button. Selection is done with a quick 1-2-1 state transition. The precise meaning of these three states varies (slightly) with the device or interaction technique that is being represented. For example, a stylus is out-of-range when it is lifted from its

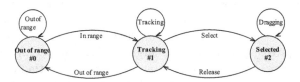

Fig. 1. Buxton's [8] three-state model for graphical input. Picture adapted from [8].

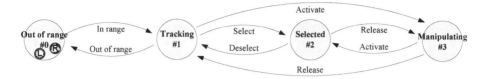

Fig. 2. Our four-state model for direct free-hand graphical input, extending the three-state model proposed by [8]. The dynamic manipulation state (#3) represents diverse tasks such as resize and activate. Tokens represent the left (L) and the right (R) hand.

tablet, a joystick has no out-of-range state (#0) because it keeps tracking when untouched and a buttonless joystick does not have a dragging state (#2).

Buxton's model can also describe direct input devices that work directly on the display surface. For such devices, for example, light pens and touch surfaces, a special case of the model applies with a direct transition between the #0 (passive tracking) and #2 (dragging) states because the system does not know what is being pointed at until contact [8]. Looking at the hands gesturing, Buxton's three-state model describes such interfaces adequately but not fully. The user is out-of-range when not addressing the screen (#0). By addressing the screen, the system switches to the track-state (#1) from which selection is possible (#2). Manipulation of any (selected) contents is, however, not always a chunking of these three steps. For example, resizing a selected object [2], activating a selected object [11] or performing a 'right-mouse'-like action on a selected object [10], cannot be described. A five-state model was proposed in which new states are added for each new mouse-button [10]. We propose a similar solution: adding a dynamic state (#3) to Buxton's three-state model to generically encompass manipulation tasks, see Figure 2. Guiard describes the human motor system with two motors that represent the hands [12]. These motors cooperate to form a kinematic chain with the non-preferred hand serving as a reference frame for the preferred hand. Based on Petri nets, we use tokens to represent the hands (R and L). These tokens move between states separately or together, capturing unimanual and bimanual interactions. Repeat transitions as in Buxton's model [8] are omitted: tokens remain in a state until an explicit transition.

3   Gestures That Come Naturally

To discover which gestures are considered natural by potential users we asked uninstructed users to issue commands through gesturing.

3.1   Methodology

Our participants were asked to manipulate a topographic map of our university's local surroundings. Participants were not expected to have knowledge of the local topography. Figure 3 shows the map and the Wizard of Oz set-up that was used[1].

---

[1] A user is fooled to believe that she is in actual control while, in fact, the wizard is.

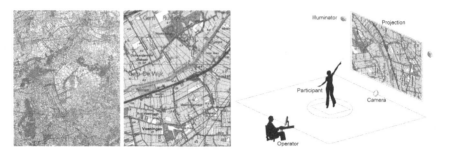

Fig. 3. The whole and a part of the map that the participants had to manipulate and the set-up for this investigation. The operator sat in the back, out of view.

Three increasingly difficult assignments were executed in which the map view needed to be moved to a specific location on a specific zoom level. Assignments were to locate and display one or more specific town(s) and to position the view port so that these target(s) would fill the screen. Participants could issue two commands to complete each assignment successfully: pan and zoom in/out. We omit the tracking state in our four-state model here because the user is either not interacting when out-of-range(#0) or she is panning (#2) or zooming (#3).

The wizard was introduced as a technician who would perform minor adjustments to a working gesture interface during a brief speak-out-loud session at the beginning of each trial. Note that during this phase, the operator chose the coupling of gesture and state-change, including the out-of-range state. The operator was instructed to respond only to hand movements and to ignore any verbal commands. Visual feedback consisted of the map panning or resizing.

Each trial was video taped with a camera facing the subject. The recorded trials were annotated in ASCII Stokoe[2] and analyzed based on occurrences in Anvil [13]. ASCII Stokoe is designed for sign language annotations. We expanded the annotation with additional symbols & and Z that represent hand movements with the same hand shape and orientation and the circumfix S(..) represented synchronized bimanual movements. We abstracted our annotations based on the assumption that similar gestures have a similar meaning [2]. For example, differences between hand orientation (slightly upwards compared to fully upwards) and hand shapes (cupped hand versus slightly stretched hand) are generalized. The operator also mentioned to have interpreted the gestures in this manner.

3.2   Results

Nine students and colleagues from our group took part in this within-subjects study. They were on average 27 years old ($\sigma = 6$), ranging from 19-36 years. One participant was female, eight were male. All participants were right handed. On a 1-3 Likert-style scale, our participants were proficient with computers ($\mu = 2.8$, $\sigma = .4$), the internet ($\mu = 3.0$, $\sigma = 0$) and map applications ($\mu = 2.8$, $\sigma = .4$). They were somewhat familiar with the local topography ($\mu = 2.1$, $\sigma = .6$).

---

[2] http://www.speakeasy.org/~mamandel/ASCII-Stokoe.txt, last checked Sep. 2009.

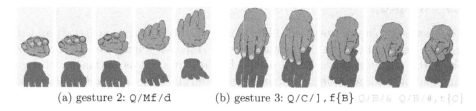

(a) gesture 2: Q/Mf/d   (b) gesture 3: Q/C/], f{B} Q/B/& Q/B/#, t{C}

Fig. 4. The two most occurring gesture for panning (notation in gray is not depicted): (a) pointing hand away from the user towards the display that moves around, relaxing the hand would release (136 occurrences in 5 subjects) and (b) relaxed/cupped hand to stretched hand that moves around for panning, relaxing or retracting the hand would release (222 occurrences in 8 subjects)

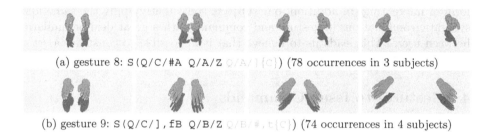

(a) gesture 8: S(Q/C/#A Q/A/Z Q/A/]{C}) (78 occurrences in 3 subjects)

(b) gesture 9: S(Q/C/], fB Q/B/Z Q/B/#, t{C}) (74 occurrences in 4 subjects)

Fig. 5. The two most occurring gestures for zooming (notation in gray is not depicted): (a) relaxed/cupped hands to pointing hands that move apart for zooming out and move together for zooming in, relaxing and retracting the hands would release and (b) relaxed/cupped hands to stretched hands that move apart for zooming out and move together for zooming in while relaxing and retracting the hands would release

We identified 14 pan and 13 zoom gestures which we reduced to 3 distinct pan and 6 distinct zoom gestures by generalizing. For panning, two gestures (IDs 2 and 3, see Figure 4) were observed to occur significantly ($p = .01$) more often and in most users. In gesture 2 the hand changes from relaxed to stretched at the beginning of the movement and back to relaxed at its end as if to press a button. In gesture 3 the hand closes with an extended index finger and back to a relaxed hand. Gestures 1 and 3 are similar but then the whole hand is closed.

For the zoom task, we observed a similar although less pronounced ($p = .07$) distinction; gestures 8 and 9 (see Figure 5) occur more for zooming than the other 4 observed gestures. These two gestures are, in fact, very similar still; differing in the hand shape only like in the pan task. Gesture 8 grabs and releases the canvas while gesture 9 will explicitly stretch the hand during the zoom movements. We identified 3 gestures made with one hand (by 5 subjects) and 3 others that were made with both hands (by 8 subjects). Subjects were consistent in their choice for using either one or two hands; some participants used both gestures.

3.3 Wrap-Up

The gestures that we observed differ mostly in the preparation (start) and retraction (end) phases of the gesture phrase [14]. We found that in the stroke phase the movements can more or less be directly used as parameter changes for panning and zooming; the hand shape during these movements does not matter much. Our subjects explicitly marked the start and end of their gesture by changing their hand shape from rest to a flat hand or pointing hand for panning and two flat or pointing hands for zooming. Subjects remarked in a post-test interview that their gesture choices were often based on their knowledge of 'mainstream' gesture interfaces such as the Apple iPhone or that they had mimicked movements that they remembered from science fiction movies such as "Minority Report"[3]. We are unsure how this has influenced our results here but it is clear that users readily accept such 'predefined' gesturing as a natural form of interacting. In addition, our subjects consistently apply the same idiosyncratic combinations of gesture and command with a great deal of similarity between users. This leads us to believe that it is possible to construct a set of gesture-commands for large display control that comes natural to the users.

4 Gestures to Issue Commands

Gesture interfaces will make use of a broader command set than just the two that we explored in our Wizard of Oz investigation. Section 2 already introduced three elementary gestures (point, select, deselect). Here we add three more gestures (activate, deactivate, resize) that address our fourth state in this model. We performed an investigation to discover which gestures are suited for these tasks.

4.1 Methodology

Three experts cannot think up a gesture set that twenty laymen can [15]. In order to fully appreciate or dislike a gesture for issuing a command we argue that the user needs to have experienced it in a working system. Getting subjective results then becomes cost-ineffective as opposed to gathering such information from a large user group online. We must rely on the extent to which these users can imagine operating the large display in the manner that we show them; placing an unknown bias on the results. This bias is expected to be minimal but that will need to be proven by comparing the results to those from a working interface.

In an online investigation[4] we asked our participants to rate gestures for each of our 6 commands. Gestures were selected from literature but also from science fiction movies and commercial gesture interfaces such as the Apple iPhone. In total, we selected 24 gestures for the 6 commands mentioned above. The commands were ordered in a predefined sequence because users would need to make up their mind first, for example, about how they would point before they could select. The gestures, then, were completely randomized per command.

---

[3] http://www.imdb.com/title/tt0181689, last checked Sep. 2009.
[4] http://fikkert.net/experiment.php, last checked Sep. 2009.

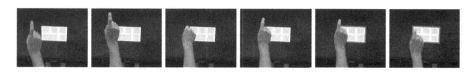

Fig. 6. *AirTap* [6]

Fig. 7. *ReferencedPullPush* from the movie Minority Report

Some examples of the gestures that we selected follow. For pointing (3 gestures) we included *RayCasting* [16] in addition to two more indirect approaches. For select (5 gestures) *AirTap* [6] and *ThumbTrigger* [17] were selected. Deselect had 4 gestures including *SelectOther* where another object is selected to deselect the current one (from MS Windows). Activate and deactivate were taken together (8 gestures) so that gestures that activate mirror those that deactivate, following [6]. We included *AirTap* and *ThumbTrigger* again but also added drawing a triangular 'play' shape that is well-known from audiovisual equipment in the household. For resize (4 gestures) we introduced moving two fingers apart as with the Apple iPhone. Also, *ReferencedPullPush*, from the movie Minority Report, showed the dominant hand serving as a reference for resizing with the distance to the other hand defining the amount, see Figure 7.

Gestures were presented in a video clip showing both hand movements and the response of the interface. The interface was an abstracted system that responded solely through visual feedback. Before the participant filled out the questionnaire we explained this interface and how it would respond. The video clips, see Figures 6 and 7, were shot in a mocked-up setting. Participants were asked how they score gestures (on 7-point Likert-style scales) intuitiveness ('1: very difficult' – '7: very intuitive'), physical effort ('1: little effort' – '7: much effort') required and if they would gesture in this way ('1: no way' – '7: for certain').

4.2   Results

99 subjects from four Western-European countries (The Netherlands, Belgium, Germany and The United Kingdom) participated in this investigation. Participants were on average 28 years old (ranging 20-60 years, $\sigma = 8$ years). Our subjects needed roughly 25 minutes to complete the entire trial. In our subject population, 22 subjects were female and 77 were male with 25 subjects who held a Bachelor degree, 53 a Masters, 12 a PhD and 9 had no degree. Our subjects were very familiar with (online) video clips in which gesture interfaces play a role ($\mu = 5.0$, $\sigma = 1.7$, with '1: unfamiliar (never seen one)' – '7: very familiar (regularly)'). They were proficient with the Apple iPhone ($\mu = 4.5$, $\sigma = 1.9$) but

Table 1. Description of our trials data ($N = 2376$)

	intuitiveness	physical effort	would use
mean	4.44	3.60	3.89
std. deviation	1.701	1.626	1.811
variance	2.892	2.643	3.280
kurtosis	-0.979	-0.769	-1.135
skewness	-0.238	0.340	0.039

only moderately so with PDAs, smart phones and similar hand-helds ($\mu = 3.7$, $\sigma = 1.6$).

The results of our analyses for normality on the collected trials indicate that we cannot assume a normal distribution of our data. A D'Agostino-Pearson K^2 analysis gave $K^2 = 80.504$ ($p < .01$) on intuitiveness, $K^2 = 85.119$ ($p < .01$) on physical effort and $K^2 = 68.474$ ($p < .01$) on whether the participant would use that gesture. This is, as is often the case in count-based data, caused by a ceiling or floor effect. We applied the non-parametric alternative to ANOVA, Kruskal-Wallis H, to assess if there is a significant difference between gestures while pairs were compared with a Mann-Whitney U analysis. Our trials data are further described in Table 1 where skewness and kurtosis are reported; the trials data are mostly deformed due to kurtosis.

Point. We found significant differences between gestures for intuitiveness ($\chi^2 = 106.098$, $p < .01$), physical effort ($\chi^2 = 61.827$, $p < .01$) and whether the participant would use this gesture ($\chi^2 = 138.275$, $p < .01$). Our Mann-Whitney U analysis results show that there are significant differences between the three gestures. *RayCasting* scored significantly higher on intuitiveness and on 'would use' than both other gestures. The difference was less pronounced regarding physical effort. Fourteen subjects commented that this is highly intuitive but that it would be fatiguing in the long run. Five subjects wondered how to stop pointing and proposed to stop when pointing off-screen.

Select. There was a significant difference between gestures for intuitiveness ($\chi^2 = 98.816$, $p < .01$), physical effort ($\chi^2 = 58.266$, $p < .01$) and whether the participant would use this gesture ($\chi^2 = 80.725$, $p < .01$). Mann-Whitney U analyes show that *AirTap* significantly scores best on intuitiveness, physical effort and 'would use'. In addition, *FistGrab* (closing the hand to a fist) and *ThumbTrigger* score significantly lower than *Encircling* (drawing a circle around the target with the on-screen pointer) for physical effort. Six subjects commented that they did not like the mouse-metaphor of *AirTap* while three subjects disliked the gun-metaphor of *ThumbTrigger*.

Deselect. We found a significant difference between gestures for intuitiveness ($\chi^2 = 47.743$, $p < .01$), physical effort ($\chi^2 = 22.817$, $p < .01$) and whether the participant would use this gesture ($\chi^2 = 51.914$, $p < .01$). Mann-Whitney U analyes show that *DropIt* (opening the hand palm-down as if dropping something on the floor) and *SelectOther* scored significantly better on intuitiveness (higher), physical effort (lower) and 'would use' (higher) than both *RetractToRest* and *JerkyRetract* where the hand retracted to rest or in a jerky way, respectively. There was no significant score difference between *DropIt* and *SelectOther* on these three topics. Twelve subjects indicated that they found selecting another target very familiar from Windows^{TM}. One of these subjects commented that although it is familiar, he would prefer 'some' other gesture.

Activate and Deactivate. There was a significant difference between gestures for intuitiveness ($\chi^2 = 140.976$, $p < .01$), physical effort ($\chi^2 = 121.518$, $p < .01$) and whether the participant would use this gesture ($\chi^2 = 154.250$, $p < .01$). Mann-Whitney U analyes show that *AirTap* combined with an exit cross scored significantly better on intuitiveness, physical effort and 'would use' than all other proposed gestures. Overall, we can distinguish three groups of gestures: the best gestures are *AirTap* and *AirTap* combined with the exit cross, the worst gestures are drawing 'play' and 'stop' shapes and using (de)activation zones [6]. The other gestures score in between with no significant differences. Eight subjects commented that it was confusing to use the *AirTap* to both activate and select.

Resize. We found a significant difference between gestures for intuitiveness ($\chi^2 = 74.200$, $p < .01$), physical effort ($\chi^2 = 64.381$, $p < .01$) and whether the participant would use this gesture ($\chi^2 = 64.117$, $p < .01$). Mann-Whitney U analyis results show no significant score difference between *FingersApart* and *HandsApart* on intuitiveness and 'would use'. In these two gestures either the fingers of one hand or the two hands are moved apart. However, with respect to physical effort, *HandsApart* scored significantly poorer (35%). *ReferencedPull-Push* scored significantly poorer on intuitiveness, physical effort and 'would use' with respect to the other three gestures. Subjects often commented (19 subjects) that *FingersApart* would be too hard to do on large displays were the larger scale is an issue. Likewise, 9 subjects commented that both *FingersApart* and *Hands-Apart* needed some way to start resizing: "needs clicking". Only three subjects mentioned the Apple iPhone as the source of these resizing gestures.

4.3   Wrap-Up

We gathered subjective ratings on 24 gestures for 6 interface commands from a large population with a similar background in our online investigation. We found significant preferences for a specific gesture to issue a command. Based on these findings we can construct a gesture set to issue commands with gestures that come naturally. Users expect a gesture-based interface to allow them to point directly at a target using pixel-precise ray-casting. For selecting, *AirTap* mimics clicking a mouse button very precisely even though no actual button can be pressed [6]. The gesture preferred for deselecting also leans heavily on existing interfaces where another target is selected to deselect the current target. The gesture used for selecting was preferred to be used for activating and deactivating targets as well. Although some subjects indicated that they found it confusing to have the same gesture for two tasks (*AirTap* for select and activate), we believe that this simplifies the interface which is indicated by the strong preference for this gesture. This also follows from the comments made by our subjects that they missed some way to 'click' for the resize command. For resizing, our subjects found that moving their fingers or hands apart was the most intuitive while some subjects wondered if moving two fingers apart would scale sufficiently to large displays. Common remarks throughout our study were how to start and stop gesturing, for example, for pointing. Like we found in our Wizard of Oz investigation, it seems that a way should be found to explicitly mark where a gesture begins and ends: when do we move to and from the null-state (out-of-range)? This is perhaps more delicate than simply pointing off-screen.

5 Discussion and Future Work

Interacting with physically large, digital surfaces through explicit command-giving can be done through the hands gesturing. A gesture is, in some cases, more suited or desired than other modalities such as touch or speech. In a Wizard of Oz investigation we found that uninstructed users independently generate the same gestures for a limited command set. The stroke phase in a gesture directly changes a parameter (zoom or pan) and the gesture was explicitly started and ended by alternating between a tensed and a relaxed hand respectively. Our follow-up study showed that such agreement is also found in a large user group for a broader and more complete command set. Moreover, similar commands, for example, select and activate, should be issued by the same gesture to simplify the interface as much as possible. Our results so far indicate that the participants in both our investigations were influenced by existing interfaces such as MS Windows and the Apple iPhone. Although biased to some extent, we feel that this made these users more open-minded to new forms of interaction that we aim to build. However, it will also have hindered them to look past existing solutions and to imagine what it really would be like to control an interface such as the one we have suggested. That is why we did not expect the *AirTap* [6] gesture to be the best candidate for the select and activate commands; users will become fatigued easily, feeling like having 'gorilla arms' when they have to extend their arms while interacting. Moreover, *AirTap* builds on the familiar mouse with tangible feedback that is not there any more, something none of our subjects mentioned. The gesture set we discovered so far will adequately control large displays but it needs to be consolidated in a working environment where users can truly experience the interaction.

We propose to continue this line of research with a third investigation in which our previous results are validated. A working prototype allows users to experience the gestures for our command set and thus provide us with a more in-depth opinion. The interactions should last long enough for the user to appreciate the gesture and to comment on it. We aim to select a focus group of participants from our online investigation so that these users are already familiar with both the gestures and how to issue commands. Using a pair of data gloves and a position tracking system we can detect both hand locations and hand shapes. The whole gesture set from our online investigation will be included to adequately validate our earlier findings. The interface needs be more elaborate than the map or abstracted applications that we used previously so that users will repeatedly issue commands through gesturing. We propose a list of search-tasks through a collection of photos where information from multiple photos needs to be cross-referenced. For example, we envision a virtual tourist application where a visitor of our university will have to look for and select landmarks on the university and to couple them to the university map.

It is surprising in some way to discover that the familiarity of the mouse has such a strong impact on our findings. We readily accept that these results would be very different when consulting a user group that does not have this type of experience, from a different culture or even from another social group. However, the standard Windows-Icon-Mouse-Pointer paradigm has, over the past decades, indoctrinated most users of the systems that we aim to control. In that respect, we might even argue that the author of this work was born after the invention of the mouse and that he, like many other users of large display systems, grew up with this input device. We feel that the mouse has become such a strong metaphor that, even though a natural interface might be defined otherwise [1], it has by now become an everyday metaphor that drives the formation of a gesture set for explicit command-giving through hand gestures.

Acknowledgements

This work is part of the BioRange program carried out by the Netherlands Bioinformatics Centre (NBIC), which is supported by a BSIK grant through the Netherlands Genomics Initiative (NGI).

References

1. Oviatt, S., Cohen, P.: Perceptual user interfaces: multimodal interfaces that process what comes naturally. Communications of the ACM 43(3), 45–53 (2000)
2. Fikkert, W., D'Ambros, M., Bierz, T., Jankun-Kelly, T.: Interacting with visualizations. In: Kerren, A., Ebert, A., Meyer, J. (eds.) GI-Dagstuhl Research Seminar 2007. LNCS, vol. 4417, pp. 77–162. Springer, Heidelberg (2007)
3. Wahlster, W.: SmartKom: Foundations of Multimodal Dialogue Systems. Cognitive Technologies, vol. XVIII. Springer, Heidelberg (2006)
4. Nijholt, A., Reidsma, D., Poppe, R.: Games and entertainment in ambient intelligence environments. In: Aghajan, H., Delgado, R., Augusto, J.C. (eds.) Human-Centric Interfaces for Ambient Intelligence. Elsevier, Amsterdam (2009)
5. Hummels, C., Smets, G., Overbeeke, K.: An intuitive two-handed gestural interface for computer supported product design. In: Wachsmuth, I., Fröhlich, M. (eds.) GW 1997. LNCS (LNAI), vol. 1371, p. 197. Springer, Heidelberg (1998)

6. Vogel, D., Balakrishnan, R.: Distant freehand pointing and clicking on very large, high resolution displays. In: Proceedings of the 18th annual ACM symposium on User interface software and technology (UIST 2005), pp. 33–42. ACM Press, New York (2005)

7. Wexelblat, A.: Research challenges in gesture: Open issues and unsolved problems. In: Wachsmuth, I., Fröhlich, M. (eds.) GW 1997. LNCS (LNAI), vol. 1371, pp. 1–11. Springer, Heidelberg (1998)

8. Buxton, W.: A three-state model of graphical input. In: Proceedings of the IFIP TC13 Third Interational Conference on Human-Computer Interaction (INTER-ACT 1990), pp. 449–456. North-Holland Publishing Co., Amsterdam (1990)

9. Bowman, D., Kruijff, E., LaViola, J., Poupyrev, I.: 3D User Interfaces: Theory and Practice. Addison Wesley Longman Publishing Co., Inc., Redwood City (2004)

10. Hinckley, K.: Input technologies and techniques. In: Sears, A., Jacko, J. (eds.) Handbook of Human-Computer Interaction: fundamentals, evolving technologies and emerging applications, pp. 151–168. Lawrence Erlbaum Associates Inc., Hillsdale (2006); Revision of 2002 chapter with lots of new material

11. Ahlstroem, D., Alexandrowicz, R., Hitz, M.: Improving menu interaction: a comparison of standard, force enhanced and jumping menus. In: Proceedings of the SIGCHI conference on Human Factors in computing systems (CHI 2006), pp. 1067–1076. ACM, New York (2006)

12. Guiard, Y.: Asymmetric division of labor in human skilled bimanual action: The kinematic chain as a model. Journal of Motor Behavior 19(4), 486–517 (1987); Slightly edited version of an article originally published

13. Kipp, M.: Gesture Generation by Imitation - From Human Behavior to Computer Character Animation. PhD thesis, Saarland University, Saarbruecken, Germany, Boca Raton, Florida (December 2004)

14. McNeill, D.: Hand and mind: What gestures reveal about thought. University of Chicago Press, Chicago (1992)

15. Wobbrock, J., Morris, M., Wilson, A.: User-defined gestures for surface computing. In: Proceedings of the 27th international conference on Human factors in computing systems (CHI 2009), pp. 1083–1092. ACM, New York (2009)

16. Bolt, R.: "put-that-there": Voice and gesture at the graphics interface. SIGGRAPH Computer Graphics 14(3), 262–270 (1980)

17. Grossman, T., Wigdor, D., Balakrishnan, R.: Multi-finger gestural interaction with 3d volumetric displays. In: Proceedings of the 17th annual ACM symposium on User interface software and technology (UIST 2004), pp. 61–70. ACM Press, New York (2004)

Gestural Attributions as Semantics in User Interface Sound Design

Kai Tuuri

Department of Computer Science and Information Systems,
FI-40014 University of Jyväskylä, Finland
krtuuri@jyu.fi

Abstract. This paper proposes a gesture-based approach to user interface sound design, which utilises projections of body movements in sounds as meaningful attributions. The approach is founded on embodied conceptualisation of human cognition and it is justified through a literature review on the subject of interpersonal action understanding. According to the resulting hypothesis, stereotypical gestural cues, which correlate with, e.g., a certain communicative intention, represent specific non-linguistic meanings. Based on this theoretical framework, a model of a process is also outlined where stereotypical gestural cues are implemented in sound design.

Keywords: gestures, user interfaces, sound design, semantics.

1 Introduction

Sound-based communication within different kinds of media has a long tradition. Sound design practices for radio-plays from as early as the 1920s have defined the basis for the communicative use of sound effects which is still relevant in today's film and video game sound design [1]. An essential part of the craftsmanship of film sound designers has concerned the creation of sound effects that reflect mental states of the story's characters. The appropriate door knock for film narration, for example, can be *urging*, *gentle* or *angry*, depending on the purpose of that door knock and the feelings and intentions of the person who is knocking. Such focus on *agency* behind sounds is frequently utilised in film sound design. It exploits the perceptual bias towards understanding the human involvement (i.e., *intentionality*) in the sound-causing action [2]. But when it comes to the sound design for human-computer interaction (HCI), such interpersonal focus on interpretation is rarely utilised in a systematic manner. This paper focuses on this agency-orientated perspective.

Due to its history, the HCI field has its roots in information theory [3] and "system-centred" design [4]. Compared to filmmaking tradition, functions of user interface (UI) sounds are more easily conceived in terms of information processing and transmission between machine and user than in terms of interpersonal communication. Such a perspective is well exemplified in the design/research

S. Kopp and I. Wachsmuth (Eds.): GW 2009, LNAI 5934, pp. 257–268, 2010.

paradigm of "earcons" [6], which usually refer to abstract user interface sounds with highly arbitrary meanings. It has adopted a linguistically orientated view of semantics which usually sees the semantic content as symbolic units of information essentially separable from its form of expression. The risk of such an approach is that design can become detached from meaningful experiences that get coupled with sounds in the interaction. It should be obvious that the role of sound cannot be as a mere carrier of symbolic information. Indeed, reflecting the ongoing shift towards user-centred design [5], contemporary trends in HCI sound research have preferred to talk about *sonic interaction design* thus emphasising the coupling of sound and its meanings with interaction [7].

The word *gesture* is used here to represent any bodily act that – observable in interaction – operates as a vehicle for interpersonal communication. Such a perspective is not restricted to hand movements, but takes all non-verbal forms of body-related communication into account. In social interaction, we express our mental states with bodily actions which can be either directly perceivable (like in hand/facial gestures or in vocal prosody), and/or indirectly perceivable as reflections of body movements (e.g., in sounds of objects which are acted on). Communication with gestures is primordial [8] and often unconscious for us. The basis for gestural communication – the physical constitution of the human body and our ways to schematise it – is universal. Gestural communication has also been suggested to have a strong phylogenetic background which precedes verbal communication [8]. As Marc Leman has put it: "Gestures form the basis of mutual adaptive behavioral resonances that create shared attention and are responsible for the feeling of being unified with other people" [2].

By suggesting the utilisation of gestural attributions (projections of motor-activity/body movement) as semantics in UI sound design, this paper emphasises bodily mediated action understanding and the role of action-relevant gestural cues in sound as constituents of meaning-creation based on a kinaesthesic foundation. In the scope of interaction design, such tacit "sensibility for movement" also accounts for a "sensibility for responses to movement" [9]. We thus stress the close engagement of interaction and meaning-creation already acknowledged within, for example, the ecological view [10] of perception. Gestural attributions, unlike linguistic ones, are not detached from the direct sensory-motor basis of social interaction. According to the embodied approach to human cognition [11], the human mind is coupled with our environment. That coupling with the environment has emerged in the course of the experiential history of using our bodies for interacting with it. Understanding is thus inseparable from the embodied experiences of the physical world including – most relevantly to this study – interactions with other people.

The aims of this paper are to promote an idea that gestural projections of body movement attributed to sounds could be used as semantics for UI sound design, and to formulate this idea into a justifiable and testable hypothesis. In addition, the aim is to outline a model of the process in which gestural cues are implemented in sound design.

2   Embodied Basis of Understanding Gestures

In the phylogenesis of social mammals, such as humans and non-human primates, it has proved to be beneficial – maybe even essential for survival – to understand the actions of others [12]. Surely, without such an ability, the social and cultural development of humans would have been impossible. In this section we discuss the embodied basis of this attunement to interpersonal relations, which involves shared body-related constituents. First, the neurological foundation of *interpersonal action understanding* is reviewed, which is then applied to the concept of body-schema and empathetic involvement in perception. Lastly, interpersonal action understanding is viewed in terms of the Brunswikian lens model.

2.1   The Human Mirror-Neuron Mechanism

Mirror neurons are a particular class of premotor neurons that discharge both when one performs a specific goal-reaching action and when one observes other individuals executing similar actions [12]. They were originally discovered in the monkey premotor cortex, but there is also evidence for the existence of a similar mirror system in humans [12].

Nowadays there exist two parallel and equally plausible hypotheses about the functional role of mirror neurons. Firstly, they mediate bodily imitation and secondly, they are related to action understanding [12]. The motor representation encoded in mirror neurons thus reflects the understanding of observed action – not object presentation. Via motor representation, mirror neurons transform sensory information into knowledge that agrees with the motor repertoire/skills of the observer [12]. In other words, the observer understands the performed action as she could perform it herself. Action understanding thus involves embodied "resonances" (or embodied simulation [13]) of the observed action.

Experiments have shown that even fragmentary clues about action presented to the observer can trigger the specific response (motor representation) in mirror neurons [12]. Therefore, the audio-visual features of the observed actions seem to be fundamental only to the point where they allow action understanding. For example, the mere sound of action seems to result in a response that matches the responses for the same action observed or executed [14]. The encoding of action in the mirror system thus seems to be highly multimodal in nature. These above aspects underline the possible role of mirror neurons in contributing schematic gestalt processes, which transforms sensory information (like hearing somebody laughing) into preconceptual structures meaningful to the observer (understanding laughing by means of mirrored motor representation of it). It is also suggested that such action understanding operates as an enabling mechanism for empathy [13].

2.2   Interpersonal Body-Schematic Transfer

The concept of *body-schema* refers to a tacit understanding of one's own body in-the-world. As suggested in *Phenomenology of Perception* by Merleau-Ponty [15], humans possess such specific schemata of our body in relation to embodied space, i.e., space in the environmental setting of our habitual actions. It is reasonable to assume that such body-schemata (or kinaesthetic image schemata [16]) are based on recurrent sensory-motor experiences of bodily interactions with the world.

According to Merleau-Ponty [15], body-schema has a crucial function in the perception of other individuals as human-beings. That function is related to *body-schematic transfer* where the movements of other individuals are perceived as the movements that the observer could imagine executing by her own action repertoire. Therefore the perception of body movements is based on the perceiver's embodied knowledge of body-schema. This theoretical idea is very much in line with the already discussed function of mirror neurons in action understanding. It is thus plausible that the mirror system is a part of the realisation of body-schematic transfer [17].

Jan Almäng [17] has proposed that, at its basic level, body-schematic transfer has at least four characteristic features, which are:

1. The perceiver observes the other as having a body-schema.
2. The perceiver can perceive the action by means of body-schema even when she is unable, e.g. due to its complexity, to perform it herself. Thus, it is sufficient that her body-schema can "read" the movement.
3. Physical similarity between the perceived and perceiver is not required for an apprehension of the movements by body-schematic transfer. Thus, it is sufficient if there appear to be kinematic similarities between observed movement and body-schematic knowledge of how to produce such movement.[1]
4. Body-schematic transfer of movements by itself does not imply that the intentionality of the other person is communicated to the perceiver. This is because understanding the mental states of someone, on the basis of physical movement, requires contextual awareness.

Because human actions arise from intentions, emotions and other affective determinants which are linked to the context, we must situate movements in the interaction where it takes place. This broader aspect of body-schematic transfer is discussed in the following section.

2.3   Empathetic Involvement in Perception

We normally perceive other people as engaged in situations that provide meaningful references to their actions. Hence, the crucial element in the Merleau-Pontyian view of understanding others (by means of body-schematic transfer) lies in the ability to automatically re-center our perception of the situation to the perspective of the other. Therefore, together with tacit perception of a person's body movements, the observer re-centers her own primordial perception of the surrounding environment – including its action affordances – to become

---

[1] This feature is evident in watching animated cartoons, where even objects can indicate such anthropomorphism in movements that they can be perceived by means of body-schematic transfer.

a perception *for* that other person [17,13]. In this way we can understand motivations and other reflections of intentionality in actions, and we are also able to anticipate possible actions of another person – as if they were actions of our own. Such an attunement to another individual, not only to body movements but also to her intentionality and action affordances, seems to be such a natural part of our interpersonal awareness that it requires no conscious reasoning.

To sum up the discussion on the embodied understanding of movements, we can assume that it is based on two parallel aspects in perception. The first aspect is related to the mimetic involvement in the mirror neuron system, by which perceived movement is understood in terms of body-schema and kinaesthesia. Such corporeal resonances can range from simple synchronisations to more specific motor mimetic attuning. The second aspect is related to empathetic involvement, in which the body-schematic "resonances" (of the first aspect) are associated with the perspective of the other individual engaged in interaction. At the lower level, this refers to mere action-based involvement with the other's movements and thus primordial apprehension of *corporeal intentionality* (i.e., motor intentionality) [2], whereas "genuine" empathy usually refers to more participative, emotional and inferential involvement with the perspective of the other. A similar distinction, between the degrees of motor-system involvement and the degrees of empathetic involvement, has also been suggested in the theory of bodily mediated experiences in music [2].

2.4   Encoding and Decoding of Gestural Cues

We finally take a look at the Brunswikian lens model scheme initially proposed as a framework for understanding how prosodic cues are encoded in a vocal expression of emotion [18]. Based on the original lens model [19], it describes the processes of various *distal cues* being situationally determined in articulation, indicating affective states of a person, and how these acoustically transmitted patterns (as *proximal cues*) play a role in the attribution of an affective state in perception. The lens model simultaneously considers *encoding* (i.e., contextual determination of cues) and *decoding* (i.e., contextual interpretation of cues). It therefore gives a neat overview of communication, where body is acknowledged as a mediator. The model, adapted for gestural communication, is illustrated in Figure 1.

In the encoding of cues, Scherer has emphasised the central role of *push* and *pull effects* [18]. Therefore intentional and affective states of a subject are situationally characterised in gestural articulation by interaction between 1) psychobiological processes, intrinsically related to mental states, that provide a natural influence on body movements (push effects) and 2) interactional processes, which involve voluntary control over body movements and are related to external conditions (pull effects). Conditions of interaction thus often requires a certain strategic display (or hiding) of intentions and other mental states.

The dominance of push effects is most evident in so-called *affect bursts*, which are mostly a result of physiological arousal. Push effects also have significant role in spontaneous expressions of, for example, pain or joy, but they also influence

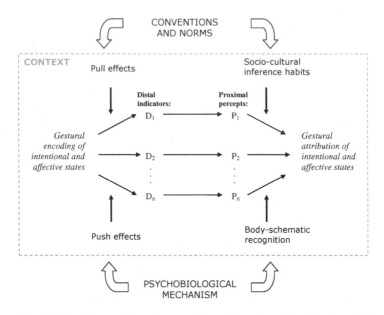

Fig. 1. The Brunswikian lens model with push and pull effects [18]

even the most premeditated acts of communication. [18] At the other end of the continuum, the dominance of pull effects is evident in expressions of an intended purpose. John R. Searle has suggested three *conditions of satisfaction* that fuel speech acts [20], but they should also apply to any acts which bear the motivation to be understood in interaction. As determinants of gestural articulation they are 1) *articulation intention*; an intention to appropriately produce a certain kind of gesture, 2) *meaning intention*; an intention to mean something with the gesture, and 3) *communicative intention*; an intention to be understood in a certain way – referring to the type of communicative intent such as *asking*. Communicative intention essentially imposes its condition of satisfaction on the conditions of satisfaction of both meaning something and producing a gesture accordingly.

According to the lens model, distal cues cannot be directly perceived. But on the basis of body-schematic transfer, the proximal cues can be perceived in terms of distal gestural movements. Proximal cues are probabilistic, partly redundant and contribute to action understanding in an additive fashion [21]. Gestural action understanding, in turn, provides cues for attributing intentionality [2]. Gestural attributions are thus contextually constructed in interaction between primordial, ecologically developed gestalts and inference based on social habits or cultural norms. These two processes can be seen as perceptual counterparts to push and pull effects, in which proximal percepts of gestural cues resonate with both body-schematic and conventional backgrounds.

3   Gestural Attributions in Sound Design

This section concentrates the discussion around a gesture-based approach to UI sound design – the principle of using sounds as the means of projecting gesturally attributable cues of movement. The basic assumption in such an approach is that human capacity for interpersonal awareness allows body movements of another individual to be understood in terms of the body movements of the perceiver. This seems to apply also in situations where the presented movement is partial or, due to its kinematic similarities with body-schematic reference, merely implies bodily movement. As already discussed earlier in the paper, action understanding is not dependent on which sensory modality is utilised in providing clues of action. Therefore the premise is that sounds can be used for presentation of action-related features.

The lens model perspective (see 2.4) demonstrates how perceptual action understanding is an emerging resonance of the mixture of several parallel cues encoded by the same gesture. In the context of HCI sound design, the strength of the lens model is that it outlines successful communication by means of probabilistic, multiple and redundant cues that allow discarding non-relevant cues for the task. Due to technical or aesthetic reasons, the designer must often conform to a selected set of acoustic cues in attributing intended characteristics to UI-sounds. Limitations should not undermine the utilisation of gestures, as there should be plenty of suitable cue combinations which compensate for the discarded ones. Indeed, it has been found that even simple acoustic cues can communicate the emotions of a musical performer or a speaker (with a general lack of cue interactions) [21]. As interaction is multimodal, the action understanding is ultimately based on the contextual whole, in which the sound instance and its cues become perceptually fused with the other aspects of interaction [22].

3.1   Gestural Articulations Projected in Sounds

From the perspective of the observer/user, gestural projections of sound refer to kinaesthetic imagery of body movement, which arise during the listening experience. The contextual creation of such gestural imagery is based on body-schematic resonances of *motor-mimetic* involvement [23] in listening. It is easiest to assume that gestural imagery is perceived in sounds that are in some way caused by bodily excitation, hence implying sound-producing gestures. But regardless of the type of sound production, motor-mimetic involvement applies to the perception of music, or *any* sound, as long as it is able to imply physical movement [23,2]. Thus, gestural imagery can even be attributed to abstract and artificially produced sounds.

From the sound designer's perspective, communication with gestural projections means defining a contextually appropriate gesture for the communicative purpose, and then articulating and implementing it in design. Gestural articulation can be a vocal act, musical expression or any physical action that itself produces, or allows its features to be transformed into, acoustic resonances. As discussed in 2.4, the articulation is bound up with the situation. When a gesture is articulated spontaneously, while being immersed in interaction, articulation is not a subjective interpretation so much as an *experience as articulated*. A sound, caused or modulated by gestural articulation consequently conveys acoustic cues of corporeal intentionality involved *in* the physical articulation.

The basic principle of using gestures as part of sound production in HCI is not new, although the idea has usually been utilised in producing immediate environmental audio feedback on the basis of the user's gestures (e.g. [24]) – not in exploiting gestures as interpersonal communication. It can be argued that traditional film sound design practices have long acknowledged the importance of gestural articulation in creating sound effects. One prominent example of this is a tradition called *foley art* [1]. Despite all the sophisticated audio technology available today, foley art still favours manual ways of producing sounds (in real-time). As noted above, gestural communication also refers to acting on material objects. This is exactly the case with foley art, in which the aim is to express through the sounds of material objects and provide "added value" to the narrative whole. We see that direct bodily involvement during sound creation – often performed concurrently with the related visual narration – enables the intentionality of a performer to be communicated via gestural projection. As illustrated in the introductory section of this paper, even simple sounds like door knocks can have much variety both in their gesturally determined qualities and in how these qualities can affect the contextual interpretations (see also [25]).

3.2   Utilising Stereotypical Gestural Cues in Sound Design

When treating gestural attributions as semantics, the sound designer can approach them from at least two directions: She can use the gesture as a starting point (thus emphasising distal cues), also accounting for the situated articulation and motivation of the gesture. Or she can focus on gesture-specific acoustic characteristics (thus emphasising proximal cues), but only if she has sufficient knowledge about the acoustic correlates of gesture-related understanding. Thus we regard it as easier for the designer to start with communicationally appropriate gestural articulation as the means to acquire and study gestural cues, which in turn can be utilised in sound production. In this way, semantics is always considered as being closely linked to the context.

In order to use gestural semantics systematically, one needs a way to categorise different types of meanings, i.e., gestural patterns that become contextually meaningful. In order to take advantage of the non-linguistic characteristics of gestures, we are especially interested in discovering *stereotypical* gestural cues. They reflect embodied meanings of a specific type of *recurrently experienced* gesture and resonate with primordial gestalts for interpersonal understanding and communication. Stereotypical cues are thus a type of gesturally perceived cues that should communicate a specific meaning robustly, without being too strongly dependent on cultural constraints. They differ from "weak cues" (like indications of direction or force), which are extremely dependent on context. They also differ from "coded cues", which communicate robustly, but are only meaningful because of coding or convention.

But how can the sound designer find gestures that convey such stereotypical meanings? We suggest using the *communicative intention* of gesture as a category of semantics. The assumption is that context-situated articulation – with specific intention to communicate – results in stereotypical physical cues of that intention as an outcome of push and pull effects. There is evidence, for example, that prosodically realised acoustic patterns specific to communicative intention exist [26,27]. Arguably, in infant-directed speech, such intention-specific prosody (e.g., for alerting or prohibiting) functions as the first regular semantic correspondence to the infant, clearly preceding any linguistically related functions of prosody [26]. Communicative intention of gestural expression thus appears to serve a fundamental and important prelinguistic function.

Prosodic patterns represent a subset of gestural patterns as they are caused by "phonetic gestures"; motor movements of the phonatory apparatus, vocal tract and respiration. Indeed, there are two reasons why prosody of vocal acts promises to be a very important source for gestural cues being utilised in sound design. Firstly, the evolution of the vocal apparatus is related to human communication [26]. Secondly, in prosody, gestural cues are directly realised as acoustic cues which are familiar and ecologically valid to us. Of course, stereotypical cues – specific in communicating different emotions or interpersonal attitudes – exist in other kinds of gestural expressions as well [28]. But in order to be encoded acoustically, non-vocal gestures need to be sonified. In everyday interactions, such sonification is a natural outcome of material resonances of motor excitation when objects and materials are acted on. However, by using physical models (e.g. [24]), the sounds of various material interactions can also be synthesised on the basis of, e.g., kinematic parameters.

Figure 2 specifies the general phases of *modelling, performing, utilising* and *evaluating* in the process of implementing gestural cues in sound design. In the first phase, the need/purpose of an UI sound element is acknowledged on the basis of the designer's model of application-user interaction. Hence the communicative functions for UI sounds can be determined. The modelling of appropriate gestural action requires mental exploration of interaction (see the discussion about action models in [22]). If the designer puts herself into the dialogue between user and machine, she is able to conceive her role as a person who is communicating with the user. The designer can thus imagine participating in the interaction, which in reality occurs via the mediation of the machine in use. From that perspective, she can mentally explore the patterns of contextual application use and – whenever sonic feedback is required – discover gestural patterns that would feel contextually appropriate for the communicative need. The communicative intention of the modelled gesture thus conforms to the communicative function of the propositional UI sound.

In the performing phase, the specified gesture is articulated. In order to achieve the spontaneity in articulation, the gesture should be performed while being immersed in interaction. To enable such immersion, a suitable scenario can be used providing the situational flow of interaction. This can be done, for example, in terms of metaphorical person-to-person interaction (see example cases

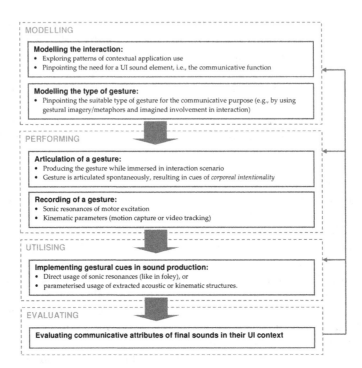

Fig. 2. The process of implementing gestural cues in sound design

in [22,27]). The articulation of a gesture needs to be recorded, either as a sound recording (of sonic resonances of action) or as a recording of selected kinematic parameters (by motion capture).

The utilisation of recorded gesture in sound production can be based on either "foleyish" direct usage of recorded sound, or – in a more analytical manner – parameterised usage of gestural cues. Parameters can be acquired, for example, by extracting selected acoustic features from sound recording (see example cases in [27,22]), or by utilising recorded kinematic parameters of gestural articulation. Parameterised gestural cues can be implemented in sounds, for example, as parameters for sound synthesis or sound manipulation. Alternatively they can be used indirectly as structural ideas in sound design and production. The last phase in the process is evaluation, where the communicative attributes of the final UI sounds are contextually tested. When required, the sound designer can iterate and re-evaluate the process starting from any of the previous phases.

4   Conclusions

We can now conclude this paper in the form of a hypothesis about using gestural projections of body movement as semantics in UI sound design. The resulting hypothesis includes the following assumptions:

- Sound design can be founded on theory which emphasises embodied cognition and interpersonal action understanding.
- By exploiting the primordial capacity for interpersonal action understanding in humans, sound design can utilise stereotypical, gesturally realised cues of social interaction, which represent non-linguistic categories of meaning.
- On the basis of the theoretical framework presented, sound design can be outlined as a process which is explicated into distinct design phases where action-relevant cues are determined in terms of interaction and gestural articulation.
- The approach presented results in ecologically valid semantics which should be communicated robustly and require less learning than semantic attributions of linguistically orientated design schemes. The ongoing research, based on the theoretical framework presented, has supported this assumption [29].

The gesture-based perspective on sound design provides an important focus on performative aspects of sound design (i.e., direct involvement with the sound creation), and bodily engagement with sonic communication (both in sound design and contextual perception). These aspects merit more explicit focus within sound design research, although they are most likely tacitly acknowledged by many professional sound designers. A linguistically orientated paradigm often considers semantics as "absolute". Such a perspective easily dismisses the communicational potential that even a simple feedback sound can have when it is designed as physical activity – and for physical activity.

Acknowledgments. This work is funded by Finnish Funding Agency for Technology and Innovation, and the following partners: GE Healthcare Finland Ltd., Suunto Ltd., Sandvik Mining and Construction Ltd. and Bronto Skylift Ltd.

References

1. Mott, R.L.: Sound effects: Radio, TV and Film. Focal Press, Boston (1990)
2. Leman, M.: Embodied Music Cognition and Mediation Technology. MIT Press, Cambridge (2008)
3. Shannon, C.E., Weaver, W.: The Mathematical Theory of Communication. The University of Illinois Press, Urbana (1949)
4. Czaja, S.J.: Systems design and evaluation. In: Salvendy, G. (ed.) Handbook of human factors and ergonomics, 2nd edn., pp. 17–40. Wiley, New York (1997)
5. Bannon, L.J.: A human-centred perspective on interaction design. In: Pirhonen, A., Isomäki, H., Roast, C., Saariluoma, P. (eds.) Future interaction design, pp. 31–51. Springer, Heidelberg (2005)
6. Brewster, S., Wright, P., Edwards, A.: A detailed investigation into the effectiveness of earcons. In: Kramer, G. (ed.) Auditory display, pp. 471–498. Addison-Wesley, Reading (1994)
7. Rocchesso, D., Serafin, S., Behrendt, F., Bernardini, N., Bresin, R., Eckel, G., Franinovic, K., Hermann, T., Pauletto, S., Susini, P., Visell, Y.: Sonic interaction design: sound, information and experience. In: CHI 2008 extended abstracts on Human factors in computing systems. ACM Press, New York (2008)

8. Rizzolatti, G., Arbib, M.A.: Language within our grasp. Trends in Neurosciences 21, 188–194 (1998)
9. Svanaes, D.: Kinaesthetic thinking. Computers in Human Behavior 13(4), 443–463 (1997)
10. Gibson, J.J.: The ecological approach to visual perception. Houghton Mifflin, Boston (1979)
11. Varela, F., Thompson, E., Rosch, E.: The Embodied Mind. MIT Press, Cambridge (1991)
12. Rizzolatti, G., Craighero, L.: The mirror-neuron system. Annual Review of Neuroscience 27, 169–192 (2004)
13. Gallese, V., Eagle, M.N., Migone, P.: Intentional Attunement: Mirror Neurons and the Neural Underpinnings of Interpersonal Relations. J. Am. Psychoanal. Assoc. 55(1), 131–175 (2007)
14. Kohler, E., Keysers, C., Umiltá, M.A., Fogassi, L., Gallese, V., Rizzolatti, G.: Hearing sounds, understanding actions: action representation in mirror neurons. Science 297, 846–848 (2002)
15. Merleau-Ponty, M.: Phenomenology of Perception. Routledge, London (1945/1996)
16. Johnson, M.: The Body in the Mind: The Bodily Basis of Meaning, Imagination, and Reason. University of Chicago, Chicago (1987)
17. Almäng, J.: Intentionality and intersubjectivity. Ph.D. thesis, Goteborg. Goteborg Universitet, Sweden (2007)
18. Scherer, K.R., Bänziger, T.: Emotional expression in prosody: a review and an agenda for future research. In: Proc. of SP 2004, Nara, Japan, pp. 359–366 (2004)
19. Brunswik, E.: Perception and the representative design of psychological experiments, 2nd edn. University of California Press, Berkeley (1956)
20. Searle, J.R.: Mind, language and society. Basic Books, New York (1998)
21. Juslin, P.N., Laukka, P.: Communication of emotions in vocal expression and music performance: Different channels, same code? Psych. Bull. 129(5), 770–814 (2003)
22. Tuuri, K., Pirhonen, A., Välkkynen, P.: Bodily Engagement in Multimodal Interaction: A Basis for a New Design Paradigm? In: Kurkovsky, S. (ed.) Multimodality in Mobile Computing and Mobile Devices. IGI Global, Hershey (2009)
23. Godøy, R.I.: Gestural-sonorous objects: embodied extensions of Schaeffer's conceptual apparatus. Organised Sound 11(02), 149–157 (2006)
24. Avanzini, F., Serafin, S., Rocchesso, D.: Friction sounds for sensory substitution. In: Proc. of ICAD 2004, Sydney, Australia (2004)
25. Vitale, R., Bresin, R.: Emotional Cues in Knocking Sounds. In: Proc. of ICMPC 10 (abstract only), Sapporo, Japan, p. 276 (2008)
26. Fernald, A.: Human maternal vocalizations to infants as biologically relevant signals: An evolutionary perspective. In: Barkow, J., Cosmides, L., Tooby, J. (eds.) The Adapted Mind: Evolutionary Psychology and the Generation of Culture, pp. 391–428. Oxford University Press, Oxford (1992)
27. Tuuri, K., Eerola, T.: Could function-specific prosodic cues be used as a basis for non-speech user interface sound design? In: Proc. of ICAD 2008, Paris, France (2008)
28. Feyereisen, P., de Lannoy, J.-D.: Gestures and speech: Psychological investigations. Cambridge University Press, New York (1991)
29. Tuuri, K., Pirhonen, A., Eerola, T.: Design and Evaluation of Prosody Based Non-Speech Audio Feedback for Physical Training Application (journal submission)

Gestural Interfaces for Elderly Users: Help or Hindrance?

Christian Stößel[1], Hartmut Wandke[2], and Lucienne Blessing[3]

[1] Zentrum für Mensch-Maschine-Systeme, Technische Universität Berlin
christian.stoessel@zmms.tu-berlin.de
[2] Institut für Psychologie, Humboldt-Universität zu Berlin
[3] Université de Luxembourg

Abstract. In this paper we investigate whether finger gesture input is a suitable input method, especially for older users (60+) with respect to age-related changes in sensory, cognitive and motor abilities. We present a study in which we compare a group of older users to a younger user group on a set of 42 different finger gestures on measures of speed and accuracy. The size and the complexity of the gestures varied systematically in order to find out how these factors interact with age on gesture performance. The results showed that older users are a little slower, but not necessarily less accurate than younger users, even on smaller screen sizes, and across different levels of gesture complexity. This indicates that gesture-based interaction could be a suitable input method for older adults. At least not a hindrance - maybe even a help.

Keywords: Gestural interfaces, aging psychology, human factors.

1 Introduction

Recent years have seen the dissemination of gestural interface technology in mass consumer products, pioneered most notably by products such as the Apple iPhone, or the Nintendo Wii video game console. Since then, manufactures of consumer electronics have included gesture control elements in a whole range of mobile electronic devices, such as laptops, cell phones, PDAs or digital cameras. While these interfaces are generally considered to provide a very direct, natural and intuitive way of interacting with a device, it remains unclear whether they also meet the needs and match the capabilities of a user group that is growing more and more important: the elderly. Demographic, structural and societal changes in most industrialized countries are leading to a dramatic increase of the percentage of elderly among the population. Even though there is not a unitary concept of *the elderly*, we refer to older adults in the following as individuals aged 60 years and above. The interaction with technology often confronts elderly people with particular problems, because devices are not designed to accommodate their special needs.

S. Kopp and I. Wachsmuth (Eds.): GW 2009, LNAI 5934, pp. 269–280, 2010.

1.1   Problems of an Aging User Related to Technology

The normal aging process is typically accompanied by sensory, perceptual and cognitive changes (see e.g. [1], for a detailed review), as well as a decline in motor skills [2]. These changes take place not only at high ages, but rather gradually across the whole life span [3], and they affect how elderly perceive and interact with the world, including technology.

All too often, unfortunately, elderly users are facing serious problems when trying to use technical devices. For instance, older users report problems related to displays that are too small and difficult to see, buttons and characters that are too small or crammed too closely together, oversupply of functions, non-intuitive menu arrangements or unclear instructions how to find certain functions and services [4]. Thus, while technology in principle could help to compensate parts of their changing physical, social and cognitive resources and enhance their quality of life, the elderly in many cases get frustrated by and disinterested in too complicated technology.

1.2   Can Gesture Technology Facilitate Technology Use?

What can be done to improve this situation and grant the older adults a better access to technology? In our view, there are different strategies that complement each other to accomplish this goal, e.g. *motivation* of the older users to bridge their initial disinclination towards technology, *training* older users with specific adaptive training concepts, or *build devices* tailored to the older user's abilities. While the best results in alleviating the use of technology for elderly users are surely achieved by a combination of these strategies, our research is centered on the problem of interface design for the older user. Finding solutions to this problem is a tightrope walk between two pitfalls: On one hand, if technology is designed only with respect to the older users' deficiencies, it runs the risk of stigmatizing them and thus being hardly accepted by the older users. On the other hand, following strictly a philosophy of "Universal Design", "Design-for-All" or "Inclusive Design" might not properly address the *specific* problems of the elderly, or lead to design compromises which are neither favored by the elderly nor by younger generations. Solutions to this predicament could emanate from new technologies, which, on one side, are sufficiently simple and intuitive to be used by the elderly, and on the other side sufficiently efficient and aesthetically pleasing to be used by a broader user community. Gesture based interaction, in our view, might be such a candidate. It remains unclear, however, how these technologies fit the needs and abilities of the elderly, and under which circumstances older adults might be able to effectively use them. Key questions that have to be addressed in this respect are:

1. **What are the requirements of gesture technologies regarding motor control and manual dexterity?** Do they match the sensory and motor control abilities of the older users? Under which boundary conditions could a match be achieved?

2. **To what extent, or under which circumstances, is gesture techno-logy intuitive for the older user?** Is there a set of gestures which are self-descriptive, easy to understand, easy to learn and easy to remember for the older users?
3. **Does gesture technology provide a benefit for the older users?** Does it compare to (or even out-perform) traditional input methods with respect to usability metrics, like efficiency, effectiveness and satisfaction?
4. **Is this technology accepted by older users?**

1.3   The Pros and Cons of Gesture Technology

Gestures, in everyday human to human interaction, are a natural and pow-erful tool of nonverbal communication and engulf everything from speech ac-companying gesticulations to highly structured sign languages. In the context of human-technology interaction, we define a gesture as *"a coordinated and intended movement of body parts to achieve communication. The information which it contains is specified by the configuration of body parts, the speed and direction of the movement and must be interpretable by its receiver"*. By this definition, we separate gesture input from simple key presses or mouse clicks where the button press itself carries no information. Gestural interfaces are implemented on a huge range of technical systems and classified roughly into *2D gestures*, operating through finger or hand movements on touchscreens or interactive sur-faces, and *3D gestures*, operating through free-form movements in space [5]. We focus our research on mobile devices, as there exist already many devices on the market that make use of 2D finger gesture input, and present the most accessibly gesture technology for elderly at the moment.

Studies comparing direct input devices (without translation or gain, e.g. touchscreen) with indirect input devices (e.g. mouse or trackball), with respect to older users have shown a general benefit of direct input devices over indirect ones (e.g.[6,7]). The direct nature of gesture input thus might facilitate inter-action for older users. However, the literature on motor control of the aging adult has documented a couple of observations which might put the suitability of finger gesture input for elderly into question: Chaparro et al. [8] found that in comparison to younger subjects (25-35), older adults (60-69) have a reduced wrist flexion and extension by 12% and 14%, respectively. As gesture input de-mands even more wrist flexibility than mouse input or simple button presses, these results might become important when deciding whether and how gestural technology can be a suitable input mechanism for the elderly. Other studies re-port that older adults have less efficient perceptual feedback systems and lack the force to produce very rapid movements [9], they make more submovements than younger ones [10], and have difficulties with continuous movements or the coordination of movements [2]. As gesture input usually demands relative precise execution of a continuous movement pattern, these findings are important when designing gesture interfaces for older users: they must be tolerant against im-precise execution of gestures, they have to provide some obvious and immediate feedback and avoid relying on fast and jerky movements.

1.4   Aim of the Study

The aim of this study is to provide a user-centered approach towards gesture technology, and targets especially the older users' abilities. This study focuses particularly on how older users meet the motor demands of finger gesture input. In order to establish boundary conditions under which this technology works for elderly, we devised an experiment to investigate how the available screen space as well as the complexity of the gesture pattern influences performance on a stationary touchscreen device. A younger and an older user group were compared with respect to velocity and accuracy measures in an imitation task of previously presented gesture patterns.

2   Methods

2.1   The Gesture Set

For the first experiment, we devised a set of 42 simple one-finger gestures. The gesture set was developed along the following goals: Overall simplicity of the gesture shapes, coverage of simple symbolic and geometric patterns which are already in use in finger gesture applications, and systematization regarding the complexity of the shape. The gesture set was inspired (among others) by Microsoft Application Gestures [11] and Apple's Trackpad Gestures [12]. The complexity of the gestures varies systematically according to the number of line segments it contains: single-line, double-line or multi-line gestures (Figure 1).

2.2   Participants and Apparatus

In total 38 participants volunteered in this experiment. The younger participants (9m, 9f), were 21-33 years old (mean 26 years; SD: 3.4 years), while the older ones (9m, 9f) were aged between 60-71 years (mean 63 years; SD: 3.2 years). All participants were right-handed, had normal or corrected-to-normal vision and no pathological condition that diminished arm, hand or finger movements on self-report. The participants were seated in front of a 15" touch screen (Eizo

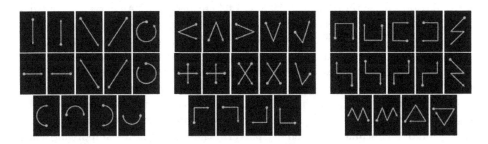

Fig. 1. Set of finger gestures used in the experiment: single-line gestures (left), double-lines gestures (middle) and multi-line gestures (right)

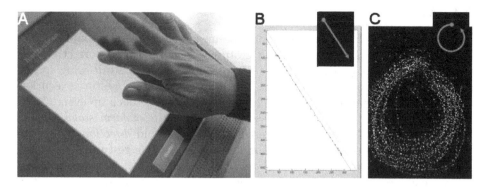

Fig. 2. A) Experimental Setup. B) Example single line gesture path, with original data (red dots), linear fit (dark blue line), and reference line (light green line). C) Example circular gesture patterns: all older users collapsed.

L353T-C) which was mounted on a supporting rack at an oblique angle (30°) and placed on a desk. (Figure 2A). The finger movements on the screen were sampled with a frequency of 50 Hz.

2.3 Procedure and Design

The task was to retrace visually presented gestures on the touch surface. The gestures were depicted as arrows (cf. Figure 1) and presented centrally on the screen at different sizes. Each gesture instruction was displayed for 1.5 seconds, and afterwards an equally sized rectangular white square appeared on the screen on which the gesture had to be retraced. The participants received no visual feedback of their drawn trajectory in order to measure original patterns without corrective movements. They were instructed to copy the presented gesture within the boundaries of the drawing area as fast and accurate as possible. The task was structured into nine blocks of 42 gestures with short breaks in between. The experiment was conducted as a 2 (AGE) x 3 (SIZE) x 3 (COMPLEXITY) factorial design. AGE varied as a between-subjects variable (younger vs. older), while SIZE (small, medium, large) and COMPLEXITY (single line, double line, multiple line) varied as within-subject variables. The three different sizes were chosen so that the medium size equals the display size of an Apple iPhone, the small size corresponded to 1/4 of this size, and the large one to four times that size. That way, the smallest size was conceived as a lower bound for possible gesture input, the medium size as a reference size for gesture input on modern mobile devices, and the largest size as an example of stationary touch screen applications. The number of lines making up the gesture was chosen as a simple means to differentiate gesture complexity. Each of the 42 different gestures was repeated 3 times per size, resulting in a total of 378 trials, organized in 9 blocks. Within each block the size was held constant while the sequence of gestures was randomized. The sequence of blocks was permuted across participants.

2.4   Analysis

The performance of gesture execution was measured through a couple of different parameters: *Errors* (when the gesture was not retraced correctly) and *boundary violations* (when the finger surpassed the designated drawing space) provided measures of task fulfillment. The *average velocity* of gesture execution was calculated between the first touch down and the last touch up event. Measures of gesture accuracy can be divided in parameters of *form stability* (e.g. how accurate was the form of the gesture preserved), and *directional stability*. These were measured differentially for linear and circular gestures. For linear gestures, the measure of *form stability* was *angular deviation* from one or more reference angles. For circular gestures, form stability was measured through the *eccentricity* value of the best ellipse fit to the data (a value of 0 denotes a perfect circle, and increasing values denote increasing asymmetry of the ellipse). *Directional stability* was measured as the average deviation from the best fitted reference line. This was an orthogonal least squares linear fit (for each line segment) for all non-circular gestures, and a geometrically fitted ellipse otherwise. The derived measures were *linear deviation* and *ellipse deviation*. All measures of velocity, form- and directional stability were analyzed only on non-erroneous gestures. For each dependent variable, a separate repeated measures analysis of variance (ANOVA) was calculated, with the between-subjects factor AGE, and the within-subjects factors SIZE and COMPLEXITY. For some analyses, the assumption of sphericity was not met, and the degrees of freedom were adjusted using the Greenhouse-Geisser estimate of sphericity.

3   Results

A summary of descriptive results can be found in tables 1 and 2. The separate parameters will be discussed more closely in the following.

Errors and Boundary Violations. For both parameters, there were no significant effects for age or complexity. The elderly performed 1.9 % more errors than the younger group, but due to huge individual differences within each group, no group effects could be observed. There was, however, a stable influence of size (=the available space to draw the gesture) on the amount of errors $[F(1.4, 48.5) = 12.94, p < .01]$ and boundary violations $[F(1.26, 43.05) = 12.96, p < .01]$: the larger the available space, the less frequent were errors observed, and, naturally, the less frequent the boundaries of the gesture space were crossed with the finger.

Average Velocity. The velocity of gesture execution was clearly influenced by age: across all complexity levels and gesture sizes, the elderly performed consistently slower than the younger users $[F(1, 34) = 6.670, p = .014]$. In addition, there was a significant effect of size on gesture execution speed: the larger the

Table 1. Comparison of the dependent variables according to *AGE*. Asterisks mark significant main effects (** $p < .01$, * $p < .05$).

parameter		younger users		older users		
		M	SD	M	SD	
errors	(%)	2,65	3,08	4,54	5,87	
boundary violations	(%)	4,50	6,00	5,00	5,79	
average velocity	(cm/s)	1,39	0,44	1,07	0,37	*
angular deviation	(deg)	5,39	0,66	5,46	1,21	
eccentricity		0,60	0,04	0,62	0,07	
line deviation	(mm)	0,69	0,15	0,68	0,14	
ellipse deviation	(mm)	0,50	0,14	0,53	0,23	

Table 2. Comparison of the dependent variables according to different levels of *SIZE* and *COMPLEXITY*. Asterisks mark significant main effects (** $p < .01$, * $p < .05$).

size:		small		medium		large		
		M	SD	M	SD	M	SD	
errors	(%)	6,09	7,19	3,30	5,18	1,39	2,77	**
boundary violations	(%)	9,14	12,48	3,62	5,59	1,48	2,07	**
average velocity	(cm/s)	0,64	0,26	1,14	0,38	1,90	0,60	**
angular deviation	(deg)	6,53	1,09	5,02	1,03	3,93	0,85	**
eccentricity		0,65	0,06	0,61	0,06	0,57	0,07	**
line deviation	(mm)	0,46	0,10	0,65	0,15	0,94	0,22	**
ellipse deviation	(mm)	0,30	0,10	0,49	0,23	0,76	0,23	**

complexity:		single		double		multi		
		M	SD	M	SD	M	SD	
errors	(%)	3,27	4,82	3,72	4,76	3,79	4,48	
boundary violations	(%)	4,60	5,83	4,65	6,36	4,99	6,17	
average velocity	(cm/s)	1,29	0,46	1,30	0,43	1,09	0,34	**
angular deviation	(deg)	3,42	0,66	6,43	1,25	5,62	1,60	**
eccentricity		0,61	0,06					
line deviation	(mm)	0,67	0,14	0,70	0,17	0,68	0,16	
ellipse deviation	(mm)	0,52	0,18					

gesture that should be retraced, the faster it was performed [$F(1.1, 37.9) = 340.3, p < .01$]. Apart from the predicted slowing effect for age, we could observe an interesting interaction of the factors size and age [$F(1.1, 37.9) = 12.139, p < .01$]: even though younger and older users both increased their drawing speed with larger sizes, the younger users could take more advantage of the largest size.

Form Stability Measures. The form stability of gesture execution as measured by angular deviation was influenced by the size [$F(2, 68) = 232.5, p < .01$] and complexity [$F(1.64, 56.58) = 83.6, p < .01$] of the gesture, but no significant differences due to age could be observed. Across all participants, the angular deviation decreased with increasing gesture space, resulting in a more accurate reproduction of the gesture pattern. The same observation could be made for circular gestures: The larger the drawing space, the smaller the eccentricity of the best ellipse fit to the gesture, resulting in a closer approximation of a perfect circle $[F(2, 68) = 60.55, p < .01]$. For both form stability measures, contrast analysis revealed a highly significant linear trend for the factor size $[F_{angle}(1, 34) = 454.27, p < .01; F_{ecc}(1, 34) = 121.67, p < .01]$, and pairwise comparisons (using Bonferroni correction) between the *small*, *medium* and *large* gesture spaces showed that performance means differed significantly across all comparisons. Comparing the angular deviation between the *single*, *double* and *multi-line* gestures revealed that all three different complexity levels differed significantly from one another, with the highest deviation values encountered at double-line gestures. Taken together, these results indicate that the form stability of gestures was not influenced by age, but it was clearly facilitated with larger screen sizes. How the complexity might have interacted with form stability is discussed below.

Direction Stability Measures. For both circular and linear gestures, we found a main effect of gesture size: with increasing gesture space, there were significantly larger deviations from the best linear fit $[F(1.4, 46.4) = 232.7, p < .01]$ or ellipse fit $[F(2, 68) = 155.54, p < .01]$ respectively. A polynomial contrast revealed clear linear trends $[F_{ellipse}(1, 34) = 324.80, p < .01; F_{line}(1, 34) = 281.27, p < .01]$ and pairwise comparisons (Bonferroni corrected) showed that all three size levels differed significantly from one another. The larger the gesture movement itself, the larger was also the movement jitter. No main effect of complexity could be found. Importantly, there was again no main effect of age, meaning that across all gestures and sizes, older and younger users did not differ in directional stability. Most interestingly, the measure of linear deviation revealed an age x size interaction effect $[F(1.4, 46.4) = 5.535, p = .015]$, with significant differences between small and medium $(p = .04)$ as well as small and large $(p = .01)$ gesture space conditions. While in the smallest gesture space the younger users were more accurate, in the medium sized space both groups are roughly equal, and in the largest gesture space the older users are more accurate than the younger users. A significant three-way interaction between *age*, *complexity* and *size* on this measure $[F(4, 136) = 5.479, p = .001]$ further differentiates the previous interaction. Contrast and pairwise comparisons analyses showed that the accuracy advantage on small screen sizes for younger users was independent of gesture complexity, but with bigger screen sizes, also the influence of complexity became stronger. It can be seen that the accuracy advantage at the largest screen size for the older users is modulated by complexity, such that the more complex the gesture gets, the bigger the direction stability difference between older and younger users.

4   Discussion

4.1   How Do Gesture Space and Gesture Complexity Influence Performance?

Across all participants of the study, it could be observed that the available space given to retrace a gesture influenced strongly the way the gesture was performed with respect to errors and boundary violations (cf. Table 2). The effects on errors and boundary violations should not raise too much concern, because first, the smallest screen size in this experiment was deliberately chosen to provide a lower bound estimate, and second, the observed overshooting of the gesture frame is most likely an artifact of our setup and cannot be generalized to physically bounded screens.

The variation of gesture space had also an effect on the average velocity with which the retracing was performed: The participants were about double as fast for the medium sized gestures, and triple as fast for the large gestures as compared to the smallest size. Thus, execution speed correlates highly with the spatial extend of the gesture. From a psychological point of view this outcome is in line with kinematic laws that describe basic principles of human motor pattern generation. It reflects a principle referred to as *"Gesetz der konstanten Figurzeit"* (Derwort, 1938, cited from [13]), which postulates that the time needed to trace identical figures of different size is constant.

With regard to accuracy, we observe that the measures of form stability and directional stability have been affected differentially by gesture size: with increasing drawing space, the form stability increased, while directional stability decreased. This seems surprising at a first glance, but can be explained in the light of a speed-accuracy tradeoff: If the user, during gesture execution, detects a deviation from the optimal path and readjusts the motor pattern, overshoots and further readjustments are more likely at higher velocities and result in a decreased directional stability. On the contrary, form stability is preserved better with larger gestures. In the case of angular deviation, this becomes obvious from the fact that the same small displacement of the finger can result in large angular deviations if the reference gestures itself is small, but results in smaller angular deviations if the reference gesture is comparably large.

The manipulation of gesture complexity as a variation of the number of lines did not result in a systematic effect across our measurements. A decrease in average velocity with increasing number of line segments is explained well by the fact that users have to decelerate and accelerate again at each turning point of the pattern. More interesting is the effect of gesture complexity on angular deviation: the highest angular deviation was found for double-line gestures, followed by multi-line gestures and single-line gestures. This pattern could be explained by the geometric properties of the gestures that make up the groups: the double-line gesture group consisted of many gestures which included an acute angle (see Figure 1, the multi-line group included more rectangular gestures, while the reference angles in the single-line group were only 90° or 45°. It seems that especially right-angled patterns can be replicated more accurate than patterns that include more arbitrary acute angles. Finally, the reason why we did not find a systematic effect of gesture complexity might be due to the fact that the initial division of single-line, double-line and multi-line gestures did not reflect the actual difficulty of the gesture. It can be easily conceived that a circular gesture poses a much higher demand on motor control than a single horizontal line, even though these appeared in the same category. Our classification was a simple one-dimensional classification approach, but the qualitative data we obtained hints at a multi-dimensional account, including for example also curvature, symmetry, direction, or familiarity of the gesture.

4.2   How Does Age Influence Gesture Performance?

The central question of this research, however, was whether there are any age-related differences in gesture execution performance. Of particular interest was whether and how age interacts with the screen size and gesture complexity variations. The results showed an influence of age on the execution speed, but not on the accuracy of gesture performance. Bearing in mind the limitations of our user and gesture samples, this suggests that elderly users have no more problems than younger users in performing accurate gesture input, even on small screen devices. In our gesture retracing task we found a slowing factor of 1.3, which is at the lower end of reported efficiency drops in studies concerned with age effects on input device performance. These studies quantify performance decline by factors ranging from 1.3 to 3 over a range of input devices, including mouse, trackball, trackpoint and touchpad [10,14,15].

In the present study, age differences were smallest (0.15 cm/s) for the smallest screen size, and largest (0.58 cm/s) for the largest screen size. It thus seems to be the case that the speed advantage found for younger users is mainly generated by their increased velocity in the largest screen size. It is known from aging psychology research that older adults prefer accuracy over speed (Salthouse, 1985, in [16]). Sülzenbrück et al. note that older people even favor accuracy if they are instructed to perform as quickly as possible, which results in higher accuracy at the cost of slowing for all tasks that exhibit a speed-accuracy tradeoff [16]. In fact, this might be the reasons why there are no obvious drawbacks in gesture accuracy for older adults in the present study.

Interestingly, in their comparison of age-related slowing effects across different motor tasks, Sülzenbrück et al. found task contingent slowing effects, and even a performance advantage of elderly users for the line-tracing task, which resembles our gesture retracing task most closely [16]. The authors explain this observation with its close relation to handwriting, in which, as has been shown previously, older adults are stronger trained with. While their highly controlled line tracing task was still of quite a different nature and this might account for the divergent findings, their results are encouraging in two ways: First, if a large sample of older adults (N=180) can outperform a younger group on a lane-tracing task which is highly similar to performing an accurate gesture pattern on the touch screen surface, then gestures as input paradigm might indeed be suitable for elderly adults. Second, considering the fact that elderly have usually a high proficiency with handwriting, they might benefit from gesture patterns that are borrowed from or similar to patterns used in cursive writing.

5   Summary and Outlook

We presented a study which was designed to provide first insights of how effectively and efficiently elderly users can produce finger gestures pattern on a touchscreen. Of particular interest were the questions whether small screens impede their interaction, and whether performance among the elderly drops as the gesture patterns become more complex. Our results show no systematic influence of age on gesture accuracy. Furthermore, no consistent interaction of complexity or size with age could be observed. This means that even on small screens (e.g. the size of current mobile phones and smart phones), older users do not fall behind younger ones in terms of accuracy. In fact, the tendency of older users to prefer accuracy over speed might prevent them from performing a gesture too fast and negligent as was observed sometimes among younger users. These results support previous findings that direct interaction, and in particular touch screen interaction is beneficial to elderly users (e.g.[17]). However, we extend existing literature by showing that not only a single touch, but also more complex gestural patterns could be handled effectively by older users. With regard to suitable gesture patterns for elderly, gestures similar to the ones we tested should be feasibly for older adults. In addition, effects like the familiarity with handwriting, or a general bias for right angles, along with curvature, direction and symmetry effects, might influence gesture performance and should be accounted for when designing simple 2D gesture commands for older users. We further observed that older users are slower than younger users in performing finger gesture input patterns. However, the slowing factor is still comparably small with regard to other input technology comparisons, and, as accuracy is not affected, this should not impede actual device usage.

The present results were obtained on a stationary touchscreen and are not automatically generalizable to a handheld device. Therefore, a second experiment is currently being conducted to investigate to which extend these results can be replicated on a mobile device (iPod Touch), and extending this research by investigating also multi-finger gestures and the effects of device posture.

Taken together, we present a user-centered approach to gesture technology, asking not only what is feasible from a technical point of view, but also how gesture technology should be designed to suit the needs and abilities of the user, and in particular the older user. There are still many important questions to be answered, including the semiotics of gestures and the acceptance of this technology among elderly. However, by pursuing this line of research we hope to contribute to the development of technology which is better suited to the older users' abilities, empowering them to actually make use of it and help them to ease their daily routine.

Acknowledgments. This research is supported by the German Research Foundation, (DFG - 1013 'Prospective Design of Human-Technology Interaction') and by the National Research Fund Luxembourg, FNR (AFR grant).

References

1. Schieber, F.: Human factors and aging: Identifying and compensating for age-related deficits in sensory and cognitive function. In: Charness, N., Schaie, K. (eds.) Impact of technology on successful aging, pp. 42–84. Springer, New York (2003)
2. Vercruyssen, M.: Movement control and speed of behaviour. In: Fisk, A.D., Rogers, W.A. (eds.) Human Factors and the Older Adult, pp. 55–86. Academic Press, San Diego (1997)
3. Schroeder, D.H., Salthouse, T.A.: Age-related effects on cognition between 20 and 50 years of age. Personality and Individual Differences 36, 393–404 (2004)
4. Kurniawan, S.: Older people and mobile phones: A multi-method investigation. International Journal of Human-Computer Studies 66(12), 889–901 (2008)
5. Saffer, D.: Designing Gestural Interfaces, 1st edn. O'Reilly Media, Sebastopol (2008)
6. Charness, N., Holley, P., Feddon, J., Jastrzembski, T.: Light pen use and practice minimize age and hand performance differences in pointing tasks. Hum. Factors 46(3), 373–384 (2004)
7. Rogers, W.A., Fisk, A.D., McLaughlin, A.C., Pak, R.: Touch a screen or turn a knob: choosing the best device for the job. Hum. Factors 47(2), 271–288 (2005)
8. Chaparro, A., Rogers, M., Fernandez, J., Bohan, M., Choi, S.D., Stumpfhauser, L.: Range of motion of the wrist: implications for designing computer input devices for the elderly. Disability & Rehabilitation 22(13), 633–637 (2000)
9. Walker, N., Philbin, D.A., Fisk, A.D.: Age-related differences in movement control: adjusting submovement structure to optimize performance. The journals of gerontology. Series B, Psychological sciences and social sciences 52(1), 40–52 (1997)
10. Smith, M.W., Sharit, J., Czaja, S.J.: Aging, motor control, and the performance of computer mouse tasks. Human Factors: The Journal of the Human Factors and Ergonomics Society 41, 389–396 (1999)
11. Microsoft Corporation: Application gestures and semantic behavior,
    http://msdn.microsoft.com/en-us/library/ms704830VS.85.aspx
    (retrieved, January 2009)
12. Apple Inc.: Multi-touch trackpad,
    http://www.apple.com/macbook/features.html (retrieved, January 2009)
13. Heuer, H.: On re-scaleability of force and time in aiming movements. Psychological Research 46(1), 73–86 (1984)
14. Chaparro, A., Bohan, M., Fernandez, J., Choi, S.D., Kattel, B.: The impact of age on computer input device use: - psychological sciences. International Journal of Industrial Ergonomics 24, 503–513 (1999)
15. Sutter, C., Müsseler, J.: User specific design of interfaces and interaction techniques: What do older computer users need? In: Universal Access in Human Computer Interaction. Coping with Diversity, pp. 1020–1029. Springer, Heidelberg (2007)
16. Sülzenbrück, S., Hegele, M., Heuer, H., Rinkenauer, G.: Generalized slowing is not that general in older adults: Evidence from a tracing task. Occupational Ergonomics (2009) (in press)
17. Murata, A., Iwase, H.: Usability of touch-panel interfaces for older adults. Hum Factors 47(4), 767–776 (2005)

Gestures in Human-Computer Interaction – Just Another Modality?

Antti Pirhonen

Department of Computer Science and Information Systems,
P.O. Box 35, FI-40014 University of Jyväskylä, Finland
antti.pirhonen@jyu.fi

Abstract. The traditional framework in human-computer studies is based on a simple input-output model of interaction. In many cases, however, splitting interaction into input and output is not necessarily appropriate. Gestures work as a good example of a modality which is difficult or inappropriate to be conceptualised within the traditional input-output paradigm. In the search for a more appropriate interaction paradigm, gestures, as modality, have potential in working as a meta-modality, in terms of which all other modalities could be analysed. This paper proposes the use of gestures and gestural metaphors in a central role in interaction design, and presents a case study as an illustration of the point.

Keywords: gesture, metaphor, human-computer interaction.

1 Introduction

In the discipline of human computer interaction (HCI), the conception of human cognition is deeply rooted in computer metaphor. The computer metaphor and the related Cartesian mind-body dualism have resulted in a fairly mechanical comprehension of the human being using a technical device. In that conception, our senses work as input devices, entering information from the environment into our central nervous system (analogous to the central processing unit, CPU, of a computer). Muscles, in turn, are seen as the output devices which work according to the neural signals generated in the central nervous system.

The claim above can be argued to be an oversimplification of contemporary HCI studies. For sure, HCI scholars who follow the related research in, for example, cognitive psychology or philosophy, have more sophisticated ideas of a human being interacting with her environment. However, the current usages of certain terms in most HCI literature indicate that the computational model of human cognition is still the dominating one in the field of HCI. For instance, the term *modality* in human-computer studies usually refers to a *communication channel*. The challenge of interaction design is to utilise these communication channels with compatible technology.

This approach reflects a model of human cognition which was already questioned several decades ago in attention studies. In it, each modality works independently of

S. Kopp and I. Wachsmuth (Eds.): GW 2009, LNAI 5934, pp. 281–288, 2010.
© Springer-Verlag Berlin Heidelberg 2010

each other [1]. When we, for instance, *see* something with our eyes, our *hearing* is – according to this model – a completely free resource to be used for something else. Even though this model has been falsified in various contexts a long time ago, its reflections can easily be seen in the usage of the term modality. For instance, only a few years ago, hands-free equipment for mobile phones was introduced as a solution to the problem of combining phone usage and driving a car. It is not far-fetched to interpret this idea as being based on a model in which the modalities employed in the usage of a phone ('hearing' as input modality, 'talk' as output modality) were independent of the modalities needed in the driving process. Even though our everyday experience as well as empirical studies [2] falsified this conception, many (including politicians) continue to believe in it. The model is easy to understand and adopt, thus all the more difficult to question.

The great success of the computer metaphor of human cognition is quite understandable in human-computer studies. In the early days of HCI, the role of the human being in HCI was explicitly formulated as to be a fluent component of the whole consisting of a technical device and its user [3]. When a machine and its user were handled as a whole, it was practical to conceptualise their functions within the same conceptual framework. Input and output, memory, information processing and many other concepts, were equally used whether it was a question of a machine or a human being.

Over time, the idea of user as a part of the system faded and new concepts were introduced. *User centred design* and *user experience*, among other new buzz-words, stress the subjective issues rather than measurable parameters of efficiency. The change indicates a clear paradigm shift in HCI. This paper continues the formulation of a new HCI paradigm by questioning the appropriateness of the computer metaphor and the related input-output conception of interaction. Gestures will be used as an illustrative example of a modality which is hard to conceptualise within a simple input-output framework.

2   Background: A Case of Conflicting User-Interface Metaphors

Some years ago, we carried out a research project about gaze-free interaction with a portable music player. The project resulted in two different versions (in Table 1 and Figure 2, referred to as v1 and v2), which had similar basic interaction principles (the design process and evaluations have been widely reported [4, 5, 6, 7]). That study was part of a pursuit of effective use of non-speech sounds in user-interfaces. We thus implemented a music player in a PDA, and decided to discover how it could be controlled without looking at the device. The rationale was the general need for learning to design human-computer interaction in mobile contexts, in which gaze is frequently engaged in other activities than in the use of a device. The potential of spatial non-speech sounds as a feedback modality was given special focus. The success was evaluated in user studies, in which the mobile context was simulated first with a stepper [4, 5] and later (v2) with an exercise bike [7]. In the evaluations, the volunteering participants were supposed to use the exercise device while listening to music from the application via headphones and following instructions (e.g., 'next track'). The instructions were given by the researcher in written form, one at a time.

Thinking back to our study, it is easy to conclude that the conceptual framework for the design of the player was the typical input-output paradigm. Our first task was to define the input and output methods for interaction. Since the primary task was to study spatial non-speech sounds, we obviously decided to use them as output (i.e., feedback). We still needed to choose an input modality. It was also necessary for input to be performed without gaze, to be part of a gaze-free interaction system. We ended up using simple hand gestures: sweeps with a finger across the touch screen of the device. That was supposed to be a robust enough solution for mobile contexts; all you would need to know is roughly where the device is, and with your finger you would easily find the edges of the screen.

A portable music player was a suitable application to study interaction for at least two reasons. First, the basic controls of a music player are few, meaning that the risk of confusion among functions is small. Second, a music player and its basic controls is such a strong convention in our culture that we could count on a certain level of common understanding about it. For instance, on the control panels of most music players, functions which are related to going backwards are on the left and going forward on the right. We called the adoption of these directions of a conventional control panel as a 'metaphor' (which in fact later resulted in questioning the way in which the term 'metaphor' is used in the context of user interface design, see [7]). The chosen directions in each basic function of the music players are listed in Table 1.

Table 1. Basic functions and related gestures

Function	TouchPlayer	GestureJukeBox
Next track	Sweep across screen left -> right	Sweep across screen left -> right
Previous track	Sweep across screen right -> left	Sweep across screen right -> left
Play / Stop	Single tap	Double tap
Volume up	Sweep from bottom -> top of screen	Circular gesture clockwise
Volume down	Sweep from top -> bottom of screen	Circular gesture anti-clockwise
Last track	-	Sweep left -> right + tap
First track	-	Sweep right -> left + tap

The interaction scenario with the application was as follows: The user of the player has the device hanging on the right hand side, fixed with a hook to the pocket seam of the trousers (Figure 1). She listens to the music via headphones, which are connected to the device. With the gestures listed in Table 1, she can browse the playlist, stop and play, as well as adjust the volume (some of the gestures are illustrated in Figure 2). In each function except volume adjustment, she hears a feedback sound as confirmation of a successful action. Each feedback sound was designed to illustrate the function it confirmed.

Fig. 1. Fixing in trousers

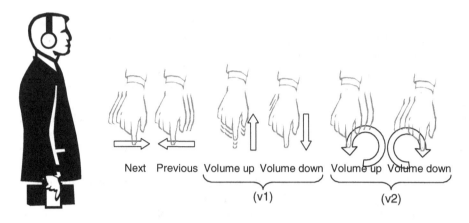

Fig. 2. Directions of some gestures

In the design of both gestures and the audio feedback, directions had a central role. As stated above, from the beginning, we talked about metaphors when referring to the cognitive link between a physical gesture or audio feedback, and the directions in a playlist. In fact, even the verbal expression of going backward or forward in a playlist, is clearly metaphorical itself. For instance, the directions could as well have been described in the vertical dimension (up and down in a playlist). Without going into the details of the design process, we will now discuss the direction-dilemma and the hypotheses that emerged.

2.1 Is It Forward-Backward or Left-Right?

The fundamental directions in control gestures were in the forward-backward dimension of the walking direction of the user. In other words, when the user wanted to browse the playlist forward (e.g., choose the next track in a playlist), she was supposed to make a sweep forward across the touch screen. To enable these directions, the device needed to be fixed to the side of the user. We soon found that if the cut of the trousers resulted in the device hanging merely in the front rather than at the side, the idea of the forward-backward dimension was more difficult to communicate. However, most of the participants in our evaluations used jeans, the cut of which was perfect for side fixing. There was another peculiar issue about the directions of sweeps: 2 out of 20 participants in two evaluations persistently made a sweep from front to back, when asked to go forward in a playlist (and vice versa). In other words, they conceptualised a hand gesture from front to back to signify 'forward'. In the post interview neither of them could argue for their behaviour. However, we later concluded that it must have been a difference in *what* they understood to be forward or backward. We as designers found it obvious that a gesture which moves from back to front denotes 'forward'. The issue is that we were focusing on the hand; and indeed it went forward. However, if one focuses on the whole body, the setting is quite the contrary. While our body is always surrounded by some material, like air or water, we must 'push' that material backwards in order to get forward. The phenomenon is familiar in many means of moving: swimming, rowing, cross-country skiing, to name but a few. In other words: if we link the coordinates to the hand, moving a hand backwards means backward. If we, on he contrary, fix the coordinates to the whole body, moving the hand(s) backward denotes an impact forward. It has to be stressed, though, that the confusion of forward-backward gestures only concerned 10 percent of the participants of the evaluations.

Physical directions were central in the design of feedback sounds as well. We argued that we used the 'control panel metaphor' in the design of non-speech feedback sounds. By this we meant that we had a typical control panel of any music player in mind – the order of push-buttons in particular. The position of each function was thus illustrated with the means available. Pitch change (e.g., forward: increasing pitch) was important in both player versions. Since the user was supposed to use headphones, we could use panning of sound as well: functions related to going backwards were from the left, while pointing forward was from the right hand side. We assumed that practically all potential users have a reasonable amount of experience of music players whose control panels follow this order.

The evaluations which we carried out revealed some peculiar things. Since we were primarily interested in the effectiveness of the specific non-speech feedback sounds, we tried what would happen if different sounds relating to functions were suddenly transposed. For instance, suddenly sounds relating to forward functions decreased in pitch and could be heard from the left. What we found out was surprising; even if the participants in the evaluation knew that at some point of time the sounds would be changed (and they were asked to hold up their hand when they noticed the change), only one participant ever noticed the change. In the post-interview, all argued that the feedback sounds were an essential part of the interaction. We concluded that the sounds were important but their design failed to illustrate the directions.

What went wrong with the sound design, then? In the post-interview, the participants found them quite relevant. The sounds just did not communicate what they were supposed to communicate. This mystery made us consider the use of metaphors again. In the control gestures (or "input"), the gestures utilised the back-front dimension. However, the sounds relied on the left-right dimension. We thus had two conflicting dimensional metaphors. Since metaphors are highly subjective elements of the human meaning creation process [8], it can be argued that when the user constructs her own dimensional metaphor on the basis of interaction with the application, she will need to choose between these conflicting dimensional cues. The fact that the participants in our evaluations did not utilise the dimension-related audio cues at all and that they used the gestures in an extremely consistent manner (even the two participants behaving exceptionally were consistent in the dimensions they adopted), leads to the conclusion that the dimensional metaphors related to gestures overrode the audio ones.

3   The Peculiarity of Gestures as Interaction Modality

The design example above and especially the related evaluation provoked more questions than answers. Was the observed difference between gestural and audio metaphors a result of some fundamental difference between gestures and audio as modalities? Or was there some other difference than the orientation between the metaphors?

Recent studies based on the notion of embodied cognition provide us with an interesting perspective on our dilemma. They also challenge the relevance of the traditional input-output paradigm of human-computer interaction.

3.1 Thinking through Action and Acting by Thinking

The shift from Cartesian mind-body dualism has led to different concepts about the nature of the human being and the relationship between a human being and the world. The embodied cognition model focuses on the central role of bodily experience in all our thinking. In particular, the claim that mental events activate a similar kind of neural activity as physical performance [9] opens up a new perspective for considering interaction.

In our music player design case, interaction was conceptualised as a combination of input and output. However, were gestures just a way to enter information into the application? And, respectively, were the feedback sounds just output signals to be received by the user? It has been argued, that the perception of sound is an active process in our consciousness [10]. User-interface feedback sounds as output is in this view only one side of the coin. What, then, would a more appropriate conceptualisation be?

Gestures are, in the common sense, an interaction modality which cannot be split into input and output. On the other hand, they are physically bound to bodily experience, which has been found to be a fundamental issue in the embodied cognition paradigm. In brief, it can be argued within the embodied cognition framework that gestures are both a means of interacting with our physical environment and of thinking.

3.2 Gestures as a Meta-modality

If the embodied cognition paradigm were to become the dominating framework for conceptualising interaction in the human-computer interaction community, gestures would assume a much more central role as a modality than they have done so far. For instance, in probably the most detailed analysis of interaction modalities ever done (Esprit Basic Research Action 7040, Amodeus project), physical gestures are referred to as 'touch' or 'haptics' in the analysis of output modalities [11] and 'kinaesthetics' in input [12]. However, they are only handled as representational or sensory modalities.

Vision, as an interaction modality, has dominated the conceptualisation of human-computer interaction from the very beginning of the discipline. By user-interface is usually meant the visual layouts on a VDU (visual display unit). When considering 'alternative' interaction modalities, visuals have most often been used as a basis for conceptualising other modalities. For instance, in the design of audio or tactile signs, the general name for these signs was a modification of 'icon', referring to a visual element of a graphical user-interface; ear+icon=earcon [13], tactile+icon=tacton [14].

In other words, we argue that visual modality has been the de facto meta-modality, in terms of which most of the interaction has been designed.

Visual dominance is not a unique phenomenon in human-computer interaction; it is easy to observe that our culture is strongly visually biased. For example, in the design of buildings, drawings are of great importance, as well as computerised visual modelling. Acoustics, on the contrary, is rarely given much attention.

If, for example, sounds have been conceptualised in terms of visuals, it appears that interaction elements of one modality can be used, at least metaphorically, as a basis for the design of interaction elements in another modality. If this holds, we argue that gestures would be a promising 'meta-modality'. Gestures, while being inherently and effortlessly conceivable as embodied entities, could work as a starting point for the design of interaction, in which the widely acknowledged view of the bodily engagement of cognition would be utilised.

4 Conclusions

The design case above is an example of problems which could have been avoided by relying on gestures as a primary interaction modality. If the sounds had been designed in terms of gestures, the conflict between the related metaphors would have been avoided. Ideally, articulating the same within the contemporary metaphor conception framework, both gestures and audio should have been expressions of the same metaphor.

From the point of view of metaphor theories, this challenges the way we communicate metaphors. In the Aristotelian view, metaphors were defined as figures of speech. The modern conceptualisation of metaphors, formulated by Lakoff and Johnson [8], provides us with means to analyse expressions in basically any form in terms of metaphors. Gestures thus have potential as meta-modality from the point of views of both embodied cognition and metaphor theories.

Acknowledgments

This work is funded by Finnish Funding Agency for Technology and Innovation, and the following partners: GE Healthcare Finland Ltd., Suunto Ltd., Sandvik Mining and Construction Ltd. and Bronto Skylift Ltd.

References

1. Broadbent, D.E.: Perception and communication. Pergamon, London (1958)
2. Horrey, W.J., Wickens, C.D.: Examining the impact of cell phone conversations on driving using meta-analytic techniques. Human Factors 48(1), 196–205 (2006)
3. Card, S.K., Moran, T.P., Newell, A.: The psychology of human-computer interaction. Lawrence Erlbaum Associates, Hillsdale (1983)
4. Pirhonen, A., Brewster, S.: Metaphors and imitation. In: Workshop proceedings at PC-HCI 2001, Patras, Greece, December 7-9, pp. 27–32 (2001)

5. Pirhonen, A., Brewster, S., Holguin, C.: Gestural and audio metaphors as a means of control for mobile devices. In: Proceedings of CHI 2002, Minneapolis, Minnesota, April 20-25, pp. 291–298 (2002)

6. Pirhonen, A.: What do learning curves tell us about learnability? In: Vetere, F., Johnston, L., Kushinsky, R. (eds.) Proceedings of the HF2002 Human Factors Conference, Design for the whole person - integrating physical, cognitive and social aspects, November 25-27. Swinburne University of Technology (CD-ROM –format), Melbourne (2002)

7. Pirhonen, A.: From metaphors to simulations to idioms: Supporting the conceptualisation process. In: Markopoulos, P., Eggen, B., Aarts, E., Crowley, J.L. (eds.) EUSAI 2004. LNCS, vol. 3295, pp. 279–290. Springer, Heidelberg (2004)

8. Lakoff, G., Johnson, M.: Metaphors we live by. The University of Chicago Press, Chicago (1980)

9. Gallese, V., Lakoff, G.: The brain's concepts: the role of the sensory-motor system in reason and language. Cogn. Neuropsychol. 22(2005), 455–479 (2005)

10. Godøy, R.I.: Gestural-Sonorous Objects: Embodied Extensions of Schaeffer's Conceptual Apparatus. Organised Sound 11(2) (2006)

11. Bernsen, N.O.: A toolbox of output modalities: Representing output information in multimodal interfaces. Esprit Basic Research Action 7040: The Amodeus Project, document TM/WP21 (1995)

12. Bernsen, N.O.: A taxonomy of input modalities. Esprit Basic Research Action 7040: The Amodeus Project, document TM/WP22 (1995)

13. Blattner, M., Sumikawa, D., Greenberg, R.: Earcons and icons: Their structure and common design principles. Human-Computer Interaction 4(1), 11–44 (1989)

14. Brewster, S., Brown, L.: Non-visual information display using tactons. In: CHI 2004 extended abstracts on Human factors in computing systems, pp. 787–788. ACM, New York (2004)

Body Posture Estimation in Sign Language Videos

François Lefebvre-Albaret and Patrice Dalle

IRIT : UPS-118 r. de Narbonne
31062 Toulouse cedex 9

Abstract. This article deals with the posture reconstruction from a mono view video of a signed utterance. Our method makes no use of additional sensors or visual markers. The head and the two hands are tracked by means of a particle filter. The elbows are detected as convolution local maxima. A non linear filter is first used to remove the outliers, then some criteria using French Sign Language phonology are used to process the hand disambiguation. The posture reconstruction is achieved by using inverse kinematics, using a Kalman smoothing and the correlation between strong and week hand depth that can be noticed in the signed utterances. The article ends with a quantitative and qualitative evaluation of the reconstruction. We show how the results could be used in the framework of automatic Sign Language video processing.

Keywords: Sign Language, Posture Reconstruction, Inverse Kinematics, Mono Vision.

1 Introduction

Recent technological progress in the field of video capture devices, powerful hardware and new computation algorithms make it possible to develop new tools dedicated to automatic Sign Language (SL) video processing. Such tools can be used by linguists or in the framework of SL teaching. In a long run, they could also be embedded in automatic SL translation tools.

The low level treatment of SL videos is so difficult to solve in the case of SL utterances, that it is necessary to have a prior knowledge of SL. In this article, we show how a SL model can be used in SL video processing for hand and head tracking as well as in posture reconstruction.

We decided to focus on the treatment of real videos provided by SL teacher or by other SL professionals. Consequently, the videos used in the frame of this article make no use of additive markers to enhance the video processing and there is no restriction of SL utterances (limitation of the set of sign, predefined utterance structure). To be able to process the widest range of SL videos, our algorithm processes mono view videos.

Our paper first deals with SL specificities and their consequences on automatic SL video processing. Then, we briefly present other studies related to body

S. Kopp and I. Wachsmuth (Eds.): GW 2009, LNAI 5934, pp. 289–300, 2010.

tracking and posture reconstruction. We finally expose our method and show how SL specificities can be used for a more efficient posture reconstruction. The paper ends with a quantitative and qualitative evaluation of our algorithm.

2   The Specificities of Sign Languages : Consequences for Automatic SL Video Processing

French Sign Language (FSL) makes use of several parameters. **Hands** convey information with their shapes, placements, configurations and movements. **Non manual features** (facial expression, body orientation, eye gaze ...) also convey an important part of the utterance meaning. As a consequence, the video processing not only has to focus on 2D hand locations but must also consider other body parts involved in the SL production (head, shoulders, elbows).

Whereas vocal languages only use the temporal dimension, SL also use the space around the signer to build utterances [7]. An error in the sign depth estimation can therefore lead to a message misinterpretation. The posture reconstruction algorithm must then be designed to estimate hand position in the image plan as well as its depth (distance from the camera).

FSL uses the space located near the face. As a consequence, we can observe a lot of occlusions of the signer's head by the two hands. These occlusions will have to be handled by the video processing algorithm. Moreover, a lot of signs also involve hand crossings that make the hand tracking more complicated.

All the above mentioned features make the task of finding the signer's posture very hard in a context of mono-vision SL videos. However, it is possible to use SL constraint and organization principle to achieve better results.

For instance, it is possible to make use of SL phonology. As already observed by [2], there are some strong tendencies in sign formations of American Sign Language (ASL). Batison distinguished three categories of signs:

Signs where both hands are moving (involving symmetries)
Signs where one hand moves but the two hands have the same configurations.
Signs where one hand moves and the two hands have different configurations.

In the two last sign categories, Battison noticed that one hand is active and that the other one is passive. Our statistics (cf. 4.3) prove that these tendencies can also be observed for FSL.

3   State of the Art in Posture Reconstruction

In automatic SL processing, some prior knowledge can be used during the tracking. Three cues are relevant for any gesture video processing method:

An appearance model (body silhouette, body texture, skin/background colour)
A kinematic model of the body
A statistical knowledge about the posture distribution

Other cues are specific to SL and can also be used to enhance the tracking:

A phonological knowledge about SL signs (cf. 2)
A lexical model (The problem is that the standard signs can be modified by a lot of spacial flexion which involve a lot of parameter changes.)
A syntactical model (For instance, in infering the orientation of the current sign thanks to the previous entities placed in the signing space.)

Several approaches have been used to achieve a posture reconstruction. We can distinguish all the methods based on external sensors (Magnetic, Inertial) described in [30] , the methods using multiple views [8], the methods using a video already containing depth estimation (like stereo cameras, time of flight cameras) and the methods only using a monocular view. We will focus on this last set of methods . The interested reader may refer to the survey of [20] about hand and head tracking and the survey of [26] about body posture reconstruction.

The silhouette can be used to estimate the body posture [11][24]. Other studies [21] only use hand and head position and strong statistical assumptions to estimate the body posture. Even if the 2D reconstruction seems to fit the original video, this method is not accurate enough to provide an accurate 3D reconstruction of the body posture. Better results are achieved when both cues coming from silhouette and hand/head tracking are merged [22].

When all body parts have been tracked, it is necessary to use a model to find the original body posture. If the necessary body articulators have been tracked properly, it is possible to use an inverse kinematics approach [12]. Inverse kinematics with a simple view is a ill posed problem [16] as the same body articulators (shoulder, elbow and hand) can correspond to at most four different arm configurations. The pure 3D approach as already been used by [6] and the authors mention a lack of robustness of this method. Moreover, it doesn't always address the problem of hand disambiguation. On the other hand, it is possible to use a prior knowledge about postures to make the estimation from the same, or less body part locations [29] [21]. The evaluation criteria differ between the different studies, so that it is very hard to compare the methods [26].

We have not mentioned any article about SL automatic recognition. Readers interested in this problematic can refer to the excellent survey of [23].

4   Description of Our Approach

In this section, we present our posture reconstruction algorithm. The description is structured as follows: First of all, we deal with the problem of hand and head tracking in the video. Then, we present an original solution to handle hand crossings that occur during the signed utterances. We finish with a description of the way of estimating the signer's body posture by means of inverse kinematics, extended Kalman smoothing and hand depth correlation. In these two last parts, we show how SL specificities can be used to enable a more robust posture estimation.

4.1   Particle Filter Used for Hand Tracking

Unlike of other studies [12] where the signer wears coloured gloves, our tracking algorithm does not need any additional marker. The signer has to simply wear long-sleeved clothes which must be a different colour from the skin.

As the hand and head movements are highly non linear [25], we decided to track them by means of particle filters. Particle filters have already been used successfully in the frame of hand tracking and can provide very robust results even if the targets have a similar appearance [27].

In our particle filter, the signer's head and his two hands are tracked using the skin colour. Several skin models can be employed [3] to achieve an accurate colour detection. [10] [1] propose to combine the colour information with the hand motion and report some detection enhancement. We didn't use the motion cue because it leads to bad skin detection when one hand remain still, which is often the case in SL videos. Other studies [17] [28] [18] propose to update the skin colour model during the tracking to make their tracking algorithm more robust to lighting variation. In our implementation, the skin model is expressed in the HSV space and learned from a skin picture, using a skin colour histogram and a background colour histogram. The structure of our particle filter has been inspired by [9]. Each body part is tracked by a cloud of particles. One particle contains only the coordinates of one pixel of the body part that is being tracked. As it is not possible to predict the hand motion from one frame to another [25], we chose to model the 2D hand and head dynamic by a random walk.

$$s(t+1) = s(t) + \epsilon \quad with \quad \epsilon \sim N(0, \Sigma)$$

The signer's hands and its head are tracked by means of a skin colour detection. If the three particle filters remain totally independent, they might follow the same target. Some solutions have already been proposed to avoid this [14].

We decided to adapt the approach proposed by [9]. Three particle filters corresponding to the two hands and the signer's head are used for the tracking. These particle filters are made of weighted particles $\{(\mathbf{s}_t^{(0)}, \pi_t^{(0)}) \ldots (\mathbf{s}_t^{(i)}, \pi_t^{(i)})\}$ of N particles. Each particle has a state $\mathbf{s}_t = [x, y]^T$ where (x, y) represents the position of the particles at the time t. Annealed update steps are used to better fit large and non-linear movements that often occur in SL production.

Our problematic is to track multiple objects with the same appearance. Therefore, it is necessary to avoid the clouds to track the same body part (ie : two particle filters on the same hand). Each frame is then processed as follows: Firstly, the particle filter track the body part on the original skin map. Then, the clouds are alternatively subtracted from the original detection map (For example, the clouds corresponding to the two hands are subtracted form the skin detection map before the head tracking). With such an algorithm, we take into account the possible hand occlusions that can occur during the signed utterances.

4.2   Tracking of Shoulders and Elbows

In order to track elbows and shoulders in the video, we have to find the signer's silhouette. We use the same method for the background detection as for the skin detection (bayesian approach). We noticed that the shoulder appearance is quite similar in each video frame (the same holds for the elbow silhouette). We then constituted 8x8 convolution kernels corresponding to elbow and shoulder silhouettes. Those body parts are then detected as convolution maxima.

In the case of self occlusion of these body parts, their appearance can vary greatly, so that the convolution maxima indicate false detections. It is then necessary to filter the entire video sequence in order to remove those outliers. This signal processing is achieved using a non linear smoother on the whole video. The coordinates of the right elbow on the frame t will be written $E(t)(x_e(t), y_e(t))$. The goal is to select as many valid coordinates as possible, so that for any couple of valid coordinates $(E(t_1), E(t_2))$ measured at the times t_1 and t_2, the average speed of the elbow has its coordinates smaller than a predefined threshold $thres$. The optimization is solved thanks to Viterbi algorithm.

$$\forall\, t_1, t_2 \begin{cases} |x_e(t_2) - x_e(t_1)|/|t_2 - t_1| < thres \\ |y_e(t_2) - y_e(t_1)|/|t_2 - t_1| < thres \end{cases}$$

4.3 The Problem of Disambiguation

In the field of SL video processing, most of the researchers seek to estimate the signer posture, in order to effectuate a sign recognition in a specific set of signs. For this reason a lot of teams focus on the problem of hand tracking and model the two hands as blobs which can merge and split without solving the problem of hand occlusion and crossing [13]. However, hand crossing remains a real problem when processing utterances of FSL. We made statistics on a 30s long FSL video (video (1) cf. 5) and discovered that the two hands where crossed in more than 10% of the frames ! (see fig. 1). A promising method to handle occlusions and hand crossings is to use multiple cues from hand and other body parts to effectuate the hand disambiguation. [25] uses measure from head position, hand shape, hand orientation and hand position to effectuate a correct hand to blob assignment in a video and achieves very good results in the framework of communicational gesture tracking. The different criteria are aggregated by means of a bayesian network. The problem is then to know in which case such a bayesian network model learned with one signer can be used with an other signer, and what are the relevant parameters. We use a similar approach as [25] to effectuate the hand disambiguation, but we also discuss about the linguistic interpretation of those criteria in using the concept of strong and weak hand developed by [2].

In this section, we will adopt the following notation conventions at the frame t.

$E_r(t)E_l(t)$: Right and left elbow location
$H_1(t)H_2(t)$: First and second hand location (used before disambiguation)
$H_r(t)H_l(t)$: Right and left hand location (used after disambiguation)
I : hypothesis of assignment ($H_1 = H_l$ and $H_2 = H_r$)

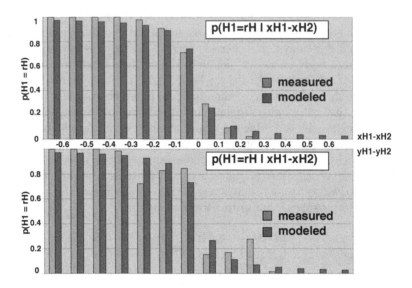

Fig. 1. Statistics on hands abscissa and ordinates, sigmoid regressions

Our disambiguation criteria are the comparison of hand abscissa, the comparison of hand ordinate and the relative position of the hands and the shoulders. Each of those criteria provides a likelihood function $P_n(I)$ (likelihood of the hypothesis I).

As a first disambiguation criterion, we naturally decided to use the comparison of hand abscissa as our statistics revealed that hands are crossed more than 10% of the time. The function $p(I|(x_{H1} - x_{H2}))$ is modelled as a sigmoid function with the equation $p(I|(x_{H1} - x_{H2})) = 1/[1 + e^{\lambda \cdot (x_{H1} - x_{H2})}]$ (fig. 1).

The second criterion is a comparison of hands ordinates. The statistics (fig. 1) show that this comparison can also be a determinant criterion. Those statistics were made for a right handed signer (whose strong hand is the right one). Those statistics can be interpreted as an outcome of the intensive use of strong hand. In fact when signing one-handed signs, the signer mostly uses his strong hand and the weak hand remains in front the bottom part of the torso. Using the hand ordinate comparison to process hand disambiguation can then only be considered in the frame of SL video processing. The likelihood function $P_2(t) = P_2(I|(y_{H1}(t) - y_{H2}(t))$ is also modelled by a sigmoid in our algorithm.

The third disambiguation criterion is the comparison between hand and elbow positions. It is a consequence of kinematic constraints. This likelyhood function can be written as $P_3(t) = P_3(I|(H_1(t), H_2(t), E_r(t), E_l(t)))$.

The first three criteria are aggregated by a nave bayesian fusion as we can not make any assumption about the independence of $P_1(t)$, $P_2(t)$ and $P_3(t)$. The confidence measure $B(t) = P_1(t).P_2(t).P_3(t)$ indicates if the first hand is the right hand. To enhance the disambiguation results, it is also possible to use the motion continuity. The fourth criterion then consists in minimizing the overall displacement of both hand. The aggregation of all the above mentioned criteria on the whole video can be written:

$$argmin \left(\sum_{t=1..T} [dist(t-1,t) + \alpha.ln(B(t))] \right)$$

$dis(t-1,t)$ is the sum of the hand displacement between the frame $t-1$ and the frame t. The parameter α has been determined empirically.

4.4   3D Posture Reconstruction

We decided to base our body model on an 3D explicit representation of the kinematic chain. As the body has a lot of degrees of freedom, we had to simplify in order to be able to find the arm posture by inverse kinematics. The head, the torso and the shoulders are assumed to remain in the same plan Π. In the following part, the depth Z is othogonal to Π.The arms segments are connected with ball joints positioned at the elbows and shoulders locations. Our model does not integrate any rotation limitation and any collision detection. It is then important to notice several important limitation of this model before exposing the posture reconstruction algorithm. We consider the hand as the extremity of the forearm segment. It is only a coarse approximation as this assumption does not take into account the wrist rotation that may cause a variation of the 3D distance between the palm and the elbow. The problem of taking the centroid of the visible hand part is also a source of imprecision because the location of this point on the hand palm will depend on the current hand configuration and on the signer's cloths. The assumption that the head and the two shoulders are in the image plane does not take into account any torso rotation although we know that those rotations have a predominant role in role shift. This limitation will have to be removed in the further versions of our posture reconstruction algorithm.

We then have to make a choice between these four possible configurations. For the following calculus, we assumed that the following order was always respected $Z_s < Z_e < Z_h$ with Z_s, Z_e and Z_h being respectively the shoulder, elbow and hand depth. We checked the validity of this hypothesis and showed that it was acceptable in the case of FSL utterances for the following reasons. Hands are most of the time in front of the elbows. The depth difference between the elbow and the shoulder is much smaller than the depth difference between the hand and the elbow when signing. The cases where the real position of the elbow is behind the shoulder ($Z_s > Z_e$) often corresponds to the weak hand rest position and the exact depth estimation of the weak hand location is then not relevant for a good comprehension of the utterance meaning. However, we noticed that those assumptions are not valid during a role shift because of the torso rotation. In this last case, we observed that one hand can frequently be behind its corresponding shoulder.

The posture reconstruction is first reconstructed thanks to an Extended Kalman Smoother approach as the relationship between the body parts 2D locations and the hand depth is not linear. The outcome of this Kalman smoothing step is an estimation of the two hand depth with their covariance. It can be noticed that the accuracy of the strong hand depth estimation with this method is much better than the depth of the weak hand. This is a consequence of the very small depth difference between the shoulder, the elbow and the hand when the weak hand is not used during signing. As mentioned in the introduction, the two hand movements are not independent. This qualitative observation is confirmed by the following measurement. There is a correlation of 0,24 between the right and left hand depth (on video (1) cf. 5). It can be noticed that the weak hand often reproduces the depth movements of the strong one, even in the signs where the weak hand is not involved. We decided to use this correlation to enhance the estimation of the weak hand depth. At the end of the Kalman smoothing, we obtain:

Strong hand depth: $Z_s^a \sim N(\mu_{Z_s^a}, \sigma_{Z_s^a})$
Weak hand depth: $Z_w^a \sim N(\mu_{Z_w^a}, \sigma_{Z_w^a})$

The a and b superscript will respectively denote the depth estimation before and after the enhancement taking into account the hand depth correlation. Refined weak hand depth estimation: $Z_w^b \sim N(\mu_{Z_w^b}, \sigma_{Z_w^b})$

$$\mu_{Z_w^b} = \mu_{Z_w^a} + \frac{(\sigma_{Z_w^a})^2}{(\sigma_{Z_w^a})^2 + (\sigma_{Z_s^a})^2.\beta} \cdot (\mu_{Z_s^a} - \mu_{Z_w^a})$$

$$(\sigma_{Z_w^b})^2 = (\sigma_{Z_w^a})^2 - \frac{(\sigma_{Z_w^a})^2}{(\sigma_{Z_w^a})^2 + (\sigma_{Z_s^a})^2.\beta} \cdot (\sigma_{Z_w^a})^2$$

The parameter β is estimated according to the dependency between the two hand depths. If those two measures are totally independent, it has to be set to $+\infty$. If on the contrary, the two hands have always the same depth, it has to be set to 1. In our experiment, we determined $\beta = 2.5$ as being the best value.

5   Evaluation

The different parts of our algorithm have been evaluated using four videos:

1. 30 second long video (706 frames) provided by Websourd society. Translation of a piece of news. Only one view.
2. 3 minute long video (5406 frames) small sentences about the health topic. One view, measured with motion capture (magnetic sensors) while filming. This video has been made in our lab by a deaf signer.
3. 2 minute long video (2973 frames) description of the September 11th events In New York. One camera facing the signer, one camera positioned at the top. (LS-Colin project : www.irit.fr/LS-COLIN).
4. 7 min 15 s long video (10905 frames) short tale. Only a front view. This video has been made in our lab by a deaf signer.

5.1   Quantitative Evaluation

The disambiguation algorithm has been tested on the video (1) where the hands were crossed in more than 10% of the frame (see fig. 1). We achieved a result of 98% good hand assignment. The question is then how to quantify the precision of the posture reconstruction. The first method consists in evaluating the 2D recovering between the estimated body shape and the corresponding body shapes in the real video. It provides a good idea about the precision of the tracking algorithm, but does not qualify the precision of depth reconstruction. A second way of evaluating the result is to compare the angle of the body joint with the real angles of the signer's body. However, it is hard to determine what angle precision has to be evaluated, as all the angle do not participate to the SL communication at the same level. A simple average of angle imprecision on a set of body joints is then hardly interpretable. The third evaluation protocol would be to evaluate the precision of the 3D position estimation of the hand location in each frame. Such a way is justified because the hand location and movement are two major parameters conveying the message in SL utterances. As the precision is much higher in the image plan that on the depth dimension, we decided to dissociate the quantitative evaluation of the hand position accuracy in (X, Y) and Z directions. The accuracy of the hand position estimation has been estimated by means of the average squared distance between the ground truth and the estimation of the hand location in the picture. The measures have been made on the video (2) and the standard error includes the errors caused by bad hands assignment during the disambiguation and bad tracking.

We obtained a 4 cm standard error which would be sufficient to make an automatic sign recognition and could be accurate enough to perform a sign reconstruction as long as no contact is involved in the sign (the restitution of contacts requires a precision of less than 0.5 cm on each hand). The case of depth dimension in the hand location should be considered separately because the two hands are located in a neutral zone around 15 cm from the torso most of the time. We measured on the video (2) that the standard deviation of the real hand depth is then no more than 6 cm. In fact, only big depth changes from this average position convey a meaning in FSL. For this reason, we decided to focus on the correlation between the ground truth and the estimated depth to give more importance to high values. The correlation measures were made on the video (3) and the two views (frontal and top) have been used to create the ground truth manually. The comparison between the ground truth and estimation showed that it is possible to gain a significant enhancement of the correlation results in using a posterior Kalman smoothing (for both hands) and in using the dependance between the two hands motions (only for the weak hand). For the weak hand, we noticed 15% of enhancement (67% thanks to the Kalman smoothing and 33% thanks to the use of the dependance between the two hands).

The evaluation showed that the method can be adapted for each signer (several persons signed in the test videos and some of them were left-handed). However, our method is not able yet to handle the case of signers wearing short sleeves or being on a cluttered background. The algorithm has been modified to run in real time. In this case, our disambiguation algorithm has the to be applied between the beginning of the video and the current frame.

5.2   Qualitative Evaluation

As we want to use this posture estimation in a further higher level SL video processing, we must test whether the depth estimation is accurate enough to convey the meaning of the signs. We distinguished two situations where the depth is particularly relevant for the sign or the sentence interpretation : the depth variation is important for the sign comprehension in signs which always include a hand movement involving depth, in directional verbs where the hand displacement reveals the entities involved in the action, and in pointing gestures.

Our aim is to test if the depth variation and comparison have the good sign during those sentence realizations. The measurements have been made on the video (4) which contains a lot of directional signs and description.

In 75% of the cases, the prediction on the movement direction was accurate. We noticed that this rate is much better for directional verbs than for other signs like pointing gestures. It could be explained because of the bigger amplitude of the directional verbs. It would then be possible to use those results in the frame of automatic video analysis.

For relative depth estimation, we achieved a result of 65% good answers. This result can be explained by the following observation. Most of the signs where the relative depth of the two hands is relevant involve hand occlusion. In this case, our particle filter becomes less precise and the posture reconstruction is then also less accurate. In fact, the human vision uses occlusion to estimate the relative depth of two objects. A good enhancement way of our algorithm would be to use this information to refine the estimation of the relative hand depth.

6   Conclusion and Perspectives

The main contribution of this article is to take into account SL features:

- The notion of dominant hand is used to process the hand disambiguation.
- The correlation between right and left hand depth has been used to enhance the weak hand depth estimation.
- The evaluation protocol takes into account the spatiality of the FSL.

We pointed out in our study that the laterality of the signer is a determinant parameter of this model adjustment. The same approach should have to be used for other parameters that could lead to enhance the posture reconstruction. Among them, the most important is certainly the head pose, because we know that the eye gaze is intensively used to assign a location to the entities before their placement by the two hands. Other criteria could also be investigated like the shoulder relative position, the hand orientations, the hand configurations that can have a linguistic interpretation. We decided to use the correlation between the two hands to enhance the depth estimation of the weak hand. This leads to an improvement of the depth estimation because the weak hand often follows the strong one. Unfortunately, SL also contains signs in which the two hands have alternative movement involving depth. The solution to handle such cases would be to detect the current kind of sign (one/two handed, kind of symmetry) and to adapt the filtering methods according to them.

The quantitative and qualitative evaluation of our method proved that it is not accurate enough to provide an accurate posture for an virtual signer automatic SL synthesis. Moreover, some parameters like the head pose, the hand orientation, the hand configuration and the face expression are still missing to achieve a full body reconstruction. However, the qualitative results showed that the results are sufficient to provide a sign characterization. The good results for directional verbs involving depth allow us to consider the use of those results in the frame of signing space modelling [5]. However, more practical applications have already been developed, as automatic sign-image generation where a simple row figures out the 3D hand path involved in the sign.

Acknowledgment. This study has been financed by the Websourd society and the Midi-Pyrenees region. It has been done in the frame of the SESCA project (System for Sign Language Pedagogy and Communication with Avatars) of the Tolosan Sign Reserch Group. Thanks to J. Dalle and E. Rigaud, our FSL experts who preformed some videos that have been used to evaluate our tracking algorithm.

References

1. Akyol, S., Alvarado, P.: Finding Relevant Image Content for mobile Sign Language Recognition. In: IASTED International Conference Signal Processing, Pattern Recognition and Application, pp. 48–52 (2001)
2. Battison, R.: Lexical borrowing in ASL. Linstok, Silver Spring (1978)
3. Brand, J., Mason, J.S.: A comparative assessment of three approaches to pixel-level human skin-detection. In: 15th ICPR, vol. 1, pp. 1056–1059 (2000)
4. Cuxac, C.: French Sign Language, the ways of Iconicity. In: Ophrys (ed.), Paris (2000)
5. Dalle, P.: High level models for sign language analysis by a vision system. In: Workshop on the Representation and Processing of Sign Language: Lexicographic Matters and Didactic Scenarios (LREC), Italy, ELDA, pp. 17–20 (2006)
6. Downton, A.C., Drouet, H.: Model-based image analysis for unconstrained human upper-body motion. In: ICIP, Venue, pp. 274–277 (1992)
7. Emmorey, K., Tversky, B., Taylor, H.A.: Using space to describe space: Perspective in speech, sign, and gesture. Spatial Cognition & Computation 2, 157–180 (2000)
8. Fontmarty, M.: Vision et filtrage particulaire pour le suivi tridimentionnel de mouvement humain, Phd thesis, LAAS, University of Toulouse (2008)
9. Gianni, F., Collet, C., Dalle, P.: Robust tracking for processing of videos of communication's gestures. In: Sales Dias, M., Gibet, S., Wanderley, M.M., Bastos, R. (eds.) GW 2007. LNCS (LNAI), vol. 5085, pp. 93–101. Springer, Heidelberg (2009)
10. Habili, N., Lim, C.C., Moini, A.: Segmentation of the face and hands in sign language video sequences using color and motion cues. IEEE Transactions on Circuits and Systems for Video Technology 14(8), 1086–1097 (2004)
11. Haritaoglu, I., Harwood, D., Davis, L.S.: Ghost: A human body part labeling system using silhouettes. In: ICPR, Brisbane, Australia, pp. 77–82 (1998)

12. Hienz, H., Grobel, K., Offner, G.: Real-time hand-arm motion analysis using a single video camera. In: Proceedings of the Second International Conference on Automatic Face and Gesture Recognition, Killington, USA, pp. 323–327 (1996)
13. Hruz, M., Campr, P., Zelezny, M.: Semi-automatic Annotation of Sign Language Corpora. In: Proceeding LREC 2008, Marrakech, Maroco (2008)
14. Jang, D.S., Jang, S.W., Choi, H.I.: 2D human body tracking with Structural Kalman filter. Pattern Recognition 35(10), 2041–2049 (2002)
15. Lenseigne, B., Gianni, F., Dalle, P.: Mono vision estimation of the arm posture using a biomechanical arm model, method and evaluation. In: 14th french-speaking congres on pattern recognition and artificial intelligence, RFIA Toulouse, France, AFRIF-AFIA, vol. (2), pp. 957–966 (2003)
16. Lenseigne, B., Gianni, F., Dalle, P.: A New Gesture Representation for Sign Language Analysis. In: LREC 2004 - Workshop on the Representation and Processing of Sign Language, Lisbonne, Portugal, pp. 85–90 (2004)
17. Li, P.H., Wang, H.J.: Object Tracking with Particle Filter Using Color Information. In: Gagalowicz, A., Philips, W. (eds.) MIRAGE 2007. LNCS, vol. 4418, pp. 534–541. Springer, Heidelberg (2007)
18. Lichtenauer, J.F., Hendriks, E.A., Reinders, M.J.: 3D Visual Detection of Correct NGT Sign Production. In: 13th Annual Conference of the Advanced School for Computing and Imaging, Heijen, Netherlands (2007)
19. Maccormick, J., Blake, A.: A probabilistic exclusion principle for tracking multiple objects. International Journal of Computer Vision 39, 572–578 (1999)
20. Mahmoudi, F., Parviz, M.: Visual Hand Tracking Algorithms. In: GMAI 2006: Proceedings of the conference on Geometric Modeling and Imaging, pp. 228–232. IEEE Computer Society, Washington (2006)
21. Micilotta, A., Bowden, R.: View-based location and tracking of body parts for visual interaction. In: BMVC 2004, Kingston, pp. 849–858 (2004)
22. Noriega, P., Bernier, O.: Multicues 3D Monocular Upper Body Tracking using Constrained Belief Propagation. In: BMVC, Warwick, pp. 57–60 (2007)
23. Ong, S.C.W., Ranganath, S.: Automatic Sign Language Analysis, A Survey and the Future beyond Lexical Meaning. PAMI 27(6), 873–891 (2005)
24. Roberts, T.J., McKenna, S.J., Ricketts, I.W.: Human Pose Estimation Using learnt probabilistic region similarities and partial configurations. In: Pajdla, T., Matas, J(G.) (eds.) ECCV 2004. LNCS, vol. 3024, pp. 291–303. Springer, Heidelberg (2004)
25. Sherrah, J., Gong, S.: Resolving Visual Uncertainty and Occlusion through Probabilistic Reasoning. In: BMVC: Proceedings of the British Machine Vision Conference, Bristol, pp. 252–261 (2000)
26. Wang, J.J., Singh, S.: Video analysis of human dynamics: a survey. Real Time Imaging 9, 321–346 (2003)
27. Wang, J., Chen, X., Gao, W.: Online selecting discriminative tracking features using particle filter. In: Conference on Computer Vision and Pattern Recognition, San Diego, USA, vol. 2, pp. 1037–1042. IEEE Computer Society, Los Alamitos (2005)
28. Wang, H., Shindler, K.: Effective Appearance Model and Similarity Measure for Particle Filtering and Visual Tracking. In: Leonardis, A., Bischof, H., Pinz, A. (eds.) ECCV 2006. LNCS, vol. 3953, pp. 606–618. Springer, Heidelberg (2006)
29. Yang, J., Timothy, R.M., Kim, H., Arora, J.S.: Abdel-Malek, K.: Multi-objective Optimization for Upper Body Posture Prediction. In: 10th AIAA/ISSMO Multidisciplinary Analysis and Optimization Conference, Albany, NY (2004)
30. Zhou, H., Hu, H.S.: A Survey, Human Motion Tracking and Stroke Rehabilitation. Technical report, Dpt. of computer sciences, university of Essex, UK (2004)

Influence of Handshape Information on Automatic Sign Language Recognition

Gineke A. ten Holt[1,2], Marcel J.T. Reinders[1], Emile A. Hendriks[1],
Huib de Ridder[2], and Andrea J. van Doorn[2]

[1] Information and Communication Theory Group, Delft University of Technology,
Mekelweg 4, 2628 CD, Delft, The Netherlands
[2] Department of Industrial Design, Delft University of Technology, Landbergstraat
15, 2628 CE, Delft, The Netherlands
{g.a.tenholt, m.j.t.reinders, e.a.hendriks, h.deridder,
a.j.vandoorn}@tudelft.nl

Abstract. Research on automatic sign language recognition (ASLR) has mostly been conducted from a machine learning perspective. We propose to implement results from human sign recognition studies in ASLR. In a previous study it was found that handshape is important for human sign recognition. The current paper describes the implementation of this conclusion: using handshape in ASLR. Handshape information in three different representations is added to an existing ASLR system. The results show that recognition improves, except for one representation. This refutes the idea that extra (handshape) information will always improve recognition. Results also vary per sign: some sign classifiers improve greatly, others are unaffected, and rare cases even show decreased performance. Adapting classifiers to specific sign types could be the key for future ASLR.

Keywords: sign language, automatic sign language recognition, handshape representation.

1 Introduction

With imaging hardware such as cameras becoming cheaper and more advanced, the interest in ambient intelligence and natural, multi-modal (i.e. speech and gesture) interfaces has grown over the last decade. As a consequence, the study of automatic sign and gesture recognition has been gaining attention steadily. Sign language signs (in their citation form) are more formal and more striclty defined than general gestures (e.g. co-speech or emblematic gestures). As such, recognition of (isolated) sign language signs is often used as a starting point for general gesture recognition methods, but it has a merit of its own, too: automatic sign language recognition techniques can facilitate communication among the deaf, and also between deaf and hearing people.

Automatic sign language recognition (ASLR) has been studied since the early 1990s — see [1] for an overview of ASLR methods, and [2] for an impression of

S. Kopp and I. Wachsmuth (Eds.): GW 2009, LNAI 5934, pp. 301–312, 2010.

the current state of the art. Focus has mostly been on methods for capturing a sign, on the choice of feature representation of a sign and on the pattern recognition algorithms to recognize or detect a sign. Derpanis et al. [3] and Vogler and Metaxas [4] are among the few who try to use sign linguistic information in their ASLR approaches. In general, little attention has been paid to the nature of signs and sign processing: issues such as "What are the important characteristics of a sign?", "Are all parts of a sign equally informative?" and "How much and what kind of variation is allowed in a sign?".

In previous work, we addressed such questions, performing recognition experiments with human signers to gain insight into the human sign recognition process [5,6]. In [7], it was discussed how the results of these studies could be applied in automatic sign language recognition. One of the conclusions was that handshapes, even in a simplified form, may be helpful for automatic sign language recognition. Because of the environment our recognition system is used in, a program for training sign language vocabulary, it is aimed specifically at recognition of isolated, citation-form signs. We therefore do not address issues of continuous sign language recognition here.

This paper describes the results of an experimental study on the implications of adding simplified handshape information to an existing ASLR system. Though handshape is an integral part of a sign language sign, our ASLR system can function reasonably well without it [8]. For this reason, we do not adopt prior assumptions about the merits of adding handshape for this system. During the study, it was noticed that results can vary substantially depending on which subdivision of the data is made to form training– and test sets. Therefore, the experiments described here were performed with several different subdivisions of the dataset and results were evaluated together. It was found that handshape information can improve recognition performance, but that results depend on the handshape representation that is used. A second interesting finding is that individual sign classifiers respond differently to the addition of handshape. Most improve, but for some, performance stays the same or even deteriorates. This concurs with the results from experiments with human signers [5], in which handshape information gave varying degrees of improvement depending on the nature of the sign tested (although here there were no cases of worsening performance). In fact, all human signer experiments showed that results vary for individual signs. This suggests that one probably should not try to develop one standard for all possible signs. Instead, the future of ASLR may lie in adapting criteria and/or methods for specific signs or sign types.

2   Method

2.1   Dataset

The dataset for training and testing consisted of 91 isolated signs from the standard lexicon of Sign Language of the Netherlands[1]. Each sign was recorded from 75 different persons (mostly non-signers). Signs were captured using two synchronized Allied Vision Technologies 'Guppy' cameras, at 25 frames per second, resolution 640 x 480 pixels. Examples of the signs in the dataset can be viewed online[2].

2.2   Sign Recognition Algorithm

For this experiment, the ASLR method described in [8,9] was used. An overview of its architecture is shown in figure 1. Stereo cameras are used to capture the sign. A skin colour model is then applied to the images, so that head and hands can be found and tracked. From the hand location in the stereo images, the 3D hand positions can be calculated, as well as several other characteristics, such as velocity, acceleration, and direction of motion (see [9] for the complete list). These feature types are extracted for each frame in a sign recording, resulting in a [*number of frames* x *number of feature types*] matrix, which is the feature representation of a sign recording (in figure 6, examples of such matrices can be seen). Each combination of feature type and frame is henceforth considered one feature. The feature values are smoothed in the time dimension using a 3-frame median filter (for outlier removal), followed by an 11-frame Gaussian filter (for further smoothing). Dynamic time warping is used to align sign examples.

With the feature representations, classifiers can be trained. For each sign in the set, a separate classifier is trained to distinguish that sign from all other signs. Examples from the target class are used as target training examples, examples of all the other classes are taken together as one large non-target class. For training, the Combined Discriminative Feature Detectors (CDFD) method is used (see [8] for details). In short, training consists of a feature selection step (based on a feature's usefulness in separating the target class from the non-target class), followed by a training of feature detectors for the selected features. Unknown signs are recognized by first applying the feature detectors of the selected features, and then combining their outputs to determine if the sign is recognized or not. The sign is recognized if a certain fraction of the selected feature detectors gives a positive response. This fraction is determined in the training phase. The sensitivity of the feature detectors can be varied to create stricter or more lenient versions of the classifiers.

Fig. 1. Overview of the ASLR system. Information from two cameras is combined to retrieve 3D position. A skin colour model is used to locate the head and hands in the frame. In the feature extraction step, certain characteristics of the hands are extracted, such as position and velocity. Signs are synchronized through dynamic time warping. Finally, a classifier is built for each sign in the dataset, distinguishing that sign from all others.

2.3   Handshape Representation

The system described in [9] was trained without the use of handshape information. To add handshape information, first a representation must be chosen.
There are several possible representations of handshape [11]. Because our system
is required to work real time, the method must be fast. In combination with the
fact that the dataset contains no zoom images of the hands, this means that
fitting detailed 3D hand models is not an option. Speed and robustness considerations caused us to select a relatively simple but efficient shape representation.
This representation is formed by taking the bounding box of a hand in a certain frame from the image (the bounding box is always aligned with the main
axes of the frame), segmenting the subimage into hand and non-hand pixels,
dividing the subimage into a fixed number of squares, and calculating the ratio
hand/non-hand pixels for each square (see figure 2 (a)). Together, these ratios
form a feature representation of the handshape, which is translation and scale
invariant, but not rotation invariant. This means that the representation carries
some information about hand orientation as well as shape (the same handshape
under a different orientation results in a different feature description). The number of squares used in the method can be varied. We chose a 4 x 4 grid (R44),
resulting in 16 values for each hand, so 32 extra feature types in total.

For comparison, two alternative methods are tried as well: a more crude version of the above one in which a 2 x 2 grid is used (R22), and the invariant
moments of the hand blob (INV), a representation which is translation, scale
and rotation invariant [10]. For the latter, the first seven moments are taken for

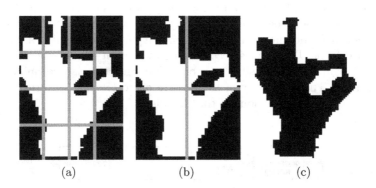

(a)   (b)   (c)

Fig. 2. Procedures for generating handshape representations. (a) Ratios of 4 x 4 grid
(R44). The bounding box of the hand is lifted from the frame and divided into
subregions. The image is then segmented with the skin color model, and the ratio
skin/background is calculated for each subregion. Together, the ratios form the shape
representation of the hand. (b) Ratios of 2 x 2 grid (R22). Same method as for (a).
The third representation (INV) is made by taking the first seven invariant moments
[10] of the raw hand blob shown in (c).

each hand. These representations result in 8 resp. 14 extra feature types in total. Figure 2 (b) and (c) refer to the alternative representations.

2.4   Missing Values

Signs where the hands overlap with each other or with the face form a problem for the handshape representation, because the skin segmentation results in a merged blob, the shape of which is not necessarily informative or representative for the shape(s) of the hand(s) involved. It was decided to extract no handshape features in these cases. As a result, the dataset is no longer complete — some feature representations contain missing values for certain handshape features. If the features were missing for only a few frames (maximally 5), the values were interpolated using a Gaussian filter in the time dimension (integrated into the filtering step). If feature values were missing for only a few examples in the dataset (maximally 10%), average values (calculated over the other examples) were imputed.

Remaining missing values in the dataset are handled as follows: if missing values remain for a feature in examples of the target class of a classifier (e.g. in the examples of the sign 'SAW' when training the classifier for 'SAW'), then this feature is rejected in the feature selection stage. Missing values in examples of the non-target class are ignored. During testing, missing values are ignored: the fraction of detected features is calculated over the existing features only.

2.5   Evaluation Method

To investigate the effects of handshape information, classifiers are trained and tested on the dataset with and without handshape features added, and the results are compared. Each classifier is trained and tested according to a five-fold cross-validation scheme. The cross-validation is repeated 10 times for different random orderings of the data. For each repetition and each cross-validation fold, four versions of the classifiers (with the three handshape representations and without handshape features) are trained and tested.

3   Results

3.1   Recognition Results

The results of the classifiers are shown as Receiver Operating Characteristic (ROC) curves (plots of the true positive rate of a classifier against the false positive rate, for a number of strictness settings). Figure 3 shows the average ROC curves over all signs, cross-validation folds and –repetitions for the original classifiers (No HS) and the three classifiers that result from training with various handshape representations. R44 produces the best curve, and R22 gives improvement as well. Adding INV representations actually worsens classification performance. To investigate whether this trend is significant, a one-way, repeated measures ANOVA was performed on the areas under the curve (AUCs)

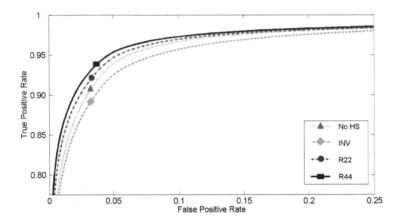

Fig. 3. Average ROC of recognition results for all four conditions over all signs, cross-validation folds and cross-validation repetitions ($N = 4550$). No HS = no handshape representation, INV = invariant moments, R22 = ratios of 2 x 2 grid, R44 = ratios of 4 x 4 grid.

of the ROCs of all classifiers, cross-validation folds and –repetitions. There was a significant effect for handshape representation ($F_{3,13647} = 546.20, p < 0.0001$). Post hoc tests, using the Bonferroni correction for multiple comparisons, showed that the four methods all differed significantly from each other (all $p < 0.0001$), with R44 giving the best performance, followed by R22, No HS, and INV — the last handshape representation made performance significantly worse. The explanation may be that the INV representation is more sensitive to noise than the other two: small changes in the skin segmentation can cause differences in the details of the hand blob shape, and thus in the higher-order shape moments. The ratio-representations are more robust against this type of noise, since the variation averages out over a subregion.

The same tests were performed for partial AUCs (AUCs for the false positive (FP) range $[0 – 0.1]$ of the ROC). The partial AUC (pAUC) is interesting because the operating point chosen for a classifier will most often lie in this range — a classifier with an FP rate of more than 10% is generally not acceptable in practice. The results for pAUCs were similar to the results for AUCs ($F_{3,13647} = 859.57, p < 0.0001$, all pairwise comparisons significant at the 99.99% level).

3.2   Individual Signs

Experiments with human signers showed that there are usually great differences between results for individual signs. In this ASLR experiment, the same effect occurs. First of all, the ROCs of individual signs can differ substantially (see figure 4). This is to be expected — the characteristics of some signs will make them more easily recognizable than others. However, there are also differences in the effects of adding handshape information. With addition of R44 features,

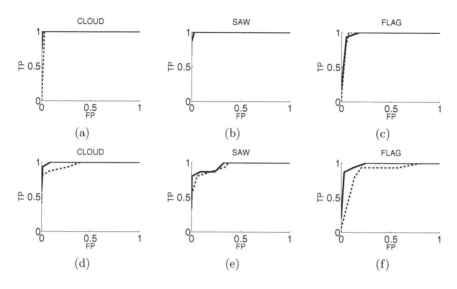

Fig. 4. ROCs for No HS (dashed) and R44 (solid), for different signs and cross-validation folds. Within each column, the difference between versions of the same sign when trained and tested with a different subdivision of the data can be seen. Within each row, differences between individual signs can be observed. (b) and (c) show cases where handshape information is not helpful.

most signs (75%) improve, but for some signs performance does not change, and for a few, there is even a decrease in performance. Paired t-tests per sign (using cross-validation folds as repetitions) were performed to investigate which sign classifiers benefit from the addition of R44 handshape information. Two measurements were used: the AUC and the partial AUC.

Table 1 summarizes the findings. For the more interesting partial AUC only one sign shows a decrease in performance. This sign, BIRD, is made by flapping the arms and hands, which will cause a lot of variation in the precise handshapes and -orientations. This, combined with the fact that the number of repetitive 'flaps' is arbitrary, makes the handshape characteristics of the sign quite variable, and thus possibly confusing rather than informative. For twenty-two signs, there is no significant difference. This is partially due to a ceiling effect: four signs already show near-perfect recognition without handshape. Another cause are the missing values: for three signs, the hands overlap for almost the entire duration of the sign, so that nearly all handshape features are missing for all examples. In these cases, it is logical that handshape information has no influence. The rest were often signs which, like BIRD, contained a lot of handshape variation, or signs with fist-like handshapes. Figure 5 shows the average partial AUC for all signs both with and without R44.

Table 1. Classification performance per sign after adding handshape information in representation R44. Significant increase or decrease in performance was determined through paired t-tests per sign over all cross-validation folds and –repetitions, $\alpha = 0.05, df = 49$.

Measurement	# Increase	# No Difference	# Decrease
AUC	69 (76%)	19 (21%)	3 (3%)
partial AUC [0 - 0.1]	68 (75%)	22 (24%)	1 (1%)

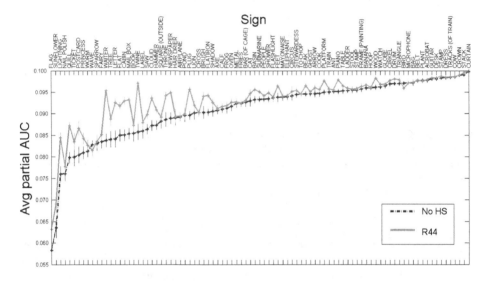

Fig. 5. Average partial AUCs (FP range [0 – 0.1]) of all signs with and without R44. Averages are taken over all cross-validation folds and –repetitions. The error bars represent the standard error of the mean.

3.3   Feature Selection

Feature selection plays an important role in the CDFD-classifier. Features that are not selected will not have any influence on classification. Since features are selected based on their ability to separate the target class from other movements, studying the feature selection can tell us more about which handshapes are informative for ASLR. Figure 6 shows the feature selections for a few classifiers trained with R44. The selections are averaged over all cross-validation folds and –repetitions (for each cross-validation fold, a different classifier with a different feature selection is trained). The gray level of a feature indicates how often it was selected, with white representing selection always. For classifier BIRD, the sign that drops in performance when R44 features are added, handshape features *are* selected. Apparently, these features appear informative during training, but prove confusing for the test examples (an indication that our feature

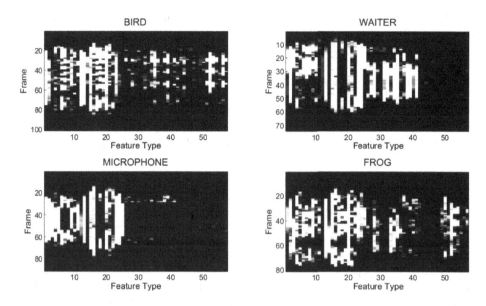

Fig. 6. Average feature selections for four signs over all cross-validation folds and – repetitions for signs with R44. Grey level indicates how often a feature was selected (white = always). Feature types 1–25 are the original, non-handshape feature types, types 26–41 are R44 of the right hand, 42–57 are R44 of the left hand. BIRD and FROG are two-handed signs, WAITER and MICROPHONE are one-handed.

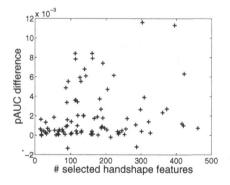

Fig. 7. Scatterplot of the average number of selected R44 handshape features versus the average increase in partial AUC (averages calculated per sign)

selection method might be improved). For classifier WAITER, many features are selected, and this classifier shows a clear increase in performance. Classifier MICROPHONE is an example of what happens when almost all handshape features are missing (in MICROPHONE, the hand is in front of the mouth, so there is facial overlap for almost the entire sign). FROG, finally, is an example of a classifier for which the feature selection varies (like for BIRD), but for which it has no significant effect on the recognition performance.

To investigate the influence of handshape feature selection (R44) on performance, the average increase in pAUC and the average number of selected handshape features were calculated for each sign. Then the linear correlation between the two was calculated. There is a slight positive correlation, which is not significant for $\alpha = 0.01$ ($\rho = 0.21, p = 0.023$). Figure 7 shows the scatterplot of the two variables. It mostly shows that when handshape features are selected, they are generally not harmful, though exceptions (such as BIRD) exist.

4   Discussion

4.1   The Merits of Adding Handshape

From the results of this experiment, it is clear that adding handshape information is in general beneficial for ASLR. However, this is not automatically true for every handshape representation. For the classification method described here, using invariant moments of the handshape blob decreased performance, probably because of its greater sensitivity to noise in combination with the low resolution of the handshape images. The more robust R22 and R44 representations did increase recognition performance. A second explanation for their success may be the fact that the ratio-representations intrinsically carry some hand orientation information as well as shape information, because they are sensitive to rotation. The INV representation is rotation invariant, which may be a disadvantage in the current situation: the orientation of the hand can be useful information for detecting a sign. But rotation sensitivity can be a disadvantage, too. Signs that show no increase or even a decrease in performance with R44 information added, are in many cases signs with much translational and rotational hand movement combined (such as BIRD or ELEPHANT). For these signs, individual examples will differ in the rotation of the handshape at different moments in the sign (because individual signers perform the combinations of translational and rotational movements in different tempos). A rotation-invariant representation would not reflect these variations (as long as the rotations were not out-of-plane). The ratio-representations, on the other hand, may reflect so much of this noisiness that the information is no longer useful for classification, or even becomes confusing.

It is not possible to give characteristics that clearly connect the signs that did not benefit from handshape information. The analysis is made difficult because there are three possible causes: a ceiling effect (the classifier can hardly improve any more), a missing values problem (there are hardly any handshape features present), or the sign is truly 'handshape-indifferent'. Removing the first two categories leaves only about fifteen signs which do not improve. These tend to contain the large variability in handshape and orientation mentioned above, or to have fist-like handshapes, which occur commonly and thus may not be helpful in distinguishing signs. However, the set is too small to test the significance of said tendencies. The set of signs that does benefit from handshape information contains all kinds of shapes, including fists, but no signs with great variability in path and orientation (like the ones mentioned above). The results demonstrate that variability in performance between individual signs occurs in ASLR as well as in human signer experiments. Future work should consider adapting recognition algorithms for individual signs, or perhaps for sign types or handshape types.

4.2 Applying Human Recognition Insights to Machine Recognition

This study was set up to implement our previous findings from human sign recognition research [7] in ASLR. Direct comparison between the results here and the outcome of our human signer experiments is not possible, because different sign sets had to be used. However, certain tendencies can be compared. Firstly, in [5], humans could only recognize a few signs based on location and motion alone. In ASLR, quite reasonable performance can be achieved under these conditions (see figure 3, 'No HS', which is basically the same condition). Of course, human beings are not used to seeing signs that way, whereas an automatic algorithm is trained to perform under certain circumstances. Secondly, in [6], it was demonstrated that the first and last part of a sign (in time) are not necessary for recognition; the central ('stroke') part suffices. The ASLR algorithm also disregards the start and end of a sign. The feature selection graphs show that selected features always come from the stroke part of the signs (see figure 6). So there are both differences and similarities between human and automatic recognition.

An important difference between human and automatic sign processing is the following: in experiments with human signers, more information never caused a deterioration in performance. But the performance of an ASLR algorithm can drop when information is added: when the INV handshape representation was used, performance of our CDFD classifiers decreased. An ASLR algorithm has the capability to find information in any feature that it is provided with. This capability probably allows it to perform so much better than human signers in recognizing signs based on location and motion alone. But the downside becomes clear when a noisy or uninformative feature is present. Even with the precaution of feature selection, meant to weed out uninformative features, the system can still over-train (try to train on noise), causing a deterioration of performance.

In conclusion, we can say that it is possible to apply results from human signer studies in ASLR — adding simplified handshape information proved beneficial for ASLR, as predicted. But the problem described above shows that such applications must be considered carefully.

Notes

[1] Standaard Lexicon Nederlandse Gebarentaal, deel 1. Stichting Nederlandse Gebarencentrum, 2002.

[2] *http://research.tenholt.nl/GW09*

Acknowledgments

This research was partly funded by the VSB-fund; grant number 2003451: project ELo, and the ICT Delft Research Center of Delft University of Technology.

References

1. Ong, S.C., Ranganath, S.: Automatic sign language analysis: A survey and the future beyond lexical meaning. IEEE Transactions on Pattern Analysis and Machine Intelligence 27(6), 873–891 (2005)
2. von Agris, U., Zieren, J., Canzler, U., Bauer, B., Kraiss, K.F.: Recent developments in visual sign language recognition. Univers. Access Inf. Soc. 6(4), 323–362 (2008)
3. Derpanis, K.G., Wildes, R.P., Tsotsos, J.K.: Hand gesture recognition within a linguistics-based framework. In: Pajdla, T., Matas, J(G.) (eds.) ECCV 2004. LNCS, vol. 3021, pp. 282–296. Springer, Heidelberg (2004)
4. Vogler, C., Metaxas, D.: Handshapes and movements: Multiple-channel american sign language recognition. In: Camurri, A., Volpe, G. (eds.) GW 2003. LNCS (LNAI), vol. 2915, pp. 247–258. Springer, Heidelberg (2004)
5. ten Holt, G.A., van Doorn, A.J., de Ridder, H., Reinders, M.J.T., Hendriks, E.A.: Signs in which handshape and hand orientation are either not visible or are only partially visible: What is the consequence for lexical recognition? Sign Language Studies 10(1) (2009)
6. ten Holt, G.A., van Doorn, A.J., de Ridder, H., Reinders, M.J., Hendriks, E.A.: Which fragments of a sign enable its recognition? Sign Language Studies 9(2), 211–239 (2009)
7. ten Holt, G.A., Arendsen, J., de Ridder, H., van Doorn, A.J., Reinders, M.J., Hendriks, E.A.: Sign language perception research for improving automatic sign and gesture recognition. In: SPIE Human Vision and Electronic Imaging XIV, vol. 7240. SPIE, Bellingham (2009)
8. Lichtenauer, J.F., Hendriks, E.A., Reinders, M.J.: Sign language recognition by combining statistical dtw and independent classification. IEEE Transactions on Pattern Analysis and Machine Intelligence 30(11), 2040–2046 (2008)
9. Lichtenauer, J.F., ten Holt, G.A., Reinders, M.J.T., Hendriks, E.A.: Person-independent 3d sign language recognition. In: Sales Dias, M., Gibet, S., Wanderley, M.M., Bastos, R. (eds.) GW 2007. LNCS (LNAI), vol. 5085, pp. 69–80. Springer, Heidelberg (2009)
10. Hu, M.K.: Visual pattern recognition by moment invariants. IRE Transactions on Information Theory 8(2), 179–187 (1962)
11. Caridakis, G., Diamanti, O., Karpouzis, K., Maragos, P.: Automatix sign language recognition: vision based feature extraction and probabilistic recognition scheme from multiple cues. In: Proceedings of ACM PETRA (2008)

Towards Interactive Web-Based Virtual Signers: First Step, a Platform for Experimentation Design

Jean-Paul Sansonnet, Annelies Braffort, and Cyril Verrecchia

LIMSI-CNRS, BP 133, F-91403 Orsay cedex, France
{firstname.lastname}@limsi.fr

Abstract. In this paper, we present a Web-based framework for interactive Sign Language using virtual signing agents. The main feature of this framework is that it is a full DOM-Integrated architecture. Firstly, we discuss the advantages and the constraints raised by the implementation of proper interactive Virtual Signers within this full DOM-integrated approach. Secondly, we discuss an experimental study about Web-based Virtual Signers that take advantage of the specific interactivity provided by our framework. This study deals with a structure of Sign Language utterances that requires dynamic handling of spatio-temporal variability and coarticulation stances in the sign generation phase.

Keywords: Web-based Virtual Signers, Sign Language dynamic generation, Sign variability, Coarticulation.

1 Introduction

Whereas animated virtual characters are proliferating on the Internet Web pages, they raise issues in terms of 1) web-oriented software architecture, 2) specification and coordination of the interactional modalities (e.g. textual interaction, gestural integration) and 3) handling the linguistic characteristics of the various groups of potential users, for example those giving preference to the usage of a Sign Language (SL) —like for example French Sign Language (LSF)— instead of oral language expressed either in vocal or written form. Virtual characters used to support Sign Language are commonly called Signing Avatars or Virtual Signers [1], the term 'signer' meaning "a person expressing, using Sign Language". There is no specific term for the Web environment mainly because there is no support for SL-based dialogical interaction now. Indeed, there is no written form for SL and SL inputs on a computer are limited to the use of Webcams (for the support of SL-chat between people of the deaf community); there is no actual solution to day for the recognition and the interpretation of real natural SL utterances.

The development of Virtual Signers on the Internet will be of main interest for the deaf community to improve the access to page content but also for the fast growing community of ordinary people that seek basic knowledge about Sign Language or want to learn it. In order to guarantee the best possible acceptability of Virtual Signers productions in the deaf community we need to focus especially on the issue of the

S. Kopp and I. Wachsmuth (Eds.): GW 2009, LNAI 5934, pp. 313–324, 2010.

precise modeling of SL inner functioning [2]. However, we have also to take into account the specific constraints imposed by the Web environment which, as showed further, can lead to some simplifications in the modeling. Then the problem is to evaluate and to assess to what extent the deployment of efficient and acceptable Virtual Signers on the Web is conceivable.

This paper is organized in three parts: next section is a presentation of the main families of Virtual Signers with a discussion of the limitations of current systems. Section 3 is dedicated to the description of the architecture of the underlying Web-oriented framework for virtual characters, called DIVA. Then, in section 4, we present an experimental study, carried out on this framework, dealing with a simplified model of two significant phenomena occurring in the dynamic generation of SL utterances: sign variability and coarticulation.

2 Virtual Signers on the Web

Sign languages, that is visuo-gestural languages as they are utilized within deaf communities can take into account all the functions fulfilled by Natural Languages. They enable people to communicate through a visual input channel and a gestural output channel. Hence they facilitate the emission of simultaneous information while using various articulators[1] (hands, arms, shoulders, torso, head, face, eyes). Similarly, the way the discourse is organized is related to the visual perceptive capacities. For example, movement and relevant utilization of the space in front of the signer (the *speaker* in SL), hence named "signing space" are intensively used in Sign Language [3]. Finally, Sign Languages also resort to iconicity both in the lexicon and in SL utterances, thanks to their unique capacity of "telling without showing" but also of "telling by showing" [4].

Up to day, most Web sites that integrate support for SL rely on videos [5]. Few studies have been carried out upon the deployment of Virtual Signers on the Web and most of them are in fact autonomous applications attached, not integrated, to the Web pages. The technique of animation for Virtual Signers is based upon two main approaches:

- *Pre-synthesized animations*: animations are synthesized *a priori* and then selected according to the context. For example, *motion capture* can be applied on non realistic simple avatars, such as the one in Fig. 1a, used in Mathsigner (see Fig. 1b), an interactive learning tool to improve the mathematical abilities of deaf children [6]. Since a few years, this technique has been introduced in order to build libraries of SL signs that in turn can be used to generate SL utterances [7]. Another pre-synthesized technique, *rotoscoping*, has been introduced successfully for the production of complete stories, such as the movie "the forest" illustrated in Fig. 1c [8].
- *Generated animations*: it consists in automatic and real-time generation of the animations. This is achieved from symbolic description languages of the animations. For example, the SigML description language [9] is based on the HamNoSys phonetic system dedicated to SL [10]. Used as input in a given signing animation

---

[1] *Articulator*: any mobile part of the human body that can be articulated voluntarily and is functional in the process of producing speech (vocal or signed).

software, it allows the generation of animations that provide a better flexibility but at the cost of *realism and naturalness*. For example, a Web application using Java applets [11] is based on this technique. Moreover the VRML format is sometimes used thus allowing some kind of limited interactivity within a Web page, as for example the Signing Science dictionary [12] (see Fig. 1d).

Discussion about the Chosen Approach: Generated animation approaches are in current progress. Presently, they cannot provide the realism and the naturalness required for deaf people acceptability and recognition of the signs. This was our main reason for choosing the pre-synthesized approach for this particular study; however, in future work, we intend to rely on generated animation approaches. Then we had to decide between motion picture and rotoscoping: the first approach is a heavy technology, requiring a post processing phase when fine animation is needed; on the contrary, rotoscoping requires less equipment (only a video recording of human subjects with two cameras face/profile and a software like 3DSmax™). However the main drawback of rotoscoping is that it relies on the artistic talent of the graphic designers in charge of the transformation of the videos into animated sequences.

Discussion about the Limited Interactivity of Existing Applications: In all the above mentioned applications, being Web-based or not, the Virtual Signer is encased into a frame (a sub window) and its interaction with the content of the Web page is minimalistic: it is often restricted to Graphical User Interface (GUI) control on the display mode (frame moving or rotating, character resizing, control of animation speed); the character cannot perform actions upon the entities of the Web page application or react dynamically to user's operations (even in the case of Fig. 1d).

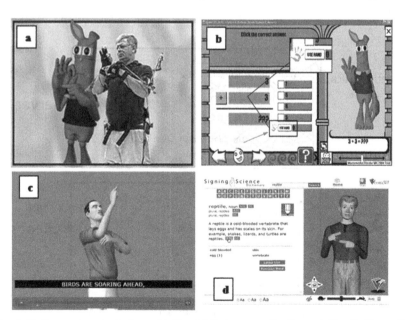

Fig. 1. a) Motion-capture technique; b) The Mathsigner application; c) The J. Stewart's 3D movie "The Forest"; d) The Web page of the Signing Science dictionary

In the next section, we present the general outline of the architecture of the web-based framework that we have chosen as a support for the deployment of the Virtual Signers with enhanced interactivity capabilities.

3 Architecture of the DIVA Framework

In the context of the research on Embodied Conversational Agents (ECA) [14, 15, 16, 17] at LIMSI-CNRS, we have developed a Web-oriented software framework, called DIVA [13]. DIVA stands for DOM Integrated Virtual Agents, emphasizing the unique feature of DIVA virtual agents that are completely integrated with the DOM (Document Object Model) tree structure of web pages. The DOM is a standard interface, independent from any language and platform which allows programs and scripts to dynamically access both in read or modify modes the content, the structure and the style of HTML or XML-based documents.

3.1 Web Architecture

The web architecture of DIVA is displayed in Fig. 2. It has two main layers:

1. A server layer dedicated to data base resources and symbolic computing (using the Wolfram Mathematica technology);
2. A rich-client layer supporting: the specific application/service web page; the animation of the graphic characters; the processing of the textual natural language interaction.

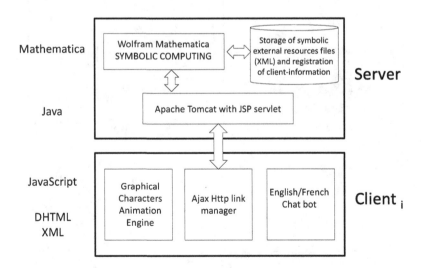

Fig. 2. Web architecture of the DIVA framework

3.2 Structure of a Virtual Character

The first objective of DIVA is to provide a high degree of interaction with the DOM-structure and the informational content of the Web page. Therefore, DIVA characters are part of the DOM structure that contains several DOM objects (mainly of type <div>) supporting various capabilities: display, drag&drop, resizing, iconifying, animation, speech display in textual 'balloons', etc. (see Fig. 3.).

Fig. 3. DOM structure of a virtual character

The animation engine also takes advantage of this integration: it is a JavaScript program that directly loads .png files from the server in <div> objects and then animates them, at the frame level on the client machine. This makes it possible to compute animations movies and to compose them in JavaScript *locally*. This feature proves to be crucial in the dynamic production of Virtual Signers utterances.

In a first version of the framework, four characters with a simple graphic 'cartoon' style were proposed (they had been originally created for experimental studies about the evaluation of ECA [18] — see 'Marco' in Fig. 3.-right). Presently, we are building realistic characters (see Fig. 3.-left) designed with rotoscoping on 3DSmax™. The resulting personification is much more realistic but at the price of a slower loading time for the client Web pages because they require larger picture files than simple cartoon characters (×10). Indeed, in a Web-based architecture, such performance issues are very frequent and they have a significant impact on the resulting software architecture; however mainly practical, these issues represent de facto technological barriers. Hence, the trade-off graphic-quality/page-loading-time remains a serious barrier for the deployment of virtual characters on the Web.

For the creation of the animations the rotoscoping was chosen because it provides a good trade-off between the time needed to produce the animations and the quality of the realistic rendering. This technique, when performed by accomplished computer graphics designers, allows the quick production of predefined animations that can be associated with SL utterances, SL signs, gestures etc.

For the creation of the animation picture files, we had to take into account the Web bandwidth constraints stated above. Thus we have to take into account both the pixel size of the frames and the number of frames for one animation. Presently, the animations' movies are composed of 6, 15 or 30 frames in 500×500 pixels in .png format (.png provides the required transparency for the avatars to move freely over the Web page). As for the animation of the characters on screen, although it is supported by a rich-client engine written in JavaScript, the animations are quite fluid, especially with Mozilla based navigators and this is bound to improve with the new generation of navigators integrating JavaScript accelerators (like Google Chrome).

A major decision was to develop an animation engine working at the frame level. As a consequence it is possible to control the animations at a very fine level. This makes it possible to dynamically generate SL utterances and to 'play' them in real time. This capability is a basic requirement for efficient interactivity between the user and the character on the Web page.

3.3 Handling Deictics

The DIVA framework provides a native support to deictic gestures within the Web page: given a target DOM object T of the application that is displayed on screen the framework can compute its physical location on screen $T_{x,y}$ (e.g. being either the top-left corner or the middle of the object display) and report them to the agent A which, according to its own physical position $A_{x,y}$ can perform the following actions:

- Move on screen, if necessary, to go nearer the target object position $T_{x,y}$;
- Perform a deictic gesture with its finger pointing on $T_{x,y}$. There are six postures corresponding to the six possible relative A/T positions. They involve the orientation of the head, of the torso and the configurations of the arm and hand[2] (see Fig. 4 left).

An example of the support of the deictics in DIVA is available on the Web page of the LIMSI-CNRS[3]. Whenever the user clicks on a balloon of the graphics that represent the scientific activities of the laboratory, the agent Elsi performs a tri modal reaction: 1) Elsi moves nearer the clicked target; 1) Elsi displays above her head a textual balloon giving a short explanation of the clicked activity and 2) in the same time, Elsi performs a pointing gesture with her finger on the middle of the clicked balloon (moreover, the clicked XY position is emphasized with a small red square).

4 Experiment

The objective of the experiment described in this section is to evaluate a method for the dynamic generation of SL utterances and their immediate animation in the context of DIVA based Virtual Signers. Also, several complex issues have to be taken into

---

[2] Other designation techniques are available like: to enlighten a cell in a HTML table, to play an animated gif picture at $T_{x,y}$, to use an arrow pointing at $T_{x,y}$ etc.

[3] LIMSI deictics demo page : http://www.limsi.fr/Individu/jps/online/diva/limsi/index.htm

account when dealing with SL utterances generation. SL functioning is completely different from the functioning of vocal languages. In the signing space, signs can have *variable realizations*, depending on the context [4]. Thus, SL utterance synthesis implies to design specific spatio-temporal grammar rules, different from the ones in use for vocal language generation. Studies on this topic have been conducted for English and German SL [22], American SL [23], and LSF [2]. Spatio-temporal rules, specific of SL, are considered in the three studies, including a representation of signing space more or less accurate, and a set of rules dealing with this representation. Approaches in [2] propose a rich representation including various kind of knowledge, including cognitive ones. Another issue concerns the coarticulation process that influences both manual and non-manual features when a sign is performed in an utterance. This phenomenon is a complex process [19] that has not yet been modeled accurately so far.

In the context of the DIVA platform and its animation engine, we handle the generation of the SL-utterances as follows:

- A SL utterance is built by a concatenation of atomic *signs*.
- Each sign is displayed as a predefined animation, built using rotoscoping, allowing a good realistic rendering.
- For all signs, the realization of which varies regarding to the context (e.g. pointing), we predefine several realizations (e.g. six for pointing; see Fig. 4 left); note that their combinatory is limited because we restrict to context-dependent utterances.
- For the coarticulation sign animations, we use one or more intermediary postures (chosen dynamically, according to the context): typically, hands are in front of the chest for signs (see Fig. 4 middle).
- Lastly, in order to build animations as realistic as possible, each utterance contains prologue and epilogue stances, allowing the virtual signer to begin and to end the utterance in a rest posture (Fig. 4 right), denoted 'rest posture', where the agent fidgets just a little to suggest life.

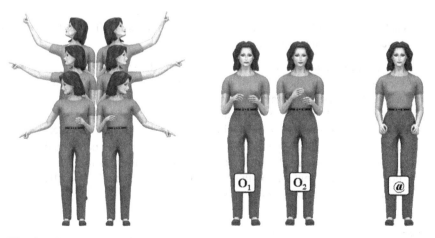

Fig. 4. a) Six pointing realizations; b) Two intermediary postures; c) The rest posture

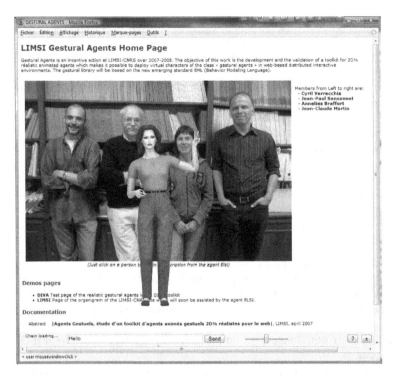

Fig. 5. Experiment page of the dynamic presentation of persons by Virtual Signer Elsi

Fig. 5 presents the Web page supporting the experiment. This experiment is currently available online at the Gestural Agents home page [20]. On this page, users can interrogate agent Elsi (a male agent 'Cyril' is also available — see Fig. 3-left) about a person displayed in the photography in two alternative ways: 1) by clicking on the person; or 2) by typing his/her name in the 'chatbox' at the bottom of the page.

In reaction to one of these user's events, agent Elsi dynamically builds a SL answer which requires four different kinds of signs:

1) One **constant** sign [SIGNNAME] which means the sign-name[4] of a person.
2) One **variable** sign, the value of which depends on the user's request. The SL variable [signname$_i$] contains the actual sign-name of the selected person. From left to right in Fig. 5, it can take four values related to the four persons.
3) Two **variable** signs, the value of which depends on the spatial context:
   - The variable [pointing$_i$] contains the deictic gesture to be performed in order to point to the person selected by the user. Depending on the relative physical position of the agent and on the selected person, it can take six different values (left/right × top/middle/bottom – see fig. 4.a).

---

[4] People of the deaf community are given a sign-name which is a specific gesture denoting the person, often related to a salient physical feature or the official name of the person.

- The variable [possessive$_i$] is associated with the sign denoting the possessive. This sign is quite like a pointing gesture in the direction of "the person who possesses something" but with a finger configuration in 'V' (the screen shot of Elsi in Fig. 5 was taken at the apex of the animation of this sign). Again, depending on the relative physical position of the agent and on the selected person, it can take several values.

Then the SL utterance synthesized for the answer has the following static structure, (its order corresponds to a usual order in LSF):

$$[\text{pointing}_i] - [\text{SIGNNAME}] - [\text{possessive}_i] - [\text{signname}_i]$$

To generate a SL utterance with a natural animation, each SL utterance begins by a rest posture which is shared by all Virtual Signers. During the animation of a SL utterance, signs are performed sequentially without interruption but they start and finish at an intermediary coarticulation posture. Consequently we use two additional constant coarticulation stances:

@ = rest posture: both arms are down, along the body;
o = intermediary posture: both hands are up in front of the torso.

To these two postures, we associate two specific animations, as shown Fig. 6:

[PROLOG] = moves the arms of the character from the @ stance to the o stance;
[EPILOG] = moves back the arms of the character from o to @.

Now the complete structure of a SL utterance U is composed of six animations containing three constant signs and three variables signs:

$$U = [\ @ \ [\text{PROLOG}] \ o$$
$$[\text{pointing}_i] \ o \ [\text{SIGNNAME}] \ o \ [\text{possessive}_i] \ o \ [\text{signname}_i]$$
$$o \ [\text{EPILOG}] \ o \ @ \ ]$$

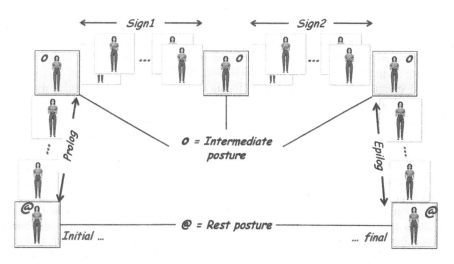

Fig. 6. SL utterance generation, using Rest and Intermediate postures, Prolog and Epilog animations

When the user puts a request to the agent (clicks on a person or puts a textual request in the chatbox) the variables [pointing$_i$], [possessive$_i$] and [signname$_i$] are instantiated in context: computation of the selected person; computation of the relative positions person/agent (note that the position of the photography in Fig. 5 is static but the agent can be positioned anywhere on the screen); the structure of U is filled; then the animation is immediately performed.

In this experiment, only one structure of SL utterance is taken into account. However this structure has been chosen to exhibit space-dependent sign realizations. It is a truly dynamic utterance that cannot be generated beforehand (e.g. with the video recording of human subjects) but has to be synthesized in real time.

In a more general manner, this kind of experiment makes it possible to evaluate how the contextual variability of the signs can be handled and also to evaluate how the coarticulation between the signs is performed. In the near future, our objective is to study the issues introduced by @ and o stances (*acceptability* factor) and their impact on the understanding of the message (*performance* factor). At the moment, we are currently undertaking an experimental evaluation of the acceptability of the produced animations along with the deaf community (this is heavy work, entailing the implementation of an evaluation protocol, the participation of SL interpreters, the recording of video sessions etc.). Following this evaluation we will initiate further research work about 1) a more generic approach to the issue of the automatic computation of various intermediary stances and 2) more general SL structures.

Although simple, this study is an illustration of the originality of our approach and of its technical feasibility (a crucial issue considered the constraints imposed by a Web-based environment). Moreover this study involves two major issues in SL utterances generation (sign variability and coarticulation).

5   Discussion

The current application scenario presented in this paper is very limited but our framework can support a larger class of SL utterances. For example, we have been able to develop another Web-based experiment (called SignTeacher [21] – available at DIVA Web page) where the pedagogical intention is to make the student familiar with some LSF grammatical rules such as the spatio-temporal structure of a sentence involving an indicating verb. In this experiment, the SL-utterances are more complex: they are composed of person names, location names, transport vehicle, transport verbs. The way to express an utterance such as "*Annelies goes from France to Italy by car*" requires three steps: 1) to 'spatialize' the two countries in the signing space, 2) to conjugate the verb in this space, by performing the movement from the departure location to the arrival location, 3) to sort the phrases in the utterance in the following way: building the spatial context (spatialization of [FRANCE] in the signing space, spatialization of [ITALY] in the signing space, person name, transport vehicle) and finally expressing the action (agreement of indicating verb).

However, not all SL utterances can be easily supported by our approach. The first limitation relates to the vocabulary size, which is limited. The generation approach, which is based on pre-synthesized animation, requires the design of several instances for each sign if its realization depends on the context. Thus, only restricted domains with few vocabulary and few sentence structures can be deployed. The second limitation is related to coarticulation aspects. As said before, coarticulation is a complex process on which we are conducting studies in order to formalize the phenomenon (forward and reverse influences across, assimilations, deletions...) [19]. It should be possible to add some automatic process in most cases, but this hypothesis has to be checked. Another issue is related to the synchronization of the various articulators into an utterance. Again, studies must be conducted to evaluate, for example, the temporal shift between gaze and spatialised signs, or the duration of facial expressions in an utterance. In this case, automatic processes should also be designed, still we will have to face the above mentioned vocabulary size limitation.

Moreover, acceptance ratings by deaf users will provide an actual evaluation of the proposed approach. A first informal evaluation provided by deaf colleagues or acquaintances is positive. Recently, we have entered a full scale experimental phase with a group of deaf subjects. This phase is progressing slowly because we have first to set bilingual questionnaires (LSF/French), including a specific one related to the socio-linguistic profile of the subjects, which is of high importance with this population (level of literacy, age of learning of sign language, etc.). The very first results computed from a group of four subjects are positives. Most criticisms are related to the pertinence of the experiment rather than the technology which is well-accepted.

6 Conclusion and Perspectives

In this paper, we have proposed a Web-based architecture for the support of Virtual Signers. In our architecture, Virtual Signers are intimately integrated into the DOM structure of Web-pages. Based on the technical constraints imposed by this framework, we have attempted a particular study about the issue of the generation of SL utterances. A solution has been proposed in order to manage 1) the contextual variability of signs by using a limited set of spatialized 'sign instances' and 2) the coarticulation between the signs of a SL utterance which involves intermediary postures.

This is a first step to the implementation of a Web application dedicated to the actual evaluation of both acceptability and performance of understanding among the deaf community. If proved successful, we hope to extend this approach and to deploy it in the Internet with more complex applications.

References

1. Losson, O., Cantegrit, B.: An assistive interface for learning lexical corpus employing a virtual signer. Technology and Accessibility 13(2), 83–94 (2000)
2. Braffort, A., Dalle, P.: Sign language applications: preliminary modeling. International journal "Universal Access in the Information Society" (UAIS), Special issue 6/4 "Emerging Technologies for Deaf Accessibility in the Information Society". Springer, Heidelberg (2007)
3. Liddell, S.: Grammar, gesture and meaning in American Sign Language. Cambridge University Press, Cambridge (2003)
4. Cuxac, C.: La Langue des Signes Française (LSF): les voies de l'iconicité. Faits de langues 15-16, Ophrys (2000)
5. ScienceSign URL, the online BSL/English glossary for science education, http://www.sciencesigns.ac.uk

6. Adamo-Villani, N., Benes, B., Brisbin, M.: A natural interface for sign language mathematics. In: Bebis, G., Boyle, R., Parvin, B., Koracin, D., Remagnino, P., Nefian, A., Meenakshisundaram, G., Pascucci, V., Zara, J., Molineros, J., Theisel, H., Malzbender, T. (eds.) ISVC 2006. LNCS, vol. 4291, pp. 70–79. Springer, Heidelberg (2006)
7. Heloir, A., Gibet, S., Multon, F., Courty, N.: Captured Motion Data Processing for Real Time Synthesis of Sign Language. In: Gibet, S., Courty, N., Kamp, J.-F. (eds.) GW 2005. LNCS (LNAI), vol. 3881, pp. 168–171. Springer, Heidelberg (2006)
8. VCom3D, http://www.vcom3d.com/vault_files/forest_asl/
9. Elliott, R., Glauert, J., Jennings, V., Kennaway, J.R.: An Overview of the SiGML Notation and SiGML Signing Software System. In: Fourth International Conference on Language Resources and Evaluation, LREC 2004, pp. 98–104 (2004)
10. Prillwitz, S., Leven, R., Zienert, H., Hanke, T., Henning, J., et al.: Hamburg notation system for sign languages: An introductory guide, Institute of German Sign Language and Communication of the Deaf, University of Hamburg. International Studies on Sign Language and the Communication of the Deaf, vol. 5 (1989)
11. Avatar Signing Dictionary: Scottish BSL, http://www2.cmp.uea.ac.uk/~jrwg/Dictionary094/
12. Signing Science Dictionary (SSD), http://signsci.terc.edu/
13. Maes, P.: Agents that reduce work and information overload. CACM 37(7), 30–40 (1994)
14. Randall, N., Pedersen, I.: Who exactly is trying to help us? The ethos of help systems in popular computer applications. In: 16th Annual Int. Conf. on Computer Documentation, pp. 63–69. ACM, New York (1998)Sallandre, M.-A.: Les unités du discours en Langue des Signes Française. Tentative de catégorisation dans le cadre d'une grammaire de l'iconicité (Discourse unit in French Sign Language. A try to categorization within the scope of a grammar of iconicity), Doctoral Thesis. University of Paris VIII (2003)Johnson, R.E., Liddell, K.S.: Sign language phonetics: architecture and description (in preparation)
15. Lester, J., Converse, S., et al.: The Persona Effect: Affective Impact of Animated Pedagogical Agents. In: CHI 1997 (1997)
16. Prendinger, H., Mayer, S., Mori, J., Ishizuka, M.: Persona Effect revisited: Using bio-signals to measure and reflect the impact of character-based interfaces. In: Rist, T., Aylett, R.S., Ballin, D., Rickel, J. (eds.) IVA 2003. LNCS (LNAI), vol. 2792, pp. 283–291. Springer, Heidelberg (2003)
17. Sansonnet, J.-P., Leray, D., Martin, J.-C.: Architecture of a Framework for Generic Assisting Conversational Agents. In: Gratch, J., Young, M., Aylett, R.S., Ballin, D., Olivier, P. (eds.) IVA 2006. LNCS (LNAI), vol. 4133, pp. 145–156. Springer, Heidelberg (2006)
18. Buisine, S., Abrilian, S., Rendu, C., Martin, J.-C.: Towards Experimental Specification and Evaluation of Lifelike Multimodal Behavior. In: Workshop on Embodied Conversational Agents at AAMAS (2002)
19. Segouat, J.: A study of sign language coarticulation. ACM SIGACCESS Accessibility and Computing (93), 31–38 (2009)
20. LIMSI Gestural Agents Home Page, http://www.limsi.fr/Individu/jps/online/diva/geste/geste.main.htm
21. Sansonnet, J.-P., Braffort, A., Segouat, J., Verrecchia, C.: SL Teacher: a Framework for teaching LSF on the Web. In: Second International Conference on ICT and Accessibility (2009)
22. Elliott, R., Glauer, J.R.W., Kennaway, J.R., Marshall, I., Safar, E.: Linguistic modeling and language-processing technologies for Avatar-based sign language presentation. In: Universaal Access in the Information Society, 6/4. Springer, Heidelberg (2008)
23. Huenerfauth, M.: Spatial, Temporal, and Semantic Models for American Sign Language Generation: Implications for Gesture Generation. Int. J. Semantic Computing 2(1), 21–45 (2008)

Toward Modeling Sign Language Coarticulation

Jérémie Segouat[1,2] and Annelies Braffort[1]

[1] LIMSI-CNRS, BP 133,
91400 Orsay, France
[2] WebSourd, Bât A, 99 Route d'Espagne,
31100 Toulouse, France
{Jeremie.Segouat, Annelies.Braffort}@limsi.fr

Abstract. This article presents a study on coarticulation modeling in French Sign Language. Our aim is to use this model to provide information to deaf people, by the mean of a virtual signer. We propose a definition for "coarticulation", based on an overview of the literature. We explain the methodology we have set up: from video corpus design to features correlations extractions, through corpus annotations and analysis. We expose first results and what are going to be the next steps of this study.

Keywords: Sign Language, Coarticulation Modeling, Corpus Design, Corpus Annotation.

1 Introduction

Our team's researches are focused on French Sign Language (LSF) processing, with an interdisciplinary point of view: linguistic and computer scientist. The goal of the study we present is to model the coarticulation phenomenon in LSF, to be used in a national project, which aim is to provide public information in LSF by "coarticulating" synthesized animations of LSF. Our work is in the field of natural language processing, and more specifically in the natural language synthesizing. Our goal is to address deaf people needs: we want to provide information in LSF that will be accepted, meaning understood, by the end users. Therefore we have to design good quality animations and coarticulate them as naturally as possible.

In this article, we present the basis we rely on in order to set up a LSF coarticulation model. To be able to create a model based on the real language, we have to accurately analyze what occurs when LSF is performed. Thus, we first need a video corpus, made with specific rules and containing specific isolated signs and utterances. Then, we have to analyze this corpus with a coarticulation point of view, and run statistics to extract relevant pieces of information. Lastly, we will establish our model thanks to the statistical results, and perform evaluation and validation steps within a display information software.

In section 2, we briefly present what sign language is, and what the constraints of this language for our study are. Then, in section 3, we expose a state of the art of the coarticulation phenomenon, and explain the definition we have chosen. In section 4, we detail our methodology: design of a video corpus, annotation, analysis, and present

S. Kopp and I. Wachsmuth (Eds.): GW 2009, LNAI 5934, pp. 325–336, 2010.

how we first qualitatively draw conclusions. Lastly, we present our very first results and what we intend to do next.

2 Sign Language

LSF is a real natural language, as Vocal Languages (VL) are. We specify we deal with French SL because there are different Sign Languages (SL) in the world. SL differ mainly on lexicon whereas they share many grammar properties [1], [2]. A difference between SL and VL is the modality in use: while vocal languages rely on audio-phonatory modalities, SL rely on visual-gestural ones. Another difference is that SL have their own grammars, which are spatial and temporal [3]. These two specificities of SL, LSF included, are to be taken into account for our study because they have an impact on the coarticulation phenomenon.

In SL, a signer uses manual and non-manual features at the same time. Manual features are hand's features: configuration, orientation, movement, etc. Non-manual features are facial expression, gaze direction, torso movement, etc. All of these features are not always used synchronously, even if they are performed at the same time. Therefore our study on coarticulation must take into account that sometimes both manual and non-manual features could be modified at the same time but not necessarily in the same way, and other times that modifications could be done asynchronously [4].

3 Coarticulation: A State-of-the-Art

Generally speaking, coarticulation in SL is what links a sign to another when used in an utterance. There are several studies in SL synthesis research field that do not take into account the coarticulation in all its complexity: they just concatenate one isolated sign or utterance to another one [5], [6], [7]. As for VL, the resulting complete utterance is not easy to understand, and sometimes it could not be understand at all. Moreover, because SL deals with the use of many features simultaneously, there could be misunderstandings if you don't consider *a minima* the coarticulation phenomenon. There are several reasons that could explain why this phenomenon hasn't been much studied in SL. One reason is that it is a very recent research field, even more for the synthesis subfield. Comparing with studies in VL, we could say that there is a gap of fifty years in research. A second reason is that the linguistic point of view on SL determines if you take into account all the complexity of phenomenon of coarticulation or not: if you consider that SL is only performed by the hands or if you consider the whole upper body, the complexity of the phenomenon is multiplied.

The coarticulation phenomenon has been studied for many years for VL [9], but it is a very new field of research for SL [10]. We have presented how the coarticulation phenomenon is defined in spoken and signed languages both in recognition and in synthesis / generation in [8]. Our choice for a definition of what we consider as "coarticulation" has been made after studying several research fields of knowledge. Signs are most of the time different when they are performed within an utterance as when they are performed isolated. Modifications could be addition, alteration, or deletion, and may occur on one or more manual or non-manual feature. They could take place at the beginning, but also at the end, and inside the sign. All these aspects constitute our definition of what "coarticulation" in SL is.

In literature, both for speech or gesture, there are two main concepts that describe a modification of one given "item" when performed within an utterance compared to its performance isolated: coarticulation and movement epenthesis.

In speech recognition and synthesis research fields, numerous articles about coarticulation effects are available. One relevant piece of information about coarticulation in speech is that, according to [11], there can be up to 6 phonemes before and after one phoneme P that can be influenced and modified because of P. Coarticulation has been defined as an "adjustment of all phoneme instantiations to their current neighbors" in [9]. More recently, coarticulation has been defined as a superficial variation of phonemes when speaking several following phonemes in opposition to isolated phonemes, and includes epenthesis, which was considered as the addition of one or more sounds to a word [12]. Thus, coarticulation implies modification of phonemes, and epenthesis implies addition of phonemes.

In SL recognition, coarticulation is defined in [13] as when a gesture influences another one, in [14] as the changing of signs when they overlap, and more accurately in [15] as when the ending of one sign and the beginning of the following are modified. Epenthesis is defined in [15] as the addition of a movement between two signs. [16] considers that it is a phenomenon that has no semantic meaning, whereas [10] declares that it is a movement that modifies signs and that have to be modeled.

In SL synthesis research field, as far as we know, there is no definition of what coarticulation is, and there are no studies on modeling it.

There are two major phenomena, coarticulation and movement epenthesis, which definitions are quite widespread and accepted in vocal research field; but when applied to SL we can notice that researchers don't agree on the same definition for coarticulation. We intend to study the coarticulation phenomenon in the largest possible point of view, thus we have chosen to keep the most generic definition. Therefore, we name "coarticulation" the modifications that occur between two signs and inside a sign, either it is addition, modification or deletion of features, when these signs are performed in utterances in comparison as when they are performed isolated.

Now we have specified our definition of coarticulation in SL, in the next section we explain the methodology we have set up to study it.

4 Methodology

The methodology we use has been described in detail in [8]. We want our model to be based on real SL, used by deaf people. We do not want to rely on a so-called "signed language" that would be based on syntax from spoken language, resulting in a mix of languages which leads to misunderstandings and false information [17]. Therefore, we rely on filmed sign language utterances and isolated signs from deaf people and analyze these videos in order to design our coarticulation model. We describe below each step we go through: firstly we design and create a video corpus, secondly we annotate it, thirdly we analyze these annotations, and fourthly we set up rules that will be the basis of our model.

4.1 Preliminaries

There are three important points regarding our study and how we present it. First point is here we use written English to detail samples of our corpus, whereas in other studies glosses are used. In both cases (using written English or glosses) it implies that the chunks (pieces of utterance) we present do not fit exactly what is performed in LSF. For example, the chunk "your attention please" is performed in LSF as "pay attention", and sometimes "pay attention, take care"). Second point is that addition or deletion of signs in a complete utterance, if compared to the same utterance created by linking isolated signs or chunks, could happen. This is because signs are very context-dependant. For example, the utterance "stay away from the edge of the platform" could not be split in "stay away" and "the edge of the platform" (for example, signs meaning "stay away" would be totally different in the utterance "stay away from the station"). Moreover there are some parts that, regarding our overall aim to provide LSF in railway station, would not be chunked. For example, the utterance "wait for the train to stop before getting in" does not contain any part that is going to be reused in another utterance, thus we won't split it. Nevertheless, the whole utterance is going to be used in several different complete utterances (for example: "train is under cleaning", "train is moving", etc.). The last point is that we do not intend to provide a coarticulation model for SL that could be use with the whole language in every situation. We focus on one signer, and one language domain (train transportation), because the very first aim of our model is to be used in a specific application, which requires a unique model of a signer for a unique language domain.

4.2 Corpus Creation

We have created a video corpus of LSF according to our final goal: providing information to deaf people, using coarticulated signs and chunks. This implies two major constraints: to be sure to provide the same information the hearing people have, and to provide this information in real SL. For the first constraint, we have had the help of a group of deaf persons who works on LSF linguistics in relation with a linguistic research group. These deaf persons are our LSF linguistic experts: they have decided, using strict criteria, what will be in the corpus, based on the vocal version of the information. For the second constraints, thanks to these experts, we are ensured that our corpus contains grammatically correct SL utterances, and correct SL lexicon. We still need to coarticulate these signs so that deaf people will understand them.

The purpose of our corpus is twofold. First we want to display information by the mean of a virtual signer. The technique of rotoscoping is used to make the 3D animations based on videos. That has been explained in [18], and we won't address this point in this article. Second, we intend to use our corpus in order to study how coarticulation occurs. This means that we have to record both isolated and in-context signs, to find out how a sign could be modified depending on the context it is performed in. Once the LSF expert group has decided what signs were going to be performed, we have cut out the utterances regarding what could change (named "variable parts", that are isolated signs, and chunks of utterances).

We want to provide information in railway stations that could be, for instance, about the departure of a train: "Your attention please, platform 10, due to a technical problem, TGV trains number 1234 and 4567, coming from Strasbourg and Reims, will arrive at 1.30 pm" (here translated in English, but in French in our corpus). There are obvious variable parts in this sentence: platform number "10", train numbers "1234" and "4567", names of the stations where they come from "Strasbourg" and "Reims", and arrival time "1.30 pm". There also are some parts that undergo changes depending of the context they are performed in. For example, the parts "platform 10", "your attention please", "TGV" (which is a type of train), "coming from Strasbourg and Reims", and "will arrive at 1.30 pm", could be used in other sentences: these other sentences could announce the delay of a train, or warn the people to stay away from the edge of the platform, etc. For instance, in the complete utterances "Your attention please. Platform 10, due to a technical problem, TGV trains number 1234 and 4567, coming from Strasbourg and Reims, will arrive at 1.30 pm.", and "Platform 10, TGV train number 4567 going to Reims is leaving. Beware of the closing doors", we can notice the reuse of the chunks "Platform 10", "4567", and "Reims". Thus, there are two kind of variable parts: ones due to information (schedule, name of the platform, etc. that followed the variable parts of the vocal information system), and others due to the specific linguistic structure of SL (chunks of coarticulated utterances are not the same as in the vocal information system).

After having established what we will constitute our video corpus, we have recorded a first one. It does not contain all the parts that will be used in the display information system: we want to build a first model, and evaluate it, so that we could eventually modify our corpus design methodology before filming the whole corpus. We have chosen a deaf translator (from written text to SL and vice and versa) who works in WebSourd[1] Company to be filmed. This person is used to perform SL in front of a camera (her work is to translate written news in LSF, to be displayed on a Web site), thus we are ensured that the quality of the signing for the purpose of our corpus is of high quality. Technically, we have used two cameras, one in front, and another on the side of the signer. This allows us to have optimal points of view on the manual and non-manual features, and avoids hand overlapping and face hiding behind the hands. We have recorded both isolated signs (Figure 1, left), chunks, and, complete and varying utterances including these signs (Figure 1, right).

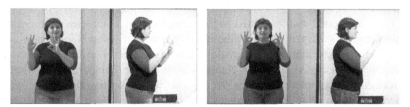

Fig. 1. Video corpus: sign $[10]_{LSF}$ performed isolated on left side, in an utterance on right side

Our corpus is made up of:

- complete utterances: warnings about different things (train is still moving, is entering, etc.), the departure (time, platform number, etc.) of a train, the arrival (time, platform number, etc.) of a train, the delay of a train;

- chunks: platform plus number or letter of the platform, reasons for a problem (delay, cancellation, etc.), and parts of utterances;
- signs: digits, letters, city names, hours.

The signs and the chunks are used in different complete utterances: for example, digits could be used for schedule, platform or train number, letters could be used for platform indication or city that has no sign name (this is called "fingerspelling": expressing a word using a letter by letter spelling, made only by the hand), the reason of a delay could be followed by a train cancellation or a platform modification, etc.

4.3 Corpus Annotation

Once the corpus has been recorded, we have annotated it thanks to Anvil annotation software [19]. This software allows displaying the video (Figure 2, (1)), and an "annotation board" (Figure 2, (2)) containing the annotations.

Fig. 2. ANVIL annotation software, with two main frames: the video (1) we are annotating, and the annotation board (2) displaying labeled temporal segmentations of what phenomenon we describe

We have annotated both isolated signs, chunks, and complete utterances. The annotation consists of temporally labeling segments of manual and non-manual features. These segmentations are made following a set of criteria, which allow analyzing how an isolated sign or a chunk is modified, in comparison as when they are performed in a complete utterance. At the time we are writing this paper, we have annotated seventeen complete utterances and sixty-nine isolated signs and isolated chunks. The annotations were firstly made on the gaze and eye aperture (Figure 3, (1)), and hand configurations (Figure 3, (3a) for right hand, (3b) for left hand). We have first decided to focus only on these features, in order to obtain a wide point of view of what occurs. In a next step we will annotate more features.

The hand configuration annotations are made on the basis of [3] (who has described 49 different hand configurations). We have chosen this annotation system because it allows us a visual view of what hand configurations are. If we do not found the configuration in the basic list, we annotate the configuration with what we think is

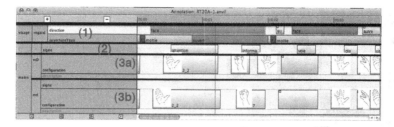

Fig. 3. Annotation sample: eye aperture (1), sign (2), right (3a) and left (3b) hand configuration

the closest hand configuration described in [3], with the addition of comments to precise what exactly the hand configuration looks like in our corpus. In a first time we have tried to make our comment as free as possible, and now we have a set of comments that we use each time we need: this set of comments correspond to a set of hand configurations that is missing in [3].

We have noticed that, for the gaze, only few locations in the signing space were used, and now we have labeled them with letters. For eye aperture, we have used three values: "open", "close", and "half"; the "close" value is used when the eyes are totally closed, and the "open" value is used when the eyes are wide open, while the "half" value is used for the remaining time of the annotation. We here have to be more accurate, and take into account the eyebrows rising: it is hard to say if eyes are wide open or half open while the eyebrows are raised.

We have annotated signs with a gloss (Figure 3, (2)). It allows us to have an idea whether a sign is shortened (or extended) when it is performed isolated or in a complete utterance. We have identified the beginning, and the ending of the sign, depending on several features (both manual and non manual features). We consider that the preparation and the retractation phase are not part of the sign. This segmentation is done upon the basis of our expertise of LSF and the context of the study: our criteria are going to be formalized in a near future.

4.4 Annotations Analysis Method

When the annotation of isolated signs and chunks, and complete utterances is done, we display them all in ANVIL.

This display of all annotations (Figure 4, (2)) simultaneously with a composition of the corresponding videos (Figure 4, (1)) allows us to easily see differences between features of one complete utterance, and features of signs and chunks that constitute it.

In the example above (Figure 4), we have displayed all the annotations we have made, both on the complete utterance "Your attention please, platform 10, due to a technical problem, TGV trains number 1234 and 4567, coming from Strasbourg and Reims, will arrive at 1.30 pm" (Figure 4, (A)), and on the chunks "your attention please" (Figure 4, (B)), "platform 10" (Figure 4, (C)), "due to a technical problem" (Figure 4, (D)), "1234", "4567", "Strasbourg", "Reims", and "1.30 pm". It means that at the same time the utterance is played, we the video of the first chunk B is displayed at the top right side, and then the chunk C is displayed at the bottom right side (Figure 4, (1) shows second and third chunks C and D, respectively at the bottom and at the top right side). They are not displayed at the same location because chunks have

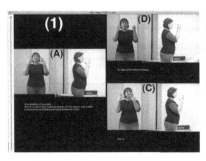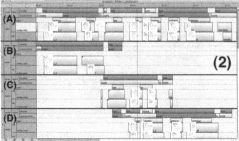

Fig. 4. Simultaneous display in Anvil: complete utterance (A), and corresponding chunks (B)(C)(D); both in video (1) and in annotations (2)

a different duration than in the complete utterance, and we want to see exactly what modifications occur within and at the border of the chunk. Thus we provide an alternative display of each chunk at the top and the bottom right side.

In our example, we can notice that there is a difference in the facial expression, and the location of the hands: in the chunk (C), facial expression is less stressed, and hand location is a little bit on the right of the face, while in the utterance (A), facial expression tends to be more concentrated, and hand location is in front of the face.

4.5   Process for Extracting Results

Thanks to the display we have decided, we can qualitatively analyze what happens when isolated signs and chunks are coarticulated in a complete utterance. We have used some facilities of the ANVIL tool, like colored and graphical annotations. This help us to gather visual information about modifications occurring both in a complete utterance as opposed to simple linked isolated ones, and between complete utterances. We had a look of each hand configuration, gaze direction and eye blinking.

We have firstly looked in the complete utterance what were happening at the beginning and the end of the corresponding isolated signs and chunks. Then we had a look at what was occurring in each isolated signs and chunks in comparison of what was in the corresponding part of the complete utterance. Lastly we went deeper into details by examining what took place between each signs of both isolated and corresponding chunk of one complete utterance. More concretely, if the complete utterance was the one listed above ("Your attention please, platform 10, due to a technical problem, TGV trains number 1234 and 4567, coming from Strasbourg and Reims, will arrive at 1.30 pm"), we first had a look at the beginning and the end of each part "Your attention please", "platform 10", "due to a technical problem", "1234", "4567", "Strasbourg", "Reims", "1.30 pm". Then we had a focus inside each isolated signs and chunks, and compare it to what occur in the corresponding part of the complete utterance. Lastly, we get deeper into details by looking at "your attention", "platform", "10", "1000", "200", "34", etc.

We now have qualitative (visual) results. Statistical analyses are going to be performed in a further step, allowing accurate comparison between isolated signs and chunks, and signs and chunks in complete utterances. We will then be able to determine very accurately what the modifications are and how they occur depending on the context.

There is one particular issue regarding our statistics. The annotation process is always evolving: when a long utterance is annotated, the annotations criteria slightly change from the beginning to the end of the process. Furthermore, annotations are made by a human person, which means the result cannot be objective. Thus, we have to balance the future statistical results regarding how the data were obtained.

5 Results and Prospects

5.1 Very First Results

We here present qualitative results from our annotations, thus we currently cannot provide numerical data about what we found (results of our statistics are going to be revealed in the near future). We explain what the phenomena we have observed are, about hand configurations, and eyes direction and blink.

Both for the dominant (the right hand for right-handed person) and the non-dominant hand, the duration of the configuration is shorter in the complete utterance. As the sign is sometimes done quite faster in the complete utterance, it seems that what takes place is a global acceleration of the chunk. Moreover, there are complete utterances where the duration of the hand configuration is shortened at the beginning and at the end of the equivalent chunk. For example, in the utterance "Platform 27, stay away from the edge of the platform. Beware of a passing train. Platform 27, stay away from the edge of the platform", the hand configuration duration for the beginning and the end of "stay away from the edge of the platform" are shortened when they are performed in the complete utterance.

Furthermore, depending on the meaning of the sentence, modifications of same chunks or isolated signs are not the same. On one hand, an utterance informing that a train is arriving from one city, at one platform, at one hour, seems to be performed with shortened hand configuration, whereas time length between each hand configuration is extended. On another hand, in an utterance informing of a delay, or a problem, hand configurations and time length between each hand configuration are shortened. One interpretation could be that in the second type of utterance, there is a hurry to provide the information.

Another important thing to be noticed is that some hand configurations are in the chunks but no longer performed in the complete utterance.

We have noticed that the gaze direction performs a pointing before the hand move to a location that is going to be used by the end: this is due to context-dependence of this feature. For example, in the chunk "Platform A" the signer's gaze still point straight forward, while in the complete utterance "Platform A, the train TGV coming from ...", the signer points his gaze to the location the hand are going to do the sign for "platform" and then get back straight forward to sign the letter of the platform.

Regarding eye's blinking, there are some complete utterances in which, if we just cut into separate pieces the utterance depending on the eyes' blink, we get the same chunks that we have decided to record in our corpus. This phenomenon is to be linked to the theory [20], which establishes that meaning units in sign language are (often) separated by a blink of the eyes.

Moreover, in several complete utterances, eyes blink after some corresponding chunks and after finger spelling or numbers performance.

5.2 To Come

Next step of our study is to annotate other features (hand location and orientation, torso movements, facial expressions), and on another hand to go deeper into annotations details by using Johnson & Liddell description model (for hand configurations, placements, movements, and orientations) [21]. Then we are going to confirm the very first results we have obtained: we are going to look at the phenomenon we have outlined, in a bigger corpus (up to eighty utterances with a total of at minimum hundred and two isolated signs and more than hundred chunks). An evaluation will be conducted, both in laboratory and in the display information system.

6   Conclusion

In this article we have presented our study on coarticulation in LSF, and some first results. This study is currently based on one signer in a restricted language domain, because of our short term aim, which is providing information in railway station. Our model will be a first step in a longer time research that will lead us to set up a more generic coarticulation model, but here we do not address this issue. We have chosen a generic definition for coarticulation in sign language, explained that this is an important research problem because we want to provide understandable information in LSF, and how we intend to study it. We have presented a several steps methodology: creation of a video corpus of LSF, annotation of this corpus with a specific software, and analysis of these annotations. This analysis has provided us with first results that are the basis for the design of a first coarticulation model. We have noticed hand configurations and eye direction and blinking modifications at the beginning, the end, and inside signs and chunks when performed in complete utterances.

We yet need to get deeper into details of our annotations, in order to set up rules that will constitute the coarticulation model. This model will be validated and improved by analyzing a bigger corpus (involving more signers), and by being implemented in a software application: the display information system in LSF. We intend to conduct an evaluation of our first model in one application that will simulate a display information system. We will implement our rules in this application, and provide an interface to adjust these rules to what the users will consider as understandable information in real LSF.

Acknowledgements

This work has been partly funded both by the European Community's Seventh Framework Programme (FP7/2007-2013) under grant agreement n°231135, and WebSourd Company.

References

1. Moody, B.: La communication internationale chez les sourds (International communication of the deaf). Rééducation Orthophonique 107, 213–223 (1979)
2. Mottez, B.: Les banquets de Sourds-Muets et la naissance du mouvement sourd (Dinners of the Deaf-Mute and root of the deaf movement). Le pouvoir des signes, pp. 170–178. INJS, Paris (1989)
3. Cuxac, C.: La langue des signes française; Les voies de l'iconicité (French Sign Language; Iconicity). In: Ophrys (ed.) Faits de Langues 15/16, Paris (2000)
4. Sallandre, M.-A.: Simultaneity in French Sign Language Discourse. In: Vermeerbergen, Leeson, Crasborn (eds.) Simultaneity in Signed Languages: Form and Function (2007)
5. Cox, S.J., Lincoln, M., Tryggvason, J., Nakisa, M., Wells, M., Tutt, M., Abbott, S.: TESSA, a system to aid communication with deaf people. In: 5th Conference on Assistive Technologies. ASSETS 2002 (2002)
6. VCom3D: SigningAvatar Frequently Asked Questions (2000),
   http://www.signingavatar.com/faq/faq.html
7. Elliott, R., Glauert, J., Kennaway, J., Marshall, I., Safr, E.: Linguistic modelling and language-processing technologies for Avatar-based sign language presentation. In: Springer (ed.) Universal Access in the Information Society (UAIS), Special issue 6/4 (2004)
8. Segouat, J., Braffort, A.: Toward the Study of Sign Language Coarticulation: Methodology Proposal. In: 2nd International Conference on Advances in Computer-Human Interactions ACHI 2009 (2009)
9. Wood, S.A.J.: Assimilation or coarticulation? Evidence from the temporal co-ordination of tongue gestures for the palatalization of Bulgarian alveolar stops. Journal of Phonetics 24(1), 139–164 (1996)
10. Vogler, C.: American Sign Language Recognition: Reducing the Complexity of the Task with Phoneme-Based Modeling and Parallel Hidden Markov Models. Doctoral Thesis. University of Pennsylvania (2002)
11. Benguerel, A.P., Cowan, H.A.: Coarticulation of upper lip protrusion in French. Phonetica 30, 41–55 (1974)
12. Marchal, A.: La production de la parole (Speech Production). Hermes Science Publications, Paris (2007)
13. Shamaie, A., Hai, W., Sutherland, A.: Hand gesture recognition for HCI. ERCIM News 46 (2001), http://www.ercim.org/publication/ErcimNews
14. Jurafsky, D., Martin, J.H.: Speech and Language Processing. Prentice Hall, Upper Saddle River (2000)
15. Yang, R., Sarkar, S., Loeding, B.: Enhanced Level Building Algorithm for the Movement Epenthesis Problem in Sign Language Recognition. In: Computer Vision and Pattern Recognition IEEE Conference, pp. 1–8, 17–22 (2007)
16. Holt, G.T., Hendriks, P., Andringa, T.: Why Don't You See What I Mean? Prospects and Limitations of Current Automatic Sing Recognition Research. Sign Language Studies 6(4) (2006)
17. Huenerfauth, M.: Generating American Sign Language classifier predicates for English-to-ASL machine translation, Doctoral Thesis. University of Pennsylvania (2006)
18. Segouat, J., Braffort, A., Bolot, L., Choisier, A., Filhol, M., Verrecchia, C.: Building 3D French Sign Language lexicon. In: 3rd Workshop on the Representation and Processing of Sign Languages: Construction and Exploitation of Sign Language Corpora. 6th international conference on Language Resources and Evaluation, LREC 2008 (2008)

19. Kipp, M.: Anvil - A Generic Annotation Tool for Multimodal Dialogue. In: 7th European Conference on Speech Communication and Technology, Eurospeech 2001 (2001)
20. Sallandre, M.-A.: Les unités du discours en Langue des Signes Française. Tentative de catégorisation dans le cadre d'une grammaire de l'iconicité (Discourse unit in French Sign Language. A try to categorization within the scope of a grammar of iconicity), Doctoral Thesis. University of Paris VIII (2003)
21. Johnson, R.E., Liddell, K.S.: Sign language phonetics: architecture and description (in preparation)

Author Index